The
American Revolution
of 1800

The
American Revolution
of 1800

Daniel Sisson
with an Introduction by Harvey Wheeler

Alfred A. Knopf   New York   1974

THIS IS A BORZOI BOOK
PUBLISHED BY ALFRED A. KNOPF, INC.

Library of Congress Cataloging in Publication Data

Sisson, Daniel.   The American Revolution of 1800.

Includes bibliographical references.
1. United States—Politics and government—Constitutional period, 1789–1809.
2. Political science—History—United States.
I.   Title.
E310.S57   320.9′73′04   73-20767
ISBN 0-394-48476-2

Manufactured in the United States of America
First Edition

In Memoriam

Douglass G. Adair

and

Scott Buchanan

"The Revolution of 1800 was as real a revolution
in the principles of our government as that of 1776 was in its form."

—THOMAS JEFFERSON

Contents

Acknowledgments

ᑐᔐᔑᑐ

The writing of this book has spanned a period of at least four years, during which time an unreasonable number of people have, out of the generosity of their hearts and a faltering faith that the book might some day be completed, given me their material aid and spiritual encouragement. My gratitude is thus extended to Ken Brown, Bruno Linde, Joseph B. Platt, and Stanley Sheinbaum for literally "keeping me alive"; to Hiden Cox and Mrs. Mary Ellen Harcourt, who believed that "scholarship stopped east of the Allegheny Mountains" but, nevertheless, took a "chance"; and to The Center for the Study of Democratic Institutions for making possible the completion of the manuscript.

Acknowledgment is extended to Dot Eberle, who gave me the kind of encouragement only a struggling writer can appreciate, and to the Utters—Don, Ruth, and D.J. I also wish to acknowledge the early help provided by Elizabeth Wrigley of the Francis Bacon Library, and by Mary Isabel Fry and Mary Wright of the Huntington Library. And a special tribute is reserved for my editor, Jane Garrett, who has shown an insight and an understanding of the ideas and materials of American history that will spoil my working relationship with any other editor for the rest of my life.

I must also mention my gratitude to a number of senior scholars who, upon my completion of the manuscript, gave me the benefit of their wisdom: Stringfellow Barr, former President of St. John's

College, Joan Coward of Claremont Men's College, Raghavan Iyer and Wilbur Jacobs of the University of California, Santa Barbara, John Niven of the Claremont Graduate School, Ralph Ross of Scripps College, Herbert Schneider of the Claremont Graduate School, and Rexford Guy Tugwell of The Center.

My acknowledgments, however, must include another group of people who have been indispensable to the writing of this book. They are the graduate students who spent countless evenings helping me refine the complex idea of revolution while tolerating my preoccupation with "those eighteenth-century bourgeois revolutionaries." Carl Dennis and Bill Burnett were indispensable here. I am indebted to John R. Seeley, a student as well as a teacher, and to Keith Berwick for a year-long seminar that became a true dialogue on the nature of revolution. In addition, Will Holdsworth, Howard Weamer, Neil Potash, Steven Jay Schnitman, and my principal critic, Dick Kipling, all gave me hours of their time and encouragement.

These students willingly contributed because of one shared assumption: we believed it was possible to develop a thesis without the formal direction of any established academic personage. To a degree we were successful, and there was only one exception to this rule. Unfortunately, of the four teachers who laid the foundation for this work, two, Douglass G. Adair and Scott Buchanan, never lived to see a portion of the manuscript. The third, Alan W. Brownsword, who started it all, reviewed the manuscript upon its completion.

The fourth was Harvey Wheeler of The Center for the Study of Democratic Institutions. His contribution has been immeasurable, and those familiar with his *Politics of Revolution* will perceive the extent to which this book draws upon his theory of the "two cities." I can only add that "whatever value this study may have, I am indebted to him for having provided me with an education . . ." Harvey will recognize the spirit as well as the origin of those words. For without his patience, in addition to his suggestive scholarship, there would never have been *The American Revolution of 1800*.

Acknowledgments

Finally, I wish to acknowledge my debt to Linda, who experienced her own revolution and whose affection lies buried in every line and page of this volume.

DANIEL SISSON

Santa Barbara, California
1974

Introduction

꧁꧂

The Revolution of 1800 unfolds a story never before told in the literature of American history. Dealing strictly with original sources, the study reveals a twenty-five-year quest by Thomas Jefferson for a theory of revolution based upon his experiences in the age of democratic revolutions. Underlying this theory of revolution is a theory of politics that establishes a dynamic relationship between the two. For once the theory was developed and applied, it became necessary to create a viable politics of revolution to implement it. Thus the book, in a new interpretation, explains the political theory and practices of the revolutionary Founding Fathers a full generation after they came to power.

Specifically, the book claims that the American Revolution did not end in 1783 but in 1800. Its thesis overturns the traditional argument for the development of political parties in the United States. It establishes a new basis for evaluating the politics of the period 1790–1800 and reveals a new and revolutionary dimension of the struggle between Jefferson and Hamilton. In a way that has not been done before, the book examines the idea of revolution in early American history, especially after 1776. It challenges the priorities set by many historians regarding the orderly consolidation of our national government after the ratification of the constitution. Finally, the book's most important contribution is that it presents a revolutionary interpretation of the early national period in American history.

In order to understand the thesis it is necessary to revise some of our concepts regarding the nature of revolution in the eighteenth century. We are accustomed to thinking of politics as peaceful electoral contests between competing parties and of revolutions as violent ideological conflicts between irreconcilable social classes. But before 1800 this distinction had not been made and, further, was not even imagined. The fact is that in the eighteenth century a much broader, classical conception of politics was held by the founders of the early American republic.

One of their assumptions, for example, was that any opposition to government in an organized fashion was potentially revolutionary. The emergence of organized political groups—they called them "factions"—constituted a threat to the administration in power. Another assumption of the founders was that, in order to achieve harmony following a period of violent revolution, the new nation required a unitary system of politics. Hence they believed in the one- or non-party state.

Both of these assumptions recognized specific characteristics of revolution that must be avoided if the state was to survive. The first held that certain *institutional* forms of political organization would lead to acts of violence against the state. The other held that certain *ideological* beliefs, in opposition to the state, would lead to violence and rebellion. Both forms of opposition created a "second city" within society. Instead of uniting the state, the "second city" would create a dual state: one half adhering to establishment values and institutions; the other half rejecting them and seeking alternatives. And this was the classical expression for an emergent revolutionary organization that would ultimately divide the state and the people against their government.

A third characteristic of revolution is its special form of crisis. When governments are in the process of breaking down, they experience a series of crises. Policies once adequate to reform a specific malady become dysfunctional, unrelated to the systemic problem of social disintegration. Instead of solving the problem, reform merely exacerbates it. Thus, revolutionary crises reveal the inadequacy of reform and demonstrate the necessity for complete structural, or revolutionary, transformation.

As revolutionary crises spread, they increase the paralysis of traditional institutions; at the same time they accelerate the articulation of the diverse infant institutions of the revolutionary "second city." With the spread of revolutionary crises the ideological and institutional foundations of the opposition come together in the form of an increasingly visible and self-conscious movement. This is the revolution.

And this is the theoretical framework the reader must keep in mind as he views the politics of faction and the various policies that the Hamiltonians pursued in order to maintain the power of the Federalist establishment. The contrast between Federalist and republican values and ideology, and their perspective on the meaning and function of American institutions all illustrate the emergence of the Jeffersonian republicans as a revolutionary "second city."

As this dynamic political organization gained strength through a series of continued crises, the Jeffersonian response in both theory and practice was a full-blown politics of revolution. This book, therefore, is a study of two basic ideas: revolution and constitutional transition. For the culmination of Jefferson's theory, combined with his politics of revolution, was the first peaceful transition of constitutional power in government, from one party to another, in western political history. The thesis, then, demands a new assessment of the idea of revolution in early American history and an extension of the meaning of the American Revolution of 1776.

HARVEY WHEELER

The Center for the Study of Democratic Institutions
Santa Barbara, California
1974

The
American Revolution
of 1800

A Note on the Historians

"Many of you may wonder why a class entitled The Early
National Period should be listed in the college catalogue,
or whether it has any relevance to life in the twentieth
century. The answer lies in this: it is only through the
study of a nation's beginnings, when the original ideas and
principles envisioned by its founders became institutionalized, that one can truly understand what the system of
government was meant to accomplish and what it, in fact,
has accomplished. In the case of the American system of
government, that period is the decade after the Constitution. By studying that era, roughly 1790 to 1800, we can
hope to develop a better understanding of the true meaning of American values and the purpose of American
institutions."

PROFESSOR ALAN W. BROWNSWORD
in a class lecture,
Long Beach State College, September 1963

The consensus among American historians who have written on
the early national period about the "Revolution of 1800" is that it
was not a "real revolution." Beginning with Henry Adams, who, in
1889, stigmatized it a "pseudo-revolution," American historians
have tended to look at Jefferson's rise to power and his accomplishments in power as a confirmation of the earlier nationalist
and centralist policies of the Federalists. Indeed, Henry Adams,
who set the original tone and interpretation of the period, dismissed Jefferson's Revolution of 1800 in one terse statement:

3

"Serious statesmen could hardly expect to make a revolution that should not be revolutionary."[1]

That statement set the stage for justifying all the younger Adams' prejudices against the man who had defeated his great-grandfather. It is in fact a statement that can be passed over too quickly. For Henry Adams was saying several things very subtly: 1. only serious statesmen can produce revolutions; 2. the Revolution of 1800 was neither serious nor revolutionary; and 3. therefore, Jefferson was neither a statesman nor a revolutionary.

From those premises all else followed. Adams concluded for successive generations of historians that the Revolution of 1800 never existed. Moreover, Adams' history, due to its brilliant literary style, won the approval of the profession as the archetypal work in American history upon which all other works were to be modeled. This uncritical acceptance by American historians unfortunately foreclosed all serious consideration of the themes that Jefferson himself had considered important.

In addition, the statement reveals something else about the logic of the historians. Not only did they dismiss the possibility of a revolution in 1800, they revealed their inability to escape the biased determinism of Adams' writing. And perhaps most seriously, they revealed that they failed to comprehend the nature of revolution. The judgment of twentieth-century historians, taking Adams as their arbiter, has been made on the basis of what executive decisions and national policy occurred *after* the revolution rather than on the process of the revolution itself. One historian echoed Adams perfectly: "Those who look back on these decades from the vantage point of the twentieth century, who know of Jefferson's policies during his eight years in office, can see nothing 'revolutionary' about this election."[2] This illustrates another

---

[1] Henry Adams, *History of the United States during the Administration of Thomas Jefferson and James Madison*, 9 vols. (New York, 1889–91), Vol. I, p. 256.

[2] Morton Borden, *The Federalism of James A. Bayard* (New York, 1955), p. 74. Another example is Noble Cunningham's categorical statement that ". . . Jefferson exaggerated when he spoke of a revolution . . ." Quoted in

point: the tendency to view the Revolution of 1800 merely as an "election" and not as a revolutionary process. Among the many professional American historians who have examined Jefferson's drive for power, none has viewed it as a fundamental revolutionary movement. Not one has given us an interpretation of Jefferson searching for ways to achieve power peacefully yet bent upon seizing power by all means necessary and utilizing every revolutionary technique known at the time.

I have not found either, from any American historian, a discussion of the influence of the French Revolution upon Jefferson's thinking and to what extent it may have modified his views on political revolution. Apart from monographs dealing with other rebellions of the period, e.g., the Fries and Whiskey rebellions, no one has treated the Revolution of 1800 as a subject important enough by itself to serve as a model for a study of revolution in America. What appears to me to be absent, then, from our historical literature is an adequate treatment of the history of revolution in America from 1789 to 1800.

American historians have, as a whole, looked upon the Revolution of 1800 as the accomplishment of a new mode of political organization, viz., that of political parties. In their analyses they have concentrated upon the emergence of political organizations, techniques, and devices that in their minds became the models for full-fledged political parties. One recent historian, whose computer-oriented scholarship would have amused Jefferson and his colleagues, summed up that approach: "Advocates of the American political system tend to view the political organization of the early Republic teleologically—as the first steps along the way to modern democracy."[3] The purpose, however, is almost always the same: to demonstrate the formation and establishment of a model not for revolution, but for modern political parties.

History of American Presidential Elections, 1798–1968, ed. Arthur Schlesinger, Jr. (New York, 1971), Vol. I, p. 101.

[3] Mary P. Ryan, "Party Formation in the United States Congress, 1789–1796: A Quantitative Analysis," *William and Mary Quarterly*, 3d Ser., XVIII (Oct. 1971), p. 523.

While authors such as Henry Adams, Wilfred Binkley, Morton Borden, William N. Chambers, Joseph Charles, Noble Cunningham, Jr., David Hackett Fischer, Richard Hofstadter, Adrienne Koch, Stephen Kurtz, Dumas Malone, Roy F. Nichols, et al., attempted to discover the historical evidence leading to the formation of these parties, I believe they failed to relate another and equally important part of the story.[4] They failed, in other words, to place themselves in Maitland's "twilight, where the past must be taken on its own terms."

Within their arguments the idea of revolution is mentioned only in passing, if at all. In no case is it discussed substantively. In many respects this aversion to the theme of revolution reveals an intellectual blind spot that few American historians of the early national period have escaped. Henry Adams so constructed his history that it was logically impossible even to have considered the possibility of revolution. Writers like Morton Borden have assumed that because violence and bloodshed were not widespread, no revolution "in the common meaning of that term"[5] occurred. Yet Borden has failed to provide us with even the hint of a definition of revolution as it was commonly understood in the eigh-

---

[4] Henry Adams, *History of the United States during the Administration of Thomas Jefferson and James Madison*, op. cit.; W. Binkley, *American Political Parties* (New York, 1943); Morton Borden, *The Federalism of James A. Bayard*, op. cit., also *Parties and Politics in the Early Republic, 1789–1815* (New York, 1967); William N. Chambers, *Political Parties in a New Nation: The American Experience, 1776–1809* (New York, 1963); Joseph Charles, *The Origins of the American Party System* (Williamsburg, Va., 1956); Noble Cunningham, Jr., *The Jeffersonian Republicans: The Formation of Party Organization, 1789–1801* (Chapel Hill, N.C., 1957); David Hackett Fischer, *The Revolution of American Conservatism* (New York, 1965); Richard Hofstadter, *The Idea of a Party System: The Rise of Legitimate Opposition in the United States 1780–1840* (Berkeley, Cal., 1969); Adrienne Koch, *Jefferson and Madison: The Great Collaboration* (New York, 1964); Stephen G. Kurtz, *The Presidency of John Adams* (Philadelphia, 1957); Dumas Malone, *The Ordeal of Liberty* (Boston, 1962); Roy F. Nichols, *The Invention of the American Political Parties* (New York, 1957).

[5] Borden, *Parties and Politics in the Early Republic, 1789–1815*, op. cit., pp. 42–58.

teenth century. He says, "In 1800–1801 people could not see things with the same clarity of the modern historians, and *they* regarded it as a revolution."[6] His commentary on Jefferson's Revolution of 1800 is an example of uncamouflaged historical determinism and self-deception. Failing to see that he has made a historical judgment affirming *their* idea of revolution, he urges us not to pay attention to those muddled eighteenth-century thinkers. He suggests, instead, that our twentieth-century notions of revolution are a better frame of reference for the eighteenth century.

Even Richard Hofstadter, one of America's greatest historians in the twentieth century, did not escape his own bias. In his *Idea of a Party System*, Hofstadter simply could not accept the fact that Jefferson believed the theme of revolution was important and that of party so negligible it was *not* worth mentioning. Here Hofstadter chides Jefferson's idea of his own fame: "When Thomas Jefferson thought of setting down the lasting achievements he wanted inscribed on his tombstone, he mentioned the writing of the Declaration of Independence and of the Virginia Statute of Religious Liberty and the founding of the University of Virginia— thus omitting almost flamboyantly all the accomplishments of his long career in national politics. Yet surely this democrat and libertarian might have taken justifiable pride in his part in creating the first truly popular party in the history of the Western world, and in his leading role in the first popular election of modern times in which the reins of government were peacefully surrendered by a governing party to an opposition."[7] Setting aside the establishment of the University of Virginia, it was inconceivable to Hofstadter that Jefferson wished to be remembered for his revolutionary contributions and not for those of party politics.

Hofstadter goes on to reflect upon Jefferson's actual statements on revolution and then completely dismisses an amount of historical evidence that contradicts the role of the historian: "The modern liberal mind has been bemused by his [Jefferson's] re-

[6] Borden, *The Federalism of James A. Bayard*, op. cit., p. 74.

[7] Hofstadter, *The Idea of a Party System*, op. cit., p. 1.

marks about the value of a little rebellion now and then, or watering the tree with the blood of tyrants, or having a complete constitutional revision every twenty or thirty years."[8] If the modern liberal mind—and especially the liberal historian's mind—has been "bemused," it is because he has failed to take Jefferson's historical accomplishment seriously.

Most historians have not purposefully misread the importance of revolution in the early republic; it simply has not occurred to them. Noble Cunningham fails to refer to the idea of revolution at all, passing it over with an oblique reference to Paine's *Rights of Man*. William N. Chambers refers to the idea of revolution in two sentences: the first, a comment by de Tocqueville meant to negate revolution in America; and the second, a note on the American Revolution of 1776. Chambers does mention the French Revolution a half-dozen times but only in the most cursory fashion.

One of the few American historians I have found who has taken the revolutionary character of the period seriously is Joseph Charles. Yet his remarks on the potential for revolution in this period are more of an intuitive than an explicitly rational analysis. While he fails to deal with the idea of revolution in any one of his three essays, he does throw out valuable suggestions that indicate he is aware of the limitations of his own analysis. In one footnote he quotes a newspaper of the period: "The election of 1800, they [the Republicans] appeared to believe, 'would fix our national character and determine whether republicanism or aristocracy would prevail. Moreover, the solution of this problem in America might perhaps turn the suspended balance in favor of liberty or despotism throughout the world.' "[9] A more fundamental statement about what the republicans considered the importance of one event in our history and the issues that confronted it could not be made. Again Charles writes, referring to Jefferson: "Years after his retirement he continued to speak of the Revolution of 1800, and the words would imply that he himself thought his election and administration of some fundamental importance.

[8] Ibid., p. 150.
[9] Charles, *The Origins of the American Party System*, op. cit., p. 6.

Anyone, therefore, who deals with Jefferson's career . . . must decide whether he failed to define his intentions or we have failed to understand them."[10]

Charles touched upon one of the true blind spots shared by most American historians: an almost universal failure to consider the idea as well as nature of revolution in the politics of the early republic. The reasons for this are manifold, but one in particular deserves mention. A review of standard works in American history will substantiate the claim that the majority of historians in America refer to only two revolutions in our national life: the one that succeeded and the one that failed. They are only too willing to accept Charles's implicit suggestion that the wily old Jefferson may have purposefully failed to define his intentions, if not because he did not always understand them himself, then at least to confuse that legion of American historians who would in later years feel compelled to ponder them.

However, another view is possible, even plausible, one which states explicitly that Jefferson was shrewd enough to create a political revolution that became one of America's fundamental contributions to world political thought. By this, of course, I mean the bloodless change of power that preserved constitutional authority and demonstrated to the world that changes in the principles of government do not always necessitate a *violent* revolutionary struggle.

However, to see, think, and write about even this view of political revolution requires a background in revolutionary theory that is seldom a part of the training of the American historian. It would appear that a fresh view of Jefferson's Revolution of 1800 requires a mind that is somehow attuned to revolutionary times, if only to gain insight into what may have been a similar mentality in the 1790s. I mention this because America, increasingly throughout the past century, has not been a consciously revolutionary nation. Consequently, our historians have reflected a nonrevolutionary mood in the spirit of the histories they have produced.

[10] Ibid., p. 75.

Their histories have, for the most part, been reformist and status quo oriented or even evolutionary, proclaiming the virtues of our "established" society.

Perhaps this has been a delusion of our century, the most revolutionary—at least since 1945—of any since the eighteenth. One example of this nonrevolutionary mood came at the turn of this century. Andrew C. McLaughlin, writing about the conceptual fallacies of that age, observed that "the men of those days could not quite see that if the[ir] Revolutionary principles were made complete . . ." they would lead "not [to] imperial organization; not [to] law and systems, but [to] personal assertion, [to] *confusions that might threaten the foundation of all reasonable order.*" "Even a man like Jefferson," said McLaughlin, "was ready to talk *nonsense* about fertilizing the tree of liberty with the blood of tyrants, and about the advisability of occasional rebellions, which ought not to be too much discouraged."[11]

Indeed, American historians in the past century have practically filtered out every revolutionary value that lay in the written material of the period 1789–1800. The works that have appeared are devoid of discussion and historical insight about the idea of revolution either during or after the Constitutional Convention.[12] Unfortunately, most historians have, with few exceptions, celebrated the triumph of stability, order, and the conservatizing of the Revolution. The best example of this is a recent book dealing with the period. Richard Buel's *Securing the Revolution: Ideology in American Politics, 1789–1815* dealt almost exclusively with the years 1789–1800 and *failed to mention even once* Jefferson's phrase "the Revolution of 1800." Thus, in an otherwise fine book, especially where foreign affairs are discussed, Buel accepted the traditional interpretations of party and ignored the significance of Jefferson's revolutionary ideology.

[11] Andrew C. McLaughlin, *The Confederation and the Constitution 1783–1789* (New York, 1905), pp. 39–40.

[12] Gordon Wood, in *The Creation of the American Republic* (Chapel Hill, N.C., 1969), p. 612, claims "the end of classical politics" and the new constitutional government made "old-fashioned popular revolutions obsolete."

His interpretation, moreover, is truly a celebration of the stability and order of the American system. He wrote near the end of his book, referring to Robert Goodloe Harper's defense of Federalist policies: "History has justified his hope, for modern historians concur in his assessment of Federalist achievements. They look back to the Federalist decade as a time when the nation's basic institutions were established and America began to acquire a distinctive identity as a commercial, industrial culture. They feel an instinctive sympathy for the Federalists and have tended to accept Harper's view that resolution of the tensions existing between the two parties in 1800 depended on the willingness of Jeffersonians to adopt their principles."[13]

The interpretation you are about to read makes the direct opposite claim. It is this book's contention that when Jefferson wrote, "The Revolution of 1800 was as real a revolution in the principles of our government as that of 1776 was in its form,"[14] he meant precisely that. This interpretation, then, claims that the real meaning of the period 1789–1800 is the triumph of principles totally opposed to those Jefferson, Madison, and their contemporaries believed the Federalists held.

This is not to suggest that Jefferson, Madison, et al., believed the American Revolution of 1776 was not revolutionary in substance or merely reflected a change in form. It is rather to place an emphasis upon Jefferson's intentions. During the period of High Federalist ascendancy Jefferson noted again and again the Federalists' lack of faith in the meaning of the first American Revolution. Thus it was Jefferson, acting as a revolutionary philosopher, who made the distinction between principles and form. Moreover, this symbolic quality, his perception that only a revolution that lived up to its principles was a true revolution, was a part of his rhetoric. It distinguished him radically from his peers and they,

13 Richard Buel, Jr., *Securing the Revolution: Ideology in American Politics, 1789–1815* (Ithaca, N.Y., 1972), p. 242.

14 Jefferson to Spencer Roane, 6 Sept. 1819. *The Writings of Thomas Jefferson*, eds. Andrew A. Lipscomb and Albert Bergh, 20 vols. (Washington, D.C., 1903), Vol. XV, p. 212 (hereafter referred to as *Writings*).

as well as many who came later, read into his statements whatever understanding of the practice of revolution they brought to them. But on this point of revolutionary principles versus practice Jefferson was attempting to address himself to a swiftly changing set of circumstances. He recognized the futility of being a pure ideologue in the midst of political crisis, of not assuming a practical approach to revolution. He knew too that he could not afford to define narrowly the meaning of his revolution, for he quickly perceived in the sober moment of taking power that rigidity would destroy the fruits of victory. He thus adopted a posture of philosophical vagueness that allowed his opponents to read into his intentions a palatable view of the future. In sum, as Joseph Charles has suggested, we simply have difficulty defining Jefferson's revolutionary intentions. And while it may appear, at times, that this author is arguing in behalf of Jefferson, the attempt has been made to balance his rhetoric and especially to avoid the black-and-white perspective of those historians who have set Jefferson against Hamilton as two cocks in a pit.

As one surveys the literature of American history and looks for those books that deal with the theme of revolution, it becomes obvious that Crane Brinton's *Anatomy of Revolution* was the only book of its kind for more than a generation. Only a small number of historians have dealt with revolutionary themes in their writings; but, perhaps more important, they captured that spirit in their teaching. Bernard Bailyn, Charles Beard, Carl Becker, Crane Brinton, Henry Steele Commager, Albert Jay Nock, and R. R. Palmer are among those who, in their scholarship and in the values they inculcated in their students, reflected a maverick quality, a nonconformist view of the American historical-political tradition that set them apart. The influence they have had in their profession has been far beyond their small numbers, and it is hoped here that they will stimulate a younger generation to turn to the study of revolution.

Such a list would not be complete without mentioning the name of Douglass Adair, who had immense influence upon the current generation of students. His teaching genius was more than a combination of his unorthodox style and dynamic personality. He seemed, at least in the eyes of his students, to actually live the characters he portrayed and to have identified completely with the eighteenth century. Adair was at first glance, and the impression grew with each successive seminar, a Walpolean character that had somehow survived unchanged; an eighteenth-century man living in the twentieth century. This was, moreover, a chosen image, one that he deliberately constructed.

In order to enhance that impression Adair had consciously surrounded himself with the accouterments of that age. He designed the furniture of his office so that it reflected his mind. The result was an institution that imparted an aura to the man, and it was no accident that every student who met him initially encountered him in that office. Leather bindings reached uniformly to the top of a twenty-foot ceiling bearing titles that most students had only vaguely heard of but never seen. Hogarth's prints and Houdon's busts stared down at freshmen graduate students waiting for the moment when Adair would stir them to life. It was a place in which any student with imagination immediately knew that Chatham, Fox, Franklin, or even Jefferson himself would have felt at home.

His reputation as one of the most knowledgeable men in early American history always preceded him, and the student, aware of this, would feel its awesome weight and sense that the bearing and confidence of the man had permeated the room. Ensconced behind a mountain of yellowed documents and fresh white term papers he would sit—the very image of what a full professor of American history should be. A warm voice would boom out a welcome followed by a question about any topic that happened momentarily to be on his mind. It was always calculated to determine what kind of material the student was made of. "Why did you choose history to study?" he would ask. "Who is your favorite nineteenth-century artist?" "When did you first meet Jefferson?" or "What do *you* mean by the word *revolution?*" (These last were the first words he ever spoke to me and they have never lost their significance.)

Thus catching the student off guard in the first moment of their encounter, Adair would proceed to regale him with an enlightening discourse on the importance of answering the question and the even greater importance of pondering the question during his graduate school career. Expecting to discuss courses, grades, registration forms, and the technicalities of being admitted to his seminar, the student often sat bewildered, staring open-mouthed at Adair's performance, a calculated posture of ranting and raving, of walking back and forth, shouting—at one moment berating the student for not answering his question properly; at another, hinting at some brilliant observation the student, in his confusion, might have uttered. The entire scene was high drama and for those who understood the subtle relationship between a teacher and a student the result was always the same: it was the ritual by which Douglass Adair baptized a new convert to his discipline. Once exposed to that charismatic personality and to those brilliant insights filling the room, the student unwittingly entered upon a love affair with the study of American history. It was as if Douglass Adair, by some magical force of his eighteenth-century personality, could intellectually hypnotize us all.

For those who persevered this dramatic introduction was only the beginning. Adair's seminars were a joy to every student who took them. Sometimes chaotic, often rambling, they were always exciting, spontaneous, revealing in nearly every session an insight which any student could take and write a good book about. Moreover, he threw those ideas out consciously. Although a polished writer himself, Adair was content to allow students, who often acted upon those insights, the luxury of pursuing their own intellectual curiosity, never insisting that he owned the idea or their research. Whether in a seminar or writing a dissertation, he created an atmosphere of complete intellectual freedom, indicating his willingness to explore any idea or historical concept. The only limits were those of the human imagination and the only standards his own academic excellence.

Consequently, Adair's students ripened the fruits of his creative insight, often publishing books and articles which had sprung, seminally, from their teacher's mind. And their numbers were many: Joseph Charles, Jack Greene, Trevor Colbourn, Cecelia Kenyon, and Caroline Robbins—to name just a few. Yet, for the most part Adair ignored all of this. More important was that students would become excited about the historical ideas he exposed them to, immersed in the subject matter they were studying, and that ultimately they would solve some problem they had discovered. It was not uncommon to see Adair's students huddled in the coffee shop of the Claremont Graduate School arguing over one of his casual remarks—thrown out like sparks—in a typical seminar. It was expected. For him *this* was the important achievement: building a fire in a student's mind, enabling him to run with one or more of those inflammable ideas. Only then did he consider himself a success. He once told me, "The best students I ever had never received their Ph.D.'s. They became interested in an intellectual problem and followed it out and their curiosity carried them elsewhere." Strange talk for a professor in a graduate school whose job it was to turn out "certified historians." But Douglass Adair was no ordinary teacher. He was unique, so much so that he can only be understood by comprehending the revolutionary nature of his mind.

His approach to the study of American history always had a maverick quality about it. He saw ideas, men, and events in a way that few of his contemporaries ever knew. There was always that strange "twist," the different "tack," so characteristic of the man. His understanding of the potential of a student, an idea, a problem, or even a lethargic publication set him apart. This scholar's "sixth sense" led him to resurrect the *William and Mary Quarterly* and establish it as the finest journal in early American history. He revolutionized the study of several fields that a legion of scholars have since made their sole preoccupation: the origins of political parties; the study of the radical Whigs in England and their influence upon the American revolutionaries; mobs and mob violence in the American Revolution; and a view of that era from the Tory perspective. He was the nation's expert on the historical background of *The Federalist* and perhaps knew more about James

Madison than anyone else, including Irving Brant. And one can only guess at the number and variety of novel teaching ideas he conjured up for his students.

Yet Adair's favorite area of study was Classical Greece and Rome and the influence he believed that period had upon the Founding Fathers. From his reading of the classics, those books read by the Founding Fathers, he developed his insights into early American history. Through this extensive process of steeping himself in the original sources of the ancients, Adair had become an eighteenth-century man. His dissertation at Yale, entitled "The Intellectual Origins of Jeffersonian Democracy," was never published; but, as he once said when a student innocently asked him in a seminar why he had never published it as a book, "it was read by everyone who counted."

That he had never published his thesis was indeed a sore point with Adair and everyone else who knew him in the profession. But it was, for many of the reasons stated above, understandable. His teaching was his first great love. His ability to ferret out new ideas ranked alongside it and the two worked in tandem. His standard of excellence for publishing was such that he warned his students at least once a week to beware of the "publish or perish syndrome." It was, he believed, a business; at best a form of intellectual corruption, and at worst, prostitution. He thus attempted to impress upon his students the central theme of his pedagogy: the fundamental difference between creativity and productivity.

Where his thesis was concerned, he knew that in spite of its brilliance it was redundant and needed improvement. He also knew that within its pages was submerged a new interpretation of early American history. With this in mind, he acted in his typical way and allowed every one of his students over a twenty-five-year period the pleasure of mining that thesis, storing up his insights for their future success. Significantly, in my case at least, Adair's spelling-out of the intellectual foundations of Jefferson's philosophy was the first inspiration for the present book and without it I do not see how I could have begun my research.

Thus, while I cannot claim to speak for those who knew him in the days at Williamsburg, those of us who were his students at Claremont, who knew him perhaps as his professional colleagues may not have, sensed all along that this was the way he wanted it. We could not escape the fact that Douglass had set an example for those he had brought into the teaching profession and his fondest hope was that we might follow his lead. For any great teacher, he would say, reward came in two ways: in fundamentally altering the lives of students and everyone close to him, and in seeing those same students publish the fruits of his labor. This was his twin legacy, to be realized more successfully than he would ever know. Belatedly, all of us have come to recognize the "old Roman" and what he did for his profession. Indeed, his fame, if there ever was any doubt, is now secure. He was, to use his favorite expression—"warts and all," the most revolutionary teacher of American history in his time.

While a few historians included "The Revolution of 1800" in their chapter headings, they made the reference casually and, for the most part, in a nonpolitical context. Lyon Gardiner Tyler, in a *History of Virginia*,[15] described the "principles" that Jefferson and the Virginia Dynasty stood for, but he did not note their revolutionary nature and, in fact, never mentioned the word. In the 1930s, John D. Hicks wrote a popular text that included a chapter entitled "The Revolution of 1800."[16] But because he dealt with political ideas in only five of the pages, Hicks was not able to delve deeply into the major problems of the period. He viewed the Jeffersonians' triumph, moreover, as the beginning of a *social* rather than a revolutionary *political* development. While Hicks's essay was a departure from the norm, i.e., treatment in terms of *"The Election* of 1800," within his lifetime it failed to provoke other historians to investigate the ideology of the period or its revolutionary implications. One modern scholar who did

15 Lyon Gardiner Tyler, *History of Virginia*, 6 vols. (Chicago, Ill.: The American Historical Society, 1924), Vol. II, pp. 307–43.
16 John D. Hicks, *The Federal Union* (Cambridge, Mass., 1937), Ch. XIII, pp. 230–50.

raise some very important issues about the "Crisis of Succession" in 1800 was Morton Grodzins. Shortly before his death, he dealt with the role of party in a little-known article that raised questions about "radical changes" and revolution in the structure of politics during the period.[17] But his essay stands alone, and because it was his last work and published "unrevised," it failed to gain the attention it deserved. More recently Pauline Maier has studied the ideology of the original American revolutionaries and paid particular attention to their political organization. More important, she has provided an interpretation of the meaning of revolution in the 1760s and '70s that enables us to translate theory into practical politics. And, unlike many who preceded her, she has demonstrated with massive evidence the connection between the two.[18]

Indeed, there are signs that we have discovered our error. The influence of outside forces, the revolutions occurring in the underdeveloped world and among the contending nations of Africa and Asia, have sparked new interest in revolution. Though late, America's deep involvement in this world struggle has forced us to reconsider our own revolutionary ideas.

There is also another side to this critical view that I am presenting, one that recognizes the constraints imposed on human nature. Most historians, like other human beings, are victims of their times and reflect the prejudices of their era. And, as we examine the literature of American politics over the last three generations, the development of political parties, not revolutions, has been the historians' preoccupation. Indeed, one might even say that until very recently the historians have concentrated exclusively upon that portion of the evidence that relates to party. For example, Noble Cunningham narrows his own limits and serves his readers notice: "Although an effort has been made to recognize ideas . . .

[17] Morton Grodzins, "Political Parties and the Crisis of Succession in the United States: The Case of 1800," in *Political Parties and Political Development*, eds. Lucien Pye and Sidney Verba (Princeton, N.J., 1966), pp. 303–27.

[18] Pauline Maier, *From Resistance to Revolution* (New York, 1972); see especially chapters 2, 5, 8, and 9.

the study is restricted to the growth of a political organization and does not treat the broader aspects of the origin and rise of Jeffersonian democracy." Yet he can say in the following sentence, "attention is focused on . . . the means by which this party gained control of the national administration" and not even mention the word revolution in his entire book.[19]

Joseph Charles, on the other hand, warns his readers: "The evidence we find among the letters of Jefferson . . . will throw little light on our problems unless we view them in relation to . . . national parties, the government policies of the period, and *above all, of the ideology* of each of the contending groups. The development of Jeffersonian democracy is the response of the Revolutionary generation to a highly complicated set of factors . . ."[20] Charles's warning is clear. The development of a large-scale popular movement, democratic in ideology and revolutionary in its political purposes, must be placed in a properly wide historical perspective and context. Narrow limits will simply not suffice for intelligent analysis.

Moreover, as Charles notes, the matter is extremely complicated. The truth of whether mature political parties were formed and/or there was a "real" revolution, as Jefferson suggested, may lie somewhere between the limits of a Noble Cunningham and a total reliance upon the ideology of the times. Yet a truly historical approach would consider both views judiciously, something which, I believe, has not been done.

A few historians, however, have begun to make inroads upon this wilderness and others will surely follow. Bernard Bailyn, who examined both ideology and political organization in his studies on the American Revolution, developed a methodology that revealed the revolutionary process as it had never been seen before. He took the pamphlets of the 1760s and '70s seriously, where those before him had simply dismissed their statements as propaganda. Bailyn noted that "there were fears, real anxieties, a sense of real danger

19 Cunningham, *The Jeffersonian Republicans*, op. cit., p. vii.
20 Charles, *The Origins of the American Party System*, op. cit., p. 89.

behind those phrases . . ."[21] Accepting their sincerity, he juxta-posed them to the official statements we have long been familiar with and then viewed both as a true historical dialectic.

Bailyn was referring, of course, to the Revolution of 1776. But I wonder whether in that age of ideology—the eighteenth century—if the beliefs and fears expressed *in the period 1790 to 1800* were not also as sincere. I see little reason to believe they were not. I see no reason to believe that we cannot approach the period 1790 to 1800 in a frame of mind and with a methodology similar to Bailyn's. By accepting the statements expressed in the pamphlets of the times, Bailyn gained new insight into the period of the American Revolution. By his refusal to accept the historical deter-minism and limits of those who preceded him, i.e., those who believed that the stated fears of the colonists amounted to nothing more than a simplified version of twentieth-century propaganda, he produced a new interpretation of one of the most "worked-over" periods in American history.

I believe that many of Bailyn's insights into the American revolutionary generation carry over as that generation matured in power. Like him, I am not convinced that suddenly, within the space of several years—even decades—those revolutionary leaders changed their appetites or human nature, much less their political ideologies. It appears reasonable to me to assume—as a working hypothesis—that Adams' and Jefferson's commitment to "ancient liberty" was as great from 1790 to 1800 as it had been from 1760 to 1776. This would also be true of their concern for republican government, their opposition to monarchy, or their fear of party.

I believe it is also realistic to assume that their revolutionary experience was as important to them in their fifties as it was in their thirties. Certainly, if we judge them by their later correspon-dence, they more than affirmed the belief that they were, all their lives, the children of revolution.

Is it reasonable then to assume that the idea of revolution did

[21] Bernard Bailyn, *The Ideological Origins of the American Revolution* (Cambridge, Mass., 1967), p. ix.

not loom larger in their minds as the years passed by? Participation in "The Revolution" was the great act of their lives. It transformed them, projected them onto the stage of world history, and guaranteed their immortality. It became the touchstone of their every subsequent action against which all else would be measured. By its standards their public acts would bear the scrutiny of history: either praise or condemnation. Indeed, that merciless standard could justify the plunging of a sword into one's own administration as well as certify the building of another revolution. For both, the standard was the same: the preservation of the revolutionary creation—its aims, its ideals, and its future success.

To fail to recognize the revolutionary character of those men's minds is to miss the fundamental reason for their existence. For us to credit their historical consciousness while at the same time denying ours—especially in the name of scholarship—is our most incredible historical irony. To assume that Jefferson did not mean it when he spoke of the necessity of revolution or when he stated, "The Revolution of 1800 was as real a revolution in the principles of our government as that of 1776 was in its form," is to risk missing the true meaning of his entire political career.

We are finally brought back to Joseph Charles's assertion regarding Jefferson's intentions and career. It is this author's contention that Jefferson defined them; only ". . . we have failed to understand them." All of us realize that Jefferson, complex man that he was, was certainly no fool. Therefore, upon those principles that he adhered to for a lifetime, we must assume that he meant what he said. We must also assume that he knew something about revolution; he'd seen two of them closer than anyone else in America. Further, Jefferson's correspondence and his actions reveal a lifelong fascination with the idea of revolution. Thus, the major problem confronting the historian is, What did Jefferson mean by "the Revolution of 1800"? Beyond that query is another: Is what he meant intelligible to us today? And if it is, what can we learn about revolution that was either new in Jefferson's time or applicable to our own?

This last point may be put into perspective by referring to

Aristotle and Polybius, two men who were infinitely closer to that revolutionary generation than to anyone in our own. One a philosopher, the other a historian, both were shrewd judges of human nature as well as nations. And both agreed that "the beginning is not merely half of the whole, but reaches out toward the end."[22] That revolutionary beginning, on July 4, 1776, like the end on July 4, 1826, without being teleologic, was symbolic for both John Adams and Thomas Jefferson. Indeed, it was almost as symbolic as that day in February 1801 when, together, they acted to preserve the spirit and the principles of the American Revolution.

[22] Hannah Arendt, *On Revolution* (New York, 1963), p. 215.

The Idea of a Non-Party State

"... for it is the nature and intention of a constitution to prevent governing by party."

THOMAS PAINE, 1795

If the historians of the early national period in America have failed to consider the revolutionary themes implicit in their period, they have more than compensated by their desire to discover and sometimes invent a modern two-party system, emerging full-blown from the minds of Jefferson, Madison, and Hamilton. Beginning with Joseph Charles's pioneering work, *The Origins of the American Party System*, the historians have queued up behind his scholarship to push the date of the formation of parties from the late, to the middle, and now to the early 1790s.[1]

Thus the concept of a "loyal party opposition" has grown in the literature of the professional historians until it has assumed the stature of our most fundamental law. Not only historians but political scientists and everyone else who has sought to explain the stability of the American governmental system have looked to the origins of parties for the confirmation of our genius. The two-party system was the dominating idea in history and political science during the twentieth century. Historians and political scientists were so mesmerized by it that they, like English Whig historians,

[1] Charles, *The Origins of the American Party System*, op. cit., the earliest years; Cunningham, *The Jeffersonian Republicans*, op. cit., Chambers, *Political Parties in a New Nation*, op. cit., and Hofstadter, *The Idea of a Party System*, op. cit., the middle years; and Ryan, "Party Formation in the United States Congress, 1789–1796," op. cit., most recently, are examples.

went back and reread all of American history (as well as British history) in order to demonstrate the continuity of the twentieth-century party system with the past. When they did so, the Revolution of 1800 dissolved. It had to.

Nor was this search for the roots of the American party system without its own historical irony. This national obsession to place the origins of political parties there has been sustained despite repeated statements that there were none by virtually everyone who participated in politics at the time. Most recently Richard Hofstadter, in the latest full treatment of the subject, wrote an entire book simultaneously asserting and denying the formation of political parties from 1790 to 1801.[2] Yet he, too, ended on the now already familiar line: Jefferson's greatest contribution was one that he had flamboyantly ignored—viz., the formation of parties. The bias, then, of the early national period historian, as well as most political scientists, not only has been antirevolutionary, it has been in favor of imposing twentieth-century political values on eighteenth-century organization. Again the historian is accused of being ahistorical.[3]

This chapter is an attempt to redress that historical perspective and to deal with the political structure of the eighteenth century as a man of the times saw it. What I am trying to do is to make a case for the politics of faction and of revolution as opposed to an emphasis on emerging political parties. If we examine the structure of politics from 1790 to 1801 and ask ourselves what Hamilton, Jefferson, Madison, et al. thought they were doing, not what historians since Henry Adams thought they were doing, a totally different picture of that political struggle will emerge.

[2] Hofstadter, *The Idea of a Party System*, op. cit., pp. 1 and 2.

[3] Chambers, *Political Parties in a New Nation*, op. cit. See his references to Max Weber and V. O. Key, both twentieth-century political analysts, for his organizational understanding of party, pp. 143 ff.; see Hofstadter, *The Idea of a Party System*, op. cit., and his references to Hans Kelsen, Robert Dahl, Herman Finer, and Robert MacIver for the shaping of his idea of party, pp. 6–8. See also *The American Party Systems*, eds. William Chambers and Walter D. Burnham (New York, 1967), pp. 3–89, as examples.

Moreover, by examining the period from a classical revolutionary perspective, rather than a nineteenth- or twentieth-century European perspective, it is possible to state several conditions not generally recognized. First, the men in power from 1790 to 1801 did not even remotely conceive of a modern two-party system. In fact, the opposite is true. They wished to consolidate and perpetuate a one-party system of politics in America and were successful in their lifetimes. Second, their view of political administration was a classical political view, necessitating only one faction in power and abhorring the existence of an "opposition." Third, because of this view it was necessary for those who were out of power to foment revolution, based upon the classical political theory of "electoral Caesarism,"[4] simply to have access to or gain power. This last point will be discussed at length in the following chapters.

In order to develop these themes it is necessary to realize that the eighteenth century had its own historical perspective. As one historian has put it, "the most fruitful point of departure in studying their careers as statesmen is acceptance of the fact that all the questions they asked and all the answers they found to them were eighteenth century questions and answers that their intensive reading had already blocked out into a systematic pattern."[5] They were not twentieth-century concepts of political organization. Any attempt, therefore, to understand that "pattern," their political ideology, must examine the assumptions upon which their political logic rested. It must also trace in detail through books, letters, diaries, and actions the degree to which the actors adhered to their "patterns"; and above all determine what, if any, influence the

---

[4] "Caesarism is the classic maneuver employed by the disaffected or thwarted members of a ruling class. Their response to being thwarted is to capitalize on the grievances of the subject population. The people are promised reforms in return for their aid in overthrowing the elite. The Gracchi initiated this maneuver in ancient Rome, but Julius Caesar made it successful." See Harvey Wheeler, *Democracy in a Revolutionary Era* (New York, 1968), p. 16.

[5] Douglass Adair, "The Intellectual Origins of Jeffersonian Democracy," unpublished Ph.D. dissertation (Yale University, 1943), p. 1 of summary.

past imposed upon their conception of politics. Nowhere is this truer than where the concepts "faction" and "party" are concerned.

While historians of early America have been confronted with these two terms for generations, most have understood them only superficially and have interpreted them literally according to their notions of when political parties were formed. Failing to examine their etymology, these historians have consigned their meaning to different periods in American history. Faction and party, it is commonly assumed, represent a kind of watershed in early American politics. The former term belongs to the period generally up to Washington's Farewell Address, where the warnings against "factions" are often considered a naïve attempt by the Chief Executive to disregard political reality. The latter term signifies the establishment of political parties or, at minimum, their origins as we know them today.

Rarely has a historian grappled with the complex meaning of these terms and never has one systematically applied them to the period in a historical sense or in a manner that reflected the written statements of the participants. Thus, for clarity's sake, and rather than discuss misconceptions of the terms party and faction by authors of secondary works in American history, it best suits our purpose to establish a working definition of the terms for an eighteenth-century politician.[6]

Common definitions before the nineteenth century treated the terms similarly, beginning in the sixteenth century. The *Oxford English Dictionary* gives a reference to "party" in 1535 as "inclined to form parties or to act for party purposes; seditious." "Faction" was described as "violent." "Sedition" held a connotation of insurrection and treason against the state, both revolu-

[6] Richard Hofstadter has come closer than any other American historian, but for unknown reasons failed to follow his research to its logical conclusions. Perhaps the title of his book *The Idea of a Party System: The Rise of Legitimate Opposition in American Politics* explains the failure. For to do so would have invalidated his thesis insofar as it applied to the period 1790–1801.

tionary kinds of activity. Lord Bolingbroke referred to faction as that which "hath no regard to National Interest."[7]

One dictionary used by contemporaries, *An Universal Etymological English Dictionary*, explained that party and faction were synonymous.[8] Samuel Johnson in his dictionary suggested two meanings that essentially merged in the examples that he cited. Giving similar descriptions of the two terms, he said faction was "a party in a state" and also "tumult, discord and dissension."[9] The examples he cited for faction in both instances were similar: 1. "He has been known to commit outrages and cherish factions," and 2. "By one of Simon's factions murders were committed." Violence and dissension were common to both terms. It remained for Thomas Hobbes, however, to give the classic revolutionary description to faction, common from Aristotle's time to Dickens' *Tale of Two Cities*. He said faction "is as it were a city within a city."[10] This was indeed recognition that potential revolutionary activity was associated with the term, for it raised the specter of the "two city" theory of revolution.

These definitions perhaps sum up, better than any other, the eighteenth century's understanding of both terms. Seditious, revolutionary, "always with an opprobrious sense, conveying the imputation of selfish or mischievous ends or turbulent or unscrupulous methods,"[11] was what characterized faction and party and sent a wave of apprehension through anyone who seriously contemplated

[7] *A New English Dictionary on Historical Principles* (later the *Oxford English Dictionary*) (Oxford, 1901), Vol. IV, F&G, p. 12.

[8] Nathan Bailey, *An Universal Etymological English Dictionary* (Edinburgh, 1800).

[9] Samuel Johnson, *A Dictionary of the English Language* (London, 1799), Vol. I. Dr. Johnson's combination of the two words can also be seen in the subsequent use of the derivative terms "factious" ("in a manner criminally dissentious or tumultuous"); "factiously" ("loud and violent in a party"); and "factiousness" ("violent clamorousness for a party").

[10] Thomas Hobbes, *Leviathan* (New York: Great Books of The Western World, 1952).

[11] *A New English Dictionary on Historical Principles*, op. cit., Vol. IV, p. 12.

them. Distinctions between party and faction were slight, if made at all. Looking upon party as both a form of political organization and as an idea of violence, "most American writers seemed to have assimilated these two senses of the word to each other."[12] Thus, in eighteenth-century America, one could speak of party violence or the violence of faction and be well understood.

Noah Webster throws additional light on the term party if for no other reason than because he was an ardent foe of Jefferson's during that turbulent decade of the '90s. Albeit after 1800, his original edition defined faction in a way that touched upon all that we have discussed—including the importance of revolution. He says a faction is:

> A party, in political society, combined or acting in union, in opposition to the prince, government or state; usually applied to a minority, but it may be applied to a majority. Sometimes a state is divided into factions nearly equal. Rome was always disturbed by factions. Republics are proverbial for factions, and factions in monarchies have often effected *revolutions.*[13]

The terms faction and party, though appearing synonymous to the average eighteenth-century American, were nevertheless partially separable. Not only did they connote violence, turbulence, and a revolutionary threat against the state—its administration and national interest—they also implied a relationship to one another based on the complexity of human nature and its involvement with politics. And there it is that our comprehension of the terms in their political and historical context must begin.

Perhaps it lies with an author read by virtually every one of the revolutionary generation, at least one who was included in their libraries, to explain the connection between the two terms:

> It is far from being an easy matter to state to you, fairly and clearly, what the words *party* and *faction* really mean. . . . A Party then, as I take it, is a set of men connected together, in

[12] Hofstadter, *The Idea of a Party System,* op. cit., p. 11.
[13] Noah Webster, *An American Dictionary of the English Language,* Vol. I (New York, 1828).

virtue of their having, or, which in this case is the same thing, pretending to have the same *private* opinion with respect to *public* concerns; and while this is confined to sentiment or discourse, without interfering with the Management of affairs, I think it wears properly that denomination; but when it proceeds further, and influences men's conduct, in any considerable degree, it *becomes* FACTION. In all such cases there are revealed *reasons*, and a reserved MOTIVE. By revealed reasons, I mean a certain set of plausible doctrines, which may be stiled the creed of the party; but the reserved motive belongs to FACTION only, and is the THIRST OF POWER. The creeds of parties vary like those of sects; but all Factions have the same motive, which never implies more or less than a lust of dominion, though they may be, and generally are, covered with the specious pretenses of self-denial, and that vehemence referred to zeal for the public, which flows in fact from AVARICE, SELF-INTEREST, RESENTMENT and other private views.[14]

Lord Viscount Bolingbroke, who had spent most of his political life opposing the administration of Robert Walpole, knew whereof he spoke. Acquainted with the motives of nearly all who objected to the Walpolean system, he could easily discern his colleagues' thirst for power no matter how they clothed it with patriotic disguises.[15]

His distinction between party and faction looms important in the politics of the early republic if merely for the reason that most American statesmen complained about party and faction on the same grounds.[16] We shall see later, when examining the idea of

[14] *Memoirs of the Life and Ministerial Conduct, of the Late Lord Visc. Bolingbroke* (London, 1752), p. 41.

[15] "The factious man is apt to mistake himself for a patriot." Berkeley, "Essay on Patriotism" (1750), *The Works of George Berkeley*, ed. A. Campbell Fraser (1901), p. 42, in *A New English Dictionary on Historical Principles*, op. cit., Vol. IV, p. 12.

[16] John Adams to Thomas Jefferson, 25 Dec. 1813, *The Adams-Jefferson Letters* (hereafter referred to as *Letters*), ed. Lester J. Cappon, Vol. II, p. 410. "Is it not laughable to hear Burke call Bolingbroke a superficial writer? To hear him ask, 'Who ever read him through?' Had I been present I would have answered him, 'I, I, myself, I have read him through, more than fifty years ago, and more than five times in my life, and once within five years past.' "

opposition, that "influencing men's behavior," making them stand in opposition to the state, was indeed "factious" and threatening behavior.

Two other observations by Bolingbroke about "motives" common to both terms deserve comment. First, members of parties or factions, despite their "revealed" motives, are men obsessed with power and a "lust for dominion." It follows then that these same men, given and perhaps even creating the opportunity, are capable of reaching for power through seditious means, which, in accordance with the contemporary definition, might be violent. This would be especially true if the administration in power considered their opposition illegal. Secondly, if parties *become* factions when their behavior affects the public realm, it is important to keep this distinction in mind. For one characteristic of eighteenth-century statesmen, little understood by twentieth-century writers, is the absolute vehemence with which they—ensconced in their own positions of power—denounced party and faction. The reasons lay in their extreme fear and anxiety of what occurred once parties became factions and began to influence public opinion. The results were almost guaranteed: disruption of the public realm. This distinction is important because it means that historians have misunderstood the terms party and faction by imputing public action only to the former. Nineteenth- and twentieth-century historians have brushed this distinction aside; and, in fact, they have *reversed* the distinction between party and faction.

David Hume's *History of England*, widely read in the colonies before, but even more after, the Revolution, described the idea of party and faction in this manner:

> Thus the nation came to be (in 1680) distinguished into petitioners and abhorrers. Factions indeed were at this time extremely animated against one another. The very names, by which each party denominated its antagonist, discover the virulence and rancour which prevailed. For besides petitioner and abhorrer, appellations which were soon forgotten, this year is remarkable for being the epoch of the well-known epithets of Whig and Tory, by which, and sometimes without any material difference, this island

has been so long divided. The court party reproached . . . their antagonists who were known as the Whigs: the country party found a resemblance between the popish banditti in Ireland, to whom the appellation of Tory was affixed: and after this manner these foolish terms of reproach came into public and general use; and even at present (1762) seem not nearer their end than when they were first invented.[17]

Here Hume implies that their origins go far back into England's past. Note how he traces the succession of party "appellations," and how quickly they change in their relation to terms such as "virulence," "rancour," and "banditti." In his *Treatise of Human Nature,* Hume wrote, "Factions subvert government, render laws impotent, and beget the fiercest animosities among men of the same nation, who ought to give mutual assistance to each other . . ." "Founders of factions," he wrote, should be "detested and hated."

Edmund Burke, who enjoyed immense popularity among Americans, spoke of party in two ways: as it existed in practice, and as he would have liked to see it ideally or philosophically. In 1770, his "Thoughts on the Cause of the Present Discontents" laid the source of England's troubles at the door of party and its relationship to the court. Describing the party system then in existence in all its ramifications, Burke went beyond theory to include the actual consequences of party practice:

The [party] machinery of this system is perplexed in its movements, and false in its principle. It is formed on a supposition that the king is something external to his government; and that he may be honored and aggrandized, even by its debility and disgrace. The [court as well as party] plan proceeds expressly on the idea of enfeebling the regulatory executory power. It proceeds on the idea of weakening the state in order to strengthen the court. The scheme depending entirely on distrust, on disconnection, on mutability by principle, on systematic weakness in every par-

---

[17] David Hume, *The History of England,* 6 vols. (London, 1841), Vol. VI, pp. 163–64.

ticular member; it is impossible that the total result should be substantial strength of any kind. . . .

All sorts of parties, by this means, have been brought into administration; from whence few have had the good fortune to escape without disgrace; none at all without considerable losses. . . . They [the party men] grow ashamed and mortified in a situation, which by its vicinity to power, only serves to remind them the more strongly of their insignificance. They are obliged either to execute the orders of their inferiors, or to see themselves opposed by the natural instruments of their office. With the loss of their dignity they lose their temper. In their turn they grow troublesome to that cabal which, whether it supports or opposes, equally disgraces and equally betrays them. . . . By this means the party goes out much thinner than it came in; and is only reduced in strength by its temporary possession of power.[18]

Burke's description of "things as they are" is a revelation of the enervating influence of party. While he states in these passages that the court may initiate much of the corruption, he demonstrates the complicity of party in policies that weaken the state. His equation of the various parties, factions, and cabals confirms the analysis of Bolingbroke and Hume, points to party undermining the constitution, and clearly implies that their influence should be limited.

Burke, however, always held out for an ideal party structure. He hoped that someday he might find a way to unite men of principle around a party organization. Though this contradicted entirely the evidence he saw around him, he indulged—in that same essay—in speculation, perhaps even wishful thinking. He even made an appeal to those "imposters" and "vulgar" politicians he so despised. "Party," he hoped to assure them, "is a body of men united for promoting by their joint endeavors the national interest upon some particular principle in which they are all agreed."[19]

When Burke became a member of Parliament four years later,

[18] *The Works of Edmund Burke*, 5 vols. (Boston, 1865), Vol. I, pp. 460–64.
[19] Ibid., Vol. I, pp. 530–31.

his speculation soon reduced to reality. Appearing before his electors, he revealed his disdain for party thusly: "As for the trifling petulance which the rage of party stirs up in little minds . . . it has not made the slightest impression on me. The highest flight of such clamorous birds is winged in an inferior region of the air."[20]

In yet another famous remark, this time on the nature of a representative, Burke indicated a total unwillingness to sacrifice his views to those of any party. Here Burke presents the theory behind his observations on practical instruction from either his district or his party:

> His [the representative's] unbiased opinion, his mature judgement, his enlightened conscience, he ought not to sacrifice to you, to any man, or any set of men living. . . . But government and legislation are matters of reason and judgement, and not of inclination; and what sort of reason is that in which determination precedes the discussion, in which one set of men deliberate and another decide, and where those who form the conclusions are perhaps three hundred miles from those who hear the arguments?[21]

A more devastating intellectual critique of the function of party could hardly be made. Refusing to become the creature of party, stating that the very rationale of party—with its willingness to dispense with deliberation and dialectical reason—contradicted the basic reason for government, Burke had made his decision on party.

For Bolingbroke, Hume, and Burke, three of the most influential writers to make an impression on the American mind, any separation of the two terms was artificial, even academic. Faction and party were, at least in the eighteenth century, logically dependent upon one another, specifically merging whenever applied to the public arena. Thus, when historians and politicians abhorred the influence of party and faction, they did so in a way that was historically intelligible to them. Their descriptions, in light of the

---

[20] Ibid., Vol. II, p. 94, "Speech to the Electors at Bristol at the Conclusion of the Poll."

[21] Ibid., pp. 95–96.

definitions of the period, reveal why the terms party and faction were used so generally in addition to their being used as terms of opprobrium.

The terms had such a long history that they were widely assumed by American statesmen to be a part of human nature. This at least was the approach taken by the two men most responsible for establishing the theoretical guidelines of the early republic. James Madison and Alexander Hamilton attempted to analyze the terms in light of their origins and influence on the political system. Their *Federalist* essays presented an analysis of party and faction that is more than consistent with the history of the terms we have reviewed. One scholar, minutely demonstrating the connection between the two, has even described Hume's influence on Madison as "a parallel march of ideas."[22]

Madison referred to "the *violence* of faction" as a "dangerous vice" characteristic of free governments. "By a faction," he says, "I understand a number of citizens, whether amounting to a majority or minority of the whole, who are actuated and united by some common impulse of passion, or of interest, *adverse* to the rights of other citizens, or to the permanent and aggregate interests of the community." After defining the term he goes on to inquire into its origins and switches from "faction" to "party" frequently, indicating that he had "assimilated" the two terms. "From the protection of different and unequal faculties of acquiring property, the possession of different degrees and kinds of property immediately results, and from the influence of these . . . ensues a division of the society into different interests and parties." He continued, "The latent causes of faction are thus sown in the nature of man; and we see them everywhere . . ." Thus party, as Madison understood it, was not something of recent origin. Parties had been around since the beginning of man.

The tendency to have different mental abilities and opinions among men has "divided mankind into parties, inflamed them

---

[22] Adair, "The Intellectual Origins of Jeffersonian Democracy," op. cit., p. 261.

with mutual animosity, and rendered them much more disposed to vex and oppress each other than to cooperate for their common good." Adding that "justice ought to hold the balance between the contending groups," Madison says, "Yet the parties are, and must be, themselves the judges; *and the most numerous party, or in other words, the most powerful faction* must be expected to prevail." He ends his essay on this note: "To secure the public good and provide rights against the danger of such a faction . . . is then the great object to which our injuries are directed."[23]

In capsule form Madison captured the essence of the terms as they were understood by his contemporaries. Madison realized that faction and party were inescapably rooted in human nature. At the same time he urged his readers to beware: faction and party produce violence, zeal, animosity, oppression, and danger—all *adverse* to the interests of the community. Madison clearly felt that ideas, opinions, attitudes, etc., were a source of property and determined one's attachment to a particular faction. This attachment could be to a wealthy group or to a group that represented the wider interests of the people. Whatever one's attachment might be, it represented his notion of his *own* self-interest. One would have thought that the great potential questions of the time would have influenced the average man's decision to join a faction or party. But the danger of faction, according to Madison, was not limited to the great political questions of the day. "Frivolous and fanciful distinctions" were often the cause of great violence. "Men of factious tempers, of local prejudices, or of sinister designs may, by intrigue, by corruption, or by other means, first obtain the suffrages, and then betray the interests of the people."[24] The rise of faction or party thus represents a constant and permanent threat of violence to the state. Their connection with "intrigue" and "sinister design" or, in other words, conspiracy and perhaps revolution, links them in Madison's mind with the subversion of

[23] James Madison, Alexander Hamilton, and John Jay, *The Federalist Papers*, ed. Clinton Rossiter (New York, 1961), #10, pp. 77–84. All quotations hereafter referred to as *Federalist*.

[24] *Federalist*, #10, p. 82.

the interests of the nation. His conclusion, then, is that their effects must be broken and controlled. They are, at all costs, not to be legitimately recognized or encouraged.

Yet Madison was not alone in his aversion to party and faction. His *Federalist* essay, written just prior to the beginning of the decade, simply happens to be the most celebrated commentary on the nature of party and faction in eighteenth-century America. His associates, who represented every faction on the political landscape and were the most important statesmen in the early republic, agreed with him. They, too, shared an abhorrence of parties and realized that unless their violence was controlled and influence diminished, the harmony cherished by every citizen would be destroyed.

Alexander Hamilton in his *Federalist* essays was in complete agreement with Madison on the danger of party. In his very first number—indeed, in almost every essay he wrote—he warns the reader, if not explicitly, in so many words of like description, to beware the seditious effects of faction. "Ambition, avarice, personal animosity, party opposition, and many other motives not more laudable than these . . ." were typical of that "intolerant spirit which has at all times characterized political parties."[25] Registering the disgust he has for faction, Hamilton continues: "A firm Union will be of the utmost moment to the peace and liberty of the States as a barrier against domestic faction and insurrection. It is impossible to read the history of the petty republics of Greece and Italy without feeling sensations of horror and disgust at the . . . rapid successions of revolutions by which they were kept in a perpetual vibration between the extremes of tyranny and anarchy."[26]

This view repeats his explanations in the sixth *Federalist*, describing the insurrections and rebellions from ancient times to the "late menacing disturbances in Pennsylvania and the actual insurrections and rebellions in Massachusetts."[27] Thus Hamilton early

[25] *Federalist*, #1, p. 34.
[26] *Federalist*, #9, p. 71.
[27] *Federalist*, #6, p. 59.

discloses a relationship between faction, party, opposition to the state, and violence and revolution. In fact, he fears the potential influence of faction and party in the new government so much that he raises the specter of what may happen if it is allowed to persist: "A successful faction may erect a tyranny on the ruins of law and order, while no succor could constitutionally be afforded by the Union to her friends and supporters of the government. The tempestuous situation from which Massachusetts has scarcely emerged evinces that dangers of this kind are *not merely speculative*. Who can determine what might have been the issue of her late convulsions if the malcontents had been headed by a Caesar or by a Cromwell?"[28]

Hamilton, along with Madison, viewed justice as the end of government and the cement that held it together. His comments in *Federalist* #81, referring to the choosing of judges by the state legislatures, more than reveal his contempt for the influence of party and faction: "The members of the legislature will rarely be chosen with a view to those qualifications which fit men for the station of judges; and as, on this account, there will be great reason to apprehend all the ill consequences of defective information, so on account of the natural propensity of such bodies to *party divisions*, there will be no less reason to fear that *the pestilential breath of faction may poison the fountains of justice*."[29]

Echoing Madison again, this time on the source of faction, Hamilton criticized a proposed dual presidency, and ingeniously forecast the role of party in American politics for the next decade. Keeping in mind the turmoil and divisions between the officers of Washington's and Adams' cabinets in the 1790s, one can readily see what Hamilton meant in *Federalist* #70 and #77:

> Whenever two or more persons are engaged in any common enterprise or pursuit, there is always the danger of difference of opinion. If it be a public trust or office in which they are clothed with equal dignity and authority, there is peculiar danger of personal

[28] *Federalist*, #21, pp. 139–40.
[29] *Federalist*, #81, pp. 484–85.

emulation and even animosity. From either, and especially from all
these causes, the most bitter dissensions are apt to spring. Whenever these happen, they lessen the respectability, weaken the
authority, and distract the plans and operations of those whom
they divide . . . *and what is still worse,* they might split the community into the most violent and irreconcilable factions, adhering differently to the different individuals who composed the
magistracy.[30]

Continuing with the same description in *Federalist* #77, he describes the influence of faction and party intrigue, connections and
"personal influence" in government in a way that was characteristic of the terms from classical times through the age of Robert
Walpole:

Every mere council of appointment, however constituted, will be
a conclave in which cabal and intrigue will have their full scope.
Their number, without an unwarrantable increase of expense, cannot be large enough to preclude a facility of combination. And as
each member will have his friends and connections to provide for,
the desire of mutual gratification will beget a scandalous bartering
of votes and bargaining for places.[31]

What is worth noting here, in these two long quotations, is not
only Hamilton's description of the influence of party and faction
upon an administration, but his general description of politics. He
is describing the politics of England for the past century and a
half. "Cabal," "intrigue," "friends," "connections," "bartering,"
and "bargaining" were all part of the political life of the mother
country and a style of politics that Hamilton projects for America.[32]
Thus Hamilton, at the beginning of the decade, described

[30] *Federalist*, #70, p. 246.

[31] *Federalist*, #77, p. 462.

[32] This theoretical summary by both Madison and Hamilton stands in stark
contrast to Noble Cunningham, Jr.'s remark in *The Jeffersonian Republicans:*
"It is felt, however, that the adoption of the Constitution, with its major
alterations in the framework of the national government, marked a sharp
change with respect to party development in the United States," p. ix.

politics in America as essentially vulnerable to the vicissitudes of the politics of Europe. He understood only too well that encouraging party and faction, at the theoretical as well as the practical level, guaranteed that the emergent system of American politics would be propelled into the futile violence and dissension that had plagued every republic in history.

Throughout the remainder of his political career, Hamilton reserved a special contempt for parties. At various times he caricatured them as "the petulance of party," the "rage of party spirit," "sedition and party rage," the "unaccommodating spirit of party," the "delirium of party," the "baneful spirit of party," and the "heats of party." Hamilton's latest biographer notes that he "never made room in his political science for a theory of political parties because he never imagined them as fully developed, essential, both dynamic and stabilizing adjuncts of the political process. To the end of his life he refused to believe that the party he led was a party at all. It was, rather, a kind of *ad hoc* committee of correspondence of men with a large view of America's destiny, a rudimentary instrument of the public good that had been reluctantly created by him and his friends to meet the wrongheaded challenge of men like Clinton and Jefferson."[33]

Madison and Hamilton, the architects of the new government, were in good company when it came to a distaste for party. For every intelligent politician, and especially those we consider statesmen, made his pronouncement against party and faction at one time or another. That they were sincere in professing their views is something that we, as historians, must view critically but not altogether dismiss.

Contrary to some historians' opinions, the consistency with which these statesmen held their views against faction and party in every phase of their political careers is indicative of a lifelong attachment to the antiparty cause. Moreover, they were willing to

[33] Clinton Rossiter, *Alexander Hamilton and the Constitution* (New York, 1964), p. 148.

write down their bias in theoretical terms, explaining in extreme detail the consequences of party activity. This fact alone should signify that they were not being "hypocritical."[34]

In addition, every political opinion on the spectrum was represented, an indication that the antiparty bias was part of an entire generation and not merely a few aberrant politicians. But what strikes the reader again and again, reading through the literature of the decade, is the quality of the men who expressed their opinions against party. They are without question the brightest, most reflective, often the wittiest, and easily the most philosophical men of their time. James Madison, Alexander Hamilton, George Washington, Sam and John Adams, Thomas Jefferson, James Monroe, Patrick Henry, Albert Gallatin, John Jay, Thomas Paine, John Taylor of Caroline, John Quincy Adams, Benjamin Rush, Fisher Ames—the list could go on, reading like a Who's Who of the 1790s.

Fisher Ames was one of those who took the time to write down his thoughts on the nature and influence of faction and party. He wrote:

> *Faction* is an adherence to interests foreign to the interests of the state; there is such a faction among us devoted to France. . . . There is some hope of reclaiming a very few of them; but if they travel far on the party road, or associate long with the desperadoes in the van, who explore the thorny and crooked by-ways, they will not remain honest. They will be corrupted, and so deeply, that, in every approach towards civil war and revolution, the dupes, who sincerely believe the whole creed of their *party*, will be found to go the farthest.[35]

Ames, writing in 1800, accepted the same definitions of the terms as his contemporaries. And like them, he makes a connection

---

[34] Hofstadter, *The Idea of a Party System*, op. cit., p. 18. "All these antiparty manifestos by party leaders can be set down, if we like, to hypocrisy . . ." Then, after adroitly stating this theme, Hofstadter has it both ways and says: ". . . the only justification of any party . . . was to eliminate all parties."

[35] Fisher Ames, "Laocoon No. 1," *Works of Fisher Ames*, compiled by a number of his friends (Boston, 1809), p. 107.

between faction, party, and the idea of revolution. Ames also dealt with the origins and causes of party and faction exactly as did Madison and Hamilton. He asks:

> Is it in the nature of free governments to exist without parties? Such a thing has never yet been and probably will never be. Is it in the nature of party to exist without passion? Or of passion to acquiesce, when it meets with opposers and obstacles? No, it is absurd to expect faction cold in the pursuit of great objects, reasonable in selecting means for gratifying inordinate designs, retarded by moral doubts . . . fearless of consequences. Party moderation is children's talk. Who has ever seen faction *calmly* in a rage? Who will expect to see that carnivorous monster quietly submit to eat grass?[36]

Fisher Ames's prose may seem lurid to us now, but to his contemporaries it was commonplace. The consequences of unbridled faction and party activity meant revolution, civil war, violence, and perhaps the most feared development of all—a change in the form of government. Others agreed with Ames, albeit in less colorful language. John Jay, writing to Jefferson in 1786, observed, "If faction should long bear down law and government, tyranny may raise its head, or the more sober part of the people may even think of a King."[37] It was a remark that left an indelible impression on his correspondent and was to become the most crucial issue of the next fifteen years.

More than a decade later Jay described his own history of parties from the Revolution to 1800. His analysis of those who were in opposition to the government is linked to their disapproval of the constitution, and ultimately—as they compose a faction—to their becoming a potential revolutionary force. It is also noteworthy that Jay sees a developing continuity between the Whigs and Tories of the Revolution and the parties contending for power in 1800. He does not indicate a radical break between them, i.e., the

[36] Ibid., p. 110.
[37] John Jay to Thomas Jefferson, 27 Oct. 1786, *The Papers of Thomas Jefferson*, ed. Julian P. Boyd (Princeton, N.J., 1950), Vol. 10, p. 489 (hereafter referred to as *Papers*).

establishment of a new party system; instead, he implies that their ideologies grew out of the Revolution. In both of these opinions he is in consistent agreement with his influential colleagues.

> The revolution found and left only two primary parties, *viz.* the whigs who succeeded, and the tories who were suppressed. The former were unanimous in approving the leading measures, both civil and military, which gave them victory. When the adoption of the new constitution afterwards came into question, the whigs divided into two parties; the one for it and the other against it. The party for the constitution prevailed; and they have with as great unanimity approved of General Washington's civil as of his military measures and services. The party opposed to the constitution disapproved of the government established by it; and there are very few of the important measures of that government which have escaped their censure.[38]

Tom Paine was another writer who considered party an evil that must be kept within traditional bounds. Writing in 1795, he states, ". . . for it is the *nature and intention of a constitution to prevent governing by party,* by establishing a common principle that shall limit and control the power and the impulse of party, and that says to all parties, *thus far shalt thou go and no further.* But in the absence of a constitution, men look entirely to party; and instead of principle governing party, party governs principle."[39]

Sprinkled throughout Paine's writings in the 1790s are constant references to the terms faction and party, always in an opprobrious sense. "The cloven foot of faction," "faction, acting in disguise," and "the dupes of faction" are simply a few among hundreds of like references. Yet Paine takes us a step further in our understanding of party and faction during the period. He not only implies his agreement that parties will always exist, but states that it is in the "nature and intention" of constitutional government to

[38] John Jay to Rev. Samuel Miller, 28 Feb. 1800, *The Life and Writings of John Jay,* ed. William Jay, 2 vols. (New York, 1833), Vol. II, p. 293.

[39] "Dissertation on First Principles of Government," July 1795, *The Life and Writings of Thomas Paine,* ed. Daniel Edwin Wheeler, 10 vols. (New York, 1908), Vol. 9, p. 273 (hereafter referred to as *Paine*).

"prevent governing by party." Always theoretical and often reaching to understand the basic principles of political science, Paine in several sentences has drawn out the prevailing theory and reasons for the eighteenth century's opposition to party.

Paine placed the constitution as a barrier between the violence of party and the principles of republican government. He also noted that in the absence of an effective constitution, or of rulers who adhere to the letter and spirit of the constitution, the spirit of party and faction will destroy those principles. This is an important observation as it demonstrates the reasoning that Paine, as well as most of his colleagues, agreed upon: party—if allowed to develop—would inevitably destroy the constitution, the principles of republican government, and the republic itself. And with the republic would go precious liberty.

This theme is important because it constitutes the main thrust of Jefferson's intriguing statement: "The Revolution of 1800 was as real a revolution in the principles of our government as that of 1776 was in its form."[40] The reader will do well to keep Paine's construction in mind as he ponders the relationship between the ideas of faction and revolution.

John Taylor of Caroline, another theoretical writer, and like Paine a close friend of Jefferson's, viewed party in a similar light. Only the emphasis was different. He wrote:

> The situation of the public good, in the hands of two parties nearly poised as to numbers, must be extremely perilous. Truth is a thing, not of divisibility into conflicting parts, but of unity. Hence, both sides cannot be right. Every patriot deprecates a disunion, which is only to be obviated by a national preference of one of these parties.[41]

Taylor pointed out the theme of unity necessary for any republic. Where Paine named the constitution as the binding force for the community, Taylor speaks of truth as producing that same unity or

[40] Jefferson to Spencer Roane, 6 Sept. 1819, *Writings*, Vol. XV, p. 212.

[41] John Taylor, *A Definition of Parties: or the Political Effects of the Paper System Considered* (Philadelphia, 1794), p. 2.

harmony. Since both groups could not be right (there was still one truth in the eighteenth century), Taylor implies that one party only is desirable. He states explicitly, that "two . . . nearly poised as to numbers" (our modern conception of the two-party system) "must be *extremely perilous*." At best Taylor is arguing for a one-party government; and, in his philosophical way, he is saying that a two-party system will result in disunion or civil war.

James Monroe, one of Jefferson's closest confidants, made up his mind on faction and party early in his political career. As a delegate to the Congress under the Articles of Confederation, he wrote Jefferson happily: "I have never seen a body of men collected in which there was less party, for there is not a shadow of it here . . ."[42] At the time of the Constitutional Convention Monroe was again writing his friend that the states would do themselves credit to "keep under the demon of party."[43] Fourteen years later Monroe urged Jefferson to formally create a one-party state. He wrote: "This public expects some tone to be given your Administration immediately. There is a conflict of principle, and either democracy or royalty must prevail. The opposing parties can never be united . . . because their views are as opposite as light and darkness."[44] Monroe, who took an unusually hard line, believed that the opposition could not be reconciled; therefore it must be eliminated.

[42] James Monroe to Thomas Jefferson, 16 June 1785, *Papers*, Vol. 8, p. 217. One historian has stated that "as early as 1784 patriots such as John Breckinridge, James Madison, John Taylor and James Monroe had formed a society called 'The Society for the Preservation of Liberty,' the principal object of which was to prevent the rise of faction in America." "Equally adamant for destroying party dissension . . ." was Dr. George Logan:

> If men of every party would endeavor to understand the principles of genuine liberty and the just rights of our country, it would dissolve the spirit of party, heal our divisions and unite us all in one common cause—the promoting the prosperity and happiness of ye United States.

The above quotations are from Eugene P. Link's *Democratic-Republican Societies, 1790–1800* (New York, 1942), pp. 122–23.

[43] James Monroe to Thomas Jefferson, 27 July 1787, *Papers*, Vol. 2, p. 631.
[44] James Monroe to Thomas Jefferson, 3 March 1801, Lib. Cong.

Another revolutionary figure, a Virginian, but one who could scarcely be considered a confidant of Jefferson's, also shared a horror of faction and party. Writing to Jefferson in 1785, when they still enjoyed a degree of civil rapport, Patrick Henry commented on Virginia politics: "I think we are as free from faction or party as any [state] in the Union."[45] For the remainder of his public life Henry would not change his mind. In 1799, on the occasion of his last public appearance, he dramatically called for the unity characteristic of the non-party state. Anticipating the crisis of the approaching revolution he declared: "United we stand; divided we fall. . . . Let us not split into factions which must destroy that union upon which our existence hangs. Let us preserve our strength . . . and not exhaust it in civil commotion and intestine wars."[46]

One of the clearest statements on the theory of the one- or non-party state comes from a man whom everyone admired, ironically, for every quality except his intellectual probity—viz., George Washington. Father figure, warrior, model of virtue, a monument in terms of his symbolic value to the country, he was also considered a repository of wisdom and common sense. Therefore, his specific warnings against party and faction in the Farewell Address merit special attention. Not only is it consistent with the definitions stated thus far, it was written in the context of a dissertation on the principles of constitutionalism and free government.

As a theoretical statement of politics in the 1790s, the Farewell Address mirrors Paine's expression that the constitution, in order to be preserved, must dampen down the spirit of party. And while there is now debate about the original authorship of the address, Washington embraced as his own the ideas contained in his last formal message to the country.

As stated earlier, the Farewell Address represents a "watershed" in the literature of American political history. Perhaps because of this, it is rarely read in its entirety, and is often taken for granted.

[45] Patrick Henry to Thomas Jefferson, 10 Sept. 1785, *Papers*, Vol. 8, p. 508.
[46] *Patrick Henry: Life, Correspondence & Speeches*, ed. W. W. Henry, 3 vols. (New York, 1891), Vol. II, pp. 609–10.

Accordingly, I have included this long excerpt because of the frequent charges by historians and political scientists that Washington was "naïve" in posting his warning on party and faction. It is my opinion that Washington's valedictory address successfully delineated the problems that would afflict the nation for several generations and especially underlined, in an eighteenth-century context, the disruptive role that party and faction would play in the years immediately following his retirement. The reader should judge for himself, in light of the theory of politics just reviewed, how "naïve" he was.

After "contemplating the causes which may disturb our union," Washington notes his concern over rising sectionalism. He observes that "geographical discriminations—Northern and Southern, Atlantic and Western" will attempt through *"the expedients of party* to acquire influence within particular districts" and "misrepresent the opinions and aims of other districts." He thus began the warning to his countrymen: "You can not shield yourselves too much against . . . these misrepresentations . . ." Next, Washington establishes a connection between the right to revolution, the constitution, and party opposition. These three themes continue as he launches into his attack upon party and faction:

> . . . the basis of our political systems is the right of the people to make and to alter their constitutions of government. But the constitution which at any time exists till changed by an explicit and authentic act of the whole people is sacredly obligatory upon all. The very idea of the power and the right of the people to establish government presupposes the duty of every individual to obey the established government.
>
> All obstructions to the execution of the laws, all combinations and associations, under whatever plausible character, with the real design to direct, control, counteract, or awe the regular deliberation and action of the constituted authorities, are destructive of this fundamental principle and of fatal tendency. They serve to organize *faction;* to give it an artificial and extraordinary force; to put in the place of the delegated will of the nation the will of a

party, often a small but artful and enterprising minority of the community, and, according to the alternate triumphs of different *parties,* to make the public administration the mirror of the ill-concerted and incongruous projects of *faction* rather than the organ of consistent and wholesome plans, digested by common counsels and modified by mutual interests.

However combinations or associations of the above descriptions may now and then answer popular ends, they are likely in the course of time and things to become potent engines by which cunning, ambitious, and unprincipled men will be enabled to subvert the power of the people, and to usurp for themselves the reins of government, destroying afterwards the very engines which have lifted them to unjust dominion.

. . . I have already intimated to you the danger of *parties* in the State, with particular reference to the founding of them on geographical discriminations. Let me now take a more comprehensive view, and warn you in the most solemn manner against the baneful effects of the spirit of *party* generally.

This spirit, unfortunately, is inseparable from our nature, having its root in the strongest passion of the human mind. It exists under different shapes in all governments, more or less stifled, controlled, or repressed; but in those of the popular form it is seen in its greatest rankness and is truly their worst enemy.

The alternate domination of one *faction* over another, sharpened by the spirit of revenge natural to *party* dissension, which in different ages and countries has perpetrated the most horrid enormities, is itself a frightful despotism. But this leads at length to a more formal and permanent despotism. The disorders and miseries which result gradually incline the minds of men to seek security and repose in the absolute power of an individual, and sooner or later the chief of some prevailing *faction,* more able or more fortunate than his competitors, turns this disposition to the purposes of his own elevation on the ruins of public liberty.

Without looking forward to an extremity of this kind (which nevertheless ought not to be entirely out of sight), the common and continual mischiefs of the spirit of *party* are sufficient to make it the interest and duty of a wise people to discourage and restrain it.

It serves always to distract the public councils and enfeeble the public administration. It agitates the community with ill-founded jealousies and false alarms; kindles the animosity of one part against another; foments occasionally riot and insurrection. It opens the door to foreign influence and corruption, which find a facilitated access to the government itself through the channels of *party* passion. Thus the policy and the will of one country are subjected to the policy and will of another.

There is an opinion that *parties* in free countries are useful checks upon the administration of the government, and serve to keep alive the spirit of liberty. This within certain limits is probably true; and in governments of a monarchical cast patriotism may look with indulgence, if not with favor, upon the spirit of *party*. But in those of the popular character, in governments purely elective, it is a spirit not to be encouraged. From their natural tendency it is certain there will always be enough of that spirit for every salutary purpose; and there being constant danger of excess, the effort ought to be by force of public opinion to mitigate and assuage it. A fire not to be quenched, it demands a uniform vigilance to prevent its bursting into a flame, lest, instead of warming, it should consume.[47]

In light of our examination of the meaning of party and faction, Washington's exposition needs little commentary. Aside from his remarks comparing party in a monarchy to a free society, and the inclination of party to produce a permanent despotism, it should be sufficient to point out that he recognized the natural existence of parties in society, realized that they could not be totally destroyed, and urged his countrymen to control them. Indeed, in all of this, Washington is in complete agreement with the best minds of his time.

While we have examined in some detail the thoughts on party and faction expressed by leading statesmen of the period, we have reserved for the end of our review the comments of the two leading thinkers and actors during the 1790s, John Adams and Thomas Jefferson. Their careers prior to their confrontation in 1800 had been remarkably similar. Both men were delegates to the Conti-

[47] *Messages and Papers of the Presidents*, ed. James D. Richardson (Washington, D.C., 1897), Vol. I, pp. 209–11. Italics mine.

nental Congress in its earliest days, members of the committee to draft a Declaration of Independence, fellow diplomats in Europe, and members of Washington's first administration. In addition, their families had been extremely close as anyone who has read their correspondence and sensed the affection in those letters would know. Despite this commonality of experience, differences in their backgrounds, in education, locale, temperament, and philosophy, gave them much to argue about in one of the most celebrated exchanges of ideas in American history. Yet, in spite of those differences, there was one thing upon which they were inseparably agreed: political parties and factions were dangerous to a free society.

Adams, throughout his long career, had written and spoken out against the influence of faction and party in America. As early as 1780 he wrote two truly prophetic sentences, as strong an indictment of party as anyone could possibly write: "There is nothing which I dread so much as a division of the republic into two great parties, each arranged under its leader, and concerting measures in opposition to each other. This in my humble apprehension is to be dreaded as the greatest political evil under our constitution."[48]

Once Adams had reached the pinnacle of his own power one might have thought he would mellow in his attitude toward party. But a couple of references will show how troubled, even irate, he could become on the subject. In 1797 Adams raised the issue in his Inaugural Address. Echoing Washington's Farewell, he remarked on the necessity of "preserving our constitution from its natural enemies, the spirit of sophistry, the spirit of party, and the profligacy of corruption . . ."[49]

In what was to be another prophetic line, his address dealt with the relation between party and elections. He said:

> We should be unfaithful to ourselves if we should ever lose sight
> of the danger to our liberties if anything partial or extraneous

[48] John Adams to Jonathan Jackson, 2 Oct. 1780, *The Works of John Adams*, ed. Charles Francis Adams (Boston, 1851), Vol. IX, p. 511 (hereafter referred to as *Works*).

[49] *Messages and Papers of the Presidents*, op. cit., Vol. I, p. 221.

should infect the purity of our free, fair, virtuous, and independent elections. If an election is to be determined by a majority of a single vote, and that can be procured by a *party* through artifice or corruption, the Government may be the choice of a *party* for its own ends, not of the nation for the national good.

Two years later, in his Proclamation for a National Fast, Adams implored "the Great Mediator and Redeemer" that "he would withhold us from unreasonable discontent, from disunion, *faction*, sedition, and insurrection: that he would preserve our country from the desolating sword . . ."[50]

Adams had good reason to rage against the spirit of party and faction in later years, especially in view of his experience in 1800. Therefore, it must have comforted Adams in later years to know that he could take out his frustrations on a sympathetic reader. In 1813, corresponding with Jefferson about the desirability of party in the state, Adams found himself agreeing wholeheartedly with Jefferson's remark, "The same political parties which now agitate the U.S. have existed through all time." Adams' reply could not be more in agreement:

Precisely. And this is precisely the complaint in the preface to the first volume of my defense. While all other Sciences have advanced, that of Government is at a stand; little better understood; little better practiced now than 3 or 4 thousand Years ago. What is the reason? I say Parties and Factions will not suffer, or permit improvements to be made. As soon as one man hints at an improvement his Rival opposes it. No sooner has one Party discovered or invented an Amelioration of the Condition of Man or the order of Society, than the opposite Party, belies it, misconstrues it, misrepresents it, ridicules it, insults it, and persecutes it. Records are destroyed. Histories are annihilated . . . by Popes . . . Emperors . . . Aristocratical and . . . democratical Assemblies . . . and . . . by mobs.[51]

Thus Adams, in his vitriolic attacks against party, believed that their pernicious influence went beyond simply his own political

[50] 6 March 1799, *Works*, Vol. IX, p. 173.
[51] John Adams to Thomas Jefferson, 9 July 1813, *Letters*, Vol. II, p. 351.

experience. He held party and faction responsible for the slow progress of political science over the past four thousand years. His precise connection between the parties in his own time with those that had existed, as Jefferson said, "through all time," is important for an understanding of party in the 1790s. For what Adams and Jefferson are agreeing to is an identification of party, its nature and type, not with a new variety or even a new form, but with a long tradition that reaches back into the mists of time.

Six months later, again in correspondence with Jefferson, Adams asked why the laws of antiquity have been lost:

> I say the *Spirit of Party* has destroyed them, civil, political and ecclesiastical Bigotry. Despotical, monarchical, aristocratical and democratical fury, have all been employed in this work of destruction of every thing that could give us true light and a clear insight of Antiquity. For every one of these Parties, when possessed of power, or when they have been Undermost and Struggling to get Uppermost, has been equally prone to every Species of Fraud and Violence and Usurpation.[52]

Adams seemingly held party and faction responsible for everything. In fact, it became a family tradition that hatred of party found expression in such glorified purple prose. John Quincy Adams took his turn at metaphor and compared the spirit of party to yellow fever: "It is not inconsistent . . . to suppose that the pestilence of the mind [the Whiskey Rebellion] which rages with such violence in the State [Penna.] under the name of party spirit, is intimately connected with that physical pestilence which sweeps away so many thousands of its people."[53] While Ambassador to Berlin he wrote more soberly: "The spirit of party has indeed done so much injury among us in various shapes, that it has given our very national character an odious aspect in the eyes of many . . . foreigners."[54]

[52] John Adams to Thomas Jefferson, 25 Dec. 1813, *Letters*, Vol. II, p. 412.

[53] John Quincy Adams to Abigail Adams, 14 April 1801, *The Writings of John Quincy Adams*, ed. Worthington C. Ford (New York, 1913), Vol. II (1796–1801), pp. 529–30.

[54] John Quincy Adams to Abigail Adams, 7 May 1799, ibid., p. 418.

Yet neither John nor his son could quite equal Abigail's capacity for sheer vehemence. Still smarting over the memory of her husband's defeat in 1800, she wrote a blast against party which, no doubt, reflected her husband's feelings as well as those of the person she addressed: "Party spirit is blind malevolent uncandid, ungenerous, unjust and unforgiving. It is equally so under federal as under democratic banners . . . Party hatred by its deadly poison blinds the Eyes and envenoms the heart. It is fatal to the integrity of the moral character. It sees not that wisdom dwells with moderation, and that firmness of conduct is seldom united with outrageous violence of sentiment."[55]

Jefferson agreed with every line of his friend's complaints, but would not have expressed himself so pungently. Beginning in 1789, however, he did leave a trail of evidence against party and faction that, over the years, adds up to the most severe indictment by anyone against the role they played. Jefferson characteristically began his onslaught against party by casting his opposition in philosophical and moral terms. He believed that no one could maintain his integrity or independence if he accepted a prevailing party creed. Writing to a friend who attempted to sound him out as to whether he was a party member, Jefferson advised him:

> I am not a Federalist, because I never submitted the whole system of my opinions to the creed of any party of men whatever in religion, in philosophy, in politics, or in anything else where I was capable of thinking for myself. Such an addiction is the last degradation of a free and moral agent. If I could not go to heaven but with a party, I would not go there at all. Therefore I protest to you that I am not of the party of the federalists. But I am much farther from that of the Antifederalists.
>
> . . . I am neither federalist nor antifederalist; . . . I am of neither party, nor . . . a trimmer between parties.[56]

[55] Abigail Adams to Thomas Jefferson, 18 Aug. 1804, *Letters*, Vol. I, p. 277.

[56] Thomas Jefferson to Francis Hopkinson, 13 March 1789, *Papers*, Vol. 14, pp. 650–51.

He could not be more explicit. To join a party movement would
be to sacrifice one's intellectual and moral integrity. Jefferson's
consistency in opposing party, of being neither Federalist, Anti-
federalist, or worse, a trimmer, is a position he adhered to all his
adult life. Six years later we find Jefferson using the same terminology to describe indirectly his own party feelings. Discussing a
pamphlet written by Edmund Randolph at the time of Jay's
Treaty, Jefferson points out the virtues, as well as the foibles, of
Randolph's position:

Randolph seems to have hit upon the true theory of our constitution; that when a treaty is made, involving matters confided by
the constitution to the three branches of the legislature conjointly,
the Representatives are as free as the President and Senate were,
to consider whether the national interest requires or forbids their
giving the form and the force of law to the article over which they
have a power. . . . Though he mistakes his own political character in the aggregate he gives it to you in the detail. Thus, he sup-
poses himself a man of no party that his opinions not containing
any systematic adherence to party, fell sometimes on one side and
sometimes on the other. Yet he gives you these facts, which show
that they fall generally on both sides and are complete incon-
sistencies . . .

The fact is, that he has generally given his principles to the one
party and his practice to the other, the oyster to one, the shell to
the other. Unfortunately, the shell was generally the lot of his
friends, the French and republicans, and the oyster of their antagonists. . . . Whether his conduct is to be ascribed to a superior
view of things, an adherence to right without regard to party, as
he pretends, or to an anxiety to trim between both, those who
know his character and capacity will decide. Were parties here
divided merely by a greediness for office, as in England, to take a
part with either would be unworthy of a reasonable or moral man.
But where the difference of principle is as substantial, and as
strongly pronounced as between the republicans and the monocrats of our country, I hold it as honorable to take a firm and
decided part, and as immoral to pursue a middle line, as between

the parties of honest men and rogues, into which every country is divided.

Jefferson continued with his assessment of Randolph's pamphlet, claiming the administration's attitude toward France and the "rejection of Mr. Rutledge by the Senate is a bold thing. . . . It is, of course, a declaration that they will receive none but *tories* into any department of the government."[57]

In this letter, one of the most misunderstood in our early political history, Jefferson has framed the issue that will dominate his political career for at least the next decade. It is the philosophy of republicanism and liberty versus the "monocrats," i.e., those in favor of a return to monarchy. It is not mere "greediness for office" that is at stake; it is liberty and the republic. The fact that Jefferson sees the administration nominating only Tories to official positions serves notice that the gravity of the situation transcends the normal party divisions between men.[58] The issue has, according to Jefferson in late 1795, become one of "principles" of government which will ultimately determine and even change the form of the government.

In this letter, Jefferson is more than chiding Randolph because he has failed to act upon his principles. Stating that it is "immoral to pursue a middle line" and hinting that Randolph may be a "trimmer" is Jefferson's way of saying he intends to do neither. The problem is that Randolph has not lived up to a "superior view of things" as Jefferson might have expected. Also, Jefferson's decision to take a firm stand for the principles of liberty and republicanism in opposition to policies which may have forced a return to monarchy is not the same as joining a party whose members deem

[57] Thomas Jefferson to William B. Giles, 31 Dec. 1795, *Writings*, Vol. IX, pp. 315–18.

[58] *The Anas, Writings*, Vol. I, p. 266. Jefferson noted (almost twenty-five years later) "a short review of the facts will show, that the contests of that day were contests of principle, between the advocates of republican, and those of kingly government, and that had not the former made the efforts they did, our government would have been, even at this early day, a very different thing."

themselves the "loyal opposition." And especially so in 1795. To state that this is positive proof that Jefferson was a party man (as many historians have) is to miss entirely the meaning of his description and the spirit in which Jefferson reentered the political arena. As we shall see later, this battle cry for liberty is more consistent with his attempt to preserve the constitution from the violence of party than it is a declaration of party loyalty.

In 1798 Jefferson wrote John Taylor of Caroline an analysis of party that suggests he is so wary of party violence he is afraid there may soon be civil war. After enumerating a series of crises that have taken place with England, "the land tax, stamp tax, increase of public debt, public and authentic avowals of sentiments hostile to the leading principles of the constitution"—all over a three-year period—he again reviews, in his usual manner, the origins of party. "Be this as it may, in every free and deliberating society, there must from the nature of man, be opposite parties, and violent dissensions and discords; and one of these for the most part, must prevail over the other for a longer or shorter time. Perhaps this party division is necessary to induce each to watch and relate to the people the proceedings of the other. But if on a temporary superiority of the one party, the other is to resort to a scission of the Union, no federal government can exist."

Here is no categorical statement of an endorsement of party. Jefferson's analysis is in the mode of philosophical speculation, recognizing the existence of parties yet pointing out their tendency to rule excessively—even to the point of violence. Admitting the possibility that the "federal government" may not be able to exist under party rule is a direct contradiction of Jefferson's principles. Knowing that party will resort to "scission" if necessary, Jefferson is stating implicitly that in order to keep the federal system intact it is necessary—again as Paine suggested—to dampen down the spirit of party. At the same time Jefferson realizes that critics of the government are necessary to warn the people if their liberty is endangered. Indeed, the remainder of his letter, which is almost never read, deals with this theme.

A little patience, and we shall see the reign of witches pass over, their spells dissolved and the people recovering their true sight, restoring the government to its true principles. . . . If the game must sometimes run against us at home, we must have patience till luck turns, and then we shall have an opportunity of winning back the PRINCIPLES we have lost. For this is a game where principles are at stake.[59]

Finally, as if to underscore his distrust for party, which, in his eyes had no principles, Jefferson added a postscript: "It is hardly necessary to caution you to let nothing of mine get before the public; a single sentence got hold of by the Porcupines[60] will suffice to abuse and persecute me in their papers for months."[61]

Almost nine months went by before Jefferson again wrote about the role of party, or something that might be construed as such. This time, when he spoke of a division of society, he referred directly to the revolutionary heritage of liberty implicit in his earlier letter to Taylor. Jefferson stated: "The spirit of 1776 is not dead. It has only been slumbering. The body of the American people is substantially republican."[62] This is a reference that is always used to demonstrate Jefferson's attachment to party. Yet, again, the context indicates that he is not referring to the proto-type of a modern political organization. His classification is general, republicanism with a small "r." Indeed, it is a hint of how Jefferson views the political character of society that has as its aims the preservation of liberty and the republican form of government.[63] Jefferson is really breathing a sigh of relief. For the first

[59] Thomas Jefferson to John Taylor, 1 June 1798, *Writings*, Vol. X, p. 45.

[60] The "Porcupine" was one William Cobbett, a journalist whose *Porcupine's Gazette* was one of the most vitriolic and partisan papers of the era.

[61] Jefferson to John Taylor, 1 June 1798, *Writings*, Vol. X, p. 47.

[62] Jefferson to Thomas Lomax, 12 March 1799, *Writings*, Vol. X, pp. 123–24.

[63] John Quincy Adams clarified Jefferson's point thirty years later. "The name of republicans is not a suitable denomination of a party of the United States, because it implies an offensive and unjust imputation upon their opponents, as if they were not also republicans. The truth is, as it was declared by

time in years, large numbers of people are beginning to show evidence that they have not abandoned their attachment to the earlier revolutionary principles of republican government.

This comment, strangely enough, is never connected with his first Inaugural Address. And it is that address, conspicuous by its absence in the works of those who claim Jefferson was establishing the first modern political party, which brings together—in a coherent body—his philosophy of government without party rule. On the eve of his triumph Jefferson could afford, indeed, he needed, to be conciliatory. But this does not alter the fact that he presented his philosophy of government as a set of permanent and binding principles and *not* expedient party policies. In that address Jefferson is in fact saying that we must guard against the violence of party. He notes sadly that its spirit has visited American shores. Finally, asking his listeners not to repeat the tragedies of the ancients who lost their liberty to party violence, Jefferson is making a plea for harmony and unity in his new administration. Those who remain in "opposition," he says, will stand as "monuments," but their opposition, it is important to notice, is equated with civil war, violence, and changing the form of the government:

> Let us then, fellow citizens, unite with one heart and one mind. Let us restore to social intercourse that harmony and affection without which liberty and even life itself are but dreary things. . . . During the throes and convulsions of the ancient world, during the agonizing spasms of infuriated man, seeking through blood and slaughter his long lost liberty, it was not wonderful that the agitation of the billows should reach even this distant and peaceful shore; that this should be more felt and feared by some and less by others, and should divide opinions as to measures of safety. But every difference of opinion is not a difference of principle. We have called by different names brethren of the same

Thomas Jefferson, all and all from the Declaration of Independence have been, Republicans." John Quincy Adams, *An Eulogy on the Life and Character of James Monroe* (Boston, 1831).

principle. We are all Republicans, we are all Federalists. If there be any among us who wish to dissolve this Union or to change the republican form, let them stand as undisturbed monuments . . .[64]

Jefferson's comment "We are all Republicans, we are all Federalists" is an appeal to every citizen to forsake party and return to the original principles of the American Revolution, the constitution, and the republic—principles which, as Jefferson viewed them, rise above party and are the common property of everyone. Years later, Jefferson would recollect the "sad realities" of the years before his successful drive for the presidency and remark, "I fondly hope, we may now truly say, 'we are all republicans, all federalists,' and that the motto of the standard to which our country will forever rally, will be, 'federal union, and republican government,' . . ."[65]

This, then, appears to be the true meaning of Jefferson's oft-quoted statement. What Jefferson expected was not the continuation of the Federalist party in opposition, but the recognition by those Federalists that they had a dual responsibility to the government: to uphold the principle of federalism (the division of the Union's power into state and national jurisdictions) and the principles of republicanism (guaranteeing the people's right to self-government through the representative system). This was the central theme of his revolution: the renewal of a decentralizing process that had begun with the American Revolution.

Nearing the end of his address, Jefferson makes an explicit connection between the principles of the American Revolution and those of his republican victory. In Jefferson's mind there was no difference:

These principles form the bright constellation which has gone before us and guided our steps through an age of revolution and reformation. The wisdom of our sages and blood of our heroes have been devoted to their attainment. They should be the creed of our political faith, the text of our civic instruction, the touch-

---

[64] *Messages and Papers of the Presidents,* op. cit., Vol. I, p. 310.
[65] *The Anas, Writings,* Vol. I, p. 282.

stone by which to try the services of those we trust; and should we wander from them in moments of error or of alarm, let us hasten to retrace our steps and to regain the road which alone leads to peace, liberty and safety.[66]

That Jefferson viewed the Revolution of 1800 as a recurrence of the Revolution of 1776 is exemplified in this closing observation. He was expressing the belief that the return to republican principles was the "touchstone" for the nation. By appealing to the people he had been able to avoid the elitism that had alarmed the country. Instead, through "electoral Caesarism" they had "regained the road" to republicanism—the road the nation had taken in the years following the Declaration of Independence.

After Jefferson came into power in 1801, he wrote to a friend confirming his long-held antiparty bias: ". . . I learn from all quarters that my inaugural address is considered as holding out a ground for conciliation and union. . . . I was always satisfied that the great body of those called federalists were real republicans as well as federalists."[67]

Here is Jefferson's optimism overflowing. He expected not only to absorb the opposition, he actually believed, or says he believed, that most of the Federalists were republicans, in sentiment, all the time. This would indicate that he was thinking in terms other than those we know today as party affiliations. He had written to General Knox: "believing that (except the ardent monarchists) all our citizens agreed in ancient whig principles, I thought it advisable to define and declare them and let them see the ground on which we could rally. And the fact proving so that they agreed in these principles, I shall pursue them with more encouragement."[68]

Indeed, this is Jefferson's notion of principles (in his Inaugural Address) challenging the effects of party and appealing not to a new political party but to an "ancient" set of Whig ideas imbedded in a century-old political tradition. I hardly need point out

[66] *Messages and Papers of the Presidents*, op. cit., Vol. I, p. 312.

[67] Thomas Jefferson to Henry Knox, 27 March 1801, *Writings*, Vol. X, pp. 245–46.

[68] Ibid.

that party and faction in the eighteenth century were devoid of principles, which makes it incumbent upon us to ask, What exactly do these constant references to principles mean? The revolutionary principles of 1776? If we take Jefferson and his Inaugural Address seriously, I think we must conclude that it was the principles of the American Revolution to which he is referring.[69]

Jefferson, in order to demonstrate his faith in a non-party system, reiterated his feelings to Levi Lincoln in 1802: "The opinion I originally formed has never been changed, that such of the body of the people as thought themselves federalists, would find they are in truth republicans, and would come over to us by degrees." By following a policy of "economy and peace," Jefferson added his hope that "federalism" will sink "into an abyss from which there will be no resurrection for it."[70] Not only did Jefferson wish to see the Federalists disappear from sight, he intended to remove from federal office anyone who gave evidence of "electioneering activity, or open and industrious opposition to the principles of the present government, legislative and executive."[71]

---

[69] *Alexander Graydon's Memoirs of His Own Time*, ed. J. S. Littell (Philadelphia, 1846). Alexander Graydon was a Federalist and an unusually perceptive observer of the political scene in Pennsylvania. He noted the connection between republicanism and the American Revolution that preceded the formation of the constitution: "The term republicans was embraced as recognizing the principles of the revolution, and as indicative perhaps of tenets, which admitted the utility of modifications and restraints, in a system resting on the broad base of general suffrage and popular sovereignty. The word *democrat* was not yet much in use, neither was the distinction established between a democrat and a republican, which appears to consist in the idea, that the former is for placing the whole governing power in the 'multitude told by the head'; the latter, for giving it some checks, and infusing into it a leaven of what is termed by Mr. Burke, the natural aristocracy of a country," p. 331. It is interesting to observe Jefferson's long-held attachment to Burke's and Graydon's definition of republicanism. As late as October 28, 1813, Jefferson wrote John Adams on the difference between an "artificial" and a "natural aristocracy."

[70] Jefferson to Levi Lincoln, 25 Oct. 1802, *Writings*, Vol. X, p. 338.

[71] Ibid., p. 340.

Jefferson's belief in the non-party state had been expressed in absolute terms: an opposition was not even to raise its head!

As President, Jefferson referred to party and faction only rarely for the next decade. But after resuming his correspondence with John Adams, he again warmed to the topic. Having the advantage of leisure, as well as five years' distance from the political wars, we may take Jefferson seriously as he waxed philosophic on the theory and history of party in America:

> Men have differed in opinion and been divided into parties by these opinions, from the first origin of societies; and in all free governments where they have been permitted freely to think and to speak. The same political parties which now agitate the U.S. have existed thro' all time. . . . And in fact the terms of whig and tory belong to natural, as well as civic history. They denote the temper and constitution of mind of different individuals. To come to our own country, and to the times when you and I became first acquainted, we well remember the violent parties which agitated the old Congress and their bitter contests. There you and I were together, and the Jays, and the Dickinsons, and the other anti-independents were arrayed against us. They cherished the monarchy of England; and we the rights of our government. When our present government was passing . . . from Confederation to Union, how bitter was the schism between the Feds and the Antis. . . . But as soon as it [the Constitution] was put into motion, the line of division was again drawn, we broke into two parties, each wishing to give a different direction to the government. . . . Here you and I separated for the first time; and as we had been longer than most others on the public theater, and our names were therefore most familiar to our countrymen, the party which considered you as thinking with them placed your name at their head; the other, for the same reason, selected mine. But neither decency nor inclination permitted us to become the advocates of ourselves, or to take part personally in the violent contests which followed. . . .
>
> To me, then, it appears that there have been differences of opinion, and party differences, from the first establishment of governments, to the present day; and on the same question which now divides our own country; that these will continue thro' all

future time: that everyone takes his side in favor of the many, or of the few, according to his constitution, and the circumstances in which he is placed: that opinions, which are equally honest on both sides, should not effect personal esteem, or social intercourse: that as we judge between the Claudii and the Gracchi . . . of past ages, so of those among us . . . the next generations will judge, favorably or unfavorably . . .[72]

Jefferson's commentary on the history and role of party has an air of detachment about it that reveals his philosophic disposition toward one of the most burning issues of his, or any, time. Noting that party is a part of our "natural, as well as civic history," Jefferson is agreeing with the consensus of his time: the party agitation he experienced was not something new, it had been characteristic of man "thro' all time." His letter is also an apologia—an attempt to soften any remaining indignation that may still be harbored by his adversary of 1800. An expression of aloofness, a feeling that "neither decency nor inclination" permitted either man to submit himself finally to party spirit, pervades the statement. Jefferson would like us to believe that he and Adams were always above party. In this context, Jefferson's letter might have been written for posterity as it places considerable confidence in the judgment of future generations. He believes, of course, that history will vindicate the stand he and Adams took on party. We might also note the historical perspective that Jefferson reveals. The Gracchi brothers, who, two thousand years before, had dealt with party agitations of a similar nature, had, according to their constitutions, taken the side of the people. Jefferson, it seems, identified with them and not with Appius Claudius Caecus, one of the despotic emperors in Roman history. This identification was "natural," as the Gracchi had provided the model for Jefferson's democratic Revolution of 1800.

Jefferson's final and complete statement on party was made to La Fayette in 1817. Relating the facts of the aftermath of the War of 1812, Jefferson told his friend that "its best effect has been *the*

---

[72] Jefferson to John Adams, 27 June 1813, *Letters,* Vol. II, pp. 335–38.

complete suppression of party. The federalists who were truly American, and their great mass was so, have separated from their brethren who were mere Anglomen, and are received with cordiality into the republican ranks." Continuing his letter with a discussion of their mutual "hobby," i.e., politics, Jefferson noted: "Nor is the election of Monroe an inefficient circumstance in our felicities. Four and twenty years, which he will accomplish, of administration in *republican forms and principles*, will so consecrate them in the eyes of the people as to secure them against the danger of change. The evanition of party dissensions has harmonized intercourse, and sweetened society beyond imagination."[73]

Thus concluded Jefferson's sentiment on party after a lifetime of politics. In retrospect, it was exactly what Jefferson's struggles had been about—"the complete suppression of party"—and the creation of the non-party state. The consistency with which Jefferson maintained this position should now be obvious. His opinions against party had been the result of long study and reflection, an expression of moral and constitutional conviction. His observations on party agitations were placed in historical perspective, in terms

[73] Thomas Jefferson to Marquis de La Fayette, 14 May 1817, *Writings*, Vol. XV, pp. 115–16. It is interesting that another revolutionary patriot, one who had participated as fully as Jefferson in the great events of the times, also wished to see the "complete suppression of party." Answering the Philadelphia Committee of Correspondence in 1816, shortly before his death, Gouverneur Morris wrote: "But, Gentlemen, let us forget party and think of our country. That country embraces both parties. We must endeavor, therefore, to save and benefit both. This cannot be effected while political delusions array good men against each other. If you abandon the contest, the voice of reason, now drowned in factious vociferation, will be listened to and heard. The pressure of distress will accelerate the moment of reflection; and when it arrives, the people will look out for men of sense, experience and integrity. Such men may, I trust, be found in both parties; and if our country be delivered, what does it signify, whether those who operate her salvation, wear a federal or democratic cloak? Perhaps the expression of these sentiments may be imprudent; but when it appears proper to speak the truth, I know not concealment. It has been the unvarying principle of my life, that the interest of our country must be preferred to every other interest." In *The American Quarterly Review* (Philadelphia: Carey & Lea, March and June 1832), Vol. XI, p. 459.

of both their natural origins and their linkage to the Revolution of 1776. That spirit had more than burned brightly in Jefferson's mind throughout the decades. In his mind the real importance of that spirit had been twofold: along with producing independence, it had guaranteed liberty and the continuation of republican principles for two generations.

Indeed, this was the crucial distinction that Jefferson continued to make. Time and time again he referred to the "principles" that needed to be preserved, "the game of principles," "principles at stake," etc. Jefferson was saying that it was not merely enough to preside over the form of republican government, one had to live according to its principles too. And if those principles were ever lost sight of, then the danger of losing the form was imminent. In Jefferson's mind, nothing disregarded those principles more savagely than party violence. Left to the struggles of faction and party, liberty would soon perish. This reflected a consensus that appealed not just to Jefferson, but to the best men of the age: once raise the embers of faction and party to a flame, and inevitably they would consume the republic. The only solution was a non-party state.

The notion of the non-party state was accepted not only in America but in Europe as well. The politics of England under George III had remained relatively constant in regard to parties, even though the paraphernalia of party sentiment and organization was always present. If anything, the increasing role and power of that monarch made parties even less significant. Sir Lewis Namier made a point about the 1760s in England that applies equally to the 1790s in America; and especially since a "superstructure" of party organization has been constructed by American historians interpreting the politics of that period.[74]

Indeed, when Thomas Paine wrote ". . . it is the nature and intention of a constitution to prevent governing by party," he

[74] "There were no proper party organizations about 1760, though party names and cant were current; the names and the cant have since supplied the material for an imaginary superstructure." Lewis Namier, *The Structure of Politics at the Accession of George III* (London, 1930), p. x.

summarized the theory of an age. A citizen of the world, Paine had witnessed firsthand the violence of party in England, France, and America. And believing, like Jefferson, that party violence would always exist, he had attempted to construct a rationale—respect for the constitution—that would keep parties within bounds.

That history of party violence in France and England which confronted Americans during the 1790s could hardly be considered an example for a two-party system. France, which nearly drowned itself in sanguinary factional strife, had seen its constitution destroyed and the last vestige of liberty vanish in despotism. England, however, provided the most compelling lessons as it had been a past model for the structure of politics in America. More important, though, was the fact that England's mixed constitution was vulnerable to the same excesses of party violence as America's. The politics that characterize England during the period we are investigating points out the validity of Paine's theory.

During the 1780s and '90s Toryism entered a decline. The constitutional Whigs had narrowed in number as well as in influence, and numerous factions had begun to emerge eager to replace those that had been prominent for so long. This posed certain problems for the crown that, when examined closely, reveal that nation's dependency on the lack of a strong party system. Richard Pares makes the point that it was impossible for the king's ministers to appeal from Whigs to Tories because "there were no effective Tories to answer the appeal."[75] Out of 658 members of Parliament at the turn of the century, one third were either "doubtful," "whimsical," or never attended. Other factions existed among the remaining 450 which were allied to powerful lords and members of the administration. Personal friendship, often a euphemism for corruption, was the connection that cemented ambition with place and created a bond stronger than party. As descriptions by Bolingbroke and Burke reveal, many of the great lords were not admirers of party and preferred to maintain their

[75] Richard Pares, *King George III and the Politicians* (Oxford, 1953), p. 72.

power through private manipulation and artifice. These leaders, moreover, disdained the propriety of concerted opposition.

But overriding this seemingly corrupt system was a respect for the English constitution and the principles that enabled it to endure. For more than forty years, roughly 1760 to 1800, adherence to rigid attitudes, extreme defense of others—often policies that had failed—produced a barrier to any real cooperation among the politicians. The result was that the formation of parties in England simply did not occur in any modern sense. "No. leader of a coalition could ever hope to find, as Lord Chesterfield said, enough pasture for the beasts he had to feed."[76]

The structure of politics in both England and America came down, for all practical purposes, to the idea of the one- or non-party state. Opposition was tolerated in legislative chambers, but not among the citizens of the nation. A degree of neutrality and moderation was expected from the opposition's attitude (what there was of it) toward all government policy. At the same time constitutional principles were to govern party, to take precedence over factional sentiment. One anonymous author described a theory regarding party that in its breadth and perspective paralleled for English politics anything that Madison, Jefferson, or anyone else in America had written:

> . . . that there have always been in this country persons who leaned towards arbitrary power, and persons who leaned towards too popular a government. In all mixed governments, there must be such men, and such parties: some will admire the monarchical, and some the democratical part of the constitution; and speaking very generally, the rich and the timid, and the indolent, as well as the base and the servile, will have a natural tendency to the one side; and the poor, the enthusiastic, and enterprising, as well as the envious and the discontented, will be inclined to range themselves on the other. These things have been always; and always must be. They have hitherto been without mischief or hazard; and might be fairly considered as symptoms at least, if not as causes,

[76] Ibid., p. 88.

of the soundness and vigor of our political organization. But this has been the case, only because the bulk of the nation has hitherto, or till very lately, belonged to no party at all. Factions existed only among a small number of irritable and ambitious individuals; and, for want of partizans, necessarily vented themselves in a few speeches and pamphlets—in an election riot, or a treasury prosecution. . . . If they had divided the whole nation among them, the little breaches of the peace and of the law at Westminster, would have been changed into civil war . . . and the constitution of the country would have perished in the conflict. In those times, therefore, the advocates of arbitrary power and of popular license were restrained, not merely by the constitutional principles of so many men of weight and authority, but by the absolute neutrality and indifference of the great body of the people. They fought like champions in a ring of impartial spectators; and the multitude who looked on, and thought it sport, had little other interest than to see that each had fair play.[77]

The fear among English, as well as American, political observers was that a division of the nation into two great parties—aristocrats versus democrats and republicans—would swallow up those who were capable of playing a conciliatory role among the factions. In its train, this nearly equal division would produce arrogance on the part of the aristocracy and popular discontent among those who believed there was no recourse against the wealthy, corrupt, and arrogant except revolution. When this occurred at the turn of the century in England, the salvation of the state against party violence lay in encouraging those who were influential to "soothe and conciliate" the parties, ". . . to moderate the public passions" and "not stand by and see the constitution torn to pieces because they could not approve entirely of either of the combatants."[78] In America, the "salvation lay in the elimination of political criticism, the creation of a one-party press . . . and eventually a one-party

[77] "Short Remarks on the State of Parties at the Close of the Year 1808," in *The Modern British Essays*, ed. Lord Jeffrey (Philadelphia, 1852), p. 605.
[78] Ibid., p. 609.

system."[79] The most desirable end in both cases was the establishment of a political system that placed principles and a concern for constitutionalism above party. And historically, the only proven system known that could accomplish that end was the one- or non-party state.

Here we conclude an overview of the idea of faction and party held by the revolutionary generation of the 1790s. Now, in order to verify their collective understanding of the idea we will make a few concluding remarks about faction and the non-party state. The definitions of party and faction remained consistent throughout the eighteenth century. The terms held connotations of violent, seditious, often revolutionary activity. Men of every political persuasion, from Fisher Ames to Thomas Jefferson, at one time or another, expressed their hatred and fear of party.

Examining the origins of faction and party, everyone agreed that they had existed from time immemorial, would continue to exist, and must be tightly controlled. They also agreed that the parties of the 1790s stemmed from the Revolution and were simply a continuation of that Whig-versus-Tory struggle. Many statesmen believed it was the responsibility of the constitution to prevent governing by party; others believed the administration should prevent any opposition from even raising its head. Everyone, it seems, would have agreed that a two-party system—even as to numbers—was perilous to the republic.

A consensus did exist that could be expressed thus: parties were incapable of realizing the truth; they were totally without regard to principle and they were against the national interest. They were, in addition, capable of corrupting the administration, enervating the principles of republican government, eroding the constitution and the spirit of the American Revolution, and ultimately of causing the dissolution of the republic itself.

The final observation is one that links the concern over party violence with the most important argument of all. As Jefferson

[79] Leonard W. Levy, *Legacy of Suppression* (Cambridge, Mass., 1960), p. xvii.

framed the issue, it came down to a choice between "kingly government" and the principles of the American Revolution. It was a centuries-old battle in which everyone, according to Jefferson, made his natural choice. Indeed, Jefferson saw his and his contemporaries' efforts to construct a non-party state contained within that ancient framework: the struggle of liberty against despotism. And this was, after all, the story of revolution throughout history.

The Idea of Revolution

"But what do we mean by the American Revolution?
Do we mean the American war? The Revolution was
effected before the war commenced. The Revolution was
in the minds and hearts of the people; . . . . This radical
change in the *principles, opinions, sentiments and affections of the people, was the real American Revolution*."

JOHN ADAMS to HEZEKIAH NILES
13 February 1818

"The Revolution of 1800 was as *real a revolution* in the
principles of our government as that of 1776 was in its
form."

THOMAS JEFFERSON to SPENCER ROANE
6 September 1819 (italics added)

While it is the purpose of this chapter to demonstrate the continuity of revolutionary ideas from the 1760s through the 1790s, I
intend to analyze the idea of revolution during the period after the
Constitutional Convention and refer to the period before 1787
only when necessary. Anyone who has read Bernard Bailyn's *The
Ideological Origins of the American Revolution* will realize that to
begin my narration in the 1760s would be mere repetition. Indeed,
those who are revolutionary "quick-witted" will have already
noted, by their perusal of the table of contents, my indebtedness
to Bailyn's masterful work.

What I do intend, however, is to establish an ideological framework for revolution as it developed during the decade after the
constitution. From that perspective this chapter will deal with the

idea of revolution, what its components were, and how it remained, at least in a definitional sense, a constant force in the minds of the revolutionary generation.

The most logical starting point, one used by Bailyn, is John Adams' oft-quoted remark on the American Revolution written fifty-five years after he believed it had begun. I begin with Adams' query because it throws into sharp relief, perhaps more succinctly than any other in eighteenth-century America, the most important elements regarding the nature of revolution.

It was characteristic of Adams to raise important questions like this and fortunate for us that he did so with Jefferson, because it provoked a lengthy as well as an intriguing discussion between the two on the idea of revolution. They had both been pondering the American Revolution for years, writing back and forth, assessing the importance of that great event in their own lives and observing the success and failure of all the revolutions that had taken place since then.[1] Indeed, one can easily claim that their exchange of

[1] That Adams considered himself a student of revolutions as well as constitutions is borne out in a letter he wrote late in life. And though he may have viewed them more skeptically than Jefferson, he nevertheless saw them much in the same light. Here he recounts his involvement: "I had been plunged head and ears in the American revolution from 1761 to 1798 (for it had been all revolution during the whole period). Did [anyone] . . . think that I had trod upon feathers, and slept upon beds of roses, during those thirty-seven years? I had been an eye-witness of two revolutions in Holland; one from aristocracy to a mongrel mixture of half aristocracy and half democracy, the other back again to aristocracy and the splendid restoration of the Stadtholder. Did [anyone] . . . think that I was so delighted with these electric shocks, these eruptions of volcanoes, these *tremblements de terre,* as to be ambitious of the character of the chemist, who could produce artificial ones in South America? I had been an ear-witness of some of the first whispers of a revolution in France in 1783, 1784, and 1785, and had given all possible attention to its rise and progress, and I can truly say, that it had given me as much anxiety as our American revolution had ever done. The last twenty-five years of the last century, and the first fifteen years of this, may be called the age of revolutions and constitutions. We began the dance, and have produced eighteen or twenty models of constitutions, the excellences and defects of which you probably know better than I do." John Adams to James Lloyd, 29 March 1815, *Works,* Vol. X, pp. 148–49.

letters on the political events of their time reads as a commentary on the nature of revolution as much as any other topic they introduced.

Adams always worried that his ideas were "peculiar, perhaps even singular." And often, as befits an irascible individual, they were. But when Adams asked Jefferson: "What do we mean by the [American] Revolution?" he was not being stubborn or peculiar. He was seeking clarification of the most significant event of their lives and the most complex political phenomenon known to man. Adams, aware that limitations had already been placed on understanding that revolution, that the secrecy of the major decisions had made it impossible to discern the truth, that adequate histories were not being written, even in his own lifetime,[2] must have had posterity in mind when he addressed Jefferson:

> What do we mean by the Revolution? The War? That was no part of the Revolution. It was only an Effect and Consequence of it. The Revolution was in the Minds of the People, and this was effected, from 1760 to 1775, in the course of fifteen years before a drop of blood was drawn at Lexington. The records of thirteen Legislatures, the Pamp[h]lets, Newspapers in all the Colonies ought [to] be consulted, during the Period, to ascertain the Steps by which the public Opinion was enlightened and informed concerning the authority of Parliament over the Colonies. The Congress of 1774, resembled in some respects, tho' I hope not in many, the Counsell of Nice in Ecclesiastical History. It assembled the Priests from the East and the West, the North and the South, who compared Notes, engaged in discussion and debates and formed Results by one Vote and by two Votes, which went out to the world as unanimous.[3]

Adams ought not to have believed he was alone in his distress over the subject of the American Revolution. For a voluminous amount of evidence exists today that indicates his contemporaries

[2] John Adams to Jefferson, 18 May 1817, *Writings*, Vol. XV, p. 120.

[3] John Adams to Jefferson, 24 Aug. 1815, *Letters*, Vol. II, p. 455. See also John Adams to Dr. J. Morse, 29 Dec. 1815, *Works*, Vol. X, p. 182; John Adams to Thomas McKean, 26 Nov. 1815, ibid., p. 180.

were capable of making, and in fact did make, many of the same distinctions he alluded to. One of those distinctions, Adams stated explicitly, was that revolution was separate from war. Adams believed that revolution had occurred over a long span of time and that *not one drop of blood* had been shed. Revolution, then, had everything to do with ideas and opinions; less to do with battlefield confrontations. In his view the changing of ideas and opinions through the then known media—newspapers, pamphlets, and legal records—was the real revolution. What Adams was describing was a complete change of people's minds regarding the principles of their constitution (i.e., between their rights and the authority of Parliament).

Indeed, if one were to use the eighteenth-century definition of the term revolution, and compare it to Adams' description, the meanings would be identical. In the Enlightenment, all revolutions, whether political or mechanical in nature, were referred to in terms of the physical universe. The metaphors of the earth revolving around the sun, the full circle, and completion of a cycle were used by every writer to describe the nature of political revolutions. After all, this was precisely what the American Revolution had been: the cyclical turning back to an original British constitution at the time of the Glorious Revolution.

John Adams, far from being "singular," was supported by many of his generation in a general understanding of the term. For most of them revolution referred to the action of turning over an idea in the mind, reflection and consideration. Nathan Bailey described revolution as "the turning round, or motion of any body, till it returns to the same place that it was before," "a rolling back or change in government." Dr. Johnson said revolutions, while "changing the state of a government or country," were also characterized by "anything which returns to the point at which it began to move."[4] Noah Webster gave several meanings to revolution that had a common theme: all dealt with change in the principles

---

[4] Bailey, *An Universal Etymological English Dictionary*, op. cit.; and Johnson, *A Dictionary of the English Language*, op. cit., Vol. II.

of a constitution. Webster viewed revolution thus: "In politics, a material change or entire change in the constitution of government. Thus the revolution in England, in 1688 produced . . . the restoration of the constitution to its primitive state." Webster also referred to "revolutionized" as "changing the form and principles of a constitution"; and "revolutionize" as "effect[ing] an entire change of principles in . . ."[5]

Rufus King observed that ". . . by the newspapers . . . Italy will be overturned. Venice is no more and Genoa has been completely revolutionized."[6] John Quincy Adams noted how the change in people's minds related to revolution in this way: "For if the people once discover (and you cannot conceal it from them long) that you maintain the war for the army, while you tell them you maintain the army for the war, you lose their attachment forever, and their good sense will immediately side against you. . . . You will have effected in *substance* if not in form *a total revolution* in the government . . . , and the chaos of civil war will ensue."[7]

The younger Adams' observation is worthy of notice because it points to more than simply a change in ideas; it calls attention to what he says is the "substance" of revolution. In Adams' mind it was not necessary to change the form of government in order to have a revolution. Like his father, John Quincy Adams also made a distinct separation between revolution and war.

John Adams was explicit on one other point regarding the nature of revolution. He referred to actions taken in the state legislatures, and indirectly to actions in Parliament. He also mentioned the establishment of Congress in 1774. He thus brought within his compass of understanding revolution the influence that constitutions and legislative bodies have in the formation of

[5] Webster, *An American Dictionary of the English Language*, op. cit., Vol. II.

[6] *Life and Correspondence of Rufus King*, ed. Charles R. King, 6 vols. (New York, 1895), Vol. II, p. 195.

[7] J. Q. Adams to William Vans Murray, 27 Jan. 1801, *The Writings of John Quincy Adams*, op. cit., Vol. II.

revolutionary ideas. As we shall see later on, this relationship to constitutional forms and processes is one of the most important aspects of the idea of revolution in eighteenth-century America.

Implicit in Adams' remarks is another distinction: the intellectual separation of violence from revolutionary change. This refers to physical violence, of course, unless one wishes to include psychological anguish, a form of violence that tears one's affections from family, friends, and the institutions we have been taught to revere. It ought to be noted that this is an intellectual distinction only, and does not rule out the fact that violence may follow or accompany actual revolution.

If one ponders Adams' query for still another moment, it is possible to detect perhaps the most important and enduring fact of all revolutions throughout history, viz., the democratic nature of the revolutionary process as it occurred from 1760 to 1775. The appeal to the people through the written and verbal forms, the election of representatives to a congress, and the rational discussion and debate that defined the course of revolution were all calculated to extend revolutionary ideas to as many people as possible. This last point, the influence of reason in discussion, also implied that revolution, at least as it was understood by the revolutionary generation, was not an irrational phenomenon. The ability to reason in the midst of political crisis was indeed one of their proudest achievements and seems lost to most twentieth-century anatomists of revolution.

While the Adams quotation succinctly raises many important questions regarding the fundamental nature of revolution, his colleague, Jefferson, in rambling fashion and over a longer period of time, provides us with a more extensive treatment of the subject in both theory and practice. Like Adams' comments, Jefferson's reveal a lifelong fascination with the idea. Yet Jefferson's letters go beyond Adams and his attempts to understand the subject philosophically. Jefferson, throughout his correspondence, revealed a passionate commitment to and an involvement with revolution that not only surpassed any other American statesman's, but spanned his entire adult life.

Whatever differences there were between them stemmed from their basic attitudes toward governmental authority, despite the fact that they had had similar, almost identical, political careers. It was Adams who nearly suffered a nervous breakdown making the psychological commitment to revolution in the 1760s. By contrast, Jefferson, as a young lawyer, never gave the slightest evidence that he suffered in his decision to undermine British authority. Jefferson had a belief, as we shall see later, that authority, especially constitutional authority, was limited in duration and ought to be renewed periodically; that governments should adapt to change like a man who refuses to wear the coat of a boy. His was a "generational" idea of change. Adams, on the other hand, saw government and even administration as the repository of authority and, certainly in a new nation, even of tradition. No one admired tradition, especially the tradition of the British constitution, more ardently than John Adams.

Adams also had a longer view of constitutional government than Jefferson. He believed that continuity, over time, provided stability without which any government would fail. Consequently, Adams' view of government was one that spanned many generations. His faith in human nature, more pessimistic than Jefferson's, failed to believe that man could change rationally or reasonably in a short time. For Adams, men were creatures of habit. Writing to Jefferson in 1794 he remarked, "The Social compact and the laws must be reduced to writing. Obedience to them becomes a national habit and they cannot be changed but by Revolutions which are costly things. Men will be too economical of their blood and property to have recourse to them very frequently."[8]

This view expressed by Adams may be the source of their disagreement, for Jefferson firmly believed that rebellions and revolutions, like "storms in the atmosphere," should be as frequent as necessary. Adams saw stable governments resisting or putting to rest all fears and threats of revolution. Contrarily, Jefferson, committed to his belief that any government could not

[8] John Adams to Jefferson, 11 May 1794, *Letters*, Vol. I, p. 254.

enjoy stability for long, was certain there could be *no* postrevolutionary society.

This meant that Jefferson, more than Adams, feared that the social compact and the laws would have only limited success in checking the power of government. Revolution would then become a necessity to maintain liberty against the encroachments of tyranny. At the same time Jefferson realized that the state had been the enemy of revolution in history and this was why revolutions had been so bloody and costly. He knew that if a people once lost their liberty, there was one recourse which the state would oppose over all others: viz., revolution. For revolution was always directed against the existing political order, those who were currently in power and would resist being overthrown with all the resources at their command. Despotic rulers would, almost by instinct, develop engines of repression that in turn would make revolution inevitable. To Jefferson, this dynamic struggle had seemed to be the entire history of western civilization.

There was another dimension to this reasoning which placed Jefferson in sharp opposition to Adams. As we have seen, Jefferson was deeply committed to principles and to substantive change. This might be described more accurately, especially in reference to a revolutionary theory, as "systemic change." Jefferson's constant references to despotic regimes indicate that he viewed them as a system with an internal logic of their own. That logic had, as its prime motivation, the aggrandizement of wealth and power for a privileged few at the expense of the many. "History has informed us," said Jefferson, "that bodies of men as well as individuals, are susceptible of the spirit of tyranny."[9] As his statements about the character of parties and the men who choose sides according to the "few or the many" show, tyranny manifested a character and condition that could only be broken by a complete constitutional (read systemic) revolution. This tension, this necessity to break apart an old system and replace it with a new one, was the primary

[9] *Autobiography, Writings,* Vol. I, p. 180.

reason Jefferson believed revolutions would continue throughout history.

Despite their basic disagreements, however, they did find many areas in which their opinions overlapped. Here is Jefferson anticipating Adams' separation of war and revolution almost thirty years before the latter's famous query:

> There is always war in one place, revolution in another, pestilence in a third interspersed with spots of quiet. These chequers shift places, but they do not vanish; so that to an eye which extends itself over the whole earth there is always an uniformity of prospect.[10]

Jefferson is recording here a profound observation on the nature of revolution: revolution is a permanent force in the world we inhabit. It does not vanish; it merely breaks out in another place. Jefferson's recognition of this permanence of revolutionary activity was in the classical political tradition. It meant that Jefferson saw revolution as others saw wars—a recognizable, permanent phenomenon in history that could be studied, analyzed and, perhaps, made predictable. But this was an old story. Polybius, one of the few who had grasped the significance of revolution in ancient times, saw that all societies were subject to the dynamics of revolution and could look forward to one immediately or in some future time. This was a cyclical view of history, simplified of course, but nonetheless true in eighteenth-century America.

What Jefferson, like Polybius, was pointing to was a historical dialectic of revolution. Because the cycle of governments revealed a state of constant change—in principle as well as in form—it meant that the changes, no matter what they might be (monarchy, aristocracy, democracy, polity, or oligarchy), would be constantly challenged by revolutionary forces and ideas. From time immemorial, revolution had been in opposition to the state. Indeed, that was the very meaning of the word—against the regime in power. It was, therefore, the antithesis of "the system,"

---

[10] Jefferson to James Currie, 27 Sept. 1785, *Papers*, Vol. 8, p. 558.

hated, feared, and detested by rulers throughout history. By viewing itself as a negating force, revolution could be successful; otherwise, it would be coopted, mere reform; or worse, it would signify a return to greater repression. These conditions, recognized by Jefferson, fulfilled the requirements of a true dialectic in history and made his theory revolutionary.

In Jefferson's mind, the Revolution of 1776 had taken on this dialectical, negating quality, that over the years influenced the checkered pattern of war and revolution on the globe. In fact, Jefferson, at the end of his life, saw the Revolution of 1776 as a permanent revolutionary force in the world. Included in this idea was the implication that the forces unleashed in a particular revolution—if universalized—might be the catalyst for revolutions elsewhere. That is, if a revolutionary "engine" could be developed that was capable of destroying the "engines" of despotism, systemic change would be accomplished on a world scale. This was really the dream of a true revolutionary: the creation of a theory of revolution that could be applied to any and every condition of man.

The evidence that Jefferson believed he had formulated a revolutionary ideology can be seen at varying intervals throughout his career. His family motto, "Rebellion against tyrants is Obedience unto God," nearly summed up his entire political philosophy. Jefferson's original Declaration of Independence firmly established the "right to revolution" among all mankind and introduced a notion of equality that, he believed, would democratize the idea of revolution. It was in this context of speaking for all men, in all future ages—"the memory of the American revolution will be immortal . . ."[11]—that one can see Jefferson's identification with a world revolutionary perspective.

During the period of the French Revolution Jefferson endorsed Paine's universal application of the Rights of Man. All his life he subscribed to the revolutionary ideology of republicanism, which,

[11] Jefferson to Hilliard d'Auberteuil, 20 Feb. 1786, *Papers*, Vol. 9, pp. 290–91.

at the time, no one knew how to translate successfully into a functional government. Like the socialist regimes in 1917, republicanism was revolutionary simply because no one—at least for two thousand years—had seen a republic. Yet, reminiscing on the origins of the nation's commitment to republicanism, Jefferson revealed that at the first idea of independence the revolutionaries were determined to try it: "From the moment that to preserve our rights a change of government became necessary, no doubt could be entertained that a republican form was most consonant with reason [and] with right . . ."[12]

Jefferson perceived that the ideology of republicanism, much like the Marxist ideology of the nineteenth and twentieth centuries, would strike terror in the minds of the absolutist regimes in Europe. He thus made it a principle to urge it upon others whenever possible. In 1792, informing Ambassador Pinckney how to conduct himself in France, Jefferson laid "down the catholic principle of republicanism, to wit, that every people may establish what form of government they please and change it as they please . . ."[13] The very idea that men could change their government was, in the eighteenth century, revolutionary.

Jefferson's notion of America acting as the revolutionary agent in the world, the equivalent of a twentieth-century Comintern, is further evidence that Jefferson believed his revolutionary ideas went beyond his immediate experience. "We feel," he wrote Priestley in 1802, "that we are acting under obligations not confined to the limits of our own society. It is impossible not to be sensible that we are acting for all mankind . . ."[14] Seven years later Jefferson would carry the torch of revolution even further, and define the United States as a revolutionary state: "The station which we occupy among the nations of the earth is honorable, but awful. Trusted with the destinies of this solitary *republic of the world*, the only monument of human rights, and the sole deposi-

12 "Address to the General Assembly of Virginia," 16 Feb. 1809, *Writings*, Vol. XVI, p. 333.

13 *The Anas*, *Writings*, Vol. I, p. 330. Entry under Dec. 1792.

14 Jefferson to Joseph Priestley, 19 June 1802, *Writings*, Vol. X, p. 324.

tary of the sacred fire of freedom and self government, from hence it is to be lighted up in the other regions of the earth . . ."[15]

Twelve years later Jefferson wrote Adams a letter that showed his consistent faith in the power of the revolutionary ideas he had helped formulate:

> . . . I will not believe our labors are lost. I shall not die without a hope that light and liberty are on a steady advance. We have seen indeed once within the records of history a compleat eclipse of the human mind continuing for centuries. And this too by swarms of the same Northern barbarians; conquering and taking possession of the countries and governments of the civilized alone, and the vast dissemination of books, will maintain the mind where it is, and raise the conquering ruffians to the level of the conquered, instead of degrading these to that of their conquerors. And even should the clouds of barbarism and despotism again obscure the science and liberties of Europe, this country remains to preserve and *restore* light and liberty to them. In short, the flames kindled on the 4th. of July 1776. have spread over too much of the globe to be extinguished by the feeble engines of despotism. On the contrary they will consume those engines, and all who work them.[16]

Thus Jefferson observed the struggle that has throughout history characterized the nature of revolution: i.e., the struggle of men to become free of despotism. Speculating on the rising tide of despotism, conjecturing that in the dialectical struggle between the two it was possible that these final stirrings of liberty might vanish in Europe as they had centuries earlier, he placed his hopes for liberation in ideas and opinions, in the power of science and the press and, most particularly, in the democratic forces unleashed in 1776. We might also note ironically that Jefferson firmly believed the spirit of 1776 crystallized in the election of 1800 would make it impossible that this nation would ever ally itself with the despotic forces in the world, but would work to destroy them.

[15] "To the Citizens of Washington," 4 March 1807, *Writings*, Vol. XVI, pp. 347–48.
[16] Jefferson to John Adams, 12 Sept. 1821, *Letters*, Vol. II, pp. 574–75.

Jefferson's optimism, within realistic bounds, had always comprehended a time span that reflected his understanding of the historical forces at work in the eighteenth century. Writing to Adams two years later, but this time regarding other countries, Jefferson concurred with him on the difficulty that revolutions experience in their transition from despotism to freedom. In the letter Jefferson supplies us with his notion of revolution in history:

> The generation which commences a revolution can rarely compleat it. Habituated from their infancy to passive submission of body and mind to their kings and priests, they are not qualified, when called on, to think and provide for themselves and their inexperience, their ignorance and bigotry make them instruments often, in the hands of the Bonapartes and Iturbides to defeat their own rights and purposes.
>
> This is the present situation of Europe and Spanish America. But it is not desperate. The light which has been shed on mankind by the art of printing has eminently changed the condition of the world. As yet that light has dawned on the midling classes only of the men of Europe. The kings and the rabble of equal ignorance, have not yet received its rays; but it continues to spread. And while printing is preserved, it can no more recede than the sun return on his course. A first attempt to recover the right of self-government may fail; so may a 2d. a 3d. etc. but as a younger, and more instructed race comes on, the sentiment becomes more and more intuitive, and a 4th. a 5th. or some subsequent one of the ever renewed attempts will ultimately succeed.[17]

Jefferson's observation that the bourgeoisie, or "midling class," was emerging as a revolutionary class is worth noting here, because it reveals Jefferson's dependence upon it to advance the idea of revolution. Of course, Jefferson's observation on class is not, strictly speaking, a pre-Marxian analysis. Jefferson saw society divided into the "few and the Many," as Aristotle did. But he viewed the fusion of political and religious power, not economics, as the deciding factor which, concentrated in the hands of one or more men, produced despotism. Jefferson's division of society into

[17] Jefferson to John Adams, 4 Sept. 1823, *Letters*, Vol. II, p. 596.

classes had more to do with a classical notion of justice, a notion that included a variety of factors in addition to economics. Identifying the despots as "monarchists," Jefferson waged a lifelong struggle to root them out of the political affairs of the nation, a struggle comparable in intensity to the nineteenth- and twentieth-century Marxist efforts to eliminate the bourgeoisie.

Pervading this statement is a doctrine of inevitability, as if the forces of revolution represented in the dialectic of history are so powerful that they cannot be denied. In fact, what Jefferson was hinting at in the latter portion of the letter is a theory that reflects not just an emerging revolutionary dialectic, but the logic of faction and the non-party state mentioned in the preceding chapter. Jefferson's description of revolution deals with a similar idea. Taking this view, one can read his letter as an analysis of the basic components of the idea of revolution.

The first component, Jefferson's description of "an eminently changed condition in the world," reflects his recognition of the potential for revolutionary societies in Europe and Latin America. Here, Jefferson is painting a picture of the dual character of societies in which two cities exist, each opposing the other. This opposition, according to Jefferson, has taken on among the younger generation an ingrained "instinct," which in time produces "two competing cultural systems warring against each other in the same society."[18]

Next, Jefferson described the "institutional" and "ideological" components in this emerging two-city thesis. The institutions were monarchy and its trappings—religious superstition and ignorance —versus the more enlightened institutions of "self-government." The ideological components were the divine right theories of the state versus the emerging republican ideology. The monarchical types represent the "establishment," the successive generations

[18] Harvey Wheeler, *The Politics of Revolution* (Berkeley, Calif., 1971), p. vii. Wheeler's two-city thesis of revolution should be examined by every student of this period. I cannot exaggerate its value in providing insights for my own studies that ultimately led to my writing this volume. "The Politics of Revolution," *The Center Magazine*, Vol. I, No. 3 (March 1968), pp. 49–65.

represent the competing classes or counterculture. Jefferson's notion of "intuitive" sentiment is merely another way of expressing the strengthening of the second city, the faction in society that challenges the establishment.

In the third component, represented by the historical view that Jefferson held, the revolutionary dialectic would increase in intensity until a crisis situation was reached. The influence of science and the printing press would spread among the younger generation, almost invisibly; yet it would be denied by the kings and priests who refused to receive its rays. This was, and is, the characteristic behavior of an establishment that fails to respond or to solve its crises. It also signaled to Jefferson that the second city would grow in strength and resolve. It might be ten, forty, or sixty years in the future, but when the crises occurred, when traditional institutional, ideological, and cultural reforms failed, the revolution would inevitably succeed.

Jefferson's realistic sense of what must be accomplished over generations was not limited to time. Included in his assessment was the toll that permanent revolution would exact in violence. He completed his letter to Adams by warning the price would not be cheap:

> . . . to attain all this however rivers of blood must yet flow, and years of desolation pass over. Yet the object is worth rivers of blood, and years of desolation for what inheritance so valuable can man leave to his posterity?[19]

This notion of leaving a legacy of revolution and violence to posterity was not the idle speculation of a philosopher in old age. Jefferson had, as a young man of thirty-three, been immersed in the violence of the Revolutionary War. He had also seen, firsthand, limited violence at the beginning of the French Revolution and knew of the purges that had followed his departure. Thus a recognition of potential violence had been a consistent part of Jefferson's experience from the beginning.

This recognition expressed itself in the references that Jefferson

[19] Jefferson to John Adams, 4 Sept. 1823, *Letters*, Vol. II, pp. 596–97.

made to rebellion and revolution. Strangely, Jefferson seemed to have merged the two. At least he was not careful about making distinctions between them. But from past experience, Jefferson felt that revolt or rebellion was directed against individual rulers or specific abuses and not against states. He also felt that rebellion was spontaneous, often reacting to specific grievances that had nothing to do with the society as a whole. Yet, "rebellion against tyrants is obedience unto God" was Jefferson's credo, and the inference is that he saw rebellion on a continuum with revolution. Had he lived in the seventeenth century, he might have founded a divine-right theory of revolution; as it was, the Declaration nearly amounted to the same thing.

While Jefferson might have acknowledged that rebellions rarely threaten the state, they had the potential to, and that made them important. Rebellions also had the potential to enlarge—at least in a ruler's mind—and therefore, their utility lay in keeping rulers honest. There was also another characteristic of rebellion that appealed to Jefferson's principles: viz., their actions were often directed against a consolidating and distant power. This consolidation of power was something that Jefferson feared. Moreover, if rebellions could prevent the gradual growth of power in the state, he wished to encourage them. If they occurred regularly, they would have the effect of maintaining society on a course consistent with its principles of government. Thus Jefferson, in what amounted to a convergence theory of (or simply a confusion over) revolt and revolution, might be regarded as a rebel who was profoundly revolutionary. Incapable of tolerating injustice in any form, Jefferson seemed unwilling, like many nineteenth- and twentieth-century revolutionaries, to play a counterrevolutionary role. Rather than wait for the opportune moment in history, when the "objective conditions" were favorable, Jefferson simply wished to see injustice eradicated. Since injustice would always exist in an imperfect world, a theory of permanent rebellion emerged along with his idea of revolution through history.

Violence, therefore, could not be divorced from either rebellion or revolution. Referring to the "rivers of blood" that would flow in the future revolutions of Europe and Latin America, Jefferson believed—in the classical sense—that liberty could grow and flourish only through bloodshed. Indeed, it was as if violence against tyrants was liberty's "natural manure." Referring to Shays's Rebellion at the time of the Constitutional Convention, Jefferson stated explicitly his notion of rebellion and its relation to violence. No American statesman, before or since, has so completely embraced the idea of violence as a means to realize the end of the state. He wrote:

> Can history produce an instance of a rebellion so honorably conducted? I say nothing of its motives. They were founded in ignorance, not wickedness. God forbid we should ever be 20. years without such a rebellion. The people can not be all, and always well informed. The part which is wrong will be discontented in proportion to the importance of the facts they misconceive. If they remain quiet under such misconceptions it is a lethargy, the forerunner of death to the public liberty. . . . What country before ever existed a century and a half without a rebellion? And what country can preserve it's [*sic*] liberties if their rulers are not warned from time to time that their people preserve the spirit of resistance? *Let them take arms.* The remedy is to set them right as to facts, pardon and pacify them. What signify a few lives lost in a century or two? The tree of liberty must be refreshed from time to time with the blood of patriots and tyrants. It is its natural manure . . .[20]

In this letter a relationship is made between opinion—construed rightly or wrongly—and rebellion. Here we perceive one important distinction that Jefferson might have made between rebellion and revolution. Since Jefferson linked his idea of revolution to a constitution, he must have been considering total and systemic change. Revolution, then, must have a plan; it must be systemic in its approach. Rebellion, on the other hand, labors under misconception and ignorance. Therefore, it could not be systemic in the changes it wrought, unless, of course, it became something else.

[20] Jefferson to William Smith, 13 Nov. 1787, *Papers*, Vol. 12, p. 356.

In that same year, 1787, Jefferson again expressed his strong commitment to the idea of rebellion. Writing to James Madison in January of that year, he said with a warning:

> I hold it that a little rebellion now and then is a good thing, and as necessary in the political world as storms in the physical. Unsuccessful rebellions indeed generally establish encroachments on the rights of the people which have produced them. An observation of this truth should render honest republican governors so mild in their punishment of rebellions, as not to discourage them too much. It is a medicine necessary for the sound health of government.[21]

The warning was specifically meant for those rulers of republican governments who wished to preserve liberty. Jefferson is acknowledging here another distinction between rebellion and revolution. Rebellion, he admits, generally results in repression; while revolution—at least in his experience—could afford to be more lenient. This leniency that Jefferson referred to (and we must remember this is 1787, not 1789) had been shown in the American Revolution. After the war ceased, there had been no executions, no bloody purges; and revolutionaries welcomed all who had opposed them to support the new government. Such restraint in the transition of either a revolutionary government or an established one putting down a rebellion was, Jefferson saw, necessary as well as desirable.

Jefferson's next epistle on rebellion was written almost mischievously, to one of his ultraconservative correspondents, and casually stated that he wished rebellion could become a permanent force in the body politic:

> The spirit of resistance to government is so valuable on certain occasions, that I wish it to be always kept alive. It will often be exercised when wrong, but better so than not to be exercised at all. I like a little rebellion now and then. It is like a storm in the Atmosphere.[22]

---

[21] Jefferson to James Madison, 30 Jan. 1787, *Papers*, Vol. 11, p. 93.
[22] Jefferson to Abigail Adams, 22 Feb. 1787, *Papers*, Vol. 11, p. 174.

Shays's Rebellion was one of those thunderstorms that Jefferson felt were necessary. Comparing the political events of Europe with those in America, he had determined that the furor over Shays's Rebellion was highly exaggerated. In strong language to his friend Madison, Jefferson warmed to his favorite theme—the topic of rebellions:

> . . . no country should be so long without one. Nor will any degree of power in the hands of government prevent insurrections. France with all it's [*sic*] despotism, and two or three hundred thousand men always in arms, has had three insurrections in the three years I have been here every one of which greater numbers were engaged than in Massachusetts and a great deal more blood was spilt. In Turkey, which Montesquieu supposes more despotic, insurrections are the events of every day. In England, where the hand of power is lighter than here [France], but heavier than with us they happen every half dozen years. Compare again the ferocious depredations of their insurgents with the order, the moderation and the almost self extinguishment of ours.[23]

What seems different about this letter is the comparison Jefferson is making between despotism and free governments and their relationship to rebellion. Normally one assumes that a free society is the most tumultuous. Jefferson, however, seems to be saying the opposite; in those states where absolutism prevails, the citizens tend toward greater extremes of violence. His reference to "insurrection" is unclear in the sense that he is drawing a sharp distinction between it and revolution. Yet the implication of his first sentence is crystal clear: no "degree of power" held by the state will prevent either rebellion or revolution from occurring. Both are natural phenomena.

As Jefferson went about his duties in France, the Constitutional Convention was meeting to decide the future of the American states. It is obvious from Jefferson's letters that, while his mind was officially occupied with the situation in France, he was also concentrating on the new event in America. This event loomed significantly in Jefferson's mind, for as we shall see later, it held

[23] Jefferson to James Madison, 20 Dec. 1787, *Papers*, Vol. 12, p. 442.

the connotations of a "second" American revolution. Keeping the Convention in mind, Jefferson was gradually coming around to a note of restraint. In his letter to Madison he referred to one of his main principles: "that the will of the majority always prevail."[24] Thus his awareness of the Convention and what he expected to come out of it indicate that his revolutionary fervor could be tempered by the deliberations of its representatives. This was not incompatible with his earlier statements on rebellion and revolution. Quite the contrary, the spirit of resistance was a tension that he felt would ensure responsible government. Indeed, that spirit "prevents the degeneracy of government, and nourishes a general attention to the public affairs."[25]

In one of his mathematical moments Jefferson had even gone so far as to introduce a kind of calculus of revolution. Thinking about the insurrection in Massachusetts and attempting to put it into a calmer perspective, he wrote: "For thus I calculate. An insurrection in one of the 13 states in the course of 11 years that they have subsisted amounts to one in any particular state in 143 years, say a century and a half. This would not be as many as has happened in every other government that has ever existed . . ."[26] And, after repeating the first two sentences in another letter on the same day, he added, "This will not weigh against the inconveniences of a government of force, such as are monarchies, and aristocracies. You see I am not discouraged by this little difficulty, nor have I any doubt that the results of our experiment will be that men are capable of governing themselves without a master."[27]

Jefferson's optimism is reminiscent of his time and can be compared to the belief of a contemporary, Jeremy Bentham, in the "felicific calculus." For Jefferson, the greatest good for the greatest number, in revolutionary terms, would be a rebellion every 143 years. That would ensure the preservation of liberty and self-government.

[24] Ibid., p. 442.
[25] Jefferson to James Madison, 30 Jan. 1787, *Papers*, Vol. 11, p. 93.
[26] Jefferson to David Hartley, 2 July 1787, *Papers*, Vol. 11, p. 526.
[27] Jefferson to Thomas Brand Hollis, 2 July 1787, *Papers*, Vol. 11, p. 527.

While Jefferson was arguing that we ought to have a revolution every century and a half, he was also pointing to the object of the revolution, viz., despotism or governments "of force." In his mind those governments were synonymous with monarchies and aristocracies, the kinds of regimes whose power to abuse was rarely limited. This is important because it registers the eighteenth century's great concern for the forms of government and the influence that form had on the conduct of administration. On this last point, Jefferson seems to be sliding over distinctions between insurrection and revolution. The comparison between American and European governments keeps the distinction; but his hope is that a revolutionary change—in principle and systemic in nature—will emerge from insurrection: the proof that men can govern themselves without kings. This would indicate that the relationship between the two is almost indistinguishable for Jefferson in 1787.

The role that violence would play in any revolution—measured against the nature of the regime—was crucial to the success that the revolution would enjoy. Jefferson had agreed with Adams that revolution was separate from war. He had even observed to a friend that "war is not the most favorable moment for divesting . . . a . . . monarchy of power. On the contrary it is the moment when the energy of a single hand shews itself in the most seducing form."[28]

Although Jefferson was, in this instance, observing the emerging revolution in France, his statement is in the form of a principle and can be generalized. His idea of revolution, which always seemed to be opposed to monarchy or aristocracy, was becoming practical. Thus, despite his assertions about the frequency and bloodiness of rebellions or the necessity for countries like France to experience revolution, Jefferson was developing an idea of peaceful revolution.

This emerging theory of nonviolent consolidation of the revolution can be understood, however, only by thinking of it as a

---

[28] Jefferson to St. John de Crevecoeur, 9 Aug. 1789, *Papers*, Vol. 13, p. 485.

complex living tissue with three interconnected layers. The first or outside layer is the influence that information and intelligent opinion have in setting the stage for revolution. The second is opinion's relationship to violence, always beneath the surface. The third, and deepest, layer is their connection to the constitution and the role it plays in preventing violence, translating the goals of revolution into reality and serving as the unifying force of the revolution. Attempt to separate any one of these layers from the others and the entire tissue may hemorrhage.

Jefferson was cognizant that each of these layers depended upon the others, that they must grow together or else the revolution would abort. In fact, throughout his writings from 1787 on, he rarely mentions the idea of revolution without explicitly referring to at least two of these factors. As the years passed, Jefferson's interest in the revolutions taking place around him appeared to become more intense.

He was already aware of the connection between the idea of revolution and his own fame. His authorship of the Declaration of Independence had established his reputation as a hero to the most "ardent spirits" in Europe, and especially to those in France. Wherever revolutionary activity was potential, contemplated, or in the process of taking place, Jefferson was a man to be consulted. His colleagues at home, many of whom did not understand, often caricatured him as a "man of some acquirements . . . but [having] opinions upon Government . . . the result of fine spun theoretic systems, drawn from the ingenious writings of Locke, Sydney and others of their cast which can never be realized."[29]

While this was true of those he would later accuse of courting the principles of "kingly government,"[30] his admirers in France and elsewhere appreciated his talents with deeper understanding. Even at the risk of violating his diplomatic neutrality, Jefferson was willing to engage in revolutionary intrigue. Once, after presiding over a revolutionary dialogue in his own home "truly worthy of

[29] *Papers*, Vol. 17, p. 63. See editor's comment.
[30] See the explanatory notes in *The Anas, Writings*, Vol. I, pp. 265–66.

being placed in parallel with the finest dialogues of antiquity," Jefferson felt moved to explain his behavior to the French minister Count Montmorin. Montmorin's guarded reply furnishes a good insight into Jefferson's ability to influence, in a practical way, the developing idea of revolution. "He told me [Jefferson] . . . he earnestly wishes I would habitually assist at such conferences, being sure I should be useful in moderating the warmer spirits, and promoting a wholesome and practicable reformation only."[31]

From time to time his more intimate friends in America gave him encouragement and perhaps even flattered him in his revolutionary undertakings. Thomas Shippen wrote from America praising Jefferson's influence on opinions and noted, in addition, the formation of the constitution as the culmination of the American Revolution:

> . . . this seems the age of revolutions in favor of liberty, and that presiding Goddess seems to triumph over every opposition to her mild and happy reign. You have greatly contributed Sir [*sic*] to setting the example in America which Europe seems now anxious to follow, that of refusing obedience to a tyrannical government and establishing a good one in its stead on the broad basis of the people's choice. Ours is by this time nearly completed, nothing remains wanting to its organization but the assembling of the Deputies already chosen.[32]

But in truth Jefferson did not need encouragement or flattery. He had been acting in his revolutionary advisory capacity for a number of years. Indeed, it was the way Jefferson had found to add to, and refine, his own ideas of revolution. By May of 1787, he was already writing long letters to his friends in America keeping them abreast of the progress of the idea of revolution throughout the world. Referring to Brazil he wrote:

> . . . the men of letters are those most desirous of a revolution. The people are not much under the influence of their priests, most

[31] *Autobiography of Thomas Jefferson,* ed. Adrienne Koch and William Peden (New York, 1944), pp. 108–9.
[32] Thomas Lee Shippen to Jefferson, 3 Feb. 1789, *Papers,* Vol. 14, pp. 517–18.

of them read and write, possess arms and are in the habit of using them for hunting. The slaves will take the side of their masters. In short, as to the question of revolution, there is but one mind in that country. But there appears to be no person capable of conducting a revolution, or willing to venture himself at its head, without the aid of some powerful nation. . . . There is no printing press in Brasil. They consider the North American revolution as a precedent for theirs. . . . [And] in case of a successful revolution, a republican government in a single body, would probably be established.[33]

Here Jefferson is making a distinction between those who may be expected to participate in revolution and those who will continue to languish in despotism. Jefferson's assessment seems to be made on the basis of the population's *literary* skills and how receptive they are to *written* appeals. Noting the absence of a printing press, he seems to believe that this device, used to disseminate revolutionary ideas, is crucial—in practical terms—to a burgeoning revolution.

He also recognizes, in a limited way, that certain objective conditions must exist in the society before revolution is possible. In order for revolution to occur, there must be someone who has the will to lead it, someone who can assimilate a view of a future society and act upon his vision. Jefferson's association between literacy and the recent historical perspective referred to above may have been acute for his estimate of Brazil's revolutionary potential. For revolution to occur—Jefferson would have argued—men must have some awareness of their place in history. They must know or realize from past examples that they can actually complete a revolution. At the same time Jefferson is implying that the people themselves must be conscious of their role in a revolution. They must understand, like their leaders, the idea of liberty sufficiently to expand it. If they are either ignorant or illiterate, with no understanding of the potential of a constitutional system, they merely endanger their lives and the few rights they enjoy.

[33] Jefferson to John Jay, 4 May 1787, *Papers*, Vol. 11, pp. 340–41.

We ought to note, too, that Jefferson *assumes* a "probable" connection of the revolutionary ideology of his time—"republicanism"—to the *successful* outcome of revolution. This would imply that Jefferson, like revolutionaries in all ages, linked the prevailing ideology to any successful revolution, whether probable, potential, or actual.

The degree to which Jefferson became involved in revolutionary activity has always been a matter of conjecture. But as his correspondence continues after 1787, one sees constant references to revolutions in countries all over the world. Such a reference was made to two Latin American nations—Brazil and Mexico—in this letter to John Jay:

> I took care to impress on him thro' the whole of our conversation that I had neither instructions nor authority to say a word to anybody on this subject, and that I could only give him my own ideas as a single individual: which were that we were not in a condition at present to meddle nationally in any war; that we wished particularly to cultivate the friendship of Portugal, with whom we have an advantageous commerce. That yet a successful revolution in Brasil could not be uninteresting to us.[34]

It is interesting to observe Jefferson's ambivalence toward his official function as an ambassador and his deep interest in revolutionary ideas. While assuring his friends in America that he was aware of the diplomatic "thin ice" he had been treading on, he nevertheless could not restrain his instincts to further a revolution.

To emphasize the relationship between opinion and the possibility of revolution, Jefferson mentioned to Jay in the same letter his conversations with another Latin American. Estimating Spanish Mexico's potential for a successful revolution, Jefferson gave evidence that he could counsel restraint: "I was still more cautious with him than with the Brasilian, mentioning it as my private opinion (unauthorized to say a word on the subject other-

[34] Ibid., p. 341.

wise) that a successful revolution was still at a distance with them; that I feared they must begin by enlightening and emancipating the minds of their people . . ."[35]

Jefferson's suggestion to the Mexican was more than practical, it was aimed at avoiding unnecessary bloodshed. His concern for "enlightening and emancipating the minds" of the people was uppermost in his notion of what was important in an emerging revolution. It was, he felt, the very first consideration one had to make in assessing the possibility of revolution. Jefferson was aware that you simply could not say you were going to begin a revolution and then have one. For a good harvest, one first had to prepare the soil.

To show his consistency on this position he was still concerned about educating these same people thirty years later. His advice had changed but only slightly. He seemed to believe it was better to have revolution piecemeal than endure a violent confrontation that would set back the cause of liberty, perhaps for generations. Answering a query from John Adams on the revolutionary potential in South America, he wrote:

> I enter into all your doubts as to the event of the revolution of S. America. They will succeed against Spain. But the dangerous enemy is within their own breasts. Ignorance and superstition will chain their minds and bodies under religious and military despotism. I do believe it would be better for them to obtain freedom by degrees only; because that would by degrees bring on light and information, and qualify them to take charge of themselves understandingly; with more certainty . . . as may keep them at peace with one another.[36]

Thus Jefferson, serving in the capacity of a revolutionary advisor, was always tailoring his advice to the conditions he found locally or nationally. No blanket theorist, he found himself making distinctions regarding the potential for revolution in a way that many critics—and even a few revolutionaries—in the twentieth century have lost sight of. Jefferson was always speaking of an "appeal to

[35] Ibid., p. 342.
[36] Jefferson to John Adams, 17 May 1818, *Letters*, Vol. II, p. 524.

the nation . . . and yet not so much as to endanger an appeal to arms."[37] His greatest fear was that revolutionaries would act prematurely, before the "public mind was ripened by time and discussion and was one opinion on the principal points."[38] Jefferson seemed to believe that without an understanding of what the forces of power were, what the delicate balance of the constitution was, even what was worth fighting for, any revolution would be strangled in its cradle. At the same time Jefferson also kept in mind that unity or agreement among the people was essential if only to demonstrate that a sufficient force of public opinion existed in the state. That was the first objective of any revolution. Means must be found to communicate that force to those in power, who, hopefully, would then change their policies or realize that resistance was futile. Jefferson never abandoned his hope that revolution could be successful without a resort to arms. Dwelling on the corruption in Greece and the potential for revolution there, he wrote John Adams decades later, indicating a consistency in his approach to the idea of revolution:

> I consider their government as the most flagitious which has existed since the days of Philip of Macedon, whom, they make their model. It is not only founded in corruption itself, but insinuates the same poison into the bowels of every other, corrupts its councils, nourishes FACTIONS, STIRS UP REVOLUTIONS, and places its own happiness in fomenting commotions and civil wars among others. . . . The effect is now coming home to itself. It's [sic] first operations will fall on the individuals who have been the chief instruments in its corruptions, and will eradicate the families which have, from generation to generation been fattening on the blood of their brethren: and this scoria once thrown off, I am in hopes a purer nation will result, and a purer government be instituted, one which, instead of endeavoring to make us their natural enemies, will see in us, what we really are, their natural friends. . . . I look therefore to their REVOLUTION with great interest. I wish it to be as moderate and bloodless, as will effect the desired object

[37] Jefferson to Moustier, 13 March 1789, *Papers*, Vol. 14, p. 652.
[38] Jefferson to Thomas Paine, 17 March 1789, ibid., p. 671.

of an honest government, one which will permit the world to live in peace, and under the bonds of friendship and good neighborhood.[39]

As we have noted above, Jefferson was in a position to know directly what the course of the French Revolution might be. His conversations with ministers and members of the French aristocracy enabled him through correspondence to keep his friends in America informed of its progress. But of greater importance, at least to his posterity, is the fact that Jefferson's letters present a month-to-month account of the French Revolution in its earliest stages, and detail what aspects he felt were most important. Thus Jefferson writes Washington informing him what the issue of revolution has been so far: ". . . the nation [France] is pressing on fast to a fixed constitution. Such a revolution in the public opinion has taken place that the crown already feels it's [sic] powers bounded, and is obliged by it's [sic] measures to acknowledge limits."[40] Here Jefferson points to the influence of opinion in the nation and what he believes the reaction of the rulers will be to that opinion. In addition, he has focused the revolutionary struggle on the development of the constitution.

Three months later, Jefferson described the politics of three nations—France, Holland, and America—to illustrate the relationship between a constitution, violence, and revolution. Note how Jefferson designates the constitution's establishment as the "second revolution" in America. This second revolution, which is nonviolent and constitutional, now emerges as Jefferson's ideal of what a revolution should be. The changes that he describes, whether between success and failure, or between form and principle, are systemic. In the one, the representatives of the nation, i.e., parliament, emerge as the true leaders at the expense of the single monarch and the "despotic party." Jefferson seems to believe that the "well-tempered constitution," which reflects a new alignment of power, will effect a permanent change in the life of the nation.

[39] Jefferson to John Adams, 25 Nov. 1816, *Letters*, Vol. II, p. 498.
[40] Jefferson to George Washington, 2 May 1788, *Papers*, Vol. 13, p. 126.

The point of interest here is that Jefferson thinks these gains have been guaranteed by incorporating them into the constitution. They are gains, moreover, not limited to form; they include principles of governing as well. Indeed, this is an idea of revolution that Jefferson will keep in mind—testing and refining—for the next three decades. By contrast, Holland represents the failure, its citizens victims of party spirit and violence. No systemic change is recognized because the status quo is preserved. Principle is lost and the constitutional issue guarantees nothing. As Jefferson so despairingly implies, it is a revolution that failed. One more factor we might notice is that Jefferson is again placing the idea of revolution in a dialectical framework: the forces of despotism (monarchy and aristocracy) versus the democratic aspirations of the people. Addressing a French citizen then living in America, he wrote:

> While our second revolution is just brought to a happy end with you, yours here is but cleverly under way. For some days I was really melancholy with the apprehension that arms would be appealed to, and the opposition crushed in its first efforts. But things seem now to wear a better aspect. While the opposition keeps at its highest wholesome point, government, unwilling to draw the sword, is not forced to do it. The contest here [in France] is exactly what it was in Holland: a contest between the monopoly of despotism over the people. . . . In Holland the people remained victims. Here [France] I think it will take a happier turn. The parliamentary party of the aristocracy is alone firmly united. The Noblesse and clergy, but especially the former, are divided partly between the parliamentary and the despotic party, and partly united with the real patriots who are endeavoring to gain for the nation what they can both from the parliamentary and the single despotism. . . . [They] will probably end in . . . a well tempered constitution.[41]

Thus, while Jefferson is keeping the model of the second American revolution in mind, he is studying the emerging constitutional

[41] Jefferson to St. John de Crevecoeur, 9 Aug. 1788, *Papers*, Vol. 13, pp. 485–86.

revolution in France—hoping that it would continue its nonviolent course during the period of consolidation. One critical factor in furthering the revolution was to "cleverly" prevent any violent turn from taking place. It was the responsibility of the leaders to nurture a rational policy that would not provoke those in power to "draw the sword." Indeed, Jefferson's reflections on the future of France, placed in the context of the favorable issue of the second American revolution, raised the question of whether other nations could imitate America.

As Jefferson had seen just two months earlier, the forces of despotism in France were so powerful that a peaceful solution was by no means guaranteed. Another critical factor mentioned above, and one that he sees as a problem for any revolution, is the question of the army. Writing to a friend, he notes rather sharply the tragic role that party and the armed forces may play in producing counterrevolution:

> We can surely boast of having set the world a beautiful example of a government reformed by reason alone without bloodshed. But the world is too far oppressed to profit of the example. On this side the Atlantic [France] the blood of the people is become an inheritance, and those who fatten on it, will not relinquish it easily. The struggle in this country is as yet of doubtful issue. It is in fact between the monarchy, and the parliaments. The nation is no otherwise concerned, but as both parties may be induced to let go some of it's [sic] abuses to court the public favor. The danger is that the people, deceived by a false cry of liberty may be led to take side with one party, and thus give the other a pretext for crushing them still more. If they can avoid an appeal to arms, the nation will be sure to gain much by this controversy. But if that appeal is made it will depend entirely on the dispositions of the army whether it issue in liberty or despotism.[42]

By the middle of 1788, as the first sentence would imply, Jefferson has the model of the second American revolution firmly in mind. Moreover, he is now projecting that model on a world scale, explicitly stating that other nations would do well to imitate

[42] Jefferson to Edward Rutledge, 18 July 1788, *Papers*, Vol. 13, p. 378.

America's example. His is a recommendation for revolution without violence and bloodshed. Yet, nothing is lost in the sense that he and Adams defined the term almost three decades later. Pondering the potential violence of the emerging French Revolution, Jefferson made a distinction between the ongoing revolution and civil war. This separation anticipated his agreement with John Adams twenty-seven years before his colleague's famous query. In addition, it asserted the optimism of the author, who, mentally comparing France to America, hoped that reason and not violence would prevail:

> I have hoped this country would settle her internal disputes advantageously and without bloodshed. As yet none has been spilt, tho' British newspapers give the idea of general civil war. Hitherto I have supposed both the king and parliament would lose authority, and the nation gain it, through the medium of it's [sic] states general and provincial assemblies. But the arrest of the deputies of Bretagne two days ago, may kindle a civil war. Its issue will depend on two questions: 1. Will other provinces rise? 2. How will the army conduct itself?. . . Happy for us . . . that . . . we are able to send our wise and good men together to talk over our form of government, discuss its weaknesses and establish its remedies. . . . The example we have given to the world is single, that of changing the form of government under the authority of reason only, without bloodshed.[43]

By March of 1789 Jefferson was still optimistic that France would avoid bloodshed. One reason for his optimism was a belief that the idea of revolution must be accepted by the people. And from his vantage point in Paris, he daily saw the public becoming deeply involved. Jefferson traced this involvement in a letter that outlined the essential politics of a developing revolution. The conditions included: 1. the nation's intellectual potential to become aware of a political crisis; 2. the role of the press in shaping public opinion; 3. an economic crisis, especially one related to taxes; 4. the degree and rate of nonviolent change; 5. the difference

---

[43] Jefferson to Ralph Izard, 17 July 1788, *Papers*, Vol. 13, p. 373.

between the newly emerging and past forms of government; 6. their relation to the constitutional powers present in the government of the day and even of the hour; and 7. the degree of liberty expressed in a declaration of rights toward which the revolution aims. Each of these points must be seen in relation to the others as they occur. Considered collectively, they comprise an idea of revolution. Judged singly, they simply represent another problem in government or administration that can be adjusted to or solved. In this letter to his friend Humphreys, Jefferson is conveying the picture of a "complete revolution":

The change in this country, since you left it, is such as you can form no idea of. The frivolities of conversation have given way entirely to politics—men, women and children talk nothing else. . . . The press groans with daily productions. . . . A complete revolution in this government has, within the space of two years (for it began with the Notables of 1787) been effected merely by the force of public opinion, aided indeed by the want of money which the dissipations of the court had brought on. And this revolution has not cost a single life, unless we charge to it a little riot lately in Bretagne which begun about the price of bread, became afterwards political and ended in the loss of 4 or 5 lives. The assembly of the States general begins the 27th of April. The representation of the people will be perfect. . . . The first great question they will have to decide will be Whether they shall vote by orders or persons. And I have hopes that the majority of the nobles are already disposed to join the tiers etat in deciding that the vote shall be by persons. This is the opinion a la mode at present, and mode has acted a wonderful part in the present instance. . . . The king stands engaged to pretend no more to the power of laying, continuing or appropriating taxes, to call the States general periodically, to submit letters de cachet to legal restriction, to consent to freedom of the press, and that all this shall be fixed by a fundamental constitution which shall bind his successors. He has not offered a participation in the legislature, but it will surely be insisted on. The public mind is so ripened on all these subjects, that there seems to be now but one opinion. . . . The writings published on this occasion are some of them very valuable: because, unfettered by the prejudices under which the English labour, they give a full scope to reason, and strike out truths as yet unperceived and unacknowledged on the other side of the channel . . . In fine I believe this nation will in the course of the present year have as full a portion of liberty dealt out to them as the nation can bear at present, considering how uninformed the mass of their people is.[44]

Jefferson throughout 1789 appears immersed in what he termed "the spirit of revolution." His correspondence fairly bristles with references to revolutions in Denmark, Sweden, Turkey, France, Poland, and even such little noticed states as the Bishopric of Liège and the tiny state of Brabant. In all he is engrossed with the essential political forces. He says:

A revolution has been effected very suddenly in the Bishoprick of Liege. Their constitution had been changed by force by the reigning sovereign about 100 years ago. This subject had been lately revived and discussed in print. The people were at length excited to assemble tumultuously. They sent for their prince, who was at a country seat, and required him to come to the town house to hear their grievances. Tho' in the night, he came instantly, and was obliged to sign a restitution of their ancient constitution, which took place on the spot, and all became quiet, without a drop of blood spilt. This fact is worthy notice only as it shews the progress of the *spirit of revolution*.[45]

Periodically noting the progress of revolution, Jefferson jotted down this observation to a friend: "Affairs in France go on slowly but steadily. The revolution in Brabant is very doubtful."[46] These examples of peaceful constitutional revolutions, promoted by the engines of the press, were all good signs to Jefferson. They indicated that the American influence of forming revolutions might become accepted in Europe.

At the same time Jefferson's optimism regarding the avoidance

[44] Jefferson to David Humphreys, 18 March 1789, *Papers*, Vol. 14, pp. 676–77.
[45] Jefferson to John Jay, 27 Aug. 1789, *Papers*, Vol. 15, pp. 358–59.
[46] Jefferson to Alexander Donald, 13 June 1790, *Papers*, Vol. 16, p. 488.

of bloodshed was not without qualification. Writing to William Carmichael he reported, "We have had in this city a very considerable riot in which about 100 people have been probably killed. It was the most unprovoked and is therefore justly the most unpitied catastrophe of that kind I ever knew. Nor did the wretches know what they wanted, except to do mischief. It seems to have had no particular connection with the great national questions now in agitation."[47] Jefferson is attempting here to make a clear separation between violence and revolution. But less than a year later, he is not quite sure the separation is complete. He even seems to be saying that despite all precautions, some merging of the two is inevitable. In what was to be a prophetic warning to his friend La Fayette, Jefferson revealed his pessimism regarding the future progress of the French Revolution. On the eve of his departure he wrote:

> So far it seemed that your revolution had got along with a steady pace: meeting indeed occasional difficulties and dangers, but we are not to expect to be translated from despotism to liberty, in a feather-bed. I have never feared for the ultimate result, tho' I have feared for you personally . . . Take care of yourself, my dear friend. For tho' I think your nation would in any event work out her salvation, I am persuaded were she to lose you, it would cost her oceans of blood, and years of confusion and anarchy.[48]

Again Jefferson is placing the revolution in the context of despotism versus liberty and indicating that any revolution entails the greatest risks to civil society.

As Jefferson contemplated the idea of revolution during the year before he left France, he could not help but believe that the most important concern of any revolutionary movement must be the constitutional process. From his own experience in the 1770s he realized that only when the ideals of a revolution were written into law was it possible for the people to realize them. If ideals re-

---

[47] Jefferson to William Carmichael, 8 May 1789, *Papers*, Vol. 15, p. 104.
[48] Jefferson to La Fayette, 2 April 1790, *Papers*, Vol. 16, p. 293.

mained mere rhetoric they would continue to divide the people and lead to confusion and anarchy.

One major part of this concern was the process of electing officials to represent the people. Elections had played a major role in Jefferson's rise to power during the American Revolution. Being a delegate to the Continental Congress had thrust him suddenly onto the national stage. But more significant was the fact that elections had made the Revolution appear legitimate in the eyes of the people. In France, as we have seen, Jefferson paid particular attention to the politics of the election process which, he foresaw, would determine the peaceful or violent future of the revolution. Writing to perhaps the only person alive who had more experience with revolutions than himself, Jefferson is careful to note the different stages of the election process:

> This country is entirely occupied in it's [*sic*] elections which go on quietly and well. The Duke d'Orleans is elected for Villers-Cotterets. The Prince of Condé has lost the election he aimed at: nor is it certain he can be elected any where. We have no news from Auvergne whither the Marquis de la Fayette is gone. In general all the men of influence in the country are gone into the several provinces to get their friends elected or be elected themselves. Since my letter to you . . . four or five lives were lost. They are now quieter, and this is the only instance of a life lost as yet in this revolution. The public mind is now so far ripened by time and discussion that there seems to be but one opinion on the principal points. The question of voting by persons or orders is the most controverted; but even that seems to have gained already a majority among the Nobles. I fear more from the number of the assembly than from any other cause. 1200 persons are difficult to keep to order, and will be especially till they shall have had time to frame rules of order.[49]

This letter was consistent with Jefferson's earlier experience in promoting a full-scale revolution. Like the "men of influence" in France, in the midst of revolution in America, Jefferson had resigned his seat in Congress and taken his "place in the legislature

[49] Jefferson to Thomas Paine, 17 March 1789, *Papers*, Vol. 14, p. 671.

of Virginia" to accomplish those same ends. There he introduced
bills in 1776 that had as their goal the complete destruction of the
British administration. Among them were the "establishment of
courts of justice" and "trial by jury," a "bill declaring tenants in
tail to hold their lands in fee simple," a "bill to prevent . . . the
. . . further importation" of slaves, abolish primogeniture, abolish
the tyranny of the church of England, "establishing religious freedom," and finally an attempt to revise the "whole code" of laws
and adopt them to "our republican form of government.[50]

These were the revolutionary aims that Jefferson had in mind in
1789, and he hoped that the French might also. Certainly, he believed they were capable of promoting those aims. In a letter to
Paine Jefferson gave a "recapitulation" of the important constitutional aims of the French Revolution. He described the outline of the National Assembly's proceedings:

> Declaration of the rights of man. Principles of the monarchy.
> Rights of the nation. Rights of the king. Rights of the citizens.
>
> Organization and rights of the National Assembly. Forms
> necessary for the enactment of laws. Organization and functions
> of the Provincial and Municipal Assemblies. Duties and limits of
> the judiciary power. Functions and duties of the military power.
>
> You see that these are the materials of a superb edifice, and
> the hands which have prepared them, are perfectly capable of
> putting together, and of filling up the work of which these are
> only the outlines.[51]

His experience of constitution making had become an integral
part of Jefferson's notion of how a revolution was to proceed. A
reflection of his American experience, it emphasized principles,
organization, and functions of every governmental entity. Indeed,
this emphasis was, in Jefferson's eyes, necessary for all the other
revolutions that he saw occurring in the world. He never tired of
believing that America could set an example that would ultimately
provide a way of avoiding civil wars. Thus in 1787, before he could

---

[50] *The Autobiography of Thomas Jefferson*, op. cit., pp. 38–47.

[51] Jefferson to Thomas Paine, 11 July 1789, *The Life and Selected Writings of Thomas Jefferson*, op. cit., p. 480.

know its results, he remarked upon hearing of the Constitutional Convention:

> . . . there is a general disposition through the states to adopt what they shall propose, and we may be assured their propositions will be wise, as a more able assembly never sat in America. Happy for us that when we find our constitutions defective and insufficient to secure the happiness of our people, we can assemble with all the coolness of philosophers and set it to rights, while every other nation on earth must have recourse to arms to amend or to restore their constitutions.[52]

The emphasis upon reason to avoid violence could hardly have been more pronounced. Jefferson's faith that America was peacefully consolidating its revolution became even stronger eighteen months later when the results of the Convention became known. He shared his optimism with David Humphreys:

> The operations which have taken place in America lately, fill me with pleasure. In the first place they realize the confidence I had that whenever our affairs get obviously wrong, the good sense of the people will interpose and set them to rights. The example of changing a constitution by assembling the wise men of the state, instead of assembling armies, will be worth as much to the world as the former examples we have given them.[53]

The transfer of constitutional power from one form of government to another, from one set of principles to another, peaceably, with the will of the majority presiding, was for Jefferson the only successful idea of revolution. This was systemic change, the true characteristic of revolution, achieved peacefully. Any other transfer of power that failed to produce an expansion of liberty, that remained attached to principles of monarchy or aristocracy—both forms of despotism—was not revolution at all.

If a compromise had to be made regarding principles, the progress of the revolution must continue, else the monarch would seek to regain his lost power. Because the latter could be accom-

[52] Jefferson to C. W. F. Dumas, 10 Sept. 1787, *Papers*, Vol. 12, p. 113.
[53] Jefferson to David Humphreys, 18 March 1789, *Papers*, Vol. 14, p. 678.

plished only by force, oppression, and terror, it failed to advance the interests of mankind. It was, indeed, a return to those dark ages when the "clouds of barbarism and despotism" had obscured the liberties of Europe, a true counterrevolution. Because of this continual possibility, the principles of government became just as important for revolution as the form. The fact was, as Jefferson had recognized earlier, those successive generations that "instinctively" demanded greater freedom were the core of the second city. As they continued to expand their idea of freedom, gradually and through written constitutional guarantees, the growth of the revolution—based on the principles of a new value system—was assured.

Jefferson saw that it did nothing for mankind to advocate revolution and then discover that the reasons for turning to revolution had been lost in the struggle. This is why he expressed concern over the failure of the "wise men" in Philadelphia to incorporate the rights of man into the constitution itself. Declaring his willingness to accept the majority view, he nevertheless stated those rights which, if abused collectively in the minds of the people, formed the right to revolution. Commenting on the new constitution, he wrote:

> I am one of those who think it a defect that the important rights, not placed in security by the frame of the constitution itself, were not explicitly secured by a supplementary declaration. There are rights which it is useless to surrender to the government, and which yet, governments have always been fond to invade. These are the rights of thinking, and publishing our thoughts by speaking or writing: the right of free commerce; the right of personal freedom. There are instruments for administering the government, so peculiarly trustworthy, that we should never leave the legislature at liberty to change them. The new constitution has secured these in the executive and legislative departments; but not in the judiciary. It should have established trials by the people themselves, that is to say by jury.
>
> There are instruments so dangerous to the rights of the nation, and which place them so totally at the mercy of their governors,

that those governors, whether legislative or executive, should be restrained from keeping such instruments on foot but in well defined cases. Such an instrument is a standing army. We are now allowed to say such a declaration of rights, as a supplement to the constitution where that is silent, is wanting to secure us in these points.[54]

While Jefferson's optimism regarding the successful conclusion of the American Revolution remained strong, his imagination ranged over the possibilities of using reason and the "coolness of philosophy" to ensure that revolution in a single society would be permanent as well as bloodless. By now he was not content to simply see the "chequers" shifted on the board. Recognizing that tensions in society which cause revolutions often result from oppressive regimes that over time have lost all touch with current problems or the needs of a new generation, Jefferson sought to provide a rationale that would prevent those tensions from accumulating.

If we recall his reference to the Constitutional Convention as the second American revolution, we may gain an insight into his idea of revolution. Perhaps, he believed, a society dedicated to rational principles could institutionalize revolution in a constitutional form. In a little known and even less understood essay entitled *The Earth Belongs to the Living*, Jefferson was apparently sounding out his most trusted colleague, Madison, to this possibility. Written at the height of his involvement with the emerging French Revolution, it answers the problems he saw developing there and elsewhere in the world.

. . . no society can make a perpetual constitution, or even a perpetual law. The earth belongs always to the living generation. They may manage it then, and what proceeds from it, as they please, during their usufruct. They are masters too of their own persons, and consequently may govern them as they please. But persons and property make the sum of government. The constitution and the laws of their predecessors extinguished then in their

[54] Ibid.

natural course with those who gave them being. This could preserve that being till it ceased to be itself, and no longer. Every
constitution then, and every law, naturally expires at the end of
19 years. If it be enforced longer, it is an act of force, and not of
right.—It may be said that the succeeding generation exercising
in fact the power of repeal, this leaves them as free as if the constitution or law had been expressly limited to 19 years only. In
the first place, this objection admits the right, in proposing an
equivalent. But the power of repeal is not an equivalent. It might
be indeed if every form of government were so perfectly contrived
that the will of the majority could always be obtained fairly and
without impediment. But this is true of no form. The people
cannot assemble themselves. Their representation is unequal and
vicious. Various checks are opposed to every legislative proposition. *Factions* get possession of the public councils. Bribery corrupts them. Personal interests lead them astray from the general
interests of their constituents; and other impediments arise so as
to prove to every practical man that a law of limited duration
is much more manageable than one which needs a repeal.

This principle that the earth belongs to the living, and not to
the dead, is of very extensive application and consequences, in
every country, and most especially in France. It enters into the
resolution of the questions Whether the nation may change the
descent of lands holden in tail? Whether they may change the ap-
propriation of lands given antiently to the church, to hospitals,
colleges, order of chivalry, and otherwise in perpetuity? Whither
they may abolish the charges and privileges attached on lands, including the whole catalogue ecclesiastical and feudal? It goes to
hereditary offices, authorities and jurisdictions; to perpetual monopolies in commerce, the arts and sciences; with a long train of et
ceteras . . .[55]

The essay turned out, in Jefferson's own words, to be the
"dream of a theorist," for he never attempted to have it written
into law. In truth, Jefferson's essay was too revolutionary even for
his most intimate colleagues—all members of the power structure.
Reading it over, they most likely realized that nothing in the

---

[55] Jefferson to James Madison, 6 Sept. 1789, *Papers*, Vol. 15, pp. 395–97.

society would remain untouched or unchanged; no one's base of power would or could remain secure. Jefferson's departure from the one-dimensional vision of change that characterized nearly all of his eighteenth-century contemporaries was too powerful. In fact, it was *so* revolutionary in its potential for systemic change that not even his closest friend would breathe a word of it—to anyone. Perhaps Madison, whom Jefferson trusted to "circulate" it, being fresh from the "realistic compromises" of the Convention, thought it too ethereal. At any rate, he suggested that changing a constitution every generation would encourage "pernicious factions . . . and agitate the public mind more frequently and more violently than might be expedient."[56]

Aside from Madison's comments contained in several letters, no evidence exists that the essay went further than this letter. Yet the idea had profound revolutionary implications. As Jefferson realized, its principle had very "extensive application" and would serve as an obstacle to despotism around the globe. The essay's application went to the heart of every important power relationship in the commonwealth, specifically those that Jefferson, in his own revolutionary experience, had drafted legislation to remedy. But most significant, within Jefferson's essay were leveling principles—institutionalized—that would democratize the idea of revolution.

What Jefferson saw himself doing was anticipating the normal development of a prerevolutionary situation. Those conditions he enumerated at the end of his letter had been present in all despotisms throughout history and were particularly characteristic of the ancient regimes yet in power. Further, they could be summarized as those conditions that existed in America from 1760 to 1775: attempts by the government in power to maintain its authority were gradually undermined; laws became arbitrary; "obligations," once bearable, "became impositions"; traditional loyalties faded and new forms of attachment (outside the existing circle of government) became noticeable—the "second city"; the idea of

---

[56] Madison to Thomas Jefferson, 4 Feb. 1790, *The Writings of James Madison*, ed. Gaillard Hunt, 9 vols. (New York, 1900–10), Vol. V, pp. 438–39.

community—defined by the establishment—no longer held people's attention to the interests of the nation; factions arose that exploited the frustrated classes in society; representatives no longer were representative, but spoke for a privileged few; accepted forms of wealth and income suddenly appeared corrupt or "ill-gained"; existing concepts of prestige changed; those in positions of power were viewed with hostility and suspicion; finally, those people with talent, normally integrated into the society, began to feel "left out." Indeed, this is the picture of an emerging two-city theory of revolution: a "dialectic of two competing cultural systems warring against each other in the same society."[57]

This was a condition that, if allowed to develop over a long period of time, would inevitably produce a "crisis of community"—"political, economic, psychological, sociological, personal, and moral at the same time."[58] The conflict of values could plunge the nation into civil war. Revolution need not be the culmination of these conflicts; but the loss of liberty and harmony most certainly would be. What was needed at a time like this, and Jefferson had seen this condition in America and in France, was the intelligent search for a new sense of community, a new set of principles or a return to older ones, a way to reestablish conditions that would become acceptable to those who were disillusioned and felt "left out."

A constitution every generation was one way to establish this new sense of community. It was an exercise guaranteed to keep the government responsive to the people while inhibiting the growth of factions that established oligarchies and corrupted the laws. It would, Jefferson pointed out, make government and constitutions respect the rights of the individual and not become the instruments of force. If every generation had to decide what to throw away, as well as what to keep, in a constitution, it would be an educational process that would force it to understand, as well as to protect, its rights. This was consistent with Jefferson's belief that

[57] Wheeler, *The Politics of Revolution*, op. cit., p. 9.

[58] R. R. Palmer, *The Age of Democratic Revolution* (Princeton, N.J., 1959), Vol. I, p. 21.

the Rights of Man were at the heart of every revolutionary struggle.

Jacques Ellul has observed that in the eighteenth century the idea of "revolution was a juridical concept that met the demands of reason . . ."[59] Jefferson's revolutionary essay was an expression of this eighteenth-century—the Age of Reason—belief in reason as the supreme arbiter in society. It was also a recognition of the political nature of revolution. Only reason could avoid the fanaticism, the excesses, and the bloodshed that ultimately defeated the cause of liberty. Accordingly, Jefferson's essay was this juridical concept carried to its logical conclusion: a system of abstract laws designed to ensure that each generation would be able to construct its own system of political relationships. Jefferson's system was not likely—as other revolutions would prove—to perpetuate and increase the power of the state at the expense of the individual.

His theory was designed to do the opposite: to signal a radical departure from the theme of centralization that has characterized all revolutions before or since. His theory would enable each generation to use established institutions and laws to decentralize anew the power of the state every twenty years. Implicit in this was the theme that liberty would be preserved through a restructuring or revision of the constitution; that the revolution itself would not absorb liberty. Further, Jefferson, in his long essay, guaranteed that every twenty years there would be a certain amount of chaos in the transition of the new government. This meant that the state, instead of increasing its power by placing succeeding generations in awe of its immortal sovereignty and majesty, would become a means to an end and not the end in itself. The essence of Jefferson's revolution every twenty years was to humanize the prospects of remodeling society.

It meant that and more: Jefferson's essay was the philosophic expression of a device that, assuming the worst situation developed, any trend toward tyranny would be abolished or altered every second decade; that those who accumulated wealth at the

---

[59] Jacques Ellul, *Autopsy of Revolution* (New York, 1971), p. 79.

expense of their fellow men would see it redistributed; that class rivalry would be eliminated or started anew; that mobility would be ensured. Finally, the hope was that liberty and justice would be renewed with each generation. Because of its thoroughness, its near complete alteration of the relations of established society, it was a system that would channel all of society's discontents and integrate them in a radical, yet nonviolent, solution.

Jefferson's logic culminated in what would be the greatest benefit of all. Since each generation would have complete control over its own life span, plus the ability to enact laws regulating its behavior, it would have no need to resort to violence or civil war in order to change the government's form or principles. Liberty and the Rights of Man embedded in the constitution would, therefore, never be endangered. In sum, *The Earth Belongs to the Living* was intended by Thomas Jefferson to be a theoretical statement of the possibility of institutionalizing permanent, peaceful, and constitutional revolution.[60]

What we have been describing thus far is an idea of revolution propounded by two eighteenth-century men and a few of their contemporaries. But not every part of that description has been limited to the pure idea of revolution. Necessarily, a portion of the description has included the tangible political forms that the idea of revolution assumed. This relationship has been established not merely for illustrative purposes, but for a deeper, even intrinsic reason. The dominance of politics, in an architectonic sense, has asserted itself in every phase of revolution that we have discussed and will discuss.

The nature of revolution in eighteenth-century America was, above all, political. Neither Jefferson nor Adams, nor anyone else who discussed the topic, ever divorced it from its classical political framework. Constitutions, ideologies, wars, committees, factions, and congresses are political ideas and forms that were known in

[60] For an extended commentary on the nonrevolutionary implications of Jefferson's essay, see Adrienne Koch's *Jefferson and Madison: The Great Collaboration*, op. cit., pp. 62–96.

and even before Aristotle's time, in the eighteenth century, and—as Jefferson put it—by one's natural political constitution. This framework, then, was rooted in human nature and as old as man himself. While many of these concepts relate to forms as well as ideas, they have a dialectical relationship of their own that makes it impossible to discuss one meaningfully without the other. It is important then, in rounding out the idea of revolution, to consider these forms in some detail and establish their connection with the politics that will be reviewed in the remaining chapters.

We have seen both Adams and Jefferson associate their revolutionary experience in the 1770s with revolutions that occurred for the rest of their lives. Their concern for opinion, elections, constitutional forms, declaration of rights, the power of the press, and so forth, were all carry-overs from those earlier forms of political organization. As they well knew, those specific kinds of organization had given form and energy to the American Revolution. Jefferson, in his search for a new mode of revolution, was attempting to maintain a similar energy level, enough—through the principles of 1776—to maintain success, but not so much that it would commit revolution to violence.

This distinction is important because it reveals Jefferson's imagination at work spinning out a theory that would enable him to realize his goal of permanent world revolution. He knew already that governments are not free once and then for all time. He realized, perhaps more fully than anyone in his century, that the nature of man made it inevitable that he would sooner or later founder in corruption. When this occurred, the two-city thesis of revolution asserted itself. Principles needed to be reestablished, constitutions reaffirmed, and liberty renewed in an ongoing natural process. It was this transition in the cycle of revolutions, this division of society into "two warring camps," that fascinated Jefferson and spurred him on in pursuit of a nonviolent theory of revolution.

What I am asserting here and will attempt to demonstrate in the succeeding chapters is that the cycle of revolution in America had occurred at least three times within Jefferson's lifetime. The Revolution of 1800 was, in more ways than not, a repetition of the Revolution of 1776 and—by Jefferson's own description—of the early phases of the French Revolution of 1789. This was especially true where organization was concerned. The one major difference was a shift from form to principle almost exclusively; another lay in the peaceful transition made by the Revolution of 1800. Yet this peaceful transition did not occur by accident.

We have seen how Jefferson always placed the framework of revolution in a struggle between the principles of despotism and those of freedom, i.e., between monarchy or aristocracy and the democratizing efforts of the people. This formulation of principles had looked back to Jefferson's original revolutionary experience—a classic example of an imperial power opposed to the freedoms of a colonial people. As the concern for principle arose, he again looked to his own experience and discovered that he must rely on the trusted "old-fashioned" or classical forms of organization.

Of the organizational principles used to combat despotism all over the world, quite a number had been invented in America and had become—after the 1770s—the bag and baggage of revolutionaries everywhere. The formation of conspiratorial caucuses "to concentrate leadership abilities," the organization of clubs, committees of correspondence, the post, circular letters, newspapers, pamphlets, broadsides, speeches, elections, legislative resolves, and constitutional resolutions were all used to advance the cause of revolution.

The culmination of these political forms *after* the election of congresses was the establishment of courts of law and provisional governments. These organizational forms and principles all took place within, but were opposed to, the existing system of government. They were literally "the state within the state," "the city within a city"; the result of a group of organized factions cooperating to achieve similar revolutionary ends. Together they created a democratic ideology and fashioned unity. They won the minds and the hearts of the people and laid the foundation for building the new government.

This was the essence of the two-city thesis and "electoral Caesarism," both concepts that recognized the dual nature of revolution. Revolution looked to the past as well as to the future. Like Tiberius Gracchus, "whose political views were of the past," Jefferson attempted simply to enforce the principles and laws "that were already in existence."[61] By appealing to the principles of the Revolution of 1776 and utilizing the forms of organization of that period, Jefferson was able to preserve what he thought was best in the society. By appealing to the people over the heads of their ruling elite, he challenged the state and revived the "old-fashioned" idea of classical, popular revolution. This was the nature of Jefferson's attempt to consolidate the revolution from form to substance.

Yet, past revolutionary history might become prologue. When the Revolution of 1775–76 was achieved, these men subsequently saw it spill over into violence and then war. In the "second American revolution" the same men had been more fortunate. But did a revolution necessarily have to culminate in war? Could the unending cycle of revolution, violence, and then war be broken? This was the intriguing question for Jefferson and his colleagues after 1789.

Indeed, Jefferson had wrestled with this question for thirteen years following his experience in 1776. In France, as he saw the revolution developing, he, along with Tom Paine, applied the formula that had brought success in America. Only the formula took time, years in fact, to change opinion so that all agreed on the "main points." And Jefferson, ending his diplomatic career, had finally run out of time and influence. As he left France he believed the revolution was in good hands, the possibilities of a peaceful constitutional settlement real.[62]

It was only later, when Jefferson was in America, that he would see the French Revolution take the worst possible turn and plunge wildly into an abyss of violence. Nothing could have reinforced his conviction more than the tragedy of the French Revolution that

[61] Ellul, *Autopsy of Revolution*, op. cit., p. 111.
[62] Jefferson to Monsieur Barré de Marbois, 14 June 1817, *Writings*, Vol. XV, p. 129.

violence would destroy freedom. It was therefore to be avoided at all possible costs. And while Jefferson's earlier statements indicated that there was no guarantee that the idea of revolution would be nonviolent, he was determined in the future to keep it as bloodless as possible.

It is in this framework that we must view Jefferson's approach to politics and revolution in the coming decade. Knowing his deep concern for republican principles and the revolutionary spirit of 1776, plus his absence of nearly six years, we might place his idea of revolution into a perspective that has not been made explicit before. That perspective, moreover, is one consistent with the classical definition of revolution in the eighteenth century: a cyclical return to the time when the rights and liberties of the people were untainted with corruption; when the ideals and principles of the American Revolution were accepted by all; and when the American Revolution was—in a word—glorious.

Jefferson in 1789, enthused with the optimism of the emerging French Revolution, contemplated his return to America. He wrote to a friend: "I hope to receive soon permission to visit America this summer, and to possess myself anew, by conversation with my countrymen, of their *spirit and their ideas*. I know only the Americans of the year 1784. They tell me this is to be much a stranger to those of 1789. This renewal of acquaintance is no indifferent matter to one acting at such a distance . . ."[63] As he would soon find out, the distance between ideas was great, if not greater than the width of the ocean he would cross. And it would take time, almost a decade in fact, before he could report that "the spirit of 1776 was not dead, . . . it [had] only been slumbering."[64]

[63] Jefferson to David Humphreys, 18 March 1789, *Papers*, Vol. 14, p. 679.
[64] Jefferson to Thomas Lomax, 12 March 1799, *Writings*, Vol. X, pp. 123–24.

The Idea of Revolution

CONSPIRACY AND COUNTERREVOLUTION

"Every republic at all times has it[s] Catalines and its
Caesars."

ALEXANDER HAMILTON, 1792

The role of conspiracy as the breeding ground for resistance and
revolution is known to every student of early American history.
For conspiracy, as a latent behavioral trait and characteristic of the
American mind, was part of the birthmark of the new nation. But
the literature of American history dealing with conspiracy ante-
dates even that founding act. The 1770s, for example, are filled
with constant charges by English and American pamphleteers of
the British ministry "having formed a conspiracy against the liberties of their country."[1]

The wide belief in the idea of conspiracy, which gained easy
acceptance in America, and the relationship it has to revolution
can be translated as follows: the fundamental rights of all citizens
under the constitution, and indeed the constitution itself, are
endangered; and tyranny, in the guise of a few unscrupulous men
seeking power, threatens. A fear then arises that the principles by

[1] Bailyn, *The Ideological Origins of the American Revolution*, op. cit., p.
94. The most informative treatment on the fears of conspiracy in early American politics can be seen in Bailyn's book. See especially chapters III, IV, and
"A Note on Conspiracy."

which the laws operate are under assault. The additional fear that the laws are being corrupted—whether they are or not—nevertheless appears real and serves to trigger a right to revolution in the minds of the people.

Equally important was a belief in the likelihood of a conspiracy that produced paranoia in the minds of the generation fighting for American independence. That belief took on the character of a permanent suspicion and distrust—a requirement to scrutinize the behavior of every public official, every politician, at every level of the new government. From the 1770s on, knowledge that the principles of free government had been under assault by politicians considered sinister in the British Parliament, by cabinet officials in the administration, even by the king himself, was transferred across the Atlantic and held in reserve for their administrative counterparts in America.

Indeed, to the generation of Adams and Jefferson, a conspiracy to destroy the principles of the American Revolution and the constitution could happen in America just as easily as it had happened in Great Britain. The fear of a counterrevolution to restore monarchy in America was a fact for more than an entire generation.

The role that history had played in the formation of these suspicions must not be overlooked. Fear of conspiracy became a permanent scar on the American mind *during* the Revolution. No amount of healing, no accretion of scar tissue built up over two decades, could erase that generation's suspicions, nor make them forget where the conspiracy against their liberties had originated. No group of people then living were more knowledgeable or more jealous of their constitutional and revolutionary principles. For this was the foundation of American liberty: a total distrust of governmental power. It was believed by almost everyone that the motives, as well as the actions, of every public official must be examined. Living up to this standard of public scrutiny was the measure of virtue demanded by the electors in the new republic. Moreover, it was felt to be a check against conspiracy. And liberty, it was said, could be maintained only with eternal vigilance.

Edmund Burke's comment that Americans could "snuff tyranny in the breeze" was as much a description of their education, character, and disposition, as it was of their reaction to the designs of the British ministry. Founders of a republican form of government, the first since classical times, the revolutionary generation reacted against the intrigues of elitist aristocracies, those of ancient times as well as those in the history of sixteenth-, seventeenth- and eighteenth-century England. Bred to the classics, almost every American who assumed a position of leadership was familiar with Thucydides' description of conspiracies in Athens, with Cleon and Dionysius of Syracuse, with the conspiracies of Tarquin and Cataline of Rome. And they were especially familiar with the conspiracy of Julius Caesar, the man who overturned the liberties of the Roman Republic.

A unique and sinister connotation was attached to Caesar's name. It was linked with every revolutionary plot, cabal, or conspiracy that arose. Indeed, "Caesarism" had become a symbol synonymous with demagoguery and, because Caesar had established one, even a return to monarchy. Caesarism thus became a stigma associated with any and every attempt to enervate the principles of the republic. An example of this can be seen in one of Jefferson and Adams' discussions on the merits of aristocracy. The latter could have been speaking of conspiracy in its broadest sense:

> When Aristocracies, are established by human laws and honor Wealth and Power are made hereditary by municipal Laws and political Institutions, then I acknowledge artificial Aristocracy to commence: but this never commences, till corruption in Elections becomes dominant and uncontrollable. But this artificial Aristocracy can never last. The everlasting envys, jealousies, rivalries and quarrels among them, their cruel rapacities upon the poor ignorant People, their followers, compell these to SETT UP A CAESAR, a Demagogue to be a Monarch and Master. . . . Here you have the origin of all artificial Aristocracy, which is the origin of all monarchy.[2]

[2] John Adams to Thomas Jefferson, 15 Nov. 1813, *Letters*, Vol. II, p. 400.

From a republican point of view, this was the greatest fear that haunted the founders of the American republic, only recently (in a national sense) liberated from the tentacles of monarchy. Adams' quote captured the essence of a conspiracy to return monarchy to America. Factional rivalries and jealousies, corruption in elections, undue regard for wealth and honors, all of these signs would characterize the politics of the 1790s. And to perceptive observers like Jefferson, Madison, Henry, and others, all that was necessary was a man to play the role of Caesar.

The idea of conspiracy was, moreover, entwined with the meaning of revolution, in more than a superficial sense. Revolutions, so called, that failed to live up to the expectations of those who began them were called rebellions; and so were conspiracies. A successful rebellion always had a few key conspirators; likewise, successful conspiracies were normally considered, at least by those in the establishment, as counterrevolutions. Yet the legal definition of conspiracy differed substantially from the common understanding of the term. Dr. Johnson's rendering of the term seemed to indicate that it had an application beyond the strict definition of the law.[3] Conspirators themselves were generally

---

[3] Dr. Samuel Johnson, A *Dictionary of the English Language,* op. cit., Vol. I. Conspiracy is "a private agreement among several persons to commit some crime; a plot; a concerted treason." "In law, an agreement of men to do any thing; always taken in the evil part. It is taken for a confederacy of two at the least." "A concurrence; a general tendency of many causes to one event." Definitions of conspiracy in law were, by nature, more precise. Sir William Blackstone's *Commentaries on the Laws of England,* Notes by Edward Christian, 4 vols. (London, 1803), said that to issue a writ of conspiracy "the conspirators, for there must be at least two to form a conspiracy, may be indicted at the suit of the king, and were by the ancient common law to receive *villenous* judgement," Vol. IV, p. 136. Christian, the editor, noted that "every confederacy to injure individuals or to do acts which are unlawful, or prejudicial to the community, is a conspiracy." He added, "In a prosecution for a conspiracy, the actual fact of conspiracy need not be proved, but may be inferred from circumstances, and the concurring conduct of the defendents . . ." The object of conspiracies, noted Christian, "is to injure by fraud, falsehood or perjury . . ."; *The Code of Virginia* (Richmond, 1860) equated conspiracy with treason, punishable by death; *Stephens Commentaries on the Laws of*

regarded as men whose political characters were identified with a lust for power or dominion. Always energetic, proud, even arrogant, they were men with forceful personalities and political aspirations that knew no bounds. They often appealed to the pride and vanity of a birthright, their own fallen status, or the continuance of one they had recently become wedded to. They were often men whose experience was of a military nature, which enabled them to develop a constituency independent of the civilian society. Because of this support, suspicion attended their involvement in the open politics of society. If they suffered the disappointment of a lost electoral candidacy, the fear always arose that they would attempt to recoup their losses through armed force or corruption. It was characteristic of political conspirators to instigate legislation that appealed to class interests, the sole intent of which was to increase their own personal power. These character traits culminated in the suspicion that the conspirator would stop at nothing short of total power; that he would not be deterred by principles or tradition; and that, ultimately, he would change the form of the constitution in order to perpetuate his own power. This, briefly, was the common understanding of the meaning of conspiracy linked with "Caesarism," "Cromwell[ism]," and "Bonapartism" among the revolutionary generation. These three names, so familiar to the generation of the 1790s, were constantly linked with revolution, monarchy, and the loss of liberty.

Alexander Hamilton, in 1792, set down a description of conspiracy in the new republic that could have been directed only at Jefferson and the republican faction. But what is so remarkable about his description is that it revealed so much about its author:

England (London, 1841), Vol. IV, p. 218, gave this definition: "Conspiracy in general may be described as a combination or agreement between two or more persons to do an unlawful act, or to do a lawful act by unlawful means; whether such act be directed against some individual, or against the public at large. . . . The essence of the offense [i.e., conspiracy] lies in the agreement; and it is not necessary to constitute the offense that the act agreed to be done by the conspirators should have been committed."

There is yet another class of men, who in all the stages of our republican system, either from desperate circumstances, or irregular ambition, or a mixture of both, will labour incessantly to keep the government in a troubled and unsettled state, to sow disquietudes in the minds of the people and to promote confusion and change. Every republic at all times has it[s] Catalines and its Caesars.

Men of this stamp, while in their hearts they scoff at the principles of Liberty, while in their real characters they are arbitrary persecuting intolerant and despotic, are in all their harangues and professions the most zealous, nay if they are to be believed, the only friends to Liberty. Mercenary and corrupt themselves, they are continually making a parade of their purity and disinterestedness and heaping upon others charges of peculation and corruption. Extravagant and dissipated in their own affairs, they are always prating about public economy and railing at the Government, for its pretended profusion. Conscious that as long as the confidence of the people shall be maintained in their tried and faithful servants, in men of real integrity and patriotism, their ambitious projects can never succeed, they leave no artifice unessayed, they spare no pains to destroy that confidence and blacken the characters that stand in their way. Convinced that as long as order and system in the public affairs can be maintained their schemes can never be realized, they are constantly representing the means of that order and system as chains forged for the people. Themselves the only plotters and conspirators they are forever spreading tales of plots and conspiracies—Always talking of the republican cause, and meaning nothing but the cause of themselves and their party, virtue and Liberty constantly on their lips, framed usurpation and tyranny in their hearts.[4]

Hamilton thus succinctly placed into perspective the genuine fears of those who would be involved in American politics for the next eight years. With incredible insight, he framed the outline of charge and countercharge, mutual accusation, and violent expectation of those who believed conspiracy and counterrevolution were

[4] "The Vindication No. 1," *The Papers of Alexander Hamilton*, eds. Harold C. Syrett and Jacob E. Cooke (New York, 1961–), Vol. XI, p. 463. This essay was never published, though written in May–August 1792.

imminent. It is not surprising then to find among the leading statesmen of the period, of every political persuasion, that the fear of a return to monarchy was real. We have often assumed that the struggle between monarchy and the republican form, complete with democratic principles, was ended once and for all with the Declaration of Independence. But to many, especially the Federalists, this apparently was not the case. The fact was there were many citizens who believed that monarchy was the only way in which a stable government could be achieved. Indeed, a case can be made that the revolution, instead of deciding the issue, simply polarized the sentiment between the advocates of monarchy and republicanism. Alexander Graydon wrote: "Nothing can be further from the truth than the idea propagated for party purposes, that the Declaration of Independence was an option made between the monarchical and democratical form of government. The measure was adopted with extreme reluctance, as the effect of dire necessity alone, as the only means of uniting and giving efficiency to the opposition, and of obtaining foreign aid . . ."[5]

John Adams, we have noted, hinted at the lack of agreement and the deciding of issues by "ones and twos" that "came out as unanimous."[6] But the implication was always that monarchy had been put to rest in the minds of Americans by the events following the Revolutionary War, the Articles of Confederation, and the constitution. Yet the issue still remained viable. William Maclay, a senator from New York, expressed his hopes as well as his fears in a *Journal*:

> . . . that the motives of the actors in the late Revolution were various cannot be doubted. The abolishing of royalty, the extinguishing of patronage and dependencies attached to that form of government, were the exalted motives to many revolutionists, and these were the improvements meant by them to be made of the war which was forced on us by British aggression—in fine, the amelioration of government and bettering the condition of man-

[5] *Alexander Graydon's Memoirs of His Own Time*, op. cit., p. 329.
[6] John Adams to Jefferson, 24 Aug. 1815, *Letters*, Vol. II, p. 455.

kind. These ends and none other were publicly avowed, and all our constitutions and public acts were formed in this spirit. Yet there were not wanting a party whose motives were different. They wished for the loaves and fishes of government, and cared for nothing else but a translation of the diadem and scepter from London to Boston, New York or Philadelphia; or, in other words, the creation of a new monarchy in America, and to form niches for themselves in the temple of royalty.

This spirit manifested itself strongly among the officers at the close of the war, and I have been afraid the army would not have been disbanded if the common soldiers could have been kept together. This spirit developed in the Order of Cincinnati, where I trust it will spend itself in a harmless flame and soon become extinguished.[7]

Maclay's implicit fear that the flame might *not* be extinguished had been expressed earlier by Jefferson. Writing his "Observations on the Encyclopedie Methodique" in 1786, he addressed himself to the future of the Order of Cincinnati and revealed a conspiratorial mentality:

As to the question then, whether any evil can proceed from the institution as it stands at present, I am of opinion there may. 1. From the meetings. These will keep the officers formed into a body; will continue a distinction between civil and military which it would be for the good of the whole to obliterate as soon as possible; and military assemblies will not only keep alive the jealousies and the fears of the civil government, but give ground for these fears and jealousies. For when men meet together, they will make business if they have none; they will collate their grievances, some real, some imaginary, all highly painted; they will communicate to each other the sparks of discontent; and these may engender a flame which will consume their particular, as well as the general, happiness.[8]

[7] *The Journal of William Maclay*, ed. Charles Beard (New York, 1927), pp. 11–12.

[8] "Observations on the Encyclopedie Methodique," 1786, *Papers*, Vol. 10, p. 53.

To Washington, Jefferson expressed himself in even stronger terms, knowing full well that the former commander-in-chief had it within his power to stamp out that "germ" of aristocracy:

> What has heretofore passed between us on this institution, makes it my duty to mention to you that I have never heard a person in Europe, learned or unlearned, express his thoughts on this institution, who did not consider it as dishonorable and destructive of our governments, and that every writing which has come out since my arrival here, in which it is mentioned, considers it, even as now reformed, as the germ whose development is one day to destroy the fabric we have reared . . . tho' the day may be at some distance, beyond the reach of our lives perhaps, *yet it will certainly come*, when, a single fibre left of this institution, will produce an hereditary aristocracy which will change the form of our government from the best to the worst in the world. . . . I shall think little also [of our government's] longevity unless this germ of destruction be taken out.[9]

Jefferson was not nearly as hopeful as Maclay for the extinguishing of the monarchical sentiment in this country; in fact, he predicted its inevitable triumph. The connection between monarchy, aristocracy, titles, and the pomp and ceremony of the military life, all opposed to the simple egalitarianism inherent in a republic, was perhaps more obvious to Jefferson, the philosopher, than to Maclay, the politician.

It was all the more striking to Jefferson because he had known of a discussion among the military council of war at the close of the Revolution. As he described the discussion in *The Anas*, the issue came to a head "whether all [the states] should be consolidated into a single government . . . and whether that national government should be a monarchy or a republic. . . . Some officers of the army, as it has always been said and believed, (and Steuben and Knox have ever been named as the leading agents), trained to monarchy by military habits, are understood to have proposed to General Washington to decide this great question by

[9] Jefferson to George Washington, 14 Nov. 1786, *Papers*, Vol. 10, pp. 532–33.

the army before its disbandment, and to assume himself the crown on the assurance of their support."[10]

Jefferson praised Washington for his answer and consequent rejection of their advice. He then went on to describe the "Cincinnati's" attempts to "ingraft" onto "the future frame of government" a "hereditary order"[11] during the time of the army's disbandment. Jefferson, it seemed, always feared the latent monarchical tendencies in America. In 1789, he had written Madison matter-of-factly that since their generation had been "educated in royalism: [it is] no wonder if some of us retain that idolatry still." He noted, too, that "there are some among us who would now establish a monarchy. But they are inconsiderable in number and weight of character." He could add "our young people are educated in republicanism [and] an apostacy from that to royalism is unprecedented and impossible."[12]

Yet, as Jefferson would acknowledge more than twenty-five years later, "a short review of the facts will show, that the contests of the day were contests of principle, between the advocates of republican, and those of kingly government . . ."[13] The issue was in doubt for longer than Jefferson cared to remember and the issue "might well have been . . . a very different thing," than a republic.

In the period which saw the transition from the confederation to the constitution, Jefferson had ample reason to wonder if the experiment in liberty might be going sour. Shays's Rebellion, though played down by Jefferson, was a portent of the future to others. Rumors of dissension abounded. One of the first hints of "scission," as Jefferson called it, initiated with two New Englanders. Theodore Sedgwick raised the point to Caleb Strong:

[10] *The Anas, Writings*, Vol. I, p. 267.

[11] Ibid., p. 267. Years later, William Branch Giles would say on the floor of Congress (19 Nov. 1794) that "there existed a self created society, that of the Cincinnati, the principles of which were . . . hereditary succession . . ." *Porcupine's Works*, 12 vols. (London, 1801), Vol. II, p. 177.

[12] Jefferson to James Madison, 15 March 1789, *Papers*, Vol. 14, p. 661.

[13] *The Anas, Writings*, Vol. I, p. 266.

It well becomes the eastern and middle States, who are in interest one, seriously to consider what advantages result to them from their connection with the Southern States. They can give us nothing, as an equivalent for the protection which they derive from us but a participation in their commerce. This they deny to us. Should their conduct continue the same, and I think there is not any prospect of an alteration, an attempt to perpetuate our connection with them, which at last too will be found ineffectual, will sacrifice everything to a mere chimera. Even the appearance of a union cannot in the way we are now be long preserved. It becomes us seriously to contemplate a substitute.[14]

Indeed, seven months earlier, Jefferson had foreseen that sentiment arising and had expressed his opinion by dividing Whigs from Tories and the latter's attachment to monarchy:

I do not believe there has ever been a moment when a single whig in any one state would not have shuddered at the very idea of a separation of their state from the Confederacy. The Tories would at all times have been glad to see the Confederacy dissolved even by particles at a time, in hopes of their attaching themselves again to Great Britain.[15]

Correspondents in Europe and America speculated that the states would separate, engage in civil war, and soon return to monarchy. John Adams, writing on the possibility of a new convention coming up with a stable government, told Jefferson: "You are apprehensive of foreign Interference, Intrigue, Influence. So am I."[16] To Adams, as well as to Jefferson, there seemed to be a conspiracy in the air. One of Jefferson's closest friends expressed it with alarm: "If this new constitution fails I will do everything in my power to leave this country which will become the scene of anarchy and confusion."[17]

This attitude did not occur overnight. It had its origins in the

[14] Theodore Sedgwick to Caleb Strong, 6 Aug. 1786, *Papers,* Vol. 9, p. 654.
[15] "Additional queries upon Jefferson's contribution to *The Encyclopedie Methodique,*" 1786. *Papers,* Vol. 10, p. 27.
[16] John Adams to Jefferson, 6 Dec. 1787, *Papers,* Vol. 12, p. 396.
[17] St. John de Crevecoeur to Jefferson, 9 Nov. 1787, *Papers,* Vol. 12, p. 332.

aftermath of the peace settlement with Great Britain. As early as 1785, Jefferson had begun to express his antipathy toward the defeated enemy: "In spite of treaties, England is still our enemy. Her hatred is deeprooted and cordial, and nothing is wanting with her but the power to wipe us and the land we live on out of existence."[18] A year later, antipathy had been joined with fear, as Jefferson wrote John Page: "That nation hates us, and their king more than all other men."[19] To C. W. F. Dumas he even raised the specter of the final solution: "I shall not wonder to see the scenes of ancient Rome and Carthage renewed in our day; and if not pursued to the same issue, it may be because the republic of modern powers will not permit the extinction of any one of it's [sic] members. . . . But the temper and folly of our enemies may not leave this in our choice."[20] Jefferson's paranoia and fear of conspiracy had reached a new high.

During most of this period, 1785–87, Jefferson received the complaints of his correspondents and, just as often, registered his own anguish. "Everything I hear from my own country fills me with despair as to their recovery from their vassalage to Great Britain."[21] To David Ross he wrote, "I am lately returned from a visit to that country [Great Britain]. It appears to me more hostile than during the war. This spirit of hostility has always existed in the mind of the king, but it has now extended itself thro' the whole mass of people, and the majority in the public councils."[22]

If Jefferson spoke for many Americans at that time, the reasons why cannot be dismissed lightly. The suspicion that Great Britain conspired to destroy the young republic had reached a state of near hysteria among the people in positions of leadership. Few refused to dismiss or discount rumors of Britain's intentions, no matter how unfounded or how hostile those rumors might be. Thus,

[18] Jefferson to John Langdon, 11 Sept. 1785, *Papers*, Vol. 8, p. 512.

[19] Jefferson to John Page, 4 May 1786, *Papers*, Vol. 9, p. 446.

[20] Jefferson to C. W. F. Dumas, 6 May 1786, *Papers*, Vol. 9, pp. 462–63.

[21] Jefferson to Thomas Pleasants, 8 May 1786, *Papers*, Vol. 9, p. 472.

[22] Jefferson to David Ross, 8 May 1786, *Papers*, Vol. 9, p. 474.

when John Jay wrote Jefferson in late December, both could believe that a conspiracy seemed to be emerging between the Massachusetts insurgents and the British:

> A variety of considerations and some facts afford room for suspicions, that there is an understanding between the Insurgents in Massachusetts and some leading persons in Canada, but whether with or without the consent or connivance of the British government, is still to be ascertained. There is so much evidence of their having sent Emissaries to Quebec, and of propositions made to and receivd by them from a character of distinction here, that I am induced to think there is at least some Truth in it.[23]

Less than six months later, Jefferson would receive a letter that carried a chilling message: "The political struggle in Massachusetts between Bowdoin . . . and Hancock, leader of the popular party, has left the aristocratic element so angry that its adherents began to look with longing upon 'la donce securite et le calme d'un Etat monarchique; several persons, Otto stated to Vergennes, had assured him they would have no objection to the setting up of a monarchy in Massachusetts.' "[24]

Jefferson was ready to believe that such a conspiracy in fact already existed. His logic reached the point of illogic. Referring to the inevitability of war with England, he prophesied that America would be coerced into abandoning her neutrality:

> I fear the English, or rather their stupid King, will force us out of it. For thus I reason. By forcing us into the war against them they will be engaged in an expensive land war as well as a sea war. Common sense dictates therefore that they should let us remain neuter: ergo they will not let us remain neuter. I never yet found any other general rule for foretelling what they will do, but that of examining what they ought not to do.[25]

[23] John Jay to Jefferson, 14 Dec. 1786, *Papers*, Vol. 10, p. 596.

[24] Edward Carrington to Jefferson, 9 July 1787, *Papers*, Vol. 11, p. 411. In a postscript to Jefferson Carrington referred to a report from Otto, the French consul in America, to Comte Vergennes.

[25] Jefferson to John Adams, 28 Sept. 1787, *Papers*, Vol. 12, p. 190.

Over the next months, Jefferson's fear that Britain still entertained the idea of regaining her lost colonies would grow. He wrote to Jay, warning him to prepare for war:

> . . . since the accession of their present monarch, has it not been passion, and not reason, which, nine times out of ten, has dictated her measures? . . . I have little hope of his permitting our neutrality. He will find subjects of provocation in various articles of our treaty with France which will now come into view in all their consequences. . . . I suggest these doubts on a supposition that our magazines are not prepared for war, and on the opinion that provisions for that event should be thought of.[26]

In the months ahead, there was to be no abatement of suspicion. Jefferson, in his official correspondence, continued the theme of distrust. Writing one of the American consuls in Europe, he alluded to a conversation with a British minister: ". . . I never concealed from him that I considered the British as our natural enemies, and as the only nation on earth who wished us ill from the bottom of their souls."[27]

It was not as if Jefferson shared his paranoia with simply a few chosen members of his political persuasion. His correspondents, while in France, included most of those who would, in future years, take a different view of the constitution than the one he chose. In addition to Madison, Monroe, Carrington, Short, et al., men like Jay, Washington, Gouverneur Morris, and John Adams would state their fears of monarchy in their moments of reflection. John Adams, drawing on his "experience," and forswearing pessimism, nevertheless gave a dour forecast for the future of

[26] Jefferson to John Jay, 8 Oct. 1787, *Papers*, Vol. 12, p. 216.

[27] Jefferson to William Carmichael, 15 Dec. 1787, *Papers*, Vol. 12, p. 424. Almost twenty years later, John Adams would express himself in the exact same terms: ". . . Great Britain is the natural enemy of the United States. She has looked at us from our first settlement to this moment, with the eyes of jealousy, envy, hatred, and contempt." John Adams to William Cunningham, 11 Feb. 1809, in John Wood's *Suppressed History of the Administration of John Adams (from 1797 to 1801) as printed and suppressed in 1802* (New York, 1846), p. 358 (hereafter referred to as *Suppressed History*).

the republic and, more important, for their joint revolutionary struggles:

> Resolutions never to have an hereditary officer will be kept in America, as religiously as that of the Cincinnati was in the Case of General Greene's son. Resolutions never to let a Citizen ally himself with things will be kept untill an Opportunity presents to violate it. If the Duke of Angoleme, or Burgundy, or especially the Dauphin should demand one of your beautiful and most amiable Daughters in marriage, all America from Georgia to New Hampshire would find their Vanity and Pride, so agreably flattered by it, that all their Sage Maxims would give way; and even our Sober New England Republicans would keep a day of Thanksgiving for it, in their hearts. If General Washington had a daughter, I firmly believe, she would be demanded in Marriage by one of the Royal Families of France or England, perhaps by both, or if he had a son he would be invited to come a courting to Europe.—The Resolution not to call in foreign nations to settle domestic differences will be kept until a domestic difference of a serious nature shall break out.—I have long been settled in my own opinion, that neither Philosophy, nor Religion, nor Morality, nor Wisdom, nor Interest will ever govern Nations or Parties, against their Vanity, their Pride. . . . If Robert Morris should maintain his Fortune to the End, I am convinced that some foreign families of very high rank will think of Alliances with his Children. . . . In short my dear Friend you and I have been indefatigable Labourers through our whole Lives for a Cause which will be thrown away in the next generation, upon the Vanity and Foppery of Persons of whom we do not now know the Names perhaps.—The War that is now breaking out will render our Country, whether she is forced into it, or not, rich, great and powerful in comparison of what she now is, and Riches Grandeur and Power will have the same effect upon American as it has upon European minds. We have seen enough already to be sure of this.[28]

[28] John Adams to Jefferson, 9 Oct. 1787, *Papers*, Vol. 12, pp. 220–21. Less than two years later Adams would flabbergast Jefferson by requesting the Senate and House of Representatives to address the President with a royal title. See Jefferson to Madison, 29 July 1789, *Papers*, Vol. 15, p. 315. Madison,

After Adams had expressed his sentiments, the news came from
America that a constitutional convention had been called, and
would address itself to the defects of the Confederation. At first,
the news buoyed Jefferson's spirits and his optimism diverted him
from his fears of conspiracy. But gradually, his correspondents
forced him to ponder the outcome of the convention if it failed.
David Ramsay, a historian and long-time correspondent of Jefferson's,
raised the specter again: "Our eyes now are all fixed on the
continental convention to be held in Philada. in May next. Unless
they make an efficient federal government I fear that the end of
the matter will be an American monarch or rather three or more
confederacies. In either case we have not labored in vain . . ."[29]

Jefferson could hardly have agreed to the "in either case." He
hated monarchy with such passion that he was ready to scrutinize
the new constitution for its germ. Within a few months he would
write Benjamin Hawkins that while he "look[ed] up with him to
the Federal convention for an amendment of our federal affairs,"
"above all things I am astonished at some people's considering a
kingly government as a refuge."[30]

When a copy of the new constitution was sent to him he was
horrified that his countrymen would take for granted a number of
their basic freedoms and fail to include what would later be called
the Bill of Rights into the body of the document. While this
triggered a suspicion in his mind about the revolutionary fervor of
his countrymen, he could hardly understand how far it had abated.
He wrote his concern to Colonel Smith: "I fear much the effects
of the perpetual re-eligibility of the President. But it is not

---

meanwhile, pushed through the lower House a resolution that "formally and
unanimously condemned" Adams' suggestion. "This," said Madison, "will show
to the friends of Republicanism that our new Government was not meant to
substitute either Monarchy or Aristocracy, and that the genius of the people
is as yet adverse to both." Madison to Jefferson, 9 May 1789, *Papers*, Vol. 15,
p. 115.

[29] David Ramsay to Jefferson, 7 April 1787, *Papers*, Vol. 11, p. 279.

[30] Jefferson to Benjamin Hawkins, 4 Aug. 1787, *Papers*, Vol. 11, p. 684.

thought of in America, and have therefore no prospect of a change of that article. But I own it astonishes me to find such a change wrought in the opinions of our countrymen since I left them, as that three-fourths of them should be contented to live under a system which leaves to their governors the power of taking from them the trial by jury in civil cases, freedom of religion, freedom of commerce, the habeas corpus laws, and of yoking them with a standing army. *This is a degeneracy in the principles of liberty* to which I had given four centuries instead of four years."[31]

Jefferson continued to harp upon the theme of the reeligibility of the President, and as his correspondence lengthened he tied that theme into the future foreign policy of the nation. The hereditary nature of the monarch in England, transplanted to America, continued to haunt him. In a letter to Alexander Donald he revealed a guarded optimism: ". . . it will be productive of cruel distress to our country even in your day and mine. The importance to France and England to have our government in the hands of a friend or foe, will occasion their interference by money, and even by arms. . . . We must take care however that neither this nor any other objection to the new form produce a schism in our union . . . all of us going together, we shall be sure to cure the evils of our new constitution before they do great harm."[32]

But optimism could not prevail for long. Sensing the battles for ratification that would follow and the crucial issues at stake, Jefferson poured out his frustrations to the one man he felt would most likely be President. His remarks link the role of the future President to his fears of monarchy and aristocracy:

> The perpetual re-eligibility of the President. This I fear will make that an office for life first, and then hereditary. I was much an enemy to monarchy before I came to Europe. I am ten thousand times more so since I have seen what they are. There is scarcely an evil known in these countries which may n°t be traced to their king as its source, nor a good which is not derived from

[31] Jefferson to William S. Smith, 2 Feb. 1788, *Papers*, Vol. 12, p. 558.
[32] Jefferson to Alexander Donald, 7 Feb. 1788, *Papers*, Vol. 12, p. 571.

the small fibres of republicanism existing among them. I can further say with safety there is not a crowned head in Europe whose talents or merit would entitle him to be elected a vestryman by the people of any parish in America. However I shall hope that before there is danger of this change taking place in the office of President, the good sense and free spirit of our countrymen will make the changes necessary to prevent it. Under this hope I look forward to the general adoption of the new constitution with anxiety, as necessary for us under our present circumstances.[33]

Jefferson's confidence in Washington "doing the right thing" was unquestioned. What worried him was Washington's declining vigor and the influence that his advisors might have upon his decisions. This particular worry, so important in the years to come, was reinforced by one of Jefferson's closest confidants, James Monroe. In a letter to his political mentor, Monroe raised the point that would preoccupy Jefferson for the next decade: ". . . for my own part I have a boundless confidence in him [Washington] nor have I any reason to believe he will ever furnish occasion for withdrawing it. More is to be apprehended if he takes a part in the public councils again as he advances in age from the designs of those around him than from any dispositions of his own."[34]

It is difficult, if not impossible, to ascertain whether Jefferson believed that a conspiracy against liberty and the republic existed at this time. But, at a later date, he said so in *The Anas*. Describing the motives of those who attended the Annapolis Convention of 1786, he says that the "friends of monarchy confined themselves to a course of obstruction only, and delay, to everything proposed; they hoped, that nothing being done, and all things going from bad to worse, a kingly government might be usurped and submitted to by the people, as better than anarchy. . . . The effect of their maneuvers . . . resulted in the measure of calling a more general convention, to be held at Philadelphia. At this, the same party exhibited the same practices, and with the same views of preventing a government of concord, which they foresaw would be

---

[33] Jefferson to George Washington, 2 May 1788, *Papers*, Vol. 13, p. 128.
[34] James Monroe to Jefferson, 12 July 1788, *Papers*, Vol. 13, p. 352.

republican, and of forcing through anarchy their way to monarchy."[35]

Though absent on his "mission to France," some of this must have been a part of his general understanding of events in America, because his correspondents never failed to keep him informed. Thus, from the Annapolis Convention through the Philadelphia Convention, Jefferson must have watched for a counterrevolution. A trusted friend had apprised him that "an extraordinary revolution in the sentiments of men, respecting political affairs," had occurred in America.[36] This was an element that Jefferson had not considered would take place so soon, if at all; and it alarmed him greatly. Nine months before he left France, Jefferson believed the situation so dangerous that he would not send a letter about the French Revolution to Paine. Correspondence was not safe "even by the couriers of Ambassadors."[37]

During his remaining months in France, Jefferson would be busy with the revolution there and, as for his own country, pleased with the inclusion of the Bill of Rights upon the ratification of the constitution. Yet, he could not help pondering conditions in America and the mind and spirit of its citizens. A steady stream of correspondence continued to inform him of Britain's refusal to give up the frontier posts, of British threats to American commerce, of attempts to sabotage her neutrality and impress her seamen. These British "designs," coupled with, as Monroe put it, the potential political designs of Washington's advisors, reinforced a fear that has been a part of every successful revolutionary's psychology since the first revolution: i.e., the fear of counterrevolution. If such a revolution were to take place in America, it definitely meant a return to monarchy. Moreover, since Jefferson believed that the majority of the people were firmly republican, it also meant that any attempt to restore monarchy would be led by a minority faction.

Monarchy could only come about through a conspiracy. And

[35] *The Anas, Writings,* Vol. I, p. 269.
[36] David Humphreys to Jefferson, 29 Nov. 1788, *Papers,* Vol. 14, p. 300.
[37] Jefferson to Thomas Paine, 23 Dec. 1788, *Papers,* Vol. 14, p. 372.

indeed, when Jefferson returned to America, the first impressions he received unfortunately caused his mind to reel in shock and wonder. As we read his statement in *The Anas*, and recollect the mood of those who wined and dined the great revolutionary figure on his return from France, one can easily imagine Jefferson, sitting at a table amidst the sounds of clinking wine glasses, listening to the buzzing yet audible voices of elitist conversation, and forming the question ever so silently in his mind: "Is it possible that a return to monarchy is imminent?"

I returned from [France] in the first year of the new government, having landed in Virginia in December, 1789, and proceeded to New York in March, 1790 to enter on the office of Secretary of State. Here, certainly, I found a state of things which, of all I had ever contemplated, I the least expected. I had left France in the first year of her revolution, in the fervor of natural rights, and zeal for reformation. My conscientious devotion to these rights could not be heightened, but it had been aroused and excited by daily exercise. The President received me cordially, and my colleagues and the circle of principal citizens apparently with welcome. The courtesies of dinner parties given me, as a stranger newly arrived among them, placed me at once in their familiar society. But I cannot describe the wonder and mortification with which the table conversations filled me. Politics were the chief topic, and a preference of kingly over republican government was evidently the favorite sentiment. An apostate I could not be, nor yet a hypocrite; and I found myself, for the most part, the only advocate on the republican side of the question. . . .[38]

Jefferson's writing to Madame d'Houdetot that he had "found here [in America and, especially, in New York] a philosophic revolution, phylosophically effected"[39] is understandable then. By this, of course, he meant that public opinion seemed to be turning toward monarchy and away from republicanism.

At about this time, Jefferson received two letters from Short,

[38] *The Anas, Writings,* Vol. I, pp. 270–71.
[39] Jefferson to Madame d'Houdetot, 2 April 1790, *Writings,* Vol. VIII, p. 15.

both stating that the "designs of England against us [i.e., the United States] had now become so public and common that it [was] impossible not to pay attention to them."[40] As he read them, Jefferson could not help but make a connection with events in America and wonder if time was running out. As if to confirm his suspicions, John Rutledge informed him of a trip he had recently taken in which the ignorance of revolutionary principles was most noticeable: "On this jaunt I found people very anxious to have conversations with a person who had lately been in France on the subject of the french revolution; of which I found it very difficult to make them think well . . . and I was sorry to observe that many of our citizens, who pass for having intelligent and enlightened minds, possess much of the english political superstitions, which teaches, that for the good of the whole a few should have the inherent right to rule over the many, man being so contrived that he is unfit for the governing of himself. It is fortunate my dear sir for this country, that you, and your associates, in 1775 and 6 held different opinions."[41]

Jefferson and his associates still held dearly to those opinions. The question now was, How many of the nation's citizens still held them and how far were they willing to go to defend them? Jefferson's appointment as Secretary of State not only gave him the opportunity to become more closely acquainted with the opinions of his countrymen, it enabled him to influence the formation of policy in the new government. We must assume Jefferson's cognizance that every decision made, every policy taken, would be a precedent; and that cumulatively, they would determine whether the nation strengthened or abandoned its republican principles.

As Jefferson assumed his duties in Washington's cabinet in March of 1790, he quickly became aware that the principles of republicanism were under assault. Despite an ostensibly agreeable start with his future rival, Alexander Hamilton, Jefferson saw that

[40] William Short to Jefferson, 4 Aug. 1790, *Papers*, Vol. 17, p. 314; see also 5 Sept. 1790, p. 489.

[41] John Rutledge, Jr., to Jefferson, 26 Sept. 1790, *Papers*, Vol. 17, p. 521.

the gauntlet had been thrown down before him. Before he had even arrived on the scene, "Hamilton's financial system had been passed." And its "first object," Jefferson noted later, was to "exclude popular understanding and inquiry . . ."[42] That system, Jefferson would claim, was a result of the "English, half-lettered ideas of Hamilton," and "destroyed" any hopes that the republic could have been launched on its true principles.[43]

In Hamilton's first report, January 14, 1790, on the public credit, he set into operation a fiscal design incorporating the nation's foreign debt, its domestic debt, and the government's assumption of state debts. The debates over the implementation of these fiscal policies were to divide the republic on the fundamental nature of the government.[44] Before Jefferson had even arrived, it seemed that the principles of republican administration had been compromised. For it appeared to him that Hamilton had set the nation on an economic course that was at variance with Jefferson's notion of an agrarian society. Hamilton's subsequent report on a national bank was clearly intended to "consolidate" the power of the national government at the expense of the states. Indeed, Hamilton's vision of a wealthy, capitalist society and a government supported mainly by a wealthy class was a direct challenge to Jefferson's idea of the limitations imposed by the constitution and his preference for states' rights and an agricultural society.

The first inkling of this challenge was to take place within three months of Jefferson's arrival. It involved a moral as well as a financial question, i.e., who would receive payment of the "arrearages in soldier's pay." Would it be the soldiers who had fought in the war of independence and were now, many of them, penniless?

---

[42] *The Anas, Writings,* Vol. I, p. 271.

[43] Jefferson to DuPont de Nemours, 18 Jan. 1802, *The Works of Thomas Jefferson* (Federal Edition), ed. P. L. Ford, 12 vols. (New York, 1904), Vol. VIII, p. 127.

[44] *The Reports of Alexander Hamilton,* ed. Jacob E. Cooke (New York, 1964), pp. 1–45.

Or, would the speculators triumph, those men who had bought up the securities issued by the Continental Congress for a fraction of their worth? As Julian P. Boyd has remarked, the dispute over soldier's pay "brought about the first open, direct and uncompromising collision between the Secretary of the Treasury and the Secretary of State. . . . This, therefore, was a case symbolic of all that was to follow."[45]

In their separate opinions on the subject, both men revealed different approaches to the application of power. Jefferson, as he would note later, knew that "immense sums were filched from the poor and ignorant, and fortunes accumulated"[46] by those with inside information. These latter men, speculators, were allegedly friends of Hamilton. Jefferson, then, in urging Washington to veto the bill, argued that a "fraud" had occurred in the administration.[47] Hamilton ignored Jefferson's evidence of fraud and allowed that the passage of his economic policies was critical, that time was of the essence. Alluding to "Caesar's wife," Hamilton implied that he was above suspicion. Washington, confronted with the choice of remaining silent or getting to the bottom of Jefferson's allegation, chose to allow the dilemma to remain unresolved. When the bill passed, it became apparent to Jefferson that his rival was well on his way to realizing the second objective of his economic system: viz., developing "a machine for the corruption of the legislature."[48]

It would seem, then, that Jefferson should have been on his guard when Hamilton approached him regarding the passage of the assumption bill. This was a bill that would allow the federal government to assume the separate state debts built up during the Revolutionary War. But because some states had paid portions of their debt and many had not, disagreements arose in Congress as

[45] See "Editor's Note on Arrearages in Soldier's Pay, 1790," *Papers*, Vol. 16, pp. 455–62.

[46] *The Anas, Writings*, Vol. I, p. 272.

[47] "Editor's Note," op. cit., *Papers*, Vol. 16, p. 460.

[48] *The Anas, Writings*, Vol. I, p. 271.

to who would receive the federal monies. The ensuing debate "seemed to unchain all those fierce passions, while a high respect for the government and for those who had administered it had in great measure [become] restrained."[49]

Confronting Jefferson one day "before the President's door," Hamilton deplored the sad state of affairs: Congress was paralyzed, the states were disgusted with the federal government, and the danger of "secession" was clear and present. He then urged Jefferson, as a cabinet member, to unite the administration and support the President. In order to produce harmony and obtain the necessary votes for passage, Jefferson acquiesced and agreed to convince two of his fellow Southerners to vote for the bill. The price was an agreement that Georgetown would become the fixed seat of government after a decade's residence in Philadelphia.

Assumption was passed and Hamilton gained a tighter hold on his ultimate objective: "it made the Treasury's chief the master of every vote in the legislature, which might give to the government the direction suited to his political views."[50] The "real history of the Assumption," Jefferson would later protest,

> was unjust, in itself oppressive to the states, and was acquiesced in merely from a fear of disunion, while our government was still in it's [sic] most infant state. It enabled Hamilton so to strengthen himself by corrupt services to many, that he could afterwards carry his bank scheme, and every measure he proposed in defiance of all opposition: in fact it was a principal ground whereon was reared up that Speculating phalanx, in and out of Congress which has since been able to give laws and to change the political complexion of the government of the United States.[51]

Within a period of six months then, Jefferson believed he had seen the government, an independent republic with principles and separate, but equal, branches, transformed into a system dependent on corruption and the will of one man. And what was per-

[49] John Marshall, *The Life of George Washington*, 4 vols. (Philadelphia, 1804; rev. ed. 1831), Vol. II, pp. 182–83.

[50] *The Anas, Writings*, Vol. I, p. 276.

[51] Thomas Jefferson, n.r.

haps worse, he, the worldly, urbane Secretary of State, had been an unwitting tool in his rival's accomplishment.[52]

The "bank scheme," as Jefferson called it, would make the future look especially bleak. What was at stake here, and Jefferson fully realized it, was the chief principle of the constitution: federalism. Another principle was also involved, viz., the separation of powers. Realizing that Hamilton must "contrive" an "engine of influence more permanent" than the funding and assumption plans, Jefferson, Madison, and their cohort all watched with grim understanding the scenes that were playing round them. Jefferson stated much later that even at that early date, December 1790, the Congress had divided into two groups "styled republican and federal. The latter being *monarchist* in principle, adhered to Hamilton . . . as their leader in that principle, and this mercenary phalanx added . . . insured him always a majority in both Houses: so that the whole of action of legislature was now under the direction of the Treasury."[53]

In the long debate over the bank bill, begun in December of 1790, the important issue soon became not the bank itself, but the principles of the constitution. Madison rose up to remind the House of Representatives that the Convention had denied the government the powers of incorporation. He then proceeded to argue for a strict construction of the constitution. Jefferson, echoing Madison in the cabinet, warned that "a single step beyond the boundaries thus specially drawn around the powers of Congress is to take possession of a boundless field of power, no longer susceptible of any definition."[54]

Jefferson's logic had penetrated the ultimate danger to the constitution. Madison, too, perhaps even the interpreter in this instance, had begun to alter his broad nationalist construction of the constitution made only two years earlier. For both, the danger in principle was the absolute and unlimited consolidation of power

[52] Jefferson to George Mason, 4 Feb. 1791, *Papers*, Vol. 19, pp. 241–42.

[53] *The Anas, Writings*, Vol. I, p. 277.

[54] *The Works of Thomas Jefferson* (Federal Edition), op. cit., Vol. VI, p. 198.

by the central government. When they saw this possibility, in conjunction with Hamilton's domination of the legislature, the future of republican principles in the constitution to them became ominous.

But the evils lurking in Hamilton's bill were seen not just by Jefferson and Madison. James Jackson, of Georgia, raised the specter of the English precedent: "What was it that drove our forefathers to this country? Was it not the ecclesiastical corporations and perpetual monopolies of England . . . ? Shall we suffer the same evils to exist in this country? . . . If we establish the precedent now before us [i.e., the bank bill] there is no saying when it will stop." "Let us beware of following the example of Great Britain in this respect."[55]

Patrick Henry, writing in January of 1791, after Monroe had sent him a copy of Hamilton's reports, added another dimension to Hamilton's "system": viz., the specter of sectionalism. "It seems to be a consistent part of a system," Henry said, "which I ever dreaded. Subserviency of Southern to N———n interests are written in Capitals on its very front; whilst Government Influence, deeply planted and wildly scattered by preceding measures, is to receive formidable addition by this plan."[56]

Jackson's reference to the "monopolies of England" had not been merely rhetorical; it implied a relationship that was being energetically discussed at the time. Many believed that Hamilton was developing a "system" that was more than simply coincidental with the British style of administration. And many, like Henry, believed he was using the old Roman maxim—*divide et impera*— to achieve it. Jefferson himself believed it, and later stated that by Hamilton's "combination [i.e., members of Congress acting as directors for the bank] legislative expositions were given to the constitution, and all the administrative laws were shaped on the *model of England* and so passed."[57]

[55] *Annals of Congress*, II, pp. 1968, 1970. Speech on the bank bill by Rep. Lawrence of New York, quoting a speech by Rep. Jackson, Georgia.

[56] Henry, *Patrick Henry*, op. cit., Vol. II, pp. 459–61.

[57] *The Anas, Writings*, Vol. I, p. 277.

Knowing Jefferson's hatred of the British system, we can begin to understand what suspicions must have been going through his mind, even at this early date, when he contemplated the direction of the government. Gouverneur Morris, an old friend of Hamilton's, would sum up, perhaps better than Jefferson could himself, what lay at the source of his conflict with the Secretary of the Treasury:

> Hamilton apprehended a corrupt understanding between the executive and a dominating party in the legislature, which would destroy the president's responsibility; and he was *not* to be taught what everyone knows, that where responsibility ends, fraud, injustice, tyranny, and treachery, begin.[58]

Indeed, this was what Jefferson feared and suspected. He stated, "Hamilton was not only a monarchist, but for a monarchy bottomed on corruption." The proof for this assertion was, for Jefferson, an anecdote that told the full story. In April 1791, Jefferson, Adams, Knox, and Hamilton had a dinner in which the subject of the British constitution came up for discussion. Hamilton, in the course of disagreeing with Adams whether or not the British constitution needed reforming, said, "Purge it of its corruption . . . and it would become an *impracticable* government: as it stands at present, with all its supposed defects, it is the most perfect government which ever existed." Jefferson's conclusion was that Hamilton was for "an hereditary King, with a House of Lords and Commons corrupted to his will, and standing between him and the people." Jefferson further concluded that Hamilton had been "so bewitched and perverted to the British example, as to be under thorough conviction that corruption was essential to the government of a nation."[59]

Indeed, Jefferson had already tasted the fruits of Hamilton's managerial corruption.[60] The funding and assumption plans, aug-

---

[58] Jared Sparks, "Life of Gouverneur Morris," in the *American Quarterly Review,* June 1832, p. 454.

[59] *The Anas, Writings,* Vol. I, pp. 278–79.

[60] Others too had tasted the fruits of his corruption, and one John F. Mercer became embroiled in a controversy with Hamilton over his conduct of

mented by the bank bill, had given Hamilton immense leverage in the new government. Already, Hamilton had interfered in foreign policy by consulting with the British representative, Major Beckwith.[61] Within a year Jefferson would complain to Washington that over the past twelve months "the Secretary of the Treasury, by his cabals with members of the legislature . . . has forced his own system, which was exactly the reverse [of Jefferson's]. He undertook, of his own authority, the conferences with the ministers of those two nations [France and England] . . ."[62]

The consequence of this resentment was that Jefferson attempted to reduce Hamilton's influence in his own department. When a vacancy appeared in the comptroller's position, Jefferson attempted to have his friend Tench Coxe fill it.[63] Hamilton recommended Oliver Wolcott, the current auditor, and Wolcott received the appointment.[64] When the position of postmaster general became vacant several months later, Jefferson attempted to have his revolutionary friend Thomas Paine appointed. Hamilton's choice of Timothy Pickering gained the appointment.[65]

It is fair to ask, in reference to Jefferson's assertions, what Hamilton might have thought he was doing. What precedents

---

administration. Mercer accused Hamilton of "encreasing your own influence and attaching to your administration a Monied Interest as an Engine of Government . . ." See Hamilton to John Mercer, 26 Sept. 1792, *The Papers of Alexander Hamilton*, op. cit., Vol. XII, p. 575. See editors' note, pp. 481–90, on the details of the dispute.

[61] Samuel F. Bemis, *Jay's Treaty* (New York, 1924), pp. 41–48.

[62] Jefferson to George Washington, 9 Sept. 1792, *The Works of Thomas Jefferson* (Federal Edition), op. cit., Vol. VII, p. 140.

[63] Jefferson to George Washington, 17 April 1791, ibid., Vol. VI, p. 246. See also Leonard White, *The Federalists* (New York, 1948), p. 225. White's analysis of this phase in Jefferson's career reveals the intense struggle that was taking place for control of the government.

[64] Alexander Hamilton to George Washington, 19 June 1791, *Works of Alexander Hamilton*, ed. H. C. Lodge, 10 vols. (New York, 1886), Vol. VIII, p. 225.

[65] Leonard White, *The Federalists*, op. cit., p. 225.

were available at the time that he may have followed? The answer lies in the example set by "the British model" that Jefferson and his colleagues so hated. The fact was, Hamilton had been emulating the late prime minister of England, Sir Robert Walpole. In the latter's role as prime minister, he used, at different intervals, George II and George III as his "Aegis very essential," established the Bank of England and a national debt, brought the monied interests into the administration, manipulated the various factions by intrigues, distributed patronage, kept a tight rein on legislation and the timing of bills, involved himself in foreign policy, created a chain of influence around the king—all in a decidedly nonpartisan fashion.

Hamilton could only have been mirroring the politics of management which were created by Walpole in the 1720s, '30s, and '40s. This style of politics relied upon the maintenance of faction, personal connection, special interests, friendship, and all the undercurrent practices—"bottomed on corruption"—that supported the British constitution Hamilton so admired.[66]

If we attempt to ask whether Hamilton had an exact blueprint, or whether Jefferson believed he did, we are missing the point of historical analysis. Hamilton obviously had little regard for the separation of powers, and if we take Jefferson, Madison, and

[66] There is enough of a parallel between English and American politics, of which Hamilton was a particularly keen student, to suggest that he might have, in the spirit of the times, believed he was "managing" the government in the personal and factional style of Robert Walpole. William L. Smith, one of Hamilton's supporters, noted that after the establishment of the funding and assumption plans, "the Secretary of the Treasury acquired a well-earned Fame and general popularity; his reputation traversed the ocean and in distant climes his Name was mentioned among the great ministers of the age." *The Politicks and Views of a Certain Party Displayed* (n.p., 1792), p. 12.

Indeed, it is possible that Hamilton, with his admiration for the British system, knew people still alive who had witnessed the great minister Walpole, and his administration, firsthand. A description of Walpole's life by a contemporary author, Tobias Smollett, reads like a miniature biography of Alexander Hamilton.

Henry seriously, he had even less regard for the limitations on the powers of the government. In any case, Hamilton would have found it a difficult task to adapt a republican form to a monarchical one.[67]

By August of 1791, it appeared to Jefferson that Hamilton was the leader of a conspiracy to transform the government from a republic to an aristocratic form. In a conversation between them, Hamilton startled Jefferson by saying "that the present government is not that which will answer the ends of society by giving stability and protection to its rights, and that it will probably be found expedient to *go into the British form*."[68] To a man of absolute principle, this reliance upon expediency was heresy in a republican government. It was at this point that Jefferson saw it would be necessary to redouble his efforts to crush Hamilton, or republican principles would be compromised out of existence.

A controversy had been brewing over Paine's *Rights of Man*, and Jefferson, because he had written an endorsement to the book, came under attack from one Publicola, in the *Boston Columbian Centinel*.[69] Jefferson believed that attacking Paine's principles was synonymous with attacking "the principles of the citizens of the United States."[70] Accordingly, the establishment of the *National Gazette* in October 1791, by Madison, was a response to the newspaper attacks against Jefferson.[71]

But try as he might, Jefferson seemed unable to cut Hamilton down, and the Secretary of the Treasury gained in influence. Early

[67] See also the lengthy discussion of Hamilton's imitation of British finances by Martin Van Buren in *Inquiry into the Origin and Course of Political Parties in the United States* (New York, 1867), pp. 139–53; 160–68; 207–12.

[68] *The Anas, Writings*, Vol. I, p. 284. Entry date 13 Aug. 1791.

[69] Publicola turned out to be John Quincy Adams, who interpreted Jefferson's endorsement as an attack on his father's *Defenses of the Constitutions of the United States*.

[70] Jefferson to John Adams, 30 Aug. 1791, *Letters*, Vol. I, p. 250. See also Jefferson to George Washington, 8 May 1791, *The Works of Thomas Jefferson* (Federal Edition), op. cit., Vol. VI, pp. 254–57.

[71] James Madison to Edmund Randolph, 13 Sept. 1792, *The Writings of James Madison*, op. cit., Vol. I, pp. 569–70.

in 1792 Jefferson attempted to have the post office transferred from the Treasury to the State Department. Jefferson told Washington that one of his reasons was "the department of the treasury possessed already such an influence as to swallow up the whole of the executive powers, and that even the future Presidents (not supported by the weight of character which himself possessed) would not be able to make head against this department."[72] Washington's reply was a dodge that avoided Jefferson's point. He simply said he had promised the position to Timothy Pickering when he was appointed.[73]

By mid-July Jefferson was sufficiently worried about the drift of the government to have begun writing a "Note of Agenda to reduce the government to its true principles."[74] While nothing came of the essay, which seems not to be extant, it did focus Jefferson's attention, most likely, on the major differences between himself and Hamilton. This was especially true where administrative principles were concerned. Jefferson presumed that the Revolution of 1776 had "elevated both the citizen and the official to a new plane of moral responsibility."[75] This meant that the *res publica*, or public thing, had become the responsibility of every citizen; that when a man was elected to an office of public responsibility he had a moral duty to avoid a conflict of interest. Indeed, it was his moral duty to the community, meaning the nation, to do so. It was, in fact, the very reason he had been given his trust. This was Jefferson's role in government: to serve the public; not to cheat, deprive, or deceive it. The idea that a government would grow strong in proportion to the fraud, corruption, and manipulation that occurred among its leaders, or that secrecy and deception were the means by which policy was advanced, was anathema to Jefferson. As Gouverneur Morris had suggested, and what "every-

---

[72] *The Anas, Writings*, Vol. I, p. 286.

[73] Washington to Jefferson, 20 Oct. 1792, *The Writings of George Washington*, ed. John C. Fitzpatrick, 39 vols. (1931–39), Vol. 32, p. 187.

[74] *Papers*, Vol. 17, p. 208. See Editor's Note.

[75] *Ibid.*, p. 344. See also Jefferson to DuPont du Nemours, 24 April 1816, *Writings*, Vol. XIV, pp. 487–93.

body else knew," those devices produced "fraud, injustice, tyranny and treachery."

These principles of administration were fundamentally at stake in the years of Jefferson's struggle with Hamilton, and would be resolved only by the Revolution of 1800. But in 1792 Jefferson had no idea that they would be resolved in any other way than the immediate course the government seemed to be taking. And that had not been promising. By March, Jefferson's suspicions of Hamilton's involvement with the British minister Hammond had grown so great that he stated, "I believe he [Hamilton] communicated to Hammond all our views, and knew from him, in return, the views of the British court."[76]

Jefferson claimed a small victory in October, as Washington allowed the State Department to assume control of the mint rather "than to multiply the duties of the other [the Treasury]."[77] But this was to be his last success. His attempt to reduce Hamilton's control of the Treasury by splitting it into two sections, customs and internal taxes, met with failure in the Senate.[78]

Meanwhile, Hamilton had gone on the offensive. In Fenno's *Gazette of the United States* he published an attack against Jefferson which revealed that Jefferson had "embarrassed [Hamilton's] plans . . . but continued in opposition to them, after they had been considered and enacted by the legislature . . . and had been approved by the chief magistrate." Hamilton was accusing Jefferson of violating "the theory of government." He ended by calling for Jefferson to resign, to "tell the people that he could no longer continue in it [i.e., the office of Secretary of State] without fore-

[76] *The Anas, Writings,* Vol. I, p. 298. Julian P. Boyd has brought out the truth of Jefferson's suspicions in the full light of day. Boyd's *Number 7: Alexander Hamilton's Secret Attempts to Control American Foreign Policy* (London, 1965) implicated Hamilton as aiding Major Beckwith, the British representative in 1790. Boyd proved that Hamilton revealed secret information to the British minister and was ready to engage in deceit and intrigue (a conspiracy?) to such a degree that it endangered American foreign policy.

[77] Washington to Jefferson, 20 Oct. 1792, *The Writings of George Washington,* op. cit., Vol. 32, p. 187.

[78] White, *The Federalists,* op. cit., p. 228.

feiting his duty to them, and that he had quitted it to be more at liberty to afford them his best services."[79]

Hamilton could write Colonel Carrington, an old friend of his and a correspondent of Jefferson's, that the objections by Jefferson and Madison to his policies were due to Jefferson's ambitions and were personally motivated. Asserting that Jefferson "aims with ardent desire at the Presidential chair," Hamilton told his friend, his "influence, therefore, with the community becomes a thing, on ambitious and personal grounds, to be resisted and destroyed."[80] And in the same letter, Hamilton, with a certain degree of dissimulation, pleaded naïve ignorance to the cause of all the strife between himself and Jefferson:

> . . . these causes [attempts by Jefferson and Madison "to produce a commercial warfare with Great Britain"] and perhaps some others, created much sooner than I was aware of it, a systematic opposition to me, on the part of these gentlemen. My subversion, I am now satisfied, has long been an object with them. Subsequent events have increased the spirit of opposition and the feelings of personal mortification on the part of these gentlemen.[81]

In July, Washington complained to Jefferson that Freneau's paper was "exciting opposition to the government." And, he

[79] *Gazette of the United States* (Philadelphia), 24 Oct. 1792, Metellus. See *The Papers of Alexander Hamilton*, op. cit., Vol. XII, pp. 613–17.

[80] Hamilton to Col. Edward Carrington, 26 May 1792, *Works of Alexander Hamilton*, op. cit., Vol. VIII, pp. 248–65. Five months later Hamilton would reveal his uncanny foresight in intuiting Jefferson's becoming President. Hamilton seemed to believe that any serious rival was guilty of excessive ambition. In addition to his attack on Jefferson, his rival in New York, Aaron Burr, was caricatured as "the worst sort," "determined to climb to the highest honors of the State," and caring "nothing about the means of effecting his purpose." "In a word," said Hamilton, "*if we have an embryo-Caesar in the United States, it is Burr.*" His use of the word "Caesar" in this instance had all the dangerous connotations of one ready and willing to overthrow the republic. Hamilton to (unknown), 26 Sept. 1792, *Works of Alexander Hamilton*, op. cit., Vol. X, p. 22.

[81] Ibid., pp. 260–61.

added, "whatever tended to produce anarchy, tended, of course, to produce a resort to monarchical government." While Washington believed that there were a few people in the large cities who might "desire" a change to monarchy, there were no "designs" to do so. Washington expressed the belief that the "main body of the people . . . were steadily for republicanism . . ." This was also Jefferson's view, at least the part about a majority of the citizenry preferring republicanism. But he differed from Washington by pointing out the influence the Treasury had in "corrupting both branches of the legislature." Washington ignored his point and defended Hamilton's assumption plan.[82]

By October, Washington was again attempting to reconcile his two advisors.[83] When the President told Jefferson "he did not believe there were ten men in the United States" who wished to transform "this Government into a monarchy," Jefferson replied that "there were many more than he [Washington] imagined."[84] And he added that the "Secretary of the Treasury was one of these." Jefferson then told the President that Hamilton had called the constitution a "shilly shally thing, of mere milk and water which could not last long and was only good as a step to something better." Jefferson reminded Washington that at the Convention of 1787, Hamilton had attempted "to make an English constitution of it" and ended by describing the "regular system" of the Treasury as responsible for collapsing the separation of powers. As the most powerful arm of the executive, he said, it "had swallowed up the legislative houses."[85]

As Jefferson began his last year as Secretary of State, he faced the pressure to remain in office from Washington on one side, and continual opposition from Hamilton on the other. Hamilton had successfully blocked a controversy over who would succeed to the

---

[82] *The Anas, Writings*, Vol. I, pp. 311–12. Entry date 10 July 1792.

[83] Washington to Jefferson, 23 Aug. 1792; Washington to Hamilton, 26 Aug. 1792, *The Writings of George Washington*, op. cit. Vol. 32, pp. 128–34.

[84] *The Anas, Writings*, Vol. I, p. 317.

[85] Ibid., p. 318. Entry date 1 Oct. 1792. This was a topic of long debate and resulted in a combined strategy by Jefferson and Giles in the House.

presidency in case of the death of the Chief Executive and the Vice President. The Senate voted for the Chief Justice, the House for the Secretary of State.[86] A compromise was agreed upon, and the President of the Senate pro-tempore was chosen successor. Jefferson, in his attempts to undercut Hamilton's influence, was on the losing side once again. Hamilton, on his part, rationalized his efforts to block Jefferson by saying "if I had no other reason for it . . . it [was] a measure of self defence."[87]

In February, once again Washington asked Jefferson if he and Hamilton might "coalesce" in the interest of giving confidence to the government. This was a revelation to Jefferson, for it meant that Washington still had not grasped what was at stake, what he had been trying to tell him for almost two long years. His answer is also illuminating, because he based his objections on principle: "That as to a coalition with Mr. Hamilton, if by that was meant that either was to sacrifice his general system to the other, it was impossible. We had both . . . principles conscientiously adopted, which . . . could not be given up on either side."[88]

Hamilton would have agreed and, in fact, had stated so as much as nine months earlier in his letter to Carrington. Complaining about Jefferson's opposition to the funding system, Hamilton said, "I do not mean that he advocates directly the undoing of what has been done, but he censures the whole, on principles, which, if they should become general, would not but end in the subversion of the system."[89] Thus Hamiliton, nursing his own conspiratorial mentality, was accusing Jefferson, and by implication Madison, of acting in a manner that would bring about a change in not only the administration but the system of government. Placing his fears into perspective, he told Carrington, "On the whole the only

86 *Annals of Congress,* Vol. II, 1911–15. 13 January 1791 was the earliest date for discussion of the issue of succession.

87 Hamilton to Col. Edward Carrington, 26 May 1792, *Works of Alexander Hamilton,* op. cit., Vol. VIII, p. 261.

88 *The Anas, Writings,* Vol. I, p. 332. Entry date 7 Feb. 1793.

89 Hamilton to Col. Edward Carrington, 26 May 1792, *Works of Alexander Hamilton,* op. cit., Vol. VIII, p. 252.

enemy which Republicanism has to fear in this country is in the spirit of faction and anarchy."[90] Of course, Hamiliton saw Jefferson acting in the spirit of one, and producing the other. That Hamilton believed Jefferson was the leader of a faction cannot be doubted. Jefferson, he stated, was leading a "uniform opposition" involving a campaign of "whispers and insinuations." Jefferson would next complain that the Attorney General, Edmund Randolph, had joined Hamilton in his conspiracy, especially as it related to England and American neutrality. Because the cabinet was equally divided, Hamilton and Knox on one side, Jefferson and Randolph on the other, it was crucial to Jefferson that the Attorney General vote on the basis of principle. But more and more Randolph equivocated and Jefferson saw that "Anglophobia [had] seized violently on three members of our Council."[91]

In desperation, Jefferson expressed his frustrations to Madison:

[90] Hamilton to Col. Edward Carrington, ibid., p. 264. William Cobbett raised a point which bears on Hamilton's remark and throws light upon the relationship between conspiracy and revolution. Given the administrative theory of the time, wherein opposition to government was considered intolerable, Porcupine defined the struggle between the factions—with their conspiratorial mentality—as an idea of revolution. And revolution, we may recall, negates government itself. "Thus . . . I think, nobody will deny, that a hatred of the British government and that of the United States go hand in hand. Nor is the reason of this at all mysterious; it is not, as the Democrats have ingeniously observed, because 'there is some dangerous connection between Great Britain and our public affairs,' *it is because they are* both pursuing the same line of conduct with respect to clubs and conspiracies; it is because they both possess the same radical defect, a power to suppress anarchy; it is, to say all in one word, because they are governments. . . . It is not the form of a government, it is not the manner of its administration, it is the thing itself they are at war with, and that they must be eternally at war with. . . ." *Porcupine's Works*, op. cit., Vol. II, p. 34. What Porcupine refused to recognize, as did Hamilton, was that Jefferson and his colleagues were not anarchists; they had in mind a definite system of government. The only difference was, that it was based on opposite principles than those Hamilton and his quilled friend thought acceptable.

[91] Jefferson to James Madison, 13 May 1793, *Writings*, Vol. IX, p. 87.

Everything, my dear Sir, hangs upon the opinion of a single person [Randolph] and that the most indecisive one I have ever had to do business with. He always contrives to agree in principle with one, but in conclusion with the other. Anglophobia, a secret anti-gallomany, a *federalisme outree,* and a present ease in his circumstances not usual, have decided the complexion of our dispositions, and our proceedings toward *these conspirators against human liberty* . . .[92]

By this time Jefferson had made a decision to retire to private life, to leave the councils of government and submit his resignation. The weight of Hamilton's opposition had become too much for him. He saw that it was futile to remain within the highest councils, yet face defeat every time a principle he deemed important was voted upon. Only Washington's pleas to remain at his post prevented him from resigning abruptly in mid-1793. Yet the situation would grow worse in the next six months.

Three months earlier Jefferson had written a note describing how Henry Knox, the Secretary of War, had become furious in a cabinet meeting and "swore that our Government must either be entirely new modeled, or it would be knocked to pieces in less than two years; and that *he would not give a copper for it* . . ."[93] These sentiments from the Secretary of War, a man Jefferson knew had already been disposed to a return to monarchy, did not inspire confidence.[94] Nor did Jefferson's next hint of intrigue on the part of Hamilton. By June of 1793, Jefferson received a rumor that there was a possibility of Hamilton's collusion with the British. John Beckley, a clerk in the Congress, reported to Jefferson that Sir John Temple, consul general for the northern states,

[92] Ibid., pp. 87–89.

[93] *The Anas, Writings,* Vol. I, p. 344.

[94] Nor did Tobias Lear, Secretary to the President, when he told Jefferson that same day "a number of gentlemen had for a long time been endeavoring to instill into the President, that the noise against the administration of the Government was that of a little *faction* . . . detested by the people." *The Anas, Writings,* Vol. I, p. 345.

had shown him a letter stating that Hamilton and two of his friends, Rufus King and William Smith of South Carolina, were to be provided with security by the British, in fact, "an asylum," if their "machinations" backfired upon them. Sir John's letter noted that the British "considered Col. Hamilton, and not Mr. Hammond, as their effective Minister here." Jefferson's conclusion to this bit of evidence was that "they [King, Smith, and Hamilton] understand that they may go on boldly in their machinations to change the Government."[95]

Thus, for Jefferson, not only had everyone in the chief councils of the government become suspect, the circles of the conspiracy seemed to be growing wider. Jefferson had drawn the line from the cabinet to the society at large and encompassed the affluent and aristocratic portions:

> The line is now drawn so clearly as to show on one side, 1. The fashionable circles of Philadelphia, New York, Boston and Charleston, (natural aristocrats.) 2. Merchants trading on British capital. 3. Paper men, (all the old tories are found in some one of these descriptions.) On the other side are, 1. Merchants trading on their own capital. 2. Irish merchants. 3. Tradesmen, mechanics, farmers and every other description of our citizens.[96]

Jefferson had begun to see the emergence of a class division: rich against poor, the old and familiar division of a republican society verging toward revolution and a change in the form of government.

When Jefferson refused to accommodate his principles to Hamilton's, it was because he was steeped in the history of repub-

[95] Ibid., p. 354. Sir Gregory Page Turner, member of Parliament from Yorkshire, to Sir John Temple (no date of letter). Jefferson's entry is 7 June 1793. Jefferson indicated also that he did not always trust Beckley's facts verbatim. On 7 June 1793, after Beckley had reported that Governor Clinton of New York had a plan of Hamilton's to establish monarchical government in the United States, Jefferson remarked, "Beckley . . . is too credulous as to what he hears from others." Ibid., p. 356.

[96] Jefferson to Madison, 15 May 1793, *Writings*, Vol. IX, pp. 88–89.

lican governments.[97] He realized more fully than anyone in the cabinet that the first compromise with Hamilton meant ultimate victory for his rival. Unfortunately, there is little evidence that Washington understood what was at stake. Himself beyond suspicion, at least in terms of motives, he wished only to reduce the friction that he saw dividing his councils. And when Jefferson refused to compromise, Washington, while not openly siding with the Secretary of the Treasury, at least inclined his way.

This became noticeable for reasons other than those that dealt specifically with the problems of the cabinet and the administration. Philip Freneau's attacks against Hamilton in the *National Gazette* often included barbs aimed at the Chief Executive. Washington not only felt insulted, he believed that Jefferson ought to have restrained Freneau in his criticisms. When confronted by Washington, Jefferson denied that he had influenced Freneau, either "directly or indirectly," and that a free press guaranteed Freneau's right to include "pieces written against aristocratical and monarchical principles."[98] Caught in this difficult situation, Jefferson became definite regarding his resignation in July. By August he was adamant that his last day as Secretary of State would be December 31, 1793.[99]

As Jefferson prepared to leave Philadelphia, he wondered what

---

[97] James Thomson Callender wrote, "When the counsels of Mr. Hamilton shall . . . be completely unveiled, no suprize will remain at the resignation of Secretary Jefferson. The sole mystery seems to be, by what magic spell these two contending powers of light and darkness could act in unison, or even in common civility, for a single day." *Sedgwick and Co., or A Key to the Six Per Cent Cabinet* (Philadelphia, 1798), p. 35.

[98] Jefferson to Washington, *The Works of Thomas Jefferson* (Federal Edition), op. cit., Vol. VII, pp. 136–49. Jefferson not only defended Freneau's right to publish freely, he expressed the belief that "his paper had saved our constitution which was galloping fast into monarchy." *The Anas, Writings*, Vol. I, p. 353.

[99] Jefferson to Washington, 31 July 1793, *Writings*, Vol. IX, pp. 173–74. See also Jefferson to Washington 11 Aug. 1793 and 31 Dec. 1793, ibid., p. 278.

the future held for the government. Hamilton's influence, by this time pervasive, would continue to grow, even through Adams' administration.[100] But it was the influence that Hamilton had had upon Washington that was truly dangerous. For, according to Jefferson, Washington had become incompetent, if not senile. "From the moment . . . of my retiring from the administration," he wrote, "the Federalists got unchecked hold of General Washington. His memory was already sensibly impaired by age, the firm tone of mind for which he had been remarkable, was beginning to relax . . . a listlessness of labor, a desire for tranquillity had crept on him, and a willingness to let others act, and even think for him." (Hamilton, in Jefferson's eyes, had already been doing too much of that.) Finally, Jefferson concluded by observing that Washington "had become alienated from myself personally, and . . . from the republican body generally of his fellow citizens . . ."[101]

Thus Jefferson, isolated from the one man who earlier had asked him to be a "check" on his administration,[102] saw he could do nothing but return to Monticello. There he kept up a rapid but distant correspondence with Madison on the main issues confronting Congress. His emissaries were keeping watch on the Hamiltonians' every move. By March of 1794, Jefferson saw Hamilton's hand in a Senate speech by William Smith opposing Madison's bill regulating commerce. Writing to Madison, he noted, "I am at no loss to ascribe Smith's speech to its true father. Every title of it is Hamilton's except the introduction."[103] This was a sign that Hamilton's influence, like that of an English prime minister's, was

---

[100] John Adams complained of Hamilton's influence in later years and the problem Washington had of getting competent people to serve from 1794 on. "The truth is," Adams said, "Hamilton's influence over him was so well known, that no man fit for the Office of State or War would accept either. He was driven to the Necessity of appointing such as would accept." John Adams to Thomas Jefferson, 3 July 1813, *Letters*, Vol. II, p. 349.

[101] *The Anas, Writings*, Vol. I, pp. 282–83.

[102] Ibid., p. 317. Entry date 1 Oct. 1792.

[103] Jefferson to Madison, 3 April 1794, *Writings*, Vol. IX, p. 281.

reaching farther and deeper into the legislature. The question now was, How far could Hamilton go in assuming control of the government? With a lame-duck President at his beck and call, with a Secretary of War who refused to give "a copper" for the government, with a "trimming" Secretary of State, Jefferson saw no obstacle to Hamilton having his way.

But the worst was yet to come. Before Jefferson retired to Monticello, a movement had been underway that bore all the signs of a revolutionary conspiracy. Beginning in July 1791, in the "western country" of Pennsylvania, a number of farmers had complained against land speculation, trials in remote federal courts, lack of concern for their defense and navigation rights on the Mississippi, and the imposition of an excise tax on whiskey.[104] Their complaints were to lead to mass meetings over a two-year period. By late 1793 violence had repeatedly broken out against the property of local revenue inspectors. In the wake of that violence, more was inspired, until, in November 1793, an inspector's house was burned to the ground. Farmers' organizations issued "circulars" that called for further *armed* mass meetings. Newspapers, primarily the *Pittsburg Gazette*, joined in printing the arguments against the government. The Democratic societies actively opposed the government. A "liberty pole" appeared, and a series of resolutions against the authorities were passed. The culmination of the meetings came on August 1, 1794 when roughly eight thousand men marched through the town of Pittsburgh.[105]

Rumors of secession filled the air in Pennsylvania and in three counties of Virginia. State officials, from Governor Mifflin on down, recommended a policy of leniency, or at minimum non-coercion. It was even feared, by those familiar with the actual conditions, that the state militia, if called upon to fight their fellow citizens, would not obey. A large meeting with representatives from Pennsylvania and Virginia convinced a group of United

[104] Francis Wharton, *State Trials of the United States* (New York, 1849), pp. 102–97.

[105] Ibid., p. 109.

States commissioners sent to Parkinson's Ferry that leniency would not deter the rebels.[106] The stage was set for confrontation.

Meanwhile, Hamilton himself had been busy in the spring and summer of 1794 preparing for what he saw was an inevitable conflict between state and federal authority over the excise bill. The excise was crucial for Hamilton's economic policy, and the fact that a number of citizens in western Pennsylvania refused to pay it meant, in Hamilton's view, that they not only wished to embarrass the Government, but that the state authorities, who had been dragging their feet, were guilty of obstructing justice.[107] Justice James Wilson departed from an earlier position that upheld the state's right to deal with the problem and reported that "the groups opposing the laws of the United States . . . were too powerful to be dealt with by the marshal or by ordinary judicial proceedings."[108] Suddenly, Hamilton's position, as second in command of the United States Army, assumed a new significance.

Henry Knox, Secretary of War, ordered a total of 12,950 men to be requisitioned in order to put down the insurrectionists.[109] That same day, August 7, Washington, assuming that the rebels intended to continue their resistance, and that their behavior "amounted to treason," decided upon force.[110] The word of

[106] Harry Marlin Tinkcom, *The Republicans and Federalists in Pennsylvania, 1790–1801* (Harrisburg, Pa., 1950), pp. 91–109. Also Wharton's *State Trials of the United States*, op. cit., p. 116. David Bradford (one of the leaders), to the Inhabitants of Monongahela, 6 Aug. 1794: "The crisis has now come. *Submission or opposition.* We are determined on the opposition . . . [and] to form . . . [a] spirited conduct." Ibid., p. 115. See also "circular," dated Canonsburg, Pa., 28 July 1794, for advice on arms: "If any volunteer should want arms or ammunition, bring them forward and they shall be supplied." Ibid., p. 116.

[107] Hamilton to George Washington, 5 Aug. 1794, *The Papers of Alexander Hamilton*, op. cit., Vol. XVII, pp. 24–58.

[108] Tinkcom, *The Republicans and Federalists in Pennsylvania, 1790–1801*, op. cit., pp. 98–99.

[109] Ibid., p. 100.

[110] Wharton, *State Trials of the United States*, op. cit., p. 118. See also "Proclamation of George Washington," *Messages and Papers of the Presidents*, op. cit., Vol. I, pp. 150–54.

Washington's determination spread quickly over the four-county area, and in a final meeting the leaders of the insurgents agreed to obey the law. By now, though, an army of approximately fifteen thousand men had been assembled at Carlisle and was ready to march. The politicians and men who attended the government could talk of nothing else. However, as for the onlookers in Philadelphia and Monticello, another development had taken place, with potentially sinister overtones.

When Washington left Philadelphia, he had at his side General and Secretary of the Treasury Alexander Hamilton.[111] This was an unusual development which raised the eyebrows of many responsible leaders in Congress. Madison believed the consequences of Hamilton's role would be the creation of a standing army and passed on the gossip of the day: "It is said the militia will return with that doctrine in their mouths."[112] Hamilton, left in command by Washington, had suddenly assumed the role of a potential Caesar. His antidemocratic sentiments leaped out of one of his first communications to Washington: "It is long since I have learned to hold popular opinion of no value."[113]

The army left Carlisle, and the rebels, long aware of the marching columns, disappeared as soon as the soldiers approached. Hamilton found no resistance whatsoever. In the end, he captured a few ringleaders, brought them to trial and, in the process, attempted to make the demonstration of federal authority appear impressive.[114] To some, it did. To others, especially the members

[111] Wharton, *State Trials of the United States*, op. cit., pp. 159–61. See Hamilton's "detailed instructions to the Western Army," 20 Oct. 1794.

[112] Madison to Jefferson, 16 Nov. 1794, *The Writings of James Madison*, op. cit., Vol. II, pp. 18–19.

[113] Hamilton to George Washington, 11 Nov. 1794, *The Works of Alexander Hamilton*, op. cit., Vol. VI, p. 65.

[114] The seriousness of the Whiskey Rebellion, of course, depended largely on one's political faction. William Smith of South Carolina noted in a Fourth of July oration, "In a sister state, deeds have been performed, which claim the warmest tribute of applause; deeds which have more effectually destroyed the calumnies of prejudice against republicanism, than volumes of fine spun theories. At the call of the supreme magistrate, we have seen ten thousand of

of the Democratic societies, the government's assemblage of troops was viewed with contempt. To Jefferson, the entire saga had all the ingredients of tragicomedy. Writing to Madison in late December, he said, "The information of our militia . . . is uniform, that though the people there let them pass quietly, they were objects of their laughter, not of their fear; that one thousand men, could have cut off their whole force in a thousand places in the Alleghany; that their detestation of the government,[115] and that a separation which perhaps was a very distinct and problematical event, is now near, and certain, and determined in the mind of every man."[116] This was the result of Hamilton's leadership in the mountains of western Pennsylvania.

The very thought of Hamilton leading an army of fifteen

---

our countrymen, crouding around the standard of the laws, to undergo the distresses of a severe march, at an inclement season. Opulent citizens, disused to fatigue, spurned the comforts of habitual ease, to endure the toils of war, in a rugged and mountainous country; they instantly forgot the sweets of social and domestic enjoyment, and the profits of professional life; they remembered nothing but the outrage to the laws and the necessity of vindicating them; they rushed to the field, they rescued the federal edifice from the meditated attack." *An Oration delivered in St. Philip's Church* (Charleston, S.C., 1796), pp. 16–17. The other side of this opinion was expressed by James Thomson Callender, a Jeffersonian: "Now, the western army never saw a person in arms against them. They stabbed a man who was in liquor or mad. They shot a boy who was sick: and these two acts of homicide, or murder, include the whole bloodshed of the campaign. . . . The ranks were crowded by young men, altogether unacquainted with the use of arms. On the 9th of January, 1795, General Smith told the House of Representatives 'numbers of the militia did not know how to set up a tent. The Virginia militia . . . were neither trained or disciplined. As for the Marylanders, when he drew part of them out, and ordered them to load, he found that fifty of them had put down the ball *before* the charge of powder. Some of them did not even know how to lay a gun over their shoulders.' " *Sketches of the History of America* (Philadelphia, 1798), pp. 126–29.

[115] Jefferson's observation is corroborated by a report to the Pennsylvania State Legislature after the insurrection, Wharton, *State Trials of the United States*, op. cit., p. 161.

[116] Jefferson to Madison, 28 Dec. 1794, *Writings*, Vol. IX, pp. 295–96.

thousand men was almost too much for Jefferson to bear. But Washington's next act, the denunciation of the Democratic societies, was, in Jefferson's words, "one of the most extraordinary acts of boldness of which we have seen so many from the *faction* of the monocrats."[117] Jefferson believed that Washington had acted in direct consequence of the Whiskey Rebellion. If this was the policy of the government, he had no doubt that it constituted an "attack on the freedom of discussion, the freedom of writing, printing and publishing." Hamilton, it appeared, was using Washington and the Whiskey Rebellion as an excuse to assault the First Amendment to the constitution—that part of the constitution Jefferson held sacred. As he contemplated Hamilton's role as a general officer, he also pondered the relationship that his adversary had with the "society of Cincinatti, a *self-created* one, carving out for itself hereditary distinctions, lowering over our Constitution eternally, meeting together in all parts of the Union, periodically, with closed doors, accumulating a capital in their separate treasury, corresponding secretly and regularly, and . . . denouncing the democrats . . ." "Their sight," he added, "must be perfectly dazzled by the glittering of crowns and coronets, not to see the extravagance of the proposition to suppress the friends of general freedom, while those who wish to confine that freedom to the few, are permitted to go on in their principles and practices . . ."[118]

Like Senator Maclay, who had pondered the motivation of those who formed the Order of Cincinnati in the days of the Revolution, Jefferson still believed their fire had not been extinguished, that they had not given up their designs to obtain a "glittering coronet," even a "crown." He stated that he fully "expected to have seen some justification of arming one part of the society against another; of declaring a civil-war *the moment before* the meeting of that body which has the sole right of declaring war . . ."[119]

[117] *Writings*, p. 293. My italics.
[118] *Writings*, p. 294.
[119] *Writings*, p. 296. My italics.

Jefferson was describing here nothing less than a conspiracy aimed at the overthrow of the constitution, the general freedom of the people, and the republic itself. The striking image of Hamilton assuming command of the largest military force assembled since the days of the Revolution would not leave Jefferson's mind. Expressing with rare sarcasm the folly of Hamilton's adventure, he compared his performance to a series by Tom Thumb and Aesop's *Fables*. Jefferson then waited until the end of his letter to remind Madison, "Just so, the fifteen thousand men enter *after* the fables, in the speech."[120]

To Jefferson and Madison those fifteen thousand men were the frightening reality. They knew that Hamilton, poised at the head of an army, potentially a standing army, was capable of declaring a "civil war" despite the authority of Congress. James Callender had noted:

> There was ample time to have assembled Congress. Neville the inspector's house was burnt on the 17th July 1794. The first proclamation by the President was issued on the 7th of August and the second on the 25th of September following. It was not till after the latter date, that the militia were ordered to march. The seven weeks intervening between the two proclamations allowed full time for assembling the legislature. . . . Instead of this legal and practicable measure, the president and Mr. Hamilton walked straight through the constitution, through the privileges of the legislature and the duties of their own respective officers.[121]

Both Madison and Jefferson knew that Hamilton had little regard for the separation of powers, and had demonstrated it. Thus, reflecting upon the character of Hamilton in those cold December evenings of 1794, both Jefferson and Madison must have wondered if Hamilton would activate his conspiracy to overthrow the republic.

They felt he had "hatched" and "plotted."[122] Jefferson sus-

---

[120] *Writings*, p. 296. My italics.

[121] Callender, *Sketches of the History of America*, op. cit., p. 116.

[122] Dr. Johnson's definition of a "conspirator" was one who hatched and plotted. A *Dictionary of the English Language*, Vol. I.

pected his ties with Hammond and the British interests. He believed in Hamilton's loyalty to the "eternal enemy" and his institutions. Madison suspected him of attempting to create a standing army.[123] They both knew he had a thirst for power; that on occasion he used Washington; that he had a military background and no large constituency of his own; that he was sympathetic to the Cincinnati; that he believed men could be governed only by force and corruption. They also thought that Hamilton believed the present republican system wouldn't work and that he looked upon it only as a steppingstone to something else. As they viewed him at the head of an army of fifteen thousand men, they could not help but wonder what that something else was. It was not surprising, then, that they both regarded him as a modern-day Caesar, a man whose perverse genius could overturn the republic.

That genius was now at the height of his power. The chief councils of the government were close to being entirely in his hands. Poised on the banks of the Rubicon, Hamilton would be the one to decide when to cross, when to declare civil war, when to ask aid from Britain, when to risk changing the form of government from a republic to a monarchy, and, finally, when to activate the counterrevolution.

And, if there were any doubt, all that Jefferson had to do was remind Madison of an anecdote that had occurred in his home in April of 1791. A chilling recollection, it would, Jefferson observed, always serve to "delineate Mr. Hamilton's *principles*." After a special cabinet meeting held in Washington's absence, Hamilton, Adams, and Jefferson gathered in the latter's living room to converse. Jefferson speaks:

> The room being hung around with a collection of the portraits of remarkable men, among them were those of Bacon, Newton and Locke, Hamilton asked me who they were. I told him they

[123] Hamilton himself had described the basis for Madison's fear in *Federalist* #8, pp. 67–68. "But standing armies, it may be replied, must inevitably . . . strengthen the executive arm of the government, in doing which their constitutions would acquire a progressive direction towards monarchy."

were my trinity of the three greatest men the world had ever produced, naming them. He [Hamilton] paused for some time: *"the greatest man,"* said he, *"that ever lived, was JULIUS CAESAR!"*[124]

[124] Jefferson to Benjamin Rush, 16 Jan. 1811, *Writings*, Vol. XIII, p. 4. See also *The Spur of Fame*, eds. John A. Schutz and Douglass Adair (San Marino, Calif., 1966), p. 2.

The Principles of the American
and French Revolutions

"That the principles of [the] American [Revolution]
opened the Bastille is not to be doubted."
THOMAS PAINE to GEORGE WASHINGTON, 1 May 1790

One of the most influential political events in America during the
decade of the '90s, the years following Jefferson's return from
France, was undoubtedly the French Revolution. It was so influential that, in Jefferson's words, ". . . the form our own government was to take depended much more on the events of France
than anybody had before imagined."[1]

Keeping this in mind then, we will, in this chapter, examine the
principles of revolution and determine what role they played in
Jefferson's, Paine's, and their colleagues' understanding of the idea
of revolution. In addition, we will review the principal elements of
revolution mentioned in the previous chapters in order to see how
they were refined, rejected, or held constant during the middle
1790s.

None other than John Marshall agreed with Jefferson in his
assessment of the importance of the French Revolution in
America. It was a cataclysmic event, "the admiration, the wonder
and the terror of the civilized world," and it made such an impres-

[1] Jefferson to Thomas Mann Randolph, 7 Jan. 1793, *Writings*, Vol. IX,
p. 13; see also Jefferson to Edmund Randolph, 2 June 1793, ibid., p. 107;
Jefferson to Madison, 29 June 1793, ibid., p. 147.

sion on Americans and how they viewed the idea of revolution that it is impossible to comprehend the Revolution of 1800 without considering its influence. We tend to forget, viewing that event from a distance of nearly two hundred years, that the revolution in France was seen as a direct outgrowth of the American Revolution. And because the character of the French upheaval was so radically different in its violence and social consequences from all prior revolutions, we forget, too, that it had its origins in the *principles* of the American Revolution.

In addition to the drama, the changing nature of the French Revolution, from one extreme to the other, provided an ongoing model *to compare and evaluate the idea of revolution,* especially as it was understood by its American spectators. This is why the French Revolution, when considered in the context of Jefferson's phrase "the Revolution of 1800 was . . . a revolution in . . . principles . . ." assumed such importance in American politics for the next decade.

But to begin our search for the principles of the French and American revolutions we must conduct our investigation in reverse and note the expectations that Americans had of the new developments in France. Thomas Paine, an American in spirit, noted that "the independence of America, considered merely as a separation from England, would have been a matter but of little importance, had it not been accompanied by a revolution in the principles and practise of governments. She made a stand, not for herself only, but for the world, and looked beyond the advantages herself could receive."[2] The American Revolution, it was widely believed, would have repercussions far beyond its borders. This was a belief shared by a few of the crowned heads of Europe as well as Americans. John Paul Jones, for example, reported that the Empress of Russia was "persuaded the American revolution cannot fail to bring about others, and influence every other Government."[3] George Washington regarded the extension of American revolu-

[2] *Paine,* Vol. 4, p. 220.

[3] J. P. Jones to Jefferson, 9 Sept. 1788, *Papers,* Vol. 13, p. 583. See enclosure.

tionary ideas abroad as the dawn of a new epoch: "Indeed, the rights of Mankind, the privileges of the people, and the true principles of liberty seem to have been more generally understood throughout Europe since the American Revolution than they were at any former period."[4]

We have seen how Jefferson personally attempted to influence the progress of the French Revolution. As early as 1788, Jefferson was claiming that France ". . . had been awakened by *our revolution*, they feel their strength, they are enlightened, their lights are spreading and they will not retrograde."[5] Jefferson was joined in his optimism by nearly every citizen in America. One Federalist critic wrote: "In its first stage, but one sentiment respecting it prevailed; and that was a belief . . . that it would . . . promote the happiness of the human race."[6] When, in 1793, the republic was announced, the same critic wrote that "the people of the United States seemed electrified by the measure, and its influence was felt by the whole society."

Even Peter Porcupine, consistently the harshest critic of France in America, recognized the widespread support occasioned by the revolution. Reporting on public reaction to newspaper accounts of the scenes there, he stated "the mad harangues of the National Convention were all translated and circulated through the states. The enthusiasm they excited it is impossible for me to describe."[7]

But Porcupine, while finding it an "impossible" task, nevertheless devoted more space to the revolution than any writer of the times. He quotes an anonymous author to make a picture emerge of the concern for the extension of the principles of "liberty over despotism" by the average American:

> When the French Revolution commenced there were very few republican Americans, perhaps *not one*, but felt a most cordial interest in the event, and anxiously wished it complete success.

---

[4] George Washington to Jefferson, 2 Jan. 1788, *Papers*, Vol. 12, p. 490.

[5] Jefferson to George Washington, 4 Nov. 1788, *Papers*, Vol. 14, p. 330.

[6] Marshall, *The Life of George Washington*, op. cit., Vol. II, p. 250.

[7] William Cobbett, "A Summary View," *Porcupine's Works*, op. cit., Vol. I, p. 98.

It was a revolution of principles, and bid fair to give freedom and happiness to a great nation. Every account which announced its progress was read with pleasure; and aspirations of gratitude to the Supreme Disposer of human affairs, for so signal a triumph of liberty over despotism, issued from every truly American heart.[8]

The reasoning behind this favorable sentiment lay in the extraordinary parallels of principle, strategy, and tactics that were seen initially (and we must note what stage of the French Revolution we refer to) by participants in both revolutions. The parallels in the primacy of politics, in the development of public opinion, in the attempts to prevent violence, the stressing of constitutional forms, elections, the distinction between revolution and war—all dominated the thinking of those who had initiated and even encouraged the revolution in France. One writer, living in England but calling himself "an American," expressed the parallels thus: "Indeed, the Patriots in France pay us too great a compliment speaking of us, as I find they do, *as their model,* and considering themselves as imitating us."[9]

This thinking in parallel had a natural consequence in America. It set off a debate on each of these topics between the former American revolutionaries then in France and their counterparts in America. This was especially true as the nature of revolution in France changed in principle as well as in form. But it is this first point—the concern for principle in revolution—that we must comprehend.

The men who played an important role in the beginning of the French Revolution—Jefferson, La Fayette, Paine, et al.—as well as those, like Gouverneur Morris, who were early observers, all agreed that the principles of the American Revolution gave rise to the French. There were exceptions, of course. Edmund Burke and James Thomson in England and Frederick Gentz of Prussia disagreed, but we will consider their viewpoints later. In 1790, Paine described the fall of the Bastille as "the first ripe [fru]its of American principles transplanted into Europe," and wrote Wash-

---

[8] Ibid., Vol. VII, p. 283.
[9] Richard Price to Jefferson, 3 Aug. 1789, *Papers*, Vol. 15, p. 329.

ington *"that* the principles of [the] American [Revolution] opened the Bastille is not to be doubted."[10] In 1802, Paine wrote that "the principles of it [the French Revolution] were good, they were copied from America."[11] For more than a decade then, Paine's belief in a dependence of principles between the two revolutions held true.

Morris noted, before he changed his views, that "many leaders [of the French Revolution] have imbibed their principles in America, and all have been fired by our example."[12] These principles referred to by Jefferson, Paine, and Morris were, in their words, the continuation of ideas that had been asserted during the American struggle: the Rights of Man, liberty, a republican form of government—in essence, the democratic principles implicit in the Declaration of Independence. Jefferson himself wrote, at the beginning of the French Revolution, "tho' celebrated writers of this and other countries had already sketched good principles on the subject of government, yet the American war seems first to have awakened the thinking part of this nation in general from the sleep of despotism in which they were sunk."[13] Paine had expressed in March of 1791, referring to France, nearly the same sentiments: "I see in America . . . that the principle of its government, which is that of the *equal Rights of Man,* is making a rapid progress in the world."[14]

But what were these revolutionary principles that Paine and Jefferson saw as responsible for the progress of both revolutions? And how, in Paine's mind, did this idea of principle differ from past revolutions? Paine's answer, in language that reflected the sentiments of Jefferson's Declaration, was this:

[10] Paine to George Washington, 1 May 1790, *Papers,* Vol. 16, pp. 530–31.

[11] "Thomas Paine to the Citizens of the United States," 15 Nov. 1802, *Paine,* Vol. 10, p. 94.

[12] Gouverneur Morris to George Washington, 29 April 1789, *The Diary and Letters of Gouverneur Morris,* ed. Anne Cary Morris (New York, 1888), Vol. I, p. 68.

[13] Jefferson to R. Price, 8 Jan. 1789, *Papers,* Vol. 14, p. 420.

[14] *Paine,* Vol. 4, p. 165.

What were formerly called revolutions, were little more than a change of persons, or an alteration of local circumstances. They rose and fell like things of course, and had nothing in their existence or their fate that could influence beyond the spot that produced them. But what we now see in the world, from the revolutions of America and France, is a renovation of the natural order of things, a SYSTEM OF PRINCIPLES as universal as truth and the existence of man, and combining moral with political happiness and national prosperity.

I. Men are born and always continue free and equal in respect to their rights. Civil distinctions, therefore, can be founded only on public utility.

II. The end of all political associations is the preservation of the natural and imprescriptible rights of man; and these rights are liberty, property, security, and resistance of oppression.

III. The Nation is essentially the source of all Sovereignty; nor can any individual or any body of men, be entitled to any authority which is not expressly derived from it.

In these principles, there is nothing to throw a nation into confusion by inflaming ambition. They are calculated to call forth wisdom and abilities, and to exercise them for the public good, and not for the emolument or aggrandizement of particular descriptions of men or families. Monarchical sovereignty, the enemy of mankind, and the source of misery, is abolished; and sovereignty itself is restored to its natural and original place, the nation. Were this the case throughout Europe, the cause of wars would be taken away.[15]

The principles of revolution here are cast in the same mold that we saw previously: mankind versus monarchical sovereignty; freedom and equality versus despotism. Paine's assertion that men have the right of self-government and are therefore the "source of all sovereignty" is, perhaps, his key revolutionary principle. All others, in which man places himself in relation to government, are derived from it.

Paine also recognized a moral dimension to his revolutionary

[15] Ibid., pp. 196–97.

principles when he addressed himself to the "disease that afflicts all mankind," viz., war. Paine recognized the universal concern for peace and morality in a world of power politics. The power to make war was to reside in the people, not in a king or his corrupt ministers. Paine believed that reason would call forth wisdom, which, in turn, would promote the proper ends of the republic or *res publica*, the public thing.

For Paine, the principles of the revolutions in France and America were bound up in the republican ideology he espoused. "In the instance of France," he wrote, "we see a revolution generated in the rational contemplation of the rights of man, and distinguished from the beginning between persons and principles."[16] These rights included an agreement on the dignity of man. There were to be no distinctions between one class of men and another; no artificial divisions based on wealth; no titles of nobility; no tinseled aristocracy. Indeed, this was the principle upon which all governments must be founded: a distinction between arbitrary rule and the rule of law. "Every citizen is a member of the sovereignty, and, as such, can acknowledge no personal subjection; and his obedience can be only to the laws."[17]

What Paine was saying here was in complete agreement with what Jefferson would write in his last letter: ". . . the mass of mankind has not been born with saddles on their back, nor a favored few booted and spurred, ready to ride them legitimately, by the grace of God."[18] Paine's principles, like those in Jefferson's essay "The Earth Belongs to the Living," went to the heart of the state's legal machinery and those mechanisms which had enabled the few to oppress the many for centuries.

Laws based on the principles of separation of church and state, on relief from tithes and the intolerance of state-supported religion, were established to guarantee a universal right of conscience

---

[16] Ibid., p. 21.
[17] Ibid., p. 195.
[18] Jefferson to Roger C. Weightman, 24 June 1826, *The Life and Writings (Selected) of Thomas Jefferson*, ed. Adrienne Koch and William Peden (New York, 1944), pp. 730–31.

to the individual. Paine's idea of the original government compact—*not* between an individual and his sovereign or his government, but between individuals (government came after the people, not before)—was consistent in principle with his views on religion, for it enabled the individual to decide what kind of government he wanted, and thus allowed him to decide how to worship his god. Many people believed Paine, in *The Rights of Man* and, later, in the *Age of Reason*, attempted to eradicate "all sentiments of religion."[19] Thus Paine was attempting to place, as much as possible, the necessity of the individual outside the instrumentality and power of the state. The principles in *The Rights of Man* recognized the basic political nature of man, more so than any other document in the eighteenth century. They were an attempt to place man in a position where he could establish meaningful relationships both in his mode of organizing society and in his social interaction with other men.

After claiming that he had spent twenty years in "the struggle for freedom during the Revolution of the United States of America," Paine wrote, "Liberty and humanity have ever been the words that best expressed my thoughts, and it is my conviction that the union of these two principles, in all cases, tends more than anything also to ensure the grandeur of a nation [the people]."[20] These sentiments were both radical and revolutionary; radical, because they attempted to get to what Paine called the "root problem," and revolutionary, because, Paine believed, once universalized, they were capable of transforming or changing the minds of the entire world.[21]

For Paine, the idea of revolution in France was consistent with his idea of revolution in America. He defined the revolution as ". . . no more than the consequence of a *mental* revolution previ-

[19] An excerpt from Dr. Watson's "Apology for the Bible," *Porcupine's Works*, op. cit., Vol. IV, p. 110.

[20] *Paine*, Vol. 5, p. 312. See Paine's "Address delivered before the Convention on the 19th of January 1793."

[21] See Paine's preface to the French edition (7 May 1791) of *The Rights of Man, Paine*, Vol. 4, p. xxv.

ously existing in France. The *mind of the nation* had changed before hand, and the new order of things had naturally followed the new order of thoughts."[22] Revolution then was, as Adams had stated, "in the minds of the people." Moreover, the change of opinion had become the basis for substantive change in France, even before the *ancien régime* was abolished.

Criticizing Edmund Burke for misunderstanding the nature of the French Revolution, Paine wrote: "It has apparently burst forth like a creation from a chaos [i.e., to Burke] but it is no more than the consequence of a *mental revolution* previously existing in France."[23] Revolution was, upon the basis of being connected with opinions and ideas, to spread so rapidly over the world that those in power could neither anticipate nor prevent them from occurring. "From the revolutions of America and France, and the symptoms that have appeared in other countries, it is evident that the opinion of the world is changed with respect to systems of government, and that revolutions are not within the compass of political calculations. The progress of time and circumstances, which men assign to the accomplishment of great changes, is too mechanical to measure the force of the mind, and the rapidity of reflection, by which revolutions are generated."[24] Later, in a burst of enthusiasm, Paine would say, "It is an age of revolutions, in which everything may be looked for . . ."[25]

Indeed, an age of revolution was bound to produce everything, even critics. And this would be especially true of those points on which Paine had so clearly expressed himself in *The Rights of Man*. A Prussian spokesman for European conservatism, Frederick Gentz, in comparing the French and American revolutions, tried so mightily to separate the two that they might have occurred on different planets. "Never," he wrote, "in the whole course of the American Revolution, were the *Rights of Man* appealed to, for the destruction of the rights of a citizen, never was the sovereignty of

22 Ibid., p. 2.
23 Ibid., p. 4.
24 Ibid., p. 194.
25 Ibid., p. 201.

the people used as a pretext to undermine the respect, due to the laws; . . . no example was ever seen of an individual . . . who recurred to the declaration of rights . . . to renounce obedience to the common sovereign; finally, never did it enter the head of any legislator, or statesman in America, to combat the lawfulness of foreign constitutions, and to set up the American Revolution, as a new epocha . . ."

The French Revolution, on the other hand, "began by a violation of rights, every step of its progress was a violation of rights, and it was never easy, until it had succeeded to establish absolute wrong, as the supreme and acknowledged maxim of a state completely dissolved, and yet existing only in bloody ruins."[26] The French Revolution was "offensive" in its principles; the American "defensive." What he meant by that, of course, was the American Revolution did not appear, *immediately*, to threaten the institutions of monarchy, aristocracy, and the church. "As the American Revolution had exhibited a model of moderation in defense, so the French one displayed an unparalleled example of violence and . . . fury in attack."[27] Gentz could see no connection between the two revolutions, and claimed "an aversion to most of the great statesmen in America to the French Revolution, *and to all what since 1789, has been called revolutionary principles.*"[28]

[26] Frederick Gentz, *The French and American Revolutions Compared*, trans. John Quincy Adams (Berlin, 1800). Reprinted in 1955 by Henry Regnery Co., Chicago, Illinois, pp. 64–65.

[27] Ibid., p. 56.

[28] Ibid., p. 65. John Quincy Adams, then Ambassador to Berlin, translated Gentz's piece into English and later wrote him a note (June 16, 1800) that his article "cannot but afford a gratification to every American attached to his country to see its revolution so ably vindicated from the imputation of having originated, or been conducted upon the same principles, as that of France." *The Writings of John Quincy Adams*, op. cit., Vol. II, p. 463. This comment by John Quincy Adams is rather strange when one reflects upon his father's concern for the principles of revolution. In the essay "Novanglus," written in 1774, John Adams referred to another author's attempts to dismiss the ideas "that all men by nature are equal," "that kings are but the ministers of the people; that their authority is delegated to them by the people, for their good, and they have a right to resume it, and place it in other hands, or keep it themselves,

By condemning categorically all revolutionary principles, Gentz placed his fears in perspective. The old order was threatened by the new republican ideology. Paine ranted and raved against monarchy, aristocracy, and the church, as did Jefferson; and their arguments had gained force when reduced to a set of principles that clarified what the revolution was struggling for. Indeed, Gentz, along with Edmund Burke, was on the opposite side of an argument that drove straight to the heart of the problem of revolution in the late eighteenth century.

Edmund Burke made his argument almost entirely against the "new and hitherto unheard of bill of rights," i.e., the right of a people to frame a government "themselves," "choose their own governors," and "cashier their rulers."[29] Arguing from an attachment to tradition, he totally rejected the idea that a nation had a right to do any of these. Examining the Revolution of 1688 as the archetype of all revolutions, Burke claimed that "the Lords spiritual and temporal, and Commons," pledged to *"submit themselves, their heirs and posterities for ever; and do faithfully promise . . . to maintain, and defend their said majesties . . . to the utmost of their power."*[30] Burke also observed that during the establishment of "the Declaration of Right, the two houses utter[ed] not a syllable of a right to frame a government for themselves."[31]

These were the principles of perpetual monarchy, handed down

---

whenever it is made use of to oppress them." Adams then wrote, *"These are what are called revolution principles.* They are the principles of Aristotle and Plato, of Livy and Cicero, and Sidney and Harrington, and Locke; the principles of nature and eternal reason . . ." "It is therefore astonishing . . . that writers . . . should in this age and country . . . insinuate a doubt concerning them." *Works*, Vol. IV, p. 15. The elder Adams was combating the sophistry of Daniel Leonard, a Massachusetts Tory, and a rebuke certainly would have been in order for his son. Needless to say, these were the basic principles underlying both the American and French revolutions.

[29] Edmund Burke, *Reflections on the Revolution in France* (London, 1790). Dolphin edition, 1961, p. 27.

[30] Ibid., p. 31.

[31] Ibid., p. 44.

to one's "posterities for ever." They also implied an interpretation of the idea of revolution. According to Burke, the Glorious Revolution established the structure of English society for eternity; it successfully produced the *post*revolutionary society. No trauma, no constitutional crisis—no matter how great—would cause the nation to reject the king and frame a new government. Burke believed, without explicitly saying it, that the Revolution of 1688 had placed limitations on reason and the idea of revolution. He also revealed a fundamental misunderstanding of the American Revolution, a cause which he had, at times, defended ably, though within a limited sphere. Burke, in his own words, was devoted to principle; but strangely, he could not grasp the long-range significance of the Declaration of Independence and the principles asserted therein. He felt compelled, like Gentz, to make an artificial separation between the two, to ignore completely any influence that America might have had on France. In fact, Burke did not mention America once in his *Reflections*.[32] In a characteristic passage, Burke "confess[ed] . . . I never liked this continual talk of resistance and revolution, or the practice of making the extreme medicine of the constitution its daily bread."[33] Burke was really saying that his powers of reasoning were to stop at a certain point; that no dialectical process was allowed. He was not interested in the principles of liberty and constitutionalism, nor their relationship to one another. As for the logic of how constitutional grievances were translated into the language of resistance and revolution, that logic was not only uninteresting, it was abhorrent.

[32] Edmund Burke's true reason for writing his *Reflections* was discerned by Peter Porcupine in America: "In England his Majesty's right to the hereditary throne of his ancestors was a commonplace discussion among the clubs of the day. Summoned by such a terrifying necessity, Mr. Burke opposed himself to those flagitious discussions, which would have been (if not combated at that juncture) the heralds of a revolution . . ." *Porcupine's Works,* op. cit., Vol. VII, p. 107.

[33] For an excellent discussion of revolutionary principles during Burke's first years as an MP, see Pauline Maier's *From Resistance to Revolution,* op. cit., pp. 27–48. Her analysis would indicate that Burke's failure to mention America was no oversight.

Paine's answer to Burke was that "it is power and not principles that Mr. Burke venerates . . ."[34] In a perfect echo of Jefferson's essay on the *Living,* Paine took Burke to task: "There never did, there never will, and there never can exist a parliament, or any description of men, or any generation of men, in any country, possessed of the right or the power of binding and controlling posterity to the 'end of time,' or of commanding forever how the world shall be governed . . ." "Every age and generation must be as free to act for itself, *in all cases,* as the ages and generation which preceded it. The vanity and the presumption of governing beyond the grave, is the most ridiculous and insolent of all tyrannies." "Every generation is, and must be, competent to all the purposes which its occasions require. It is the living, and not the dead, that are to be accommodated. . . . I am contending for the rights of the living, and against their being willed away, and controlled and contracted for, by the manuscript assumed authority of the dead; and Mr. Burke is contending for the authority of the dead over the rights and freedom of the living."[35]

Paine's criticism of Burke was a restatement of a portion of Jefferson's letter to Madison on *The Earth Belongs to the Living.*[36] It was an assertion of a new idea of freedom and equality, based on principles that both hoped would enable mankind to destroy despotism. These principles could be expressed symbolically in one of the first acts of the French Revolution: "The fall of the Bastille," said Paine, "included the idea of the downfall of despotism."[37]

Yet another factor of singular importance was beginning to emerge that would disillusion many in their support of the revolution and separate the hard-core revolutionaries from the mere sympathizers. Many who had fought in the American Revolution, and wished to support the French struggle, began to feel uneasy about the increasing violence. Paine attempted to make a clear

[34] *Paine,* Vol. 4, p. 22.
[35] Ibid., pp. 7–8.
[36] See also p. 109 for a discussion of this essay.
[37] *Paine,* Vol. 4, p. 27.

separation between the causes of violence and revolutionary principles. He stated, "These outrages are not the effect of the
principles of the Revolution, but of the degraded mind that
existed before the Revolution, and which the Revolution is calculated to reform. Place them in their proper cause, and take the
reproach of them to your [Burke and the critics] own side."[38]

Becoming somewhat impatient with what he considered irrele-
vant criticism, Paine asked his critics to account for the influence
of human nature in a revolutionary situation:

> While the characters of men are forming, as is always the case in
> revolutions, there is a reciprocal suspicion, and a disposition to
> misinterpret each other; and even parties directly opposite in
> principle, will sometimes concur in pushing forward the same
> movement with different views [motives], and with the hope of
> its producing very different circumstances.[39]

In addition to the idea of forming a basic revolutionary character, what Paine was implying here is a convergence theory of
revolution. He is saying that it is necessary to subordinate ideological disputes to the basic character of the revolution. It is also
necessary to submerge factional, or what would later be interpreted as class, dispositions in the interests of revolution. What
Paine is alluding to is a political organization that transcends the
differences between factions.

Despite the best of intentions, however, many felt by early 1793
that the bloom had faded from the French Revolution. Jefferson,
in particular, felt compelled to convey a measure of stern, fatherly
advice to his young protégé in France, William Short. Admitting
that he felt some "pain" from the tone of Short's letters censuring
the Jacobins, Jefferson conceded that "many guilty persons fell
without the forms of trial, and with them some innocent. . . .
[But] it was necessary to use the arm of the people. . . . *The
liberty of the whole earth* was depending on the issue of the
contest, and was ever such a prize won with so little innocent

blood? . . . rather than it should have failed I would have seen half the earth desolated; were there but an Adam and Eve left in every country, and left free, it would be better than it now is." Censuring Short even further, by noting that several of his diplomatic colleagues had "broken silence" and reported actual "conversations," Jefferson attempted to rationalize Short's behavior for him, assuring his friend that he had "been hurried in a temper of mind which would be extremely disrelished if known to your countrymen." This was harsh language for Jefferson, and at the end of his letter he placed Short on the correct ideological track by saying, "I know your republicanism to be pure . . ."[40] The statement "it was necessary to use the arm of the people" reveals Jefferson's awareness that when a regime's rulers and aristocracy refuse to meet the demands of the people, they must be coerced. In addition, the revolutionaries themselves must be willing, but only as a last resort, to use force, if the liberty of the nation is at stake. They must, however, never lose sight of their principles.

In this instance, Jefferson seemed to believe, like revolutionaries in all ages, that his particular cause—"the liberty of the whole earth"—was at stake. While his tone may sound exaggerated to us, for him it apparently was not. His subsequent statements lead one to believe that his hatred of despotism was so great he had no qualms about seeing "half the earth desolated." This is the perspective either of a fool or of a world revolutionary figure whose concern for the principles of freedom allows him to yield no quarter.[41] One question we might keep in mind, therefore, is this:

[40] Jefferson to William Short, 3 Jan. 1793, *Writings*, Vol. IX, pp. 9–12.

[41] There is some evidence that Jefferson simply refused to believe the accounts of violence in the newspapers as late as May 1794. See Jefferson to Tench Coxe, 1 May 1794, *Writings*, Vol. IX, pp. 284–85. But a kinder explanation might be that Jefferson had simply lost touch with the daily events in France, which in any revolutionary situation is an easy thing to do. In a note to Tobias Lear he wrote, "All my Friends there [in France] have been turned adrift in the different stages of the progression of their Revolution." *Jefferson's Germantown Letters Together with Other Papers Relating to His Stay in Germantown During the Month of November, 1793*, ed. Charles F. Jenkins (Philadelphia, 1906), p. 37. Jefferson to Tobias Lear, 5 Nov. 1793.

If Jefferson believed in 1793 and '94 that the cause of world liberty rested with the revolution in France, how much more so would he believe that the same cause would depend upon America in the years following Napoleon's despotic rise to power?

For Jefferson, the issues of the French Revolution were those of revolutionary principles and ideology. All of this talk about violence rattled him and caused him to become even firmer in his support for the revolution. After writing his letter to Short, he would attempt to give Gouverneur Morris the same advice, but in a more subtle fashion. Noting several of Morris' written reports and the difficulty he was having with the changing leadership in France, Jefferson stated forcefully that "nevertheless, when principles are well understood, their application is less embarrassing."[42] While this may have been Jefferson's way of rationalizing his own support of the revolution, it also reflected his concern that even in America the men who criticized the French Revolution were themselves devoid of revolutionary principles. He said as much to Short when he referred to "some characters of opposite principles, some of them high in office, others possessing great wealth, and all of them hostile to France . . ." "The successes of republicanism in France have given the *coup de grace* to their prospects and I hope to their projects."[43]

When the news that France had "constituted itself as a republic" reached America, it was bound to reinforce Jefferson's enthusiasm despite the flow of blood and criticism. "Be assured, Sir," he wrote Ternant, "that the Government and the citizens of the United States view with the most sincere pleasure every advance of your nation toward its happiness, an object essentially connected with its liberty, and they consider the union of principles and pursuits between our two countries as a link which binds still closer their interests and affections."[44]

Peter Porcupine, writing from America, noted that "as the

---

[42] Jefferson to Gouverneur Morris, 12 March 1793, *Writings*, Vol. IX, p. 36.
[43] Jefferson to William Short, 3 Jan. 1793, ibid., pp. 9–12.
[44] Jefferson to Monsieur de Ternant, 23 Feb. 1793, ibid., p. 32.

[French] Revolution advanced, the enthusiasm increased; but from the moment that the French nation declared itself a REPUB-LIC the enthusiasm was changed to madness. All the means by which this change of government was to be accomplished were totally overlooked; nothing was talked about or dreamed of but the enfranchisement of the world; the whole universe was to become a republic . . ."[45] Writing from Berlin, John Quincy Adams echoed Porcupine's sentiments to his father: "You should be aware that . . . they [the leaders of the French Revolution] have seriously resumed the plan of revolutionizing the whole world . . ."[46] One author, the Englishman James Thomson, wrote in 1799, "The nature and consequence of the [republican] principles which have lately been disseminated over the world . . . are so destructive to the peace of society and so ruinous to human nature, that . . . were the French Revolution to continue for a few years more . . . men would become savages and the earth would be converted into a desert."[47]

There was another view of revolution shared by almost all Americans, not only enthusiastically but as a simple matter of principle. This was the definition of revolution stated by Marbois and it summed up eloquently the prevailing American sentiment: "I define revolution as the advent of law, the resurrection of human rights and the revival of justice."[48] Americans sympathetic with the republican ideology expressed approval of the extension of what they considered their revolution to France and, indeed,

---

[45] *Porcupine's Works,* op. cit., Vol. VIII, p. 154. As time went by and the progress of the French Revolution continued, the arch-conservative Cobbett became completely frustrated. He called for "one grand revolutionary movement to republicanize the infernal regions, and establish a democracy in hell." Vol. XII, p. 129.

[46] John Quincy Adams to John Adams, 13 Aug. 1796, *The Writings of John Quincy Adams,* op. cit., Vol. II, p. 25.

[47] James Thomson, *The Rise, Progress and Consequences of the New Opinions and Principles lately introduced into France* (Edinburgh, 1799), p. 249.

[48] Ellul, *Autopsy of Revolution,* op. cit., p. 71.

the world. And Jefferson was certainly one, if not the leader, of those who understood and foresaw that revolutions would continue. This was, for many, the real meaning of the American Revolution: the beginning of a new age of revolutions. As the news of the terror in France came to America, Jefferson and those like him would rely more and more upon their faith in principles and the necessity of revolutions. To accept the arguments of the critics of France and condemn the revolution itself would have meant giving up the principles of revolution and the reason for them. Jefferson was too principled himself, and basically too revolutionary, to do this.

The fact was Americans generally saw the French Revolution taking the same course and exhibiting the same forms as the American Revolution before it. Jefferson had written Madison about La Fayette's declaration of rights, which, he thought, contained "the essential principles of *ours* accommodated as much as could be to the actual state of things here."[49] That declaration, which essentially stated the principles of the American Revolution, was presented to the king on the 3rd of September, 1791. It stressed, in its opening paragraphs, the architectonic nature of politics. It was felt of primary importance that "acts of the legislative and executive powers of Government," be "capable of being every moment compared with the end of political institutions . . ." The chief concern of the revolutionaries during these first years of the revolution was to guarantee liberty through the most architectonic political structure known to them—a constitution. They were determined to proceed, step by step, in forming a government whose constitutional authority would be presented as a *fait accompli* to a monarch, totally changing the political nature of a regime. Article XVI stated that "society in which the guarantee of rights is not assured, nor the separation of powers, has no constitution."[50]

Jefferson had noted this ascendancy of the politics of revolution

[49] Jefferson to James Madison, 12 Jan. 1789, *Papers*, Vol. 15, pp. 232–33.
[50] Anon., *An Impartial History of the Revolution in France*, 2 vols. (London, 1794), Vol. II, p. 357.

in more than constitutional terms. Judging the temper of a revolutionary state in 1789, he described this scene: "The gay and thoughtless Paris is now become a furnace of Politics. All the world is run politically mad. Men, women, children talk nothing else . . ."[51] To Richard Price he noted, "the press, notwithstanding its shackles, began to disseminate these dictates ['the dictates of common sense and common right']"; "politics became the theme of all societies, male and female and a very extensive and zealous party was formed . . ." "The basis of the present struggle," continued Jefferson, is "the establishment of a constitution which shall assure to them a good degree of liberty. They flatter themselves they shall form a better constitution than the English."[52]

Jefferson gave an indication of how he believed the French could benefit from England's example, especially upon principle. It was Jefferson's hope that France would establish "a real constitution, which cannot be changed by the ordinary legislature; whereas England has no constitution at all; that is to say, there is not one principle of their government which the parliament does not alter at pleasure. The omnipotence of Parliament is an established principle with them."[53] Jefferson, approving the actions of the French revolutionaries, wished to see the rights of man so embedded in a "fixed constitution" that there would be no turning back, no counterrevolution. Only in this manner, slow, cautious, yet deliberate, could the fundamental alterations of power be achieved without massive violence.

After France declared a republican form, Washington would express the same sentiment as Jefferson regarding the relationship between revolution and a constitution. "I rejoice that the interesting revolutionary movements of so many years have issued in the formation of a constitution designed to give permanency to that great object for which you have contended [i.e., liberty]. . . . In delivering to you these sentiments, I express not my own feelings only, but those of my fellow-citizens, in relation to the commence-

[51] Jefferson to Anne W. Bingham, 11 May 1788, *Papers*, Vol. 13, p. 151.
[52] Jefferson to Richard Price, 8 Jan. 1789, *Papers*, Vol. 14, p. 420.
[53] Jefferson to Diodati, 3 Aug. 1789, *Papers*, Vol. 15, p. 327.

ment, the progress and the issue of the French Revolution."[54] This was the American idea of what a revolution must consider as its goal: a constitution, fixed, with the permanent guarantee of liberty for its citizens.

The constitution that was being debated and adopted by the French Assembly was, as far as Jefferson was concerned, revolutionizing the country in the manner that the original republican constitutions had in America. The objects the Assembly sought to guarantee were the same ones that Jefferson had sought to guarantee in Virginia: "a free press," "a habeas corpus law," "the rights to periodical convocation of the States," "their exclusive right to raise and appropriate money," a "participation in legislation," a "right to propose amendments," "infallibly end[ing] in a right of origination . . ."[55] The only principles lacking, according to Jefferson, were "trial by jury" and the abolishment of "a standing army."

This was a definition of the politics of revolution in principle: the coordination of ideology and institutions adapted to the changing needs of a revolutionary society. It meant involving a wide spectrum of people in novel political organizations that enabled them to become educated and prepared for political action. Ultimately, it involved dealing with those forces and institutions directly responsible for implementing a constitution. Another way of describing Jefferson's analysis would be to say that the politics of revolution finds its peculiar mode of organization and then "inevitably channels itself into institutions and constitutions."[56]

This kind of organization was not surprising to Americans, least of all to William Cobbett. "Let it never be forgotten," he wrote, "that the opinions and the systems, which have shaken Europe to its very centre, had their rise in America. . . . Not only the prin-

[54] George Washington to P. A. Adet, French Minister to the United States, in *Porcupine's Works,* op. cit., Vol. VIII, pp. 70–71. See also Alexander Hamilton to William Short, 5 Feb. 1793, *The Works of Alexander Hamilton,* op. cit., Vol. X, p. 32.

[55] Jefferson to Richard Price, 8 Jan. 1789, *Papers,* Vol. 14, p. 420.

[56] Ellul, *Autopsy of Revolution,* op. cit., p. 54.

ciples, but the mode of proceeding also, were copied from the Americans. *Declarations of Rights, Committees of Safety, Committees of Secrecy, Requisitions, Confiscations, Assignats, Mandates, etc., were they not all borrowed from America?"*[57]

Paine himself related that, by late 1789,

> societies were formed in Paris, and committees of correspondence and communication established throughout the nation, for the purposes of enlightening the people and explaining to them the principles of civil government; and so orderly was the election of the first National Assembly conducted that it did not give rise even to the rumor of tumult.[58]

Cobbett, who feared a revolution in England, saw the same forms that had pointed to the revolution in France springing up in America.[59] Or at least he expressed that fear. Quoting a congressman in 1797, he satirized: "The gentleman might have mentioned a great many other instances, in which the French revolutionists have observed a close imitation of the old Congress of America. Their committees of secrecy, of public safety (salut publique): their intriguing with the people of other countries; their various and varying addresses; their being appointed to produce conciliation, and their rendering conciliation impossible; and many other things, in which I presume Mr. Blount would not wish them to find imitators in the present Congress."[60]

[57] *Porcupine's Works,* op. cit., Vol. XII, p. 137.

[58] *Paine,* Vol. 4, pp. 124–25.

[59] A New England clergyman, Jedidiah Morse, would see the same development taking place. He told his congregation that "the Jacobin Clubs, instituted by Genet, were a formidable engine for the accomplishment of the designs of France to subjugate this country. They started into existence by a kind of magic influence, in all parts of the United States, from Georgia to New Hampshire, and being linked together by correspondence, by constitutional ties, and . . . by oaths, . . . they acted upon one plan, in concert, and with an ultimate reference to the same grand objects. . . . And," he added, "there is reason to believe their intention was . . . to produce a 'general explosion' or, in other words, a *revolution* in our country . . ." A *Sermon on the Anniversary of Thanksgiving in Massachusetts,* 29 Nov. 1798 (Boston, 1798), p. 67.

[60] *Porcupine's Works,* op. cit., Vol. VI, p. 187.

Indeed, these forms had been seen by the Americans and they knew what they meant. Jefferson would refer to them collectively as signs of the spirit of '76. Obviously, these same forms of organization gave rise to enormous amounts of energy in France. As Paine indicated, they made it possible to coordinate the activities of men in committees and clubs with elections that decided national questions. This "mode of proceeding" then, which produced results in the early years of the American and French revolutions, became for Jefferson and most Americans a model of revolutionary organization. This was the mode to be imitated, with adaptations, of course, for anyone attempting to revolutionize a nation.[61]

The "favorable issue" of revolution depended upon the mode of organization, plus the strength of a fixed constitution attained. The mode was, theoretically, nonviolent. The basic distinction made between potential violence and the progress of a "constitutional revolution" was how both related to great national questions. According to Jefferson and most of his associates, instances of violence based on local needs not affecting the entire citizenry only disrupted the revolution and distracted the people.[62] Jeffer-

[61] This was recognized by a few discerning Tories even before the outbreak of the American Revolution. Daniel Leonard of Massachusetts wrote in 1772, referring to the committees of correspondence: "This is the foulest, subtlest, and most venemous serpent ever issued from the egg of sedition. I saw the small seed when it was implanted; it was a grain of mustard. I have watched the plant until it has become a great tree." In Link's *Democratic-Republican Societies, 1790–1800,* op. cit., p. 30. Peter Porcupine echoed the same sentiments twenty-five years later. For him, the Jacobin clubs in France were, like the committees of correspondence, a prelude to revolution. "The Jacobin Club is the source of power, and those who lead it govern France. It keeps up an intimate correspondence with all the inferior clubs in the different departments, and takes care that they shall be formed of none but . . . inhabitants entirely devoted to itself. It is the seat of information and gives what impression it pleases . . ." *Porcupine's Works,* op. cit., Vol. V, pp. 192–93.

[62] Jefferson to Madison, 11 May 1789, *Papers,* Vol. 15, p. 121; Jefferson to Benjamin Vaughan, 14 Sept. 1789, ibid., p. 426; Jefferson to Ralph Izard, 18 Sept. 1789, ibid., p. 445.

son firmly believed a revolution could be advanced by the "wheedling and intimidation" of leaders in a parliamentary body, as in the case of the National Assembly. But the intimidation would be calculated always to fall short of force.[63] If any rough spots occurred in the transition of power from an aristocracy to the representatives of the people, especially within an assembly, France should follow the example of America in her "second revolution." "You must have observed, when in America," Jefferson had written dal Verme earlier, "that time and trial had discovered defects in our federal constitution. A new essay, made in the midst of the flames could not be perfect."[64] This concern for the reasoned, steady growth of a constitution was Jefferson's way of suggesting a remedy to a constitutional defect. And it was why he felt it necessary to grasp the principles of the politics of revolution. Indeed, "a political revolution," Jefferson's protégé in France echoed, "may be considered effected so far as it relates to the transfer of all power into the hands of the representatives of the people . . ."[65] If a revolution resulted in despotism, or in uncontrollable violence, Jefferson would have considered it a disaster.

Jefferson's protégé turned against the revolution in France after his mentor's departure, and like him, many Americans began to change their opinions as the revolution in France turned away from republicanism and toward the despotism of Napoleon. The enthusiastic response of Americans in the formation of Democratic clubs and Jacobin societies[66] began tailing off by 1794, especially after Washington officially denounced them as "self-created societies."[67] Tricolored cockades, once the badge of

---

[63] Jefferson to John Jay, 17 June 1789, *Papers*, Vol. 15, p. 190.

[64] Jefferson to Francis dal Verme, 15 Aug. 1787, *Papers*, Vol. 12, p. 42.

[65] William Short to John Jay, 30 Nov. 1789, *Papers*, Vol. 16, p. 3.

[66] See Link, *Democratic-Republican Societies, 1790–1800*, op. cit., pp. 13–15, for a complete list of the societies.

[67] *Messages and Papers of the Presidents*, op. cit., Vol. I, p. 155. See Washington's Sixth Annual Address, 19 Nov. 1794.

French sympathy, appeared less frequently in the streets and among the social gatherings of communities. Where toasts to "Paine and revolution forever" were once common, in their stead was found a well-regulated reserve.[68] Liberty poles, symbolic of French support, were publicly torn down or disappeared. The antics of a French ambassador, Edmund Genet, had soured many Americans;[69] while the depredations of French privateers against American commerce alienated even more.[70]

The bitterness over the progress of the French Revolution extended into the innermost recesses of Washington's cabinet.[71] According to one commentator, the divisions had become so great that "the President, [during] the whole tenor of his [last] administration was bitterly and incessantly inveighed against as hostile to liberty. The logic of democracy was extremely compendious, and therefore the more satisfactory to superficial inquirers. On the one hand it pointed to *republican* France; on the other, to a combination of despots—and this was enough. In so interesting a struggle, could any friend to his kind be neutral! And the inference was, that they who were not for France, were against her, and monarchists, tories, and tyrants of course. The name of England, too, was well calculated to rouse old resentments . . ."[72] Additionally, an increased polarization of opinion created factions within Congress and state legislatures over the leveling principles of the French Revolution. And many saw the principle of equality—applied to all forms—as an attempt to abolish religious worship.

[68] Link, *Democratic-Republican Societies, 1790–1800,* op. cit., p. 196.

[69] Jefferson to Gouverneur Morris, 16 Aug. 1793, *Writings,* Vol. IX, pp. 180–209.

[70] John Adams gives a vivid description of the problems with France in a "Special Session Message to the Senate and House of Representatives," 16 May 1797, in *Messages and Papers of the Presidents,* op. cit., Vol. I, pp. 223–29.

[71] John Quincy Adams, *The Lives of James Madison and James Monroe* (Boston, 1850), pp. 243–45; see also Jefferson's *The Anas, Writings,* Vol. I, pp. 281 ff.

[72] *Alexander Graydon's Memoirs of His Own Time,* op. cit., p. 382.

But the real culprit was violence. Americans were treated to the spectacle of violence on a scale never before dreamed of. Leaders fell almost daily. Those who attempted to act moderately were victims as easily as those who demanded excessive and ruthless policies. Mirabeau had noted the spirit of the times in a casual fashion: "In revolutions the distance was small between the Capitol and the Tarpeian Rock."[73] This seemed an understatement. To Americans, unused to prolonged terror and bloodshed, the carnage seemed unreasonable. While they had seen terror, bloodshed, and guerrilla warfare in the southern colonies and between Loyalists and Rebels in New England, nevertheless they had witnessed nothing like the wholesale bloodletting that characterized the revolution in France.

A description of revolutionary gore in Lyons, France, is typical of the articles written by William Cobbett and those who detested the revolution. Cobbett, whose flair for colorful language was surpassed by no other editor of his time, called forth all his rhetorical powers: "Reader!" he screamed, "fix your eyes on this theatre of carnage. You barbarous, you ferocious monsters!"

Accordingly, next day, the execution *in mass* began. The prisoners were led out, from a hundred to three hundred at a time, into the outskirts of the city, where they were fired upon or stabbed. One of these massacres deserves a particular notice. Two hundred and sixty-nine persons, taken indiscriminately among all classes and all ages . . . were tied to trees . . . they were fired upon with grape shot. . . . Numbers of these unfortunate had only their limbs broken by the artillery; these were dispatched with the sword or the musket. The greatest part of the bodies were thrown into the Rhone, some of them before they were quite dead; two men in particular, had strength enough to reach the opposite bank of the river. One would have thought, that thus saved as it were by a miracle, the vengeance of their enemies would have pursued them no farther; but, no sooner were they perceived, than a party

[73] "The Works of Mirabeau," *American Quarterly Review* (Paris, 1830), p. 437.

of the dragoons of Lorraine crossed the arm of the river and stabbed them, and left them a prey to the fowls of the air.[74]

It was not that every newspaper editor deliberately set out to turn the tide of American opinion for or against the idea of revolution in France. It was simply that then, as now, the violence—which became such a sensational part of the revolution—was good copy. Porcupine, one of the exceptions, was in the forefront of those denouncing the revolution. His real ambition was to begin a worldwide reactionary movement, attacking the idea of revolution in every country. He was not concerned with just a few nations abroad. As the furor arose over the Jay Treaty, and the possibility of war with Great Britain became real, he expressed the fear that America herself would become revolutionized: "The moment a war should be declared, in consequence of the rejection of the treaty, the Constitution would be thrown aside as useless lumber. A revolutionary state must succeed."[75]

This became the real fear of those opposed to the French Revolution: the influence that it would have in America. Porcupine had noted shrilly that "the elections that have lately taken place (1796) have proved that the *French faction is increasing.* There are to be found, in every beer-house, scores of fellows, who will not only justify the French in all they have done, but will tell you flat and plain, that they would *join them,* if they were to land in the country."[76]

Even such a calm observer of the political scene as Alexander Hamilton could see events from Porcupine's perspective:

> Symptoms of the too great prevalence of this system [the French revolutionary system] in the United States are alarmingly visible. It was by its influence that efforts were made to embark this country in a common cause with France . . . to induce our government to sanction and promote her odious principles. . . . It is

[74] *Porcupine's Works,* op. cit., Vol. II, pp. 126–27. This excerpt was taken from literally dozens of pages of like descriptions and was published separately as *A Bone to Gnaw.*

[75] *Porcupine's Works,* op. cit., Vol. VIII, p. 364.

[76] Ibid., Vol. VII, p. 305.

by its influence that every succeeding revolution has been approved or excused; all the horrors that have been committed justified . . . even the last usurpation, which contradicts all the ostensible principles of the Revolution has been regarded with complacency, and the despotic constitution engendered by it slyly held up as a model not unworthy of our imitation.[77]

Fisher Ames, a few years later, would sum up the revolutionary fears of the Federalists: ". . . for the French Revolution has been, from the first, hostile to all right and justice . . . and therefore, its very existence has been a state of warfare against the civilized world, and most of all against free and orderly republics, for such are never without factions, ready to be allies of France, and to aid her in the work of destruction."[78] Ames's point was really that which all other Federalists feared: the politics of revolution in France was beginning to make its appearance in America.

That the French played politics in America cannot be doubted. "The tyranny of the Robespierian principles were calculated to inveigle within the vortex of European politics, the American government and people."[79] By 1795, the attitude of many Americans, in the spirit of the French Revolution, had become rebellious. The aftermath of the Whiskey Rebellion prompted many to raise questions about the number of revolutionaries returning to this country from France. William Cobbett produced an insight that even he did not grasp the full meaning of: "I do not say that they had any immediate hand in the Western affair: but when rebels from every quarter of the world are received with open arms, as persecuted patriots, it is no wonder that rebellion should be looked upon as Patriotism."[80] Indeed, rebellion, equated with patriotism, was fast becoming a national mood.

Many Americans, despite their rebellious mood, believed the Directory was interfering unjustifiably in American affairs. Le

[77] "Fragment on the French Revolution," no date, *The Works of Alexander Hamilton,* op. cit., Vol. VII, p. 377.
[78] Ames, *Works of Fisher Ames,* op. cit., p. 126.
[79] *Suppressed History,* p. 303.
[80] *Porcupine's Works,* op. cit., Vol. II, p. 15.

Tombe,[81] the French consul in Philadelphia, attempted to implement a policy formulated by the Directory, whose chief end was the separation of the people from their government.[82] But that policy had been long in formation. When Charles Cotesworth Pinckney succeeded James Monroe as the ambassador to France, Louis-Guillaume Otto, the former chargé d'affaires in the United States, termed it "the most unpardonable . . . of all the . . . blunders" between both sides in "six years." Pinckney never met with Talleyrand, the French foreign minister, after Monroe's departure. And Delacroix, a spokesman for the ministry, told Monroe that France could "no longer recognize or receive a minister plenipotentiary from the United States" until a "reparation of grievances was made."[83]

Calmer voices and deeper insight could not prevail. Otto, respected by most Americans and a man with considerable experience in America, was ignored by Talleyrand and the Directory. Considering his government's policy toward America, Otto based his advice on more than mere diplomatic blundering. According to him, French policy was based on a fundamental misunderstanding of American politics. Here Otto confirms Jefferson's idea of the one-party state:

> Our agents wished to see only two political parties in the United States, the French party and the English party; but there is a middle party, much larger, composed of the most estimable men of the two other parties. Their party, whose existence we have not even suspected, is the American party, which loves its country above all and for whom preferences either for France or England are only accessory and often passing affections.[84]

[81] Le Tombe became French consul general in May 1797, taking over P. A. Adet's functions.

[82] Wilson E. Lyon, "The Directory and the United States," *American Historical Review*, Vol. 43 (1938), p. 523.

[83] Otto to James Monroe, 20 March 1797, in Lyon, op. cit., p. 517.

[84] "Considerations sur la conduite du Gouvernement des États-Unis envers la France depuis 1789 jusque 1797, messidor, an 5, June 19–July 18, 1797, par M. Otto, AA.E, États-Unis, Vol. 47, ff. 401–418," quoted in Lyon, op. cit., p. 414.

Ignoring Otto's advice, Talleyrand sent "propaganda documents" during the XYZ affair to Le Tombe, "with instructions to give it all possible publicity."[85] Yet this was all in character. The appeals of the French minister Genet, over the heads of the Washington administration, are well known.[86] The intrigues of Fauchet and Adet were equally shocking to many Americans. One Federalist, Stephen Higginson, wrote: "I often think that the Jacobin faction will get the administration of our government into their hands ere long. . . . Foreign intrigues will unite with the disaffected and disappointed, with seekers after places, with ambitious, popular demagogues and the vicious and corrupt of every class."[87]

When it came to understanding the motives behind French policy, perhaps John Quincy Adams had the most rational view of it all. He told his mother that Talleyrand's approach "was the result of a system of policy much more ancient than their Revolution—the system of connecting the French influence with the party in that country opposed to the existing government. This system was not always followed from a pure and disinterested love of liberty. . . . This policy was not even peculiar to the French monarchy. It is the policy natural between a great state and a small one; it is founded deep in the human character, and all history is full of it, in ancient as well as modern times."[88] John Quincy Adams was referring, of course, to the time-honored dictum of power politics: *divide et impera*.

The use of the media was equally feared by the conservatives as an instrument of subversion. Cobbett was typical of those who appealed to base emotions in an attempt to discredit his fellow

[85] Lyon, op. cit., p. 523.

[86] John Marshall, *The Life of George Washington*, op. cit., pp. 260–77. See especially Jefferson to Gouverneur Morris, 16 Aug. 1793, *Writings*, Vol. IX, pp. 180–209.

[87] Stephen Higginson to Timothy Pickering, 14 July 1795, "Letters of Stephen Higginson," *American Historical Association Report* (1896), pp. 787–88.

[88] John Quincy Adams to Abigail Adams, 27 June 1798, *The Writings of John Quincy Adams*, op. cit., p. 324.

editors. Indeed, his bombastic rhetoric was to become standard fare among demagogues then and in the future:

> The editors, perceiving the partiality of the most *numerous* class of their subscribers for this revolution, and all the novel and wild principles it has given rise to, have been seduced, by the love of gain, to flatter that partiality, by extolling those principles at the expense of everything, their own private interests excepted. Their papers, which swarm like summer flies, are become the vehicles of falsehood in place of truth, of ignorance in place of knowledge. Like the tenebriscous stars mentioned by a celebrated author, they shed darkness instead of light.
>
> A veil has been carefully drawn over the distresses and horrors resulting from the anarchical system of France; or, when this could not be done, when the editors have feared to be anticipated by their fellow laborers, they have endeavored to outvie each other in apologies for what ought to have been held up to detestation, or, at least, as an awful lesson to ourselves. Every one, even of the most destructive acts of that pretended republic, has been trumpeted forth as the effect of a liberal and enlightened policy . . .[89]

The French were so diabolical that they were using, in addition to committees of correspondence, clubs, and the newspapers, one of the notorious devices of the American Revolution: the post office. A "letter from Rhode Island" complained that: "There are two fellows from Vermont, setting up a printing-office in this town, in the cursed line of your infernal Bache. One I hear just commenced in Connecticut. This is the way the French intend oversetting our government; and unless honest men attend less to their business, and more to the general welfare, they will accomplish their ends. The Post-master General ought to have a strict eye on the post-offices throughout the United States: there are a number of them altogether in the French interest, and do much mischief . . ."[90]

Talleyrand, who had recently spent time in America, believed

[89] *Porcupine's Works,* op. cit., Vol. VIII, p. 4.
[90] Ibid., p. 165.

that the French faction was capable of influencing, perhaps even controlling, domestic politics. In the dispatches submitted to the government on the XYZ affair, it was revealed that Mr. "Y" told the American delegates (Elbridge Gerry, John Marshall, and C. C. Pinckney): "Perhaps, you believe that in returning and exposing to your countrymen the unreasonableness of the demands of this government, *you will unite them in their resistance to those demands:* you are mistaken: you ought to know that the diplomatic skill of France and the means she possesses in your country, are sufficient to enable her, with the French party in America, to throw the blame which will attend the rupture of the negotiations on the Federalists . . ."[91]

Such language was not only calculated to overawe the Americans, it was based on France's assessment of the domestic political situation in the United States. In a supposed profession of friendship, but knowing full well that any further negotiation would be delayed at least a year, Talleyrand revealed the attitude that France had held all along: "The government of the United States believed that France wished to revolutionize it; France believed that the government of the United States wished to throw itself into the arms of England."[92]

The negotiations that Talleyrand hinted would "soon" result in an "accord" proved elusive. More than a year and a half would lapse before "the Convention of 1800" was signed between the two nations. In the meantime the continuing French Revolution would cause consternation and bitterness among the factions in American politics.

Those who were cynical, who could see nothing of value in the changing nature of the revolution, who, perhaps, never truly understood what the revolution was about—even from an American viewpoint—were wont to reduce that struggle to a domestic political club. Among those was Alexander Graydon, the Pennsyl-

[91] Excerpts from the official dispatches. *Porcupine's Works*, op. cit., Vol. IX, pp. 103–4.

[92] Talleyrand to William Vans Murray, 15 Aug. 1798, in Lyon, op. cit.. p. 530.

vania Federalist: "The French Revolution then, . . . it is fair to conclude, was less beloved by them [the Jeffersonians] for any philanthropic disposition it manifested, than from its being an engine wherewith to assail its adversaries in power; and it was so much the better adapted to this purpose, as it was in conflict with Britain, that accursed island . . ."[93] Thus, Graydon recognized a conspiracy; only, in his eyes, it was a domestic one, having more to do with political partisanship than revolution.

Other Federalists, notably Fisher Ames, could excoriate the French Revolution in purple prose, but could also, on occasion, demonstrate an understanding of what was at stake. Making a connection between the causes of the American Revolution and the French, Ames condenses into one paragraph the understanding of most Americans on both sides of the political spectrum:

> The American Revolution was, in fact, after 1776, a resistance to foreign government. We claimed the right to govern ourselves, and our patriots never contemplated . . . that a mob should govern us. It is true, that the checks on the power of the people themselves were not deemed so necessary, as on the temporary rulers whom we elected: we looked for danger on the same side, where we had been used to look [i.e., faction]. . . . [By contrast] The French Revolution has been made the instrument of faction; it has multiplied popular errors, and rendered them indocile. Restraints on the power of the people, seem to all democrats, foolish, for how shall they restrain themselves? And mischievous, because, as they think, the power of the people is their liberty. Restraints, that make it less, and, on every inviting occasion for mischief and the oppression of a minority, make it nothing, *will appear to be the abandonment of its principles and cause.*[94]

Ames, like Paine, was pointing out the role of faction in destroying a concern for principle. Making a distinction between revolution and war against a foreign government, Ames implied that Americans, while acting on the principle of limiting government

---

[93] *Alexander Graydon's Memoirs of His Own Time*, op. cit., p. 363.
[94] Ames, "Equality II," *Works of Fisher Ames*, op. cit., pp. 234–35.

and its rulers, nevertheless imposed constitutional restraints upon themselves. The French partisans, on the other hand, were incapable of restraint, and gave themselves over entirely to their factional instincts. In the process, it appeared, they had abandoned the republican principles so carefully inculcated by Jefferson and Paine.

This sentiment was echoed by one who had witnessed the excesses of the revolution firsthand. James Monroe saw the tragic role that the opposition played in carrying the revolution to an extreme. Minority factions split the republican majority in the National Assembly until that majority consumed itself in terror, brought on the despotism of Napoleon, and eventually—in a true counterrevolution—the restored monarchy.

Other Americans had also begun to perceive the tragedy in France. As early as 1796, Patrick Henry warned his friends in Virginia: "I should not be surprised if the very man at whose victories you now rejoice, should *Caesar-like, subvert the liberties of his country.*"[95] Expressions such as these signaled a complete abandonment of principle, without which a revolution would slide backward. Because the French had failed to unite the nation and have their gains perpetuated by degrees in the constitution, the revolution *had* failed. Paradoxes abounded: the greater the violence, the less self-discipline was imposed; no sooner was one aspect of despotism destroyed than, suddenly, the threat of total despotism seemed even greater; the more the French did to establish the Rights of Man, the less secure they became; and the more that was done to destroy the centralized power of the monarchy, the greater became the consolidated power of the revolution.

The climax of these contradictions, as seen by Jefferson and his friends, was that an entirely new set of problems had arisen. Revolution suddenly had the opposite effect from that which was intended. The primacy of the state was enhanced at the expense of the individual. If revolution proceeded too fast and too soon, it destroyed whatever opportunities it had to guarantee liberty and

[95] Henry, *Patrick Henry*, op. cit., Vol. II, p. 576. Italics mine.

conserve principles. Jefferson had noted in 1790 that "the ground of liberty is to be gained by inches. . . . We must be contented to secure what we can get, from time to time, and eternally press forward for what is yet to get. It takes time to persuade men to do even what is for their own good."[96]

The means to gain that liberty, consistent with its spirit and with its purposes, had been in existence in the early part of the revolution. The constitution that had been presented to the king in 1791 had been the herald of a new value system. Destroying the oppressive feudal aristocracy of the *ancien régime*, it ushered in a new system of relationships, transforming completely the French citizen's notion of himself and his society. "In contemplating the French constitution," wrote Paine, in 1790, "we see in it a rational order of things. The principles harmonize with the forms, and both with their origin. It may perhaps be said as an excuse for bad forms, that they are nothing more than forms; but this is a mistake. Forms grow out of principles, and operate to continue the principles they grow from. It is impossible to practise a bad form on any thing but a bad principle. It cannot be ingrafted on a good one; and whenever the forms in any government are bad, it is a certain indication that the principles are bad also."[97]

The emphasis was placed equally upon both principle and form. The two were interconnected in a way that Jefferson, as well as Paine, understood was essential for liberty. A revolution that began upon republican principles must assume a republican form in its constitution and its governing administration. If not, the two would lack harmony and the one or the other, and ultimately both, would become corrupt. This was as true for America as it had been for France. And for Americans, the Consulate was a vivid example. As the years passed by, and the revolution in France went through its successive changes, Paine saw the implications for liberty in dark and disillusioned terms.

[96] Jefferson to Rev. Charles Clay, 27 Jan. 1790, *Papers*, Vol. 16, p. 129.
[97] *Paine*, Vol. 4, p. 103.

Three years later, Paine would write Jefferson underscoring the concern for principles that occupied their attention: "Had this revolution been conducted consistently with its principles, there was once a good prospect of extending liberty through the greatest part of Europe; but I now relinquish that hope."[98]

Jefferson himself made a connection between the form and principle of revolution in America and how they differed from the issue of the French Revolution. In a letter to Tracy, in 1811, he stated, "The republican government of France was lost *without a struggle* because the party of 'un et indivisible' had prevailed; no provincial organizations existed to which the people might rally under authority of the laws, the seats of the Directory were virtually vacant, and a small force sufficed to turn the legislature out of their chamber, and to salute its leader chief of the nation."[99]

Because the revolutionary party had become so powerful, its very slogan—used to achieve power—denied that there might be a division of power. Indeed, there was no possibility of a reversal of power to the people. The principle of liberty for "the people" had been usurped by the central government. As Jefferson implied, no institutions existed in which an alternative locus of power remained. All political power and authority had been concentrated in the Directory and, later, consolidated in the Consulate.

By comparison, the American revolutionaries had been wiser. Jefferson remarked in 1811 that "the true barriers of our liberty in this country are the State governments; and the wisest conservative power ever contrived by man, is that of which our Revolution and present government found us possessed. Seventeen distinct States, amalgamated, regularly organized . . . [by] the choice of a free people, and enlightened by a free press, can never be so fascinated by the arts of one man, as to submit voluntarily to his usurpation. Nor can they be constrained to it by any force he can possess.

[98] Thomas Paine to Jefferson, 20 April 1793, *Writings of Thomas Paine*, ed. Moncure D. Conway, 3 vols. (New York, 1895), Vol. III, pp. 132–33.
[99] Jefferson to Monsieur Destutt De Tracy, 26 Jan. 1811, *Writings*, Vol. XIII, p. 20.

While that may paralyze the single State in which it happens to be encamped, sixteen others . . . rise up on every side, ready organized for deliberation by a constitutional legislature, and for action by their governor, constitutionally the commander of the militia of the State . . ."[100]

This was a "constitutional prescription" for revolution if the need arose, or if a usurper attempted to overthrow the liberties of the people. Jefferson's description of the French Assembly, "virtually vacant," and of the French provinces, without legal organizations that had reserved powers under the law, is juxtaposed to the state legislatures in America with their powers to unite under legal auspices in rebellion against the national government. Jefferson's greatest fear was that, like France, the federal government of the United States would "consolidate" all power unto itself.[101]

This principle, i.e., a decentralized organization of states opposing a consolidation of power by a central government, was so important to Jefferson and his colleagues that they were willing to tolerate its contradictions: "to wit, that certain states . . . might attempt to secede from the Union." Jefferson noted, "This is certainly possible, and would be befriended by this kind of regular organization. But . . . if they should ever reach the majority of states they would then become the regular government . . ."[102] This was the principle that many saw could potentially lead to a confrontation like the American Civil War.

But this was also the one principle that could continue to legitimate a dynamic, changing society. It was a principle consistent with Jefferson's notion of a permanent, constitutional revolution. When the governing elite became unrepresentative, the states individually, and then reaching a majority, would validate

[100] Ibid., p. 19.

[101] Jefferson to Judge William Johnson, 12 June 1823, *Writings*, Vol. XV, p. 444. "I have been blamed for saying, that a prevalence of the doctrines of consolidation would one day call for reformation or *revolution*." See also Jefferson to Robert J. Garnett, 14 Feb. 1824, *Writings*, Vol. XVI, p. 14.

[102] Jefferson to Monsieur Destutt De Tracy, 26 Jan. 1811, *Writings*, Vol. XIII, pp. 20–21.

the revolution. The implication of this theory, applied to the states, could also be applied to the individual. Through the constitutional process, the individual could make a conscious, legitimate choice for or against revolution.

Indeed, as we view the consolidation argument posed by Jefferson as a threat to American liberty, and as we see his argument for the necessity of constitutionally reserved powers to enable states to resist national encroachments, we may better understand his concern for the purity of both principle and form. We may also clearly understand the idea of revolution that Jefferson propounded. In terms of that idea, which we have been discussing, Jefferson saw the necessity of maintaining a form that would allow and facilitate resistance but, at the same time, be consistent with the principle of revolution. This was essential for one basic purpose: to prevent counterrevolution. Learning his lesson from that "abortive" experiment abroad, Jefferson was determined that France's loss of liberty would not be duplicated in America. Indeed, as Paine's letter signaled the death of liberty in Europe, Jefferson's commitment to the idea of revolution deepened: America would not lose hers "without a struggle."

Paine, in the despair of his imprisonment in Paris, could express his loss of hope for liberty and at the same time begin writing his celebrated *Age of Reason*. A world revolutionary figure, he could not believe that man was destined to live in perpetual terror and oppression. As he languished in his cell, the very symbol of a man deprived of his civil and personal liberties, he held onto his dream: the establishment of a society in which "liberty and humanity" were denied to none.[103]

His colleague in America was cut from the same mold. In 1836, a friend described the importance that the French Revolution had for Jefferson. But more important, he explained why it was that the idea of revolution in America and in France had become "fixed forever as the ruling bias of his mind."

---

[103] "Address before the Convention, 19 January 1793," *Paine*, Vol. 5, p. 312.

In giving his approbation, his sympathy . . . to the earliest movements of the French Revolution, he found himself sustained by
the unanimous consent of all the men whose opinions could
with him be supposed to possess much value. Was it unnatural
then, that, under these circumstances, the tendency to popular
principles of government, which he carried with him to Europe,
should have been confirmed and fixed forever as the ruling bias
of his mind? Is it necessary to suppose him either imbecile,
corrupt or perverse, if, under these circumstances, he continued
to dwell habitually upon the existing abuses of Power, rather
than the possible abuses of Liberty? Is it just to represent him
as feeling, thinking, or acting under French influence, when he
was simply pursuing the same line of feeling, thought and action
as before, and was, in fact, himself one of the principal channels
through which the people of this country were . . . exercising
upon France that American influence . . .[104]

If, as noted, Jefferson believed in 1793–94 that the cause of
world liberty rested with the revolution in France, he must have
believed by 1797 that the future of liberty in the world rested in
America. And if, as Jefferson noted, the form and principles of
government in America were to be influenced by the future of the
revolution in France, he must have been more determined than
ever that a conspiracy against liberty in this country should never
succeed.

That same friend ended his "Defense of Mr. Jefferson" in 1836
on this theme: "The object of Mr. Jefferson, through life, was
. . . to increase and extend the influence of the great principle of
LIBERTY, to which he had attached his faith, and which formed, as
it were, his religion." It was a good ending because it cut straight
to the heart of the meaning of Jefferson's life. Jefferson's "religion" required a constant devotion to the principles of liberty and,
implicitly, to the principles of revolution. This was made explicit
when he wrote to Monroe that the excitement surrounding the
progress of the French Revolution, especially where it was directed

---

[104] Alexander H. Everett, "A Defense of the Character and Principles of
Mr. Jefferson," *Mr. Everett's Address* (Boston, 1836), pp. 43–44.

against England, had "rekindl[ed]" in the newspapers—"from Boston to Charleston"—"all the old spirit of 1776!"[105] Indeed, this spirit, Jefferson's own euphemism for the spirit of revolution, was to pervade American politics in the years ahead. And Jefferson, bound by his devotion, was determined to keep it alive.

[105] Jefferson to James Monroe, 5 May 1793, *Writings*, Vol. IX, p. 75.

The Politics of Faction

"Faction is to party what the superlative is to the positive:
party is a political evil, and faction is the worst of all
parties."
BOLINGBROKE, *The Idea of a Patriot King*

"The violence of faction is the MORTAL disease under
which popular governments have everywhere perished."
MADISON, *Federalist,* #10

Thus far we have explored the principles of the one-party state and
of revolution, and we have examined the ideas, as well as the fears,
of conspiracy and counterrevolution. We have seen that leading
politicians believed they were observing the development of administrative, political, and revolutionary models that were similar,
if not identical, to those in England and the revolutionary period
of the colonies. These statements would imply that the American
political system as it developed from 1787 to 1801 was not, at least
in the minds of the actors, materially different from what they had
known before. This also means that the political system, in the
context of its basic ideological conflicts, remained largely unchanged from the early 1770s to 1800. This hypothesis, if true,
contradicts the conclusion of every American historian to the
present. But before we dismiss or reject it as being out of step with
contemporary historical scholarship, let us examine the assumption
upon which this assertion rests.

Opposition to government in the eighteenth century was regarded as a political evil of the greatest magnitude. There was only one government, one administration; and everyone was bound (at least in theory) to support it. Those who failed to give their allegiance did so at their own peril. For the most part, political opposition was considered illegal, subversive, and always dangerous.

Indeed, as we have seen, those who were members of an extreme opposition faction were regarded as members of a city within a city, a state within a state, potentially violent revolutionaries. No matter what area of politics one might choose to become active in—administration, the newspaper media, pamphleteering, etc.—it was impossible to be ignorant of the fact that the purpose of the government in power was to suppress faction before it could promote civil war and thus tear apart the state.[1] In a typical passage of the times, Peter Porcupine quoted the *New York Gazette:*

> It is an axiom in republican politics that the majority must rule. This power is exercized by proxy; and whoever erects, or is accessary in erecting a systematic opposition to this proxy, or government established by the people, is a bad citizen and merits the resentment of the people. If a party be formed under the auspices of any foreign state to clog the wheels of government, it is treasonably engaged in resisting the will of the people, and of course deserves *capital* punishment.[2]

This was the theory of the one- or non-party state. Yet, clearly, more than one party or faction existed in America, just as it had in

[1] For example, "freedom of . . . political expression whether written or verbal was feared as a means of triggering conspiracies, internal disorders, wars, revolutions or some other disastrous train of events that might pull down . . . the State." In Leonard Levy, *Freedom of Speech and Press in Early American History* (Cambridge, Mass., 1960), p. 7.

[2] *Porcupine's Works*, op. cit., Vol. X, pp. 18–19. Remember, it was not until 1826 that Sir John Hobhouse, then a member of Lords, derisively commented on "His Majesty's Opposition," indicating that he believed their presence an innocuous one. Hofstadter believes the idea did not gain acceptance in England until the 1840s, a full two generations after Jefferson's victory in 1800.

every other republic in history. The ideal contemporary political theory, then, recognized that society was divided into different factions, but that for the benefit of the commonwealth they were not to raise their voice in the community. And since political parties were not allowed, they *had* to be the parties of a "foreign state." This was also characteristic of politics during the revolutionary era in America. Bernard Bailyn writes that Massachusetts' Governor "Bernard's fear of a conspiratorial faction is the main theme that runs through his extensive correspondence of the 1760's."[3]

This fear of a conspiratorial faction, one of the principal themes which we have already examined, also ran through the entire decade following the Revolution. It was characteristic of the period under the Articles of Confederation and the era immediately following the constitution. And this style of politics, dominated by faction, continued through the remainder of the 1790s. It is the purpose of this chapter, then, to point out how the politics of faction grew into a politics of revolution—ultimately climaxing in Jefferson's accession to power in 1801.

One of the principal theories of government in the eighteenth century, designed to counter the influence of faction, was harmony. Richard Hofstadter has written that "they [the Founding Fathers] were far from clear as to how opposition should make itself felt, for they valued social unity or harmony and they had not arrived at the point that opposition, manifested in organized popular parties, could sustain freedom without totally shattering such harmony."[4] This historical judgment accurately reflected Washington's attempts to "coalesce" Jefferson's and Hamilton's differing views for the sake of unity in his administration. It was also Hamilton's point in initially achieving Jefferson's agreement on the assumption plan. For even though Jefferson would later regret that the bargain with Hamilton was his greatest political

---

[3] Bailyn, *The Ideological Origins of the American Revolution*, op. cit., p. 151.

[4] Hofstadter, *The Idea of a Party System*, op. cit., p. 9.

error,[5] he had compromised on the basis that harmony in the administration was essential. To an old friend he had written: "In general I think it is necessary to give as well as take in a government like ours."[6] This would seem to reflect the theory of the constitution as well as a belief that disagreement in the formation of policy was allowed up to a certain point. Then, majority rule would assert itself upon the vote taken for any particular bill, and the opposition, in whatever branch, would acquiesce in its binding provisions. This opposition, necessary as well as natural for wise deliberation, was restricted in its most virulent form to the legislative chambers. But it, too, was limited.

Thus, in the earliest days of the new government, the fear of faction threatening the fragile harmony of the administration spread among those concerned with public affairs. Arguing over the residence bill in 1790, one political observer wrote that if the seat of government was moved, "there will be one party endeavoring to carry the bill into effect, and another . . . that will exert themselves to oppose it. . . . The influence of these factions will go into every measure of government . . ."[7] Other newspapers sounded the tocsin: "If a faction can violate the Constitution; this sacred charter of government, which they are sworn to support, may be considered as blank paper."[8] The author feared that a faction within the legislature was, by urging the change of location, undermining the "integrity and popularity of the executive."

The administrative council, too, expected that a certain amount of disagreement would assert itself in the making of policy; but it was not accustomed, or prepared, to see the opposition continue unabated. Washington certainly reflected this view when he stated that bringing someone to the highest councils "whose tenets are

[5] Jefferson to George Washington, 9 Sept. 1792, *The Works of Thomas Jefferson* (Federal Edition), op. cit., Vol. VII, pp. 137–38.

[6] Jefferson to George Mason, 13 June 1790, *Papers*, Vol. 16, p. 493.

[7] *Papers*, Vol. 17, p. 172; see also (New York) *Daily Advertiser*, 7, 8, and 9 July 1790; *Connecticut Courant*, 15 July 1790.

[8] A Citizen of America, *New York Journal*, 27 July 1790, in *Papers*, Vol. 17, p. 181. See editorial note.

adverse to the measures which the general government advocates
. . . would be a sort of political suicide."[9] From an administrative
point of view, the same fear motivated Hamilton as he contemplated Virginia's protest against the assumption bill: "A spirited
remonstrance to Congress is talked of. This is the first symptom of
a spirit which must either be killed, or it will kill the constitution
of the United States."[10] Obviously Hamilton believed such opposition reflected the spirit of a faction opposed to his policies. And
the spirit of a faction the size of Virginia, phrasing its disagreements in such terms as "subversive" and "dangerous," could lead
to serious consequences, viz., the threat of revolution against the
national government.[11]

In the spirit of the times, Hamilton also believed—to use his
own word—that that kind of opposition must be "killed."[12] He
had, moreover, good grounds for expressing his fear in such extreme language. If a faction did not expire it would theoretically
grow until it had overwhelmed the state. Jefferson shared Hamil-

---

[9] Washington to the Acting Secretary of State, 27 Sept. 1795, *Writings of George Washington*, op. cit., Vol. 34, pp. 314–16.

[10] Hamilton to John Jay, 13 Nov. 1790, *The Life and Writings of John Jay*, op. cit., Vol. II, pp. 202–3. The Virginia Assembly had passed several resolu-
tions, one of which stated: "An act making provisions for the debt of the United States as limits the right of the United States in their redemption of the public debt is dangerous to the rights and subversive of the interests of the people, and demands the marked disapprobation of the General Assembly." This was the spirit Hamilton wished killed.

[11] In *The Idea of a Party System*, op. cit., Richard Hofstadter remarked, "In America . . . party opposition . . . had been carried on in the face of a firm conviction by each side . . . that the other was not legitimate, and in a healthy state of affairs would be put out of business." P. x. The reason for extinguishing the opposition, in the absence of any clearly defined loyal party system, could only have been the fear of potential revolution against the state.

[12] Due to the chronological approach of this and a portion of the next chap-
ter and because the basic organization corresponds to the books written by Noble Cunningham, Jr., and William Nisbet Chambers, I urge the reader to make a point-by-point comparison of the evidence they have cited in support of the development of party with my use of that same evidence to argue against party and for a politics of faction.

ton's belief, at least on the assumption bill, but only as to its consequences. He wrote Monroe declaring that "unless they [Congress] can be reconciled by some plan of compromise, there will be no funding bill agreed to, our credit . . . will burst and vanish, and the states separate to take care everyone of itself."[13] Thus, starting from two different poles of reason, both Hamilton and Jefferson appeared to believe that the constitution was threatened by the politics of faction. The latter intoned to John Harvie that "if it [the assumption plan] is obdurately rejected, something much worse will happen" than his "aversion" to assumption.[14] That allusion was double: it referred to the potential failure of compromise and the death of the new government. The point we might keep in mind, however, is that a state, passing resolutions against the policies of the national government, was considered a threat to the constitution.

The spirit of opposition did not subside, however; it continued to raise its head and the ensuing political struggle between Hamilton and Jefferson implied a complete destruction of one or the other's faction. One Federalist reported to Hamilton in 1791 that it appeared as though a group were concerting together in opposition to the government. Robert Livingston, Aaron Burr, Jefferson, and Madison were all engaged in a "passionate courtship" in New York and "*Delenda est Carthago* I suppose is the maxim adopted with respect to you. They had better be quiet, for if they succeed they will tumble the fabric of the government in ruins to the ground."[15] The implication was clear: Hamilton must be destroyed. The succeeding statement also implied that any struggle between the two, if it reached a point where power changed hands, would result in the destruction of the government. It was inconceivable, because it had never happened before, that a peaceful transition of power could occur, without violent revolu-

[13] Jefferson to James Monroe, 20 June 1790, *Papers*, Vol. 16, p. 537.

[14] Jefferson to Col. John Harvie, 25 July 1790, *The Works of Thomas Jefferson* (Federal Edition), op. cit., Vol. VI, p. 109.

[15] Robert Troup to Hamilton, 15 June 1791, *The Papers of Alexander Hamilton*, op. cit., Vol. VIII, p. 478.

tion. This internecine struggle, however, was not limited to Jefferson and Hamilton. In Massachusetts, John Adams saw the politics of faction directed against his own political future. He viewed the changing alignment of power in his own state with such foreboding that he predicted his own retirement in the face of "the Stone House Faction":[16]

> It is thought by some that Mr. Hancock's friends are preparing the Way, by my destruction, for his Election to the Place of Vice President, and that of Mr. Samuel Adams to be Governor of this Commonwealth, and then the Stone House Faction will be sure of all the Loaves and Fishes, in the national Government and the State Government as they hope. The opposers of the present Constitution of Pensilvania, the promoters of Shases Rebellion and County Resolves, and many of the Detesters of the present national Government, will undoubtedly aid them. Many people think too that no small Share of a foreign Influence, in revenge for certain untractable conduct at the Treaty of Peace, is and will be intermingled. The Janizaries of this goodly Combination, among whom are three or four, who hesitate at no falshood, have written all the Impudence and Impertinence which have appeared in the Boston Papers upon this memorable Occasion.

And then, summing up the nature of the politics of faction, he laments: "I must own to you that the daring Traits of Ambition and Intrigue, and those unbridled Rivalries which have already appeared, are the most melancholly and alarming Symptoms that I have ever seen in this Country."[17] Thus John Adams, even at this early date, saw the rise of faction as a threat to both the constitution and the country.

In addition to the primary actors of the new administration, the trend toward faction was noted by other leading figures, who expressed themselves in similar terms. Oliver Wolcott noted that "faction and diversity of opinion" had produced "an unfortunate jealousy . . . too apparent in some of the most influential charac-

[16] "The Stone House Faction" was led by Adams' arch rival John Hancock, whose mansion on Beacon Hill was made of granite.

[17] Adams to Jefferson, 29 July 1791, *Letters*, Vol. I, p. 249.

ters in our country. The consequence is, that questions are not so calmly discussed, characters are not so fairly estimated, and the people are not so perfectly availed of the talents which have been selected for their use, as every honest and patriotic man must desire. Time alone can discover whether these evils proceed from permanent or temporary causes."[18]

From the generally accepted theory of faction it would appear that the causes, if understood, proceeded from permanent divisions in the nature of man. The only temporary consideration was whether the government had or did not have the power to suppress violent factions. While Hamilton shared his opinions with Wolcott, which may explain the nature of the information passed on by that trusted subordinate, the suspicions of the former produced a reaction that, to a twentieth-century observer, approached paranoia. But if what follows may appear hysterical to us, it obviously registered the deep-seated fears of Hamilton and his perception of what was going on around him:

> It was not 'till the last session that I became unequivocally convinced of the following truth—*That Mr. Madison, co-operating with Mr. Jefferson, is at the head of a faction decidely hostile to me and my administration; and actuated by views, in my judgement, subversive of the principles of good government and dangerous to the Union, peace and happiness of the country.* These are strong expressions. . . . I have not lightly resolved to hazard them. They are the result of a *Serious Alarm* in my mind for the public welfare, and of a full conviction that what I have alledged is a truth, and a truth, which ought to be told and well attended to, by all the friends of Union and efficient National Government.[19]

Hamilton, it seemed, had articulated a conspiracy theory of his own: Jefferson and Madison at the head of a faction were deter-

---

[18] Oliver Wolcott to Frederick Wolcott, 6 April 1792, George Gibbs, *Memoirs of the Administrations of Washington and Adams* (New York, 1846), Vol. I, p. 75.

[19] Hamilton to Col. Edward Carrington, 26 May 1792, *The Papers of Alexander Hamilton*, op. cit., Vol. XI, p. 429.

mined to subvert the government. In addition, Hamilton revealed what Jefferson had suspected all along. He saw himself acting as the prime minister, the head of Washington's cabinet, even labeling it "my administration." Moreover, he labeled Jefferson's and Madison's actions as "subversive," implying that "principles of good government" would not tolerate an opposition, especially from a *faction*. Indeed, Hamilton had made a separation between Jefferson and the friends of efficient national government.

Jefferson's reaction, once he heard that the terms had been applied to him personally, was one of anger. Within a month, he told Madison "you will discover Hamilton's pen . . . daring to call the republican party *a faction*."[20] The term infuriated Jefferson, and for good reason. Yet the charge was more generally applied than even he knew. Because of the strife, Washington had thought of retiring and had asked Madison to author a valedictory address for him. The request included a wish by the President to say something that would dampen down the spirit of party. But the President, postponing his retirement for four more years, failed to use the speech until 1796. Nevertheless, it indicates that the concern about faction had become grave.

Meanwhile, another cabinet member, Edmund Randolph, warned the President that the harmony of his administration was threatened by the violence of faction: "You suffered yourself to yield when the voice of your country summoned you to the Administration. Should a civil-war arise, you cannot stay at home. And how much easier will it be to disperse the factions, which are rushing to this catastrophe, than to subdue them after they shall appear in arms?"[21] Randolph was, in accordance with the theory of the times, asking the President to crush the opposition that threatened the country. Faction, he believed, should be "nipped in the bud."

But if Jefferson was outraged by Hamilton's charge, the latter

[20] Jefferson to James Madison, 29 June 1792, *The Works of Thomas Jefferson* (Federal Edition), op. cit., Vol. VII, p. 130.
[21] Henry Jones Ford, *Washington and His Colleagues* (New Haven, Conn., 1921), p. 177. No reference is cited other than a time period of mid-1792.

was continuing his attacks on everything that Jefferson was fighting for. William L. Smith, an extreme Federalist and supporter of Hamilton, attempted to ridicule Jefferson for his "pure republicanism," "affectation of simplicity," and his "pretended out[cries] against Monarchy and Aristocracy." Jefferson was further described as "the Generalissimo" and his colleague, Madison, as "the General." But though Smith was a devout Federalist, he nevertheless made an attack upon the idea of party and faction that is almost unparalleled in the literature of the period. In essence, he attacked the idea of faction and party as a "system" of illegitimate opposition. His argument, therefore, is not in favor of party; it is entirely against it. He wrote:

> I have discovered the origins, motives, progress and design of a SYSTEM as wicked, profligate and malevolent as ever disgraced the most corrupt and abandoned government, and as it nearly concerns the tranquility, order and happiness of the union, I shall disclose it to my fellow citizens. . . .
>
> Before a disclosure of this system is entered into it may not be amiss to premise that the writer is far from alledging that there are not defects in some of the measures of Congress, or defending *in toto* those which have been selected by the FACTION above alluded to as the chief objects of their animadversion; on the contrary . . . all the measures of government he wishes to see strictly but fairly scrutinized; with the eye of the judicious Patriot, not of the malevolent party-man; with the head of the cool and candid citizen, not of the disappointed, envious and crafty Politician . . .

Taking Jefferson and Madison to task for their role in the opposition, Smith goes on to ask a series of questions:

> Who proposed the plan for organizing the Treasury Department? —let it be answered the General; who advised that the Secretary of Treasury should report to Congress his plans for improving the public Revenues? answer, the General: who advised, urged and contended . . . that the President should have power of removing . . . every officer of Government?—answer, the General: . . . who advised a Funding System?—answer, the General; . . . who

voted for the Excise and would have . . . voted for the National Bank had the Charter been limited to ten years?—answer, the General. Is it conceivable that he who advised and supported the measures above recited should now be one of the *advisors, supporters and mainsprings of a* FACTION, whose daily employment is to cry down all those very measures which have any connection with the Treasury Department?

Smith then attempts to place the rise of faction in perspective:

Had anyone fore told in the year 88, that in the course of a few short years the writer of this pious patriotic prayer would have been himself the first to disturb the tranquility of government he had recommended, by destroying Union and creating Schism, by sounding the Trumpet of Discord, raising the Flag of Disunion and inlisting troops under his hostile Banners, would he have been listened to with patience? But so it is—if anyone doubts it . . . let him read the Gazette established by one of the Clerks of his Office and undoubtedly under his auspices for the express purpose of ruining the Secretary of the Treasury. . . . such proceedings must have an immediate tendency to create parties in the Government, to set the Minister of State and Finance at variance, to the great injury of the public, and to inflame against each other their respective friends and partizans, thereby destroying the Union of the States, and promoting a most fatal Schism . . .

The writer of these observations most sincerely joins, with this further prayer to the all-wise Ruler of the Universe that he will be graciously pleased to turn the hearts of the wicked and factious from their dangerous machinations, and dispose them to unite with the rest of their fellow Citizens in promoting the tranquility, order and happiness of the United States.[22]

Meanwhile, Hamilton was writing his own "general" in South Carolina:

It is to be lamented that so strong a *spirit of faction* and innovation prevails at the present moment in a great part of this Country.

[22] William L. Smith, *The Politicks and Views of a Certain Party Displayed,* op. cit., pp. 2–27.

The thing is alarming enough to call for the attention of every friend to Government. Let me not be thought to travel out of my sphere if I observe that a particular attention to the election for the next Congress is dictated by the vigorous and general effort which is making by factious men, to introduce everywhere and in every department, persons unfriendly to the measures, if not the constitution of the National Government.[23]

Thus Hamilton, while attempting to discredit the opposition by an appeal to the unity theory, continued to fear the influence of faction and especially their potential to, as he saw it, corrupt the elections. The congressional elections in Massachusetts, for example, saw the rise of partisan politics in a contest between Fisher Ames and "a Democratic enragee," Benjamin Austin, Jr. Nathaniel Cutting remarked that Austin was "an instigator and patron of faction in this town [Boston]."[24] In Rhode Island, a writer in the local newspaper wrote "may all party and local views, inconsistent with the good of our common country, be forever banished from the august assembly [Congress]."[25]

The elections of 1792 saw the emergence of political organizations that had been characteristic of the revolutionary era. In New York committees of correspondence were formed to assist in nominating, selecting, and promoting candidates for office.[26] In Philadelphia a "Rights of Man Ticket," espousing the revolutionary ideals of Tom Paine, appeared.[27] As far as presidential electors were concerned, Dr. James Hutchinson, a leading Pennsylvania politician, wrote Gallatin suggesting a list of men sanctioned by the local "corresponding society." Circulation of the candidates'

---

[23] Hamilton to General Charles Cotesworth Pinckney, 10 Oct. 1792, *The Papers of Alexander Hamilton*, Vol. XII, pp. 543–44.

[24] "Extracts from the Diary of Nathaniel Cutting," 3 Nov. 1792, *Proceedings of the Massachusetts Historical Society*, XII (1871), p. 68.

[25] *United States Chronicle* (Providence, R.I.), 23 Aug. 1792, in Cunningham, *The Jeffersonian Republicans*, op. cit., p. 32.

[26] New York *Daily Advertiser*, 2, 17, 21 April 1792.

[27] Tinkcom, *The Republicans and Federalists in Pennsylvania, 1790–1801*, op. cit., pp. 64–65; George D. Leutscher, *Early Political Machinery in the United States* (Philadelphia, 1903), p. 132.

names, he said, would "be secret and silent in this business" of electing officials. Thus, in true revolutionary style, the political leaders of Pennsylvania avoided the open character of a mature party system. Attempts to organize slates or tickets in any modern sense had failed. As Noble Cunningham, Jr., has suggested, whatever the arrangements for tickets, either among the "Federal or the Anti-Federal Interests," many of the names appeared on both lists.[28]

In Pennsylvania the lines drawn around political circles were definitely those of factions. In Virginia and Maryland voters were able to read in the newspapers about a prospective candidate who would be identified only generally as to his interests. The attempts by Jefferson, Madison, and Burr—the emergence of a Virginia–New York cooperation—were similar to the same cooperation that had taken place in the early 1770s. Exchanges of information, limited strategies, and a determination to advance the ideals of the republican ideology were what these efforts amounted to. Benjamin Rush, writing from Pennsylvania, told Burr: "Your friends everywhere look to you to take an active part in removing the monarchical rubbish of our government."[29] Rush, like Jefferson, had placed his advice in the context of republican versus monarchical principles. He had, by implication, described Burr's efforts as part of a factional struggle. "Removal" meant, in the political language of the times, the complete extirpation of his opponents.

The exuberance that Jefferson and his colleagues would show over the election of 1792 was short-lived. But while it lasted it revealed their hopes for the new republic. Jefferson realized what was at stake in his battle with Hamilton, and, by 1792, that battle had indeed surfaced in all its ugliness. He thus reported to one of his lieutenants that "the elections for Congress have produced a decided majority in favor of the republican interest. I think we may consider the tide of this government as now at the

---

[28] Cunningham, *The Jeffersonian Republicans*, op. cit., p. 44.

[29] Benjamin Rush to Aaron Burr, 24 Sept. 1792, "Some Papers of Aaron Burr," ed. W. C. Ford, *Proceedings of the American Antiquarian Society*, n.s. 29 (1919), p. 97.

fullest, and that it will, from the commencement of the next session of Congress, retire and subside into the true principles of the Constitution."[30] Jefferson was expressing the hope that for the first time since his arrival, the Secretary of the Treasury would be faced with an effective separation of powers and that his attempts to control and manipulate the legislature would be frustrated. Theodore Sedgwick, the Massachusetts Federalist, underscored the point when he noted that "the antis place absolute dependence on having a majority in the next house."[31] Sedgwick obviously saw the difference of political views in terms of the old divisions: Federalists versus anti-Federalists. Fisher Ames pointed out the solidity of the largest faction in opposition to the Hamiltonian system: "Virginia moves in a solid column, and the discipline of the party is as severe as the Prussian. . . . Madison is become a desperate party leader and I am not sure of his stopping at any point or extremity."[32] At nearly the same time, Hamilton himself was gloomily reporting his worst fears: ". . . the spirit of party has grown to maturity sooner in this country than perhaps was to have been counted upon . . ."[33] Hamilton not only saw his system threatened, he began to fear that the implications of Virginia's solid resistance might portend the end of the Union.

Jefferson was desperate. He saw Hamilton leading the attack against him in the newspapers, asserting powers for the collectors of customs that violated American neutrality, "setting up a system of espionage, destructive of the peace of society," all in the spirit of "Anglophobia."[34] Gradually he saw events unfolding that

[30] Jefferson to Thomas Pinckney, 3 Dec. 1792, *The Works of Thomas Jefferson* (Federal Edition), op. cit., Vol. VII, p. 191.

[31] Theodore Sedgwick to Ephraim Williams, 31 Jan. 1793, Sedgwick Papers, III, Massachusetts Historical Society.

[32] Fisher Ames to Timothy Dwight, Jan. 1793, in Irving Brant, *James Madison, 1787–1800: The Father of the Constitution* (New York, 1950), p. 368.

[33] Hamilton to William Short, 5 Feb. 1793, *The Papers of Alexander Hamilton*, op. cit., Vol. XIV, p. 7.

[34] Jefferson to Madison, 12 May 1793, *Writings*, Vol. IX, p. 87.

tended to "damp that energy of republicanism in our new Congress, from which I had hoped so much reformation."[35] The "republicanism" that Jefferson referred to was a set of philosophical principles he hoped would have been adhered to in the new Congress. As a result, Jefferson felt it was absolutely necessary to destroy Hamilton and his influence. Writing Madison, he urged him to "enter the lists with him [Hamilton]," to "take up your pen, select the most striking heresies and cut him to pieces in the face of the public."[36] Jefferson, by his choice of words, was in no mood to show mercy; he meant war.

Madison's response was to turn to the kind of organization that he and Jefferson had long been familiar with. He immediately wrote Jefferson that "we shall endeavor at some means of repelling the danger particularly by setting on foot expressions of the public mind in important Counties, and under the auspices of respectable names." Circular letters were accordingly sent to counties, to cities, and to individuals "modified in every particular according to the state of information and particular temper of the place."[37] Madison's estimate of the sentiment of the majority of the people was a reflection of those principles opposing the Hamiltonian system:

> They are attached to the Constitution. They are attached to the President. They are attached to the French Nation *and Revolution*. They are attached to peace as long as it can be honorably preserved. They are averse to Monarchy and to a political connection with that of Great Britain and will readily protest against any known or supposed danger that may have this change in their situation for their object. Why then cannot the sense of the people be collected on these points by the agency of temperate and respectable men who have the opportunity of meeting them.[38]

[35] Jefferson to Edmund Randolph, 2 June 1793, ibid., pp. 108–9.

[36] Jefferson to Madison, 7 July 1793, *The Works of Thomas Jefferson* (Federal Edition), op. cit., Vol. VII, p. 436.

[37] Jefferson to Madison, 2 Sept. 1793, *The Writings of James Madison*, op. cit., Vol. VI, p. 192–93.

[38] Madison to Archibald Stuart, 1 Sept. 1793, ibid., pp. 189–90.

When Madison sent Monroe a copy of the plan to oppose the Hamiltonians, the latter found that efforts had already been made to offset the Virginians. Nevertheless, the circular letters "effectually changed the current and gave direction against the antirepublican faction." In the style of the old revolutionary politics, "a meeting took place and resolutions were passed in a tone of sentiment perfectly correct and proper."[39]

Hamilton's recognition that party spirit had "matured" was tantamount to saying it constituted a threat to the government. This was particularly true where the Democratic societies were concerned. As we have already noted, Jefferson defended these societies and opposed Washington's condemnation of them. The reason they were so viciously attacked was a reflection of the nature of their activity. They were viewed as potentially revolutionary. Washington himself reflected the fears of many when he wrote Jay "that the *self-created societies* which have spread themselves over this country, have been laboring incessantly to sow the seeds of distrust, jealousy, and of course discontent, thereby hoping to effect some *revolution* in the government, is not unknown to you."[40] Indeed, the meetings, the passing of resolutions, the distribution of circular letters, the vociferous statements of opposition to the administration, the correspondence exchanged, the identification with the revolutionary fervor in France, and the Whiskey Rebellion had all added up, as Jefferson suggested, to a "rekind[ling] of the old spirit of 1776."[41]

Madison and his colleagues responded to the furor over the societies by looking for ulterior motives—specifically, the designs of a counterrevolutionary faction. Madison wrote:

It was obvious that a most dangerous game was playing against Republicanism. The insurrection was universally and deservedly

[39] Monroe to Madison, 25 Sept. 1792, *The Writings of James Madison*, op. cit., Vol. I, pp. 276–77. See also: *The Writings of James Monroe*, ed. S. M. Hamilton, 7 vols. (New York, 1898–1903).

[40] Washington to John Jay, 1 Nov. 1794, *The Life and Writings of John Jay*, op. cit., Vol. II, p. 233.

[41] Jefferson to James Monroe, 5 May 1793, *Writings*, Vol. IX, p. 75.

odious. The Democratic Societies were presented as in league with it. The Republican part of Congress were to be drawn into an *ostensible* patronage of those societies, and into an ostensible opposition to the President. And by this artifice the delusion of New England was to be confirmed, and a chance afforded of some new turn in Virginia before the elections in the Spring. What the success of this game will really be, time must decide. If the people of America are so far degenerated already as not to see, or to see with indifference, that the citadel of their liberties is menaced by the precedent before their eyes, they require abler advocates than they now have to save them from the consequences.[42]

The leader of the opposition in Congress thus saw the attempt to crush the Democratic societies as a threat to American liberty. Indeed, Madison felt the crisis so great that he spelled out the threat to his friend Monroe in even more precise terms. In the process he revealed his idea of the use of power in dealing with counterrevolution. And interestingly, he placed his reflections on power in the context of the republican ideology. Reporting on the western insurrection, he began:

The event was, in several respects, a critical one for the cause of liberty, and the real authors of it, if not in the service, were, in the most effectual manner, doing the business of Despotism. *You well know the general tendency of insurrections to increase the momentum of power.* You will recollect the particular effect of what happened some years ago in Massachusetts. Precisely the same calamity was to be dreaded on a larger scale in this case. There were enough, as you may well suppose, ready to give the same turn to the crisis, and to propagate the same impressions from it. It happened most auspiciously, however, that, with a spirit truly Republican, the people every where, and of every description, condemned the resistance to the will of the majority, and obeyed with alacrity the call to vindicate the authority of the laws. . . . If the insurrection had not been crushed in the

[42] James Madison to Thomas Jefferson, 30 Nov. 1794, *The Letters and Other Writings of James Madison* (Published by Order of Congress), 4 vols. (New York, 1884), Vol. II, p. 22.

manner it was, I have no doubt that a formidable attempt would have been made to establish the principle that a standing army was necessary for *enforcing the laws*. When I first came to this City about the middle of October, this was the fashionable language. . . . You will readily understand the business detailed in the newspapers relating to the denunciation of the "self-created Societies." . . . The game was to connect the Democratic Societies with the odium of the insurrection; to connect the Republicans in Congress with those Societies; to put the President ostensibly at the head of the other party, in opposition to both, and by these means prolong the illusions in the North, and try a new experiment on the South.[43]

That experiment, Madison believed, was an attempt to coerce the South into following the Hamiltonian policies. If Hamilton, at the head of an army, could maintain the illusion of resistance to the administration's policies, perhaps the force of a standing army could overawe the South.

Earlier in the year Madison had seen the threat coming. Referring to the lower House he wrote Jefferson, "The attempts of this Branch to give the President power to raise an army of 10,000 men, if he should please, was strangled more easily in the House of Representatives than I had expected. This is the third or fourth effort made in the course of the Session to get a powerful military establishment, under the pretext of public danger, and under the auspices of the President's popularity."[44] Now Hamilton was at the head of an army. It was not surprising, then, that Madison, in the closing days of 1794, would allude to a desperate situation facing the country. Confiding his fears to Jefferson, he described the scene in language that hinted darkly at the worst possible consequences:

The phenomenon you wish to have explained is as little understood here as with you; but it would be here quite unfashionable

[43] James Madison to James Monroe, 4 Dec. 1794, *The Writings of James Madison*, op. cit., Vol. VI, pp. 220–23.

[44] James Madison to Thomas Jefferson, 1 June 1794, *The Letters and Other Writings of James Madison*, op. cit., Vol. II, p. 18.

to suppose it needed explanation. It is impossible to give you an idea of the force with which the tide has set in a particular direction. It has been too violent not to be soon followed by a change. In fact, I think a change has begun already. The danger will then be of as violent a reflux to the opposite extreme.[45]

Jefferson concurred in Madison's pessimism and saw the train of events leading finally to the "dismembering of the Union, and setting us all afloat to choose what part of it we will adhere to."[46] For both, the politics of faction seemed to be approaching its historical conclusion: the complete destruction of the state.

As the new year came into view, Madison believed that instead of the danger decreasing, it had worsened. Within five weeks he again wrote Jefferson counseling a mood of despair:

> I am extremely sorry to remark a growing apathy to the evil and danger of standing armies. And a vote passed two days ago, which is not only an evidence of that, but, if not, the efforts of unpardonable inattention, indicates a temper still more alarming. . . . The debates brought out an avowal that the Executive ought to be free to use the regular troops, as well as the Militia, in support of the laws against our own citizens.[47]

In the wake of this extremely pessimistic discussion, opinion had polarized within the legislative branch. The previous year had seen Jefferson's retirement from the executive branch and now it appeared Madison might be heading a losing cause. Factional differences had become so great that no one had any idea, at least since December 1793, what course Congress would take: compromise or greater polarization. To another observer the longer this situation obtained, the more likely it was to have alarming consequences: ". . . the passions of many are so violent, and such the real diversity of views and interests, that the prospects of tranquility

---

[45] Madison to Jefferson, 21 Dec. 1794, ibid., p. 28.

[46] Jefferson to Madison, 28 Dec. 1794, *Writings*, Vol. IX, p. 295.

[47] Madison to Jefferson, 15 Feb. 1795, *The Letters and Other Writings of James Madison*, op. cit., Vol. II, pp. 35–36.

and permanency in our public policy has much diminished."[48]
Oliver Wolcott's "diversity" implied a multiplicity of views and
interests, a clear expression of factional politics. This was also an
indication that the members of the legislative branch had no clear
idea as to what alignments would take place. The style of politics
in the Congress was like that in the states: factional and in the
traditional sense. The proof of this lay in the nature of political
leadership in the House. Madison dominated the House of Representatives to such a degree that the republicans, or Anti's, as they
were called, were termed "Madison's party."[49]

Yet as the congressional sessions wore on, the evidence of wider
polarization became obvious—even to those who were not members of the government. One South Carolinian wrote:

> Our Information of the proceedings of Congress is very broken
> and Imperfect. We perceive however that warmth and dissention
> prevail on almost every question. Even the naturalization bill on
> which one would have hoped that no division would have arisen,
> furnished minds disposed to seek for differences an occasion to
> dispute and clamor. Your Hall appears to be an arena where the
> Combattants descend to engage, not for persuasion, but for vic-
> tory. No disciplined Prussians or enthusiastic French, adhere more
> firmly to their ranks than the different members of Congress to
> their respective standards. A few scattering Independent votes, are
> sometimes found changing sides according to the dictates of their
> Judgement, But in general the members may be classed with
> great precision and Certainty.
> This is a melancholy picture, but I fear it is too true.[50]

Again the impression Congress created for most onlookers
smacked of traditional factional politics. Victory, not persuasion,

[48] Oliver Wolcott to Oliver Wolcott, Sr., 3 May 1794, Gibbs, *Memoirs of
the Administrations of Washington and Adams*, op. cit., Vol. I, p. 136.

[49] Samuel Smith to O. H. Williams, 20 March 1794, Papers of Otho
Holland Williams, IX, No. 866, Maryland Historical Society, in Cunningham,
The Jeffersonian Republicans, op. cit., p. 69.

[50] Henry William De Saussure to Richard Bland Lee, 14 Feb. 1795, R. B.
Lee Papers, Lib. Cong.

was the end of politics; and victory in its ultimate sense meant destruction of the opponent. The lesson was clear to at least one writer who understood the role of faction and party in a free society:

> What caused the fall of Athens? Faction: the spirit of discord prevailed and liberty was destroyed. . . . The republic of Rome experienced a similar fate. Ambitious Caesar saw the moment when party blinded the vigilance of his country's friends, seized it, and triumphed. . . . This fatal shore, on which so many nations have been stranded, is destined to produce the same fate to America, unless the spirit of party be repressed. . . . Party is a monster who devours the common good, whose destructive jaws are dangerous to the felicity of nations.[51]

In April of 1794, John Taylor of Caroline, one of the finest philosophical minds in the South, addressed himself to the political situation in the country and attempted to analyze the causes of the increasing conflict. He titled his examination "A Definition of Parties" and began with a general proposition:

> The Constitution of the United States, was established for the national good, and not for the exclusive benefit of an inconsiderable number of the community.

Continuing with the recognition that we are all subject to the laws of the constitution, he said, "If it [the government] is callous, it will become the prostitute of faction—the vehicle of corrupt speculation, and the factor of private interest." He then began an attack on Alexander Hamilton's policies, claiming that the

> good of 5,000 hath . . . triumphed over that of the 5,000,000. . . . Neither the interest of all the states . . . or the preservation of the union, have stood against the circumventions of faction. Even this liberal proposition [i.e., an attempt to increase American navigation and commerce] has been successfully carricatured into the vile semblance of party. In short the general government has been an exclamation for money—more money.

[51] William Wyche, *Party Spirit: An Oration, delivered to the Horanian Literary Society* . . . (New York, 1794), pp. 15–16.

Taylor next began a critique of the economic system erected by
Hamilton: "Paper is in fact the only representative, both of
numbers and of property, bestowed by a faction upon itself . . ."
And consistently using the term "junto" interchangeably with
faction he continued:

> The politics of a junto may therefore be accurately anticipated;
> indeed its theory and practice in all ages is the same. Standing
> armies—fleets—increase of taxes—extension of influence and of
> patronage—in short, whatever will obviate all attempts for a
> reclamation of political rights, will mark its progress.

The consequence of a faction or junto active in the Congress was
that it would "speculate upon individuals by possessing the secrets
of government. It is tempted to produce fluctuations in politics,
because every fluctuation is a new game—and the divisions of a
factious spirit upon which it subsists . . . will extend the sessions
of the legislature, until in point of expense it will constitute a
second standing army, to be quartered upon the public favor."

Examining the charges of faction that filled the air on both
sides, Taylor remarked: "Yet Britain and the paper junto have
successively applied to republicanism the epithet *factious* . . ."
He denied the charge and in the context of the current political
situation, he listed the criteria by which one could recognize a
faction or junto. A faction will:

> increase taxes and increase debts . . .
> impose all taxes, receive most taxes, and pay no taxes
> borrow for the public—making the contract for the public and
> with itself
> renew the bank
> modif[y] paper credit
> raise fleets and armies to defend itself against the nation
> efface the principles of republicanism, by . . . producing unequal
> wealth and by sowing partizans, in offices created for the pur-
> pose at the public expense
> distract the public mind . . . and take advantage of the con-
> fusion generated by its own acts, avowedly to erect monarchy,
> under pretence of restoring order

endeavor to break the union itself, if the union should obstruct
its designs
render insurmountable the difficulty of reconciling state interests,
from the necessity of consulting the clashing interest of a junto
connect itself with a country governed by a paper junto . . .

Finally—"A system of public plunder will plead for itself, by pretending to secure private property; and the office of an honest
government will be thus assumed by a paper faction." Taylor then
asks the following questions: "How happens it, that the faction
cannot be defined, by geographical boundary? . . . Why then is
it, that the particles compounding the faction, are not united by
the cement of state interest, pervading an entire representation."
Going "in search of the component parts of this faction," Taylor
concluded that it was a "deadly foe to republicanism, and . . .
ha[d] been postured by a private interest, confined in every state,
to an inconsiderable number of citizens, and even largely shared by
foreigners. For the truth is," he concluded, "that a secretary of the
Treasury—an incorporated bank—and a funding system, constitute substantially a phalanx of privileged orders, if they can
influence the legislature. They are a correct representation of a
king—lords—and commons. The first will sway the legislature, by
the magic of private interest. The second is a successional body
having exclusive right and legislative weight . . . and the third is
a mode of representation, equivalent to the rotten boroughs of
England.

"Accordingly, our privileged orders have openly sympathized
with the privileged orders combined for the suppression of republicanism in France. . . . Ruminate, fellow citizens upon this
fact—trace it to all its consequences—anticipate the events of
which it is prophetic—and if you are republicans, determine,
whether at this momentous crisis, or *at any other period*, the
commonwealth can be safe in the hands of such a faction."

This was John Taylor's assessment and definition of party.[52]

His assessment was not limited to a southern viewpoint. A

[52] John Taylor of Caroline, A *Definition of Parties*, op. cit., pp. 4–16.

number of philosophical types in the northern states believed that faction was dangerous to the government and even traced its implications for revolution in a way that Taylor had ignored. One of these was Ezra Stiles, the president of Yale College, and a prophet in his own time. Stiles, in a carefully written defense of the right of the people to freedom of information at all levels of government, invoked the right to revolution and developed a relationship between faction and revolution under a repressive government. The vision he calls forth raises the specter of a number of factions coming together in "associations" and spreading, as they did in the political struggles of the revolutionary era, into a *system of revolution:*

> Nothing will kill a faction, like the body of a people if consulted. A faction may beat a faction, at a pretty fair and even conflict; but in a fair and full contest, it can never beat the people. The great art of factions is to keep the decision from the body of the people. But let a matter be fairly brought before the people, and they will not only determine it, but will judge and determine right. It is the insidious art of parties and politicians to keep things concealed from the people, or if they are alarmed and assemble, to excite parties, sow dissentions, and prevent as much as possible the question from coming up fairly before them, instead of harmoniously endeavoring in a fair, open and candid manner, to lay things clearly before them, and thus honestly endeavoring to form and obtain the public mind. And thus they ever attempt, and are too successful in deceiving, instead of a frank and open appeal to the people. . . . Almost all the civil polities on earth are become so corrupt and oppressive, as that they cannot stand before a well formed system of revolutionary societies. Those of the United States and France will sustain them without injury or aversion. The reformation of all others, must commence in associations, which by government will be considered and treated as factionary and treasonable, but will enlarge and spread into a system of revolutionary societies. In all states these will be frowned upon, and suppressed as treasonable. Their suppression and persecution will pour oil on the flame. They will burst out again and again, till they will carry all before them, till real

treason shall be accurately defined not to the sense of aristocrats or the present usurped reigning powers, but to the general sense of the community. And such a law of treason will be infallibly supported by the community. This done every association will know what it may, and what it may not do, with impunity. Till this is done, the spirit of enlightened liberty is become so great and ready to burst forth under oppressive and intolerable irritations, that it will risque all consequences, until all the present policies shall be fairly brought to the tribunal of the public sense. Then no one can doubt the result. Factionary societies begun even with the primary and direct design of overturning government, if the government or polity be supported by the general sense, will fall: otherwise they will bring on and adduce at length extensive discussions which enlighten the public, defeat insidious and partial cunning, and bring forward an open and firm support of good and acceptable government.[53]

Stiles, whose essay paralleled Jefferson's ideas, had articulated a preview of the politics of faction for the next six years. While his projections dealt with factionary societies in an international sense, the logic he propounded applied even more profoundly at home. Indeed, as we view the political events developing over the years to 1800, we should look for that "system" emerging in response to the most important issues of the time.

The next truly important event that would spur the contending factions to even greater heights was the Jay Treaty. As early as April 1794, it had been rumored that an envoy would be sent to Great Britain. The rumor, moreover, had it that Hamilton would "probably be appointed, unless overruled by an apprehension from the disgust to Republicanism and to France."[54] With Jefferson's and Madison's knowledge and suspicion of Hamilton's collusion with the British, this news no doubt caused them to worry about the future of American foreign policy. John Jay's appointment as

[53] Ezra Stiles, *A History of Three of the Judges of King Charles I* (Hartford, Conn., 1794). In *Puritan Political Ideas*, ed. Edmund M. Morgan (New York, 1965), pp. 376–77.

[54] Madison to Jefferson, 14 April 1794, *The Letters and Other Writings of James Madison*, op. cit., Vol. II, p. 10.

envoy extraordinary mollified the critics only slightly; and those who subscribed to the revolutionary ideology of republicanism and the French Revolution mounted an outcry against it.

Madison, along with Jefferson, saw the Jay Treaty as simply another step toward a reunion with the hated British. Madison wrote to Chancellor Livingston:

> Indeed, the Treaty, from one end to the other, must be regarded as a demonstration that the party to which the Envoy belongs, and of which he has been more the organ than of the United States, is a British party, systematically aiming at an exclusive connection with the British Government, and ready to sacrifice to that object, as well the dearest interests of our commerce, as the most sacred dictates of National honour. This is the true Key to this unparalleled proceeding, and can alone explain it to the impartial and discerning part of the public. The leaders of this party stand *self-condemned* . . .[55]

Nearly the same view had been expressed by John Adams when he first heard of Jay's appointment. He too saw the implications of the treaty—the introduction of a standing army and monarchy—as crucial, albeit from a somewhat different perspective:

> The President has sent Mr. Jay to try if he can find any Way to reconcile our honour with Peace. I have no great Faith in any very brilliant Success: but hope he may have enough to keep Us out of a War. Another War would add two or three hundred millions of Dollars to our Debt, raise up a many headed and many bellied Monster of an Army to tyrannize over Us, totally disadjust our present Government, and accelerate the Advent of Monarchy and Aristocracy by at least fifty Years.
>
> Those who dread Monarchy and Aristocracy and at the same time Advocate War are the most inconsistent of all men.[56]

Yet this interpretation depended entirely upon one's factional point of view. Peter Porcupine saw "the key" to understanding the furor over Jay's Treaty in diametrically opposite terms:

---

[55] Madison to Robert R. Livingston, 10 Aug. 1795, ibid., p. 45.
[56] John Adams to Jefferson, 11 May 1794, *Letters*, Vol. I, p. 255.

. . . the Madisonian system was not so directly levelled against the Executive; but it went to a direct violation of our neutrality in respect to Great Britain, and to counteract the measures of the Administration. It was to cut off all commercial intercourse, and consequently all supplies from this country to Great Britain, while that intercourse and those supplies, were to be continued to France, and consequently the whole turned to her advantage in prosecuting the war against England. Before this however, the ministry of England, apprized of the faction here, the intrigues of Americans at Paris, the cooperation of France with that faction . . . were undoubtedly alarmed and seriously expected that our government would be thrown into the balance against them; consequently begun their depredations, determined to secure what advantages they could . . . before they should be totally deprived of it. Those depredations on our commerce were, therefore, the effects of the co-operation of the French government with the opposition in America . . .[57]

Arguments over the stand that the lower house would take on the treaty became academic once the Senate ratified it in June 1795. But with an amendment pending on the approval by the British, the Jay Treaty quickly became a major political issue in Congress. Rhetoric filled the air and charges of excessive factional behavior were made all around. Porcupine wrote that in the battle "the measures of the Chief Magistrate had been most violently opposed; he had been all but menaced, in order to deter him from the exercise of powers vested in him by the Constitution; his motives had been disfigured, and his character reviled. This was to be expected from the *leaders of a faction* averse to his administration, and even to the Government."[58]

Fisher Ames, too, believed that the politics of faction had gone beyond the bounds of decency. Referring to the treaty's rough handling in Congress and in the press he wrote: "A crisis now exists, the most serious I ever witnessed. . . . The government cannot go to the halves. It would be another, a worse government,

[57] *Porcupine's Works*, op. cit., Vol. V, p. 293.
[58] Ibid., Vol. III, p. 41.

if the mob, or the leaders of the mob in Congress, can stop the lawful acts of the President, and unmake a treaty. It would be either no government, or instantly a government by usurpation and wrong."[59] Ames equated the advocates of republicanism in Congress with a mob, an indication of their status in the politics of faction.

Ames's sense of crisis was shared by the President. Washington wrote to Adams during the height of the controversy, alluding to the possibility of a "pre-concerted plan." To Washington and a number of his advisors, it seemed as if a revolutionary crisis was upon them: ". . . whether it was from the sparke which kindled the fire in Boston, that the flames have spread so extensively; or whether the torch, by a pre-concerted plan, was lit ready for the explosion in all parts so soon as the advice to ratify the treaty should be announced, remains to be developed; but as the ratification thereof, agreeably to the advice of the Senate has passed from me, these meetings in opposition to the constituted authorities are as useless as they are *at all times*, improper and dangerous."[60] In the midst of crisis the Chief Executive naturally reprobated those who were in the opposition. The non-party state could not tolerate factious opposition.

But that opposition had its claims upon the moment. At first, Madison believed he had votes to spare in expressing the House of Representatives' disapproval of the treaty. But Hamilton, displaying his acumen as a parliamentary leader, adopted a strategy of delay. When the vote finally came in April 1796, the "majority" that Madison had held disappeared "under the mercantile influence and the alarm of war."[61] Madison's attempt to inhibit legislation that would have subsequently put the treaty into effect had failed. He explained the failure to Monroe in typical factional

[59] Fisher Adams to (unknown), at Springfield, 9 March 1796, *Works of Fisher Ames*, op. cit., p. 481.

[60] George Washington to John Adams, 20 Aug. 1795, *The Writings of George Washington*, op. cit., Vol. 34, p. 280.

[61] Madison to Jefferson, 14 May 1796, *The Writings of James Madison*, op. cit., Vol. VI, p. 300.

prose: ". . . the final turn of the majority ought at least to have been sooner prepared for. This was in fact contemplated. But before some were ripe for the arrangement, others were rotten."[62] Obviously Hamilton presided over a rotten borough system in the national legislature.

Jefferson had anticipated Madison's ultimate failure with an extremely pessimistic letter. Its main theme was the description of a hopeless situation and an indictment of Washington's naïveté. Madison should not cooperate:

> . . . where a faction has entered into a conspiracy with the enemies of their country to chain down the Legislature at the feet of both; where the whole mass of your constituents have condemned this work in the most unequivocal manner, and are looking to you as their last hope to save them from the effects of the avarice and corruption of the first agent, the revolutionary machinations of others, and the incomprehensible acquiescence of the only honest man who has assented to it. I wish that his honesty and his political errors may not furnish a second occasion to exclaim, "curse on his virtues, they have undone his country."[63]

One of the reasons for Madison's failure was, of course, the nature of the struggle itself. John Jay had plumbed the depths of the struggle in a letter to Washington, and laid it to natural causes. Referring to the turmoil over his treaty, he said, "some allowances are to be made for zeal; but all my accounts agree . . . that certain virulent publications have caused great and general indignation, even among many who had been misled into intemperate proceedings, and had given too much countenance to factious leaders. . . . These are political evils, which, in all ages, have grown out of such a state of things, as naturally as certain physical combinations produce whirlwinds and meteors."[64] Thus Jay, who understood the battle over Jay's Treaty as well as anyone,

[62] Madison to Monroe, 14 May 1796, ibid., pp. 300–1.

[63] Jefferson to Madison, 27 March 1796, *Writings*, Vol. IX, pp. 330–31.

[64] John Jay to George Washington, 14 Dec. 1795, *The Life and Writings of John Jay*, op. cit., Vol. II, p. 260.

linked the politics of that struggle not to any new development but to the politics of faction of "all ages."

Four months later, Jefferson would lament the change in American politics that had become apparent in the aftermath of the Jay Treaty. Writing a letter that would later become a liability and an embarrassment to its author, Jefferson spelled out the state of factions on the national scene. In his depressed state, he returned to the one theme that had dominated his thoughts since his return from France—the fear of counterrevolution. And, as he contemplated his natural fear, he wrote in the context of an unremitting hatred for British aristocratical principles:

> The aspect of our politics has wonderfully changed since you left us. In place of that noble love of liberty and republican government which carried us triumphantly through the war, an Anglican monarchical aristocratical party has sprung up, whose avowed object is to draw over us to the substance, as they have already done the forms, of the British government. . . . Against us are the Executive, the Judiciary, two out of three branches of the Legislature, all the officers of the government, all who want to be officers, all timid men who prefer the calm of despotism to the boisterous sea of liberty, British merchants and Americans trading on British capital, speculators and holders in the banks and public funds, a contrivance invented for the purposes of corruption, and for assimilating us in all things to the rotten as well as the sound parts of the British model. It would give you a fever were I to name to you the apostates who have gone over to these heresies, men who were Samsons in the field and Solomons in the council, but who have had their heads shorn by the harlot England. In short, we are likely to preserve the liberty we have obtained only by unremitting labors and perils. But we shall preserve it; and our mass of weight and wealth . . . is so great, as to leave no danger that force will be attempted against us.[65]

[65] Jefferson to Philip Mazzei, 24 April 1796, *Writings*, Vol. IX, pp. 335–36. Note Jefferson's last sentence. Whatever "perils" he envisioned, he was determined they would not escalate into a violent confrontation. Already, it appeared, Jefferson was attempting to spin out a theory of opposition to the government that would stop short of force.

In the debate over the Jay Treaty there was no allegiance to something that we, in the twentieth century, call a political party. Politicians elected to office were normally given the right, in accordance with the Burkeian notion of a representative, to vote their conscience. Party discipline, as we know it today, did not exist.

No better proof of this assertion can be seen than Albert Gallatin's statement that between the years 1795 to 1801 *"there were but two* of those party meetings called for the purpose of deliberating upon the measures to be adopted."[66] These meetings, called caucuses, could hardly be called innovative. Caucuses were an old revolutionary device which had begun in Boston and Tom Dawes's attic in the years prior to the Revolution.[67] The fact was that in these two caucuses, strung out over a period of six years, the discipline was so lax and the freedom so great, that they simply revealed the fragmented nature of politics at that time. "On both occasions," said Gallatin, "we were divided; and on both the members of the minority of each meeting were left at full liberty to vote as they pleased, without being on that account proscribed or considered as having abandoned the principles of the party."[68] What Gallatin described was not a factional alignment, nor a party in the modern sense. He was describing a group concerned with principle and, further, one that had nothing to do with discipline or coercion. The fundamental reason that the republican interest failed to hold was that in the struggles between the personal factions then in existence, the members of the legislature were obligated to no one. Madison expressed his frustrations as the personal leader of such a faction when he wrote Jefferson:

> The progress of this business throughout has to me been the most worrying and vexatious that I ever encountered, and the more so, as the causes lay in the unsteadiness, the follies, the

[66] *The Writings of Albert Gallatin,* ed. Henry Adams (Philadelphia, 1879), Vol. III, p. 553.

[67] Kenneth Umbreit, *Founding Fathers* (New York, 1941), p. 182.

[68] *The Writings of Albert Gallatin,* op. cit., Vol. III, p. 553.

perverseness, and the defections among our friends, more than in
the strength, or dexterity, or malice of our opponents.[69]

As events shifted from the Jay Treaty to other spheres, the
importance of Madison's role as the leader of the opposition faction cannot be better or more clearly demonstrated than in the
politics that led to the selection of the presidential candidates in
1796. The nature of the election process, from a practical viewpoint, reflected the politics of "personal connexion" and friend-
ships. This "old style," traditional school of politics had been
known to Americans during the entire colonial period.[70] The old-
style method produced the selection of a candidate by a few
leaders who agreed on a man proven trustworthy and wise to the
ways of the establishment. He would then be presented to the
voters. No party primary, no truly open selection process for the
highest office in the land existed. The nominating caucuses were
closed affairs. The principal qualifications demanded were not
party loyalty or party obedience or ethnic balance—the kind we
demand in the twentieth century—but leadership ability and
experience. No provision in the constitution was made for a balanced party ticket or even for a party or a ticket. Instead, each of

[69] Madison to Jefferson, 1 May 1796, *The Letters and Other Writings of
James Madison,* op. cit., Vol. II, pp. 99–100.

[70] The continuity between the colonial and early national period styles of
politics can be illustrated. For example, John Beckley, one of the leading
political organizers of the day, was attempting to build a political structure that
would counter the existing influence of "rotten" boroughs then dominating
the old-style politics of Pennsylvania. Beckley, with inside information, no
doubt, wrote a letter just two days before Washington announced he would
not seek the presidency: ". . . a little exertion by a few good active republicans
in each County would bring the people out, and defeat the influence of your
little rotten towns such as Carlisle, Lancaster, York etc." We might assume
the et cetera included most of the people in the state, and Beckley's attempt
to enlarge the level of political organization and thus transcend the influence
of the tightly controlled rotten boroughs, was a reflection of the way politics
had been carried on in Virginia for almost two generations. John Beckley to
William Irvine, 15 Sept. 1796, Irvine Papers, Vol. XIII, Historical Society of
Pennsylvania, in Cunningham, *The Jeffersonian Republicans,* op. cit., p. 103.

the states was to submit a "list of all the persons voted for" and the "Person having the greatest Number of Votes shall be the President . . ." And, "in every Case, after the Choice of the President, the Person having the greatest Number of votes of the Electors shall be the Vice President."[71] The emphasis upon choosing the President assumed that the two best qualified men in the country would be chosen as its leaders. This logic was so completely agreeable to everyone involved in politics at the time that no specific constitutional designation was made for Vice President either in 1796 or in 1800. Everyone simply assumed that the two men chosen would work in harmony for an efficient administration.

But what was even more characteristic of the traditional or old-style school of politics was the absence of candidates campaigning openly for office. Politicians "stood for office," they did not actively seek it. The voters themselves, especially outside the few large cities, still maintained a "habit of subordination," and elites "managed political affairs."[72] In the tradition of an aristocratic political society, the spectacle of a politician overtly grasping for power reflected a distasteful tendency to democracy, still considered a corrupt form of government. Politicians, of whatever persuasion, liked to believe they were dignified and respectable. Thus it is not surprising that while electioneering and campaigning rarely entered the minds of the Founding Fathers, tight control—implicit in the machinery of the electoral college—was never very far in the back of their minds.

Washington's refusal to divulge his plans until late in the summer of 1796 was certainly part of his and his advisors' political strategy; but it also implied that he did not believe an extended party campaign, with contesting factions, was good for the country. The Farewell Address speaks eloquently to this point. Washington wished, as much as possible, to dampen down the possibil-

[71] Article II, Section 1, United States Constitution; superseded by the Twelfth Amendment.

[72] David Hackett Fischer, *The Revolution of American Conservatism*, op. cit., pp. xi–xv, 10.

ity of a virulent contest, and in so doing was in accordance with
the political theory of his time.

From the opposition's side, the theory was equally valid. For
while Madison hinted, and then declared with certainty, the fact
of Washington's retirement, he was faced with the problem of
presenting a candidate who had the wisdom and experience of an
elder statesman, yet, like the Cincinnatus of old, did not appear to
be grasping for power.[73] Fortunately, Madison did not find this a
serious problem. Jefferson, his closest friend and political mentor,
was the ideal candidate. Retired from political life for two years,
he had professed his intentions never to embark on the political
high road again. Jefferson had written Madison, "as to myself . . .
my retirement from office had been meant from all office high or
low, without exception. . . . The little spice of ambition which I
had in my younger days has long since evaporated, and I set still
less store by a posthumous than present name. . . . The question
is forever closed with me . . ."[74]

But Madison was determined, and in the style of friendship and
personal connection he simply plotted Jefferson's candidacy without gaining his consent. This first draft in American presidential
politics was one in which the student had turned the tables on his
master. For years, Jefferson had been urging Madison to become
the leader of the opposition, to take up his pen, plot the strategy,
and, finally, to direct the forces of republican interest. It was this
elevation to the forefront of national politics that gave Madison
the influence and ability to decide Jefferson's fate. Madison was
not only cunning, he was wary. He knew of Jefferson's real sentiments and although he was within a day's ride of Monticello, he

[73] Madison to Jefferson, 19 Dec. 1796, *Writings*, Vol. VI, pp. 296–300.

[74] Jefferson to Madison, 27 April 1795, *The Works of Thomas Jefferson*,
ed. H. A. Washington, 9 vols. (New York, 1884), Vol. IV, pp. 116–17. See
also Jefferson to John Adams, 28 Dec. 1796. "I have no ambition to govern
men. It is a painful and thankless task." Ibid., Vol. IX, p. 154. To Madison in
January of 1797, Jefferson noted, "for I think with the Romans of old, that
the General of today should be a common soldier to-morrow, if necessary."
Ibid., p. 155.

avoided meeting with his mentor. He wrote Monroe: "I have not seen Jefferson and have thought it best to provide him no opportunity of protesting to his friends against being embarked in the contest."[75] Knowingly then, Madison intended to hand Jefferson a *fait accompli,* thus revealing his acceptance of the time-worn method of selecting a candidate. For him the electoral process would proceed according to the style of politics that Virginians had practiced for generations: an agreement on a candidate from the gentry.

On the other side, the forces marshaled by Hamilton assumed from the start a personal tone, which indicated that in 1796 the politics of faction would be intense. It was not that Hamilton had a particular candidate in mind, it was more that he simply believed *anybody* would be better than Jefferson. "'Tis all important to our country that his [Washington's] successor shall be a *safe* man. But it is far less important who of many men that may be named shall be the person, than that it shall not be Jefferson. . . . All personal and partial considerations must be discarded, and everything must give way to the great object of excluding Jefferson."[76] In his search for a "safe" man, who would be "named," Hamilton was worried principally about protecting his system. The proof of this lies in a comment attributed to the new President-elect: "About the 22nd of December, 1796, John Adams spoke to a gentleman in Philadelphia, in these words: 'the Junto at New York have never wanted to make me President. They wish to get in Pinckney, that they may make an AUTOMATON of him.' At the head of this junto is Alexander Hamilton, and this is the way in which our Vice-President speaks of him."[77]

As the election drew nearer, those who commented on public affairs had a tendency to disavow faction and attempt to buttress

[75] Madison to Monroe, 29 Sept. 1796, in Brant, *James Madison, 1787–1800,* op. cit., p. 444.

[76] Hamilton to (unknown), 1796, *Works of Alexander Hamilton,* Vol. VIII, p. 419.

[77] James Thomson Callender, *The American Annual Register, or Historical Memoirs of the United States for the Year 1796* (Philadelphia, 1797), p. 241.

the prevailing theory of harmony in the political system. For example, a Maryland state elector addressed his constituency, warning them that he would "spare no pains to acquire the best information, to vote for that man, who to my judgement, after all information I can obtain, shall appear best qualified, and likely to support the honor, and to preserve and promote the freedom, the tranquility, and the prosperity of our common country. *I am not,* nor will I be a party man . . ."[78] It sounded as though he had been reading Edmund Burke. Electoral independence was as precious in Virginia as it was in Maryland. Charles Simms, hoping to become the elector for the Northern Neck, made it clear to his constituents that he was determined to maintain a freedom of choice, "not finally to decide on the characters for whom I shall vote until the meeting of the electors; yet I am free to declare, that if I retain my present impressions, I shall vote for Patrick Henry and John Adams."[79] Simms was asking the electorate to place their confidence in his judgment.

The issues upon which the campaign turned were few. The towering stature of Washington seemed to diminish the contenders. The time element was short to begin with, and because nothing in the way of an opposition program had been developed—especially as we view a party platform today—the election itself focused on personalities and principles. One political observer noted:

The late President gave intimation of his declining to serve, by a letter, addressed to the public at large, dated September 17, 1796. . . . No leisure was left for mutual correspondence, to ascertain characters, to balance merits, and to turn, in every point of view, a subject so important. . . . Mr. Washington, delayed the annunciation of his design till the last possible minute; so that in

[78] An Address to the Freemen of Prince George's and Montgomery Counties, signed by William Deakins, Jr., of Baltimore, *Federal Gazette*, 20 Oct. 1796.

[79] An Address to the Freeholders of the Counties of Prince William, Stafford and Fairfax, signed by Charles Simms, of Baltimore, *Federal Gazette*, 4 Oct. 1796.

some of the remote states, the citizens had not more than two or three weeks to deliberate.[80]

Under these circumstances it is highly improbable that any systematic party organization could have been developed, and local factions, deeply rooted, would have felt their power unchallenged. In reference to personalities, a typical statement was made by a candidate in North Carolina:

> If elected, I shall vote for Jefferson; in principle he is a Republican; in character and reputation, he is distinguished; in point of abilities he is equalled by few, surpassed by still fewer, within the compass of our political horizon. His election I am satisfied, will be the fairest means of giving tone to the government and supporting its *Republic* dignity, which Mr. Adams, by the introduction of foreign and *aristocratic* principles, may endeavor to shackle.[81]

The author placed his appeal in the context of the principles of a republic versus the principles of an aristocracy. His vote would be cast for a man who subscribed to a republican philosophy. As far as political rhetoric could make it, the election was a contest between republican versus aristocratic principles. John Adams was badgered for introducing monarchical principles, Jefferson defended for promoting republicanism. Adams' *Defence of the Constitutions of the United States* was brought forth and cited as evidence that he was in love with the British constitution. Voters were continually reminded of Jefferson's contribution to liberty and the Declaration. In Pennsylvania, the local handbills attempted to make the choices clear: "Thomas Jefferson is a firm REPUBLICAN—John Adams is an avowed MONARCHIST."[82] Philip Freneau's paper stated "President Washington loves a republican

[80] James Thomson Callender, *Sedgwick and Co., or A Key to the Six Per Cent Cabinet*, op. cit., p. 82.

[81] Notice to the Citizens of Chowan District, signed by John Hamilton, in *Edenton State Gazette* of North Carolina, 20, 27 Oct. and 3 Nov. 1796.

[82] Handbill signed "a Republican," 3 Oct. 1796, Broadside, Historical Society of Pennsylvania.

and hates a monarchist."[83] This division, which was to become the dominant ideological tone of the contest in 1800, revealed the fear of a suspected counterrevolution among the electorate. One example occurred in Philadelphia, where a mob was reported to have gathered at the polls yelling, "Jefferson and no king."[84]

A circular, one of the most common means of communication during the revolutionary era, especially among the committees of correspondence, was used to make the contest between Jefferson and Adams appear to be a choice between a free republic and a monarchy. While this was undoubtedly an overstatement of the effects of electing one of the candidates, the language of the circular is couched in such compelling terms that the authors must have felt that the future republic was at stake. Indeed, as John Beckley had earlier written: "It is now or never for the republican cause."[85]

That these observations had spread fear among the voters at large cannot be doubted. In New Jersey a political tract stated, "There is (the assertion, alas, is too well founded) a powerful party in the United States who have, under a variety of disguises, labored to subvert republicanism, and introduce a system inimical to liberty." There could be little doubt that that system was monarchy or that the faction in question was bent upon subverting the ideology of the republic. The writer concluded: "Mr. Jefferson must be your choice. He can alone reconcile contending parties, and steer the bark into safety."[86]

Another writer, in a Philadelphia newspaper, brought the main issues of the election into focus: eliminate divisive sentiment,

[83] Philadelphia *Gazette of the United States,* 31 Oct. 1796.

[84] William Smith to Ralph Izard, 8 Nov. 1796, "South Carolina Federalist Correspondence," *American Historical Review,* 14 (1909), pp. 784–85.

[85] John Beckley to William Irvine, 15 Sept. 1796, Irvine Papers, Vol. XIII, Historical Society of Pennsylvania.

[86] *President II, Being Observations on the Late Official Address of George Washington: Designed to Promote the Interest of a Certain Candidate for the Executive, and to Explode the Pretensions of Others* (Newark, N.J., 1796), p. 15.

SIR,   Philadelphia, Sept. 25, 1796.

The republican members of the State Legislature and of Congress from this State, before their late adjournment had a meeting to frame a ticket for electors of the President and Vice President. They at the same time appointed a committee to communicate to the citizens of Pennsylvania any information of importance on the subject of the election, which might come to their knowledge at the seat of Government.

By the Death of DAVID RITTENHOUSE, from the City of Philadelphia, a chasm has occurred, and the committee after obtaining every information in their power and consulting with some friends from different counties have agreed to recommend JAMES BOYD of Chester County to complete the ticket, as it would prove an injury to it had a blank remained.

They greatly lament in common with their Rebublican friends throughout the State, that the advocates for fair election in the last Legislature were unable to prevail in districting the State, for the choice of electors ; they are sensible of the inconvenience of the mode adopted. It was no doubt adopted to promote the views of the antirepublicans by giving full scope to their talents at intrigue and combination ; but since it has been forced upon us, let us defeat their defigns by union and activity.

The present is an important crisis. The citizen who now fills the station of chief executive magistrate of the Union has officially declined a re-election and the contest for that important office will lie between two men of very dissimilar politics, indeed—THOMAS JEFFERSON and JOHN ADAMS. It remains with the Citizens of Pennsylvania to decide, in which they will repose confidence,---the uniform advocate of equal rights among citizens, or the champion of rank, titles and hereditary distinctions;---the steady supporter of our present republican constitution ; or the warm panegyrist of the British Monarchical form of Government, one who has unqualifiedly declared as *hazardous* and *dangerous*,* our departure from his model of excellence, the British constitution, in making our Executives and Senates elective. No comment upon opinions so subersive of the basis upon which our free governments rest, need be addressed to Americans ; they will meet in the minds of every one impressions and self-evident truths, that must repel with abhorrence such doctrines.

The issue of the approaching election of President and Vice President from the best information we are able to procure is likely to depend altogether upon the exertions which shall be made in this state in the choice of electors. It is calculated, that the States to the North and South of this will be nearly balanced, so that the casting voice remains with Pennsylvania. No greater spur to unremitting exertions can exist. The first executive magistrate of the Union is to be chosen, the contest is between a tried republican and an avowed aristocrat, the balance is in our hands.

AARON BURR of New-York and THOMAS PINCKNEY of South Carolina will be the principal, it not only, candidates for the Vice Presidency ; the former will be supported by the republican interest.

Should any further information occur worth communicating we shall immediately impart it. Any information from you in return on the great objects which should now engage our undivided attention will be thankfully received.
In behalf of the Committee.

M. Leib, Chairman.

REPUBLICAN TICKET.

THOMAS M'KEAN,	Chief Justice of Pennsylvania,	PHILADELPHIA,
JACOB MORGAN,		PHILADELPHIA COUNTY,
JAMES BOYD,		CHESTER,
JONAS HARTSEL,		NORTHAMPTON,
PETER MUHLENBERG,		MONTGOMERY,
JOSEPH HEISTER,		BERKS,
WM. M'CLAY,		DAUPHIN,
JAMES HANNA,		BUCKS,
JOHN WHITEHILL,		LANCASTER,
WILLIAM IRWIN,		CUMBERLAND
ABRAHAM SMITH.		FRANKLIN,
WILLIAM BROWN,		MIFFLIN,
JOHN PIPER,		BEDFORD,
JOHN SMILIE,		FAYETTE'
JAMES EDGAR,		WASHINGTON.

A number of republican Citizens of the County of Cumberland convened in the Borough of Carlisle, and having the subject of the preceeding letter under their confideration, unanimously agreed, that the ticket therein mentioned, be recommended to their fellow citizens and request that you and all those who retain republican sentiments urge their fellow citizens to turn out to the election on the 4th day of November next, in order that our united endeavours may have the happy effect of having a President and Vice-President of republican sentiments elected.
Signed by order of the meeting
William Brown, Chairman.

October 15th 1796.

Circular by the Republican Committee of Pennsylvania, 1796
(Courtesy of the Historical Society of Pennsylvania)

disassociate oneself from party and faction, and adhere to the republican ideology. He wrote:

> Thomas Jefferson is the man. . . . He will be the cement of discordant interests and of jarring passions—*of no party* but the great party of human benefactors, he will allay the heats of our country, heal its divisions, and calm the boisterous elements of political controversy—Under the administration of a man, untinctured with party spirit, citizens may smoke the calumet of peace. . . . To promote the election of the great Jefferson ought to be the objects of every friend to republicanism and his country . . .[87]

A South Carolina Federalist, attempting to tone down the strife of faction, orated, "In spite of all the perils which we have for some time encompassed . . . we may now congratulate ourselves, that the steady adherance of the American people to their true interests, amidst the storms of faction and the persevering efforts of insidious disorganizers [i.e., those in opposition to the government], has again saved America . . ."[88]

North and South the politics of faction reminded those who had witnessed the Revolution of 1776 that the same forms of protest and organization had reappeared. Henry Cabot Lodge perceived the frustrations of the Federalists in this comment:

> Extra constitutional machinery, mass meetings of the people, semi-permanent committees of correspondence smacked of subversion and the spirit of subversion. When the Jeffersonian movement began to develop Cabot recoiled from the form as well as the substance of its protest. "After all," said Cabot, "where is the boasted advantage of a representative system over the turbulent mobocracy of Athens? If the resort to popular meetings is necessary, faction, and especially faction of great towns—always the

---

[87] Philadelphia *Aurora*, 1 Nov. 1796; Philadelphia *Gazette of the United States*, 1 Nov. 1796.

[88] William L. Smith, *An Oration Delivered in St. Philip's Church*, 4 July 1796 (Charleston, S.C., 1796), p. 38.

most powerful—will be too strong for our mild and feeble government."[89]

What Lodge had clearly described, and Cabot certainly knew, were the revolutionary politics of the 1770s.

When the election was over, and Adams proved the victor, the nation breathed a sigh of relief while realizing that the flames of party spirit had been raised to a dangerously high level. One writer expressed his alarm in terms that everyone would understand. The contest had been carried on in a manner "very objectionable, and, if continued, seems in its tendency, not only calculated to foment and keep up heats and animosities amongst us, but in no long time . . . to overset our union, or split and shiver us into many governments; and if we once begin to divide, no one can forsee the end of it." America, he said, "seemed to split itself into two parties, through predilection for two citizens; a long noted, dreadful rock, a Caesar and Pompey, a Scylla and Charybdis." Indeed, he hoped that the next contest would not even have the "appearance of countenancing parties." Then, in order to drive the main point home, the old revolutionary patriot addressed himself to the true spirit of the constitution. Complaining about the factional preferences of many of the electors, he said an "elector, who, antecedent to his appointment, has engaged to vote for any particular person, sins . . . against the *spirit and vitals* of the constitution." This was the accepted wisdom of the age, a realization that if the factious spirit were to continue it would destroy the constitution. This pamphleteer wanted each state to select its candidate, hoping thereby to frustrate "the sly emissaries, *behind the scenes,* foreign and domestic," to enable the people "to see their *deep* plan, to set us all by the ears with one another, effectually defeated."[90]

[89] George Cabot to Rufus King, 14 Aug. 1795, *Life and Letters of George Cabot*, ed. H. C. Lodge (Boston, 1877), p. 85. See also Charles Warren, *Jacobin and Junto* (Cambridge, Mass., 1931), p. 173.

[90] *A Few Observations on Some Late Public Transactions in and out of Congress, Particularly on the Dangerous and Seemingly Unconstitutional Man-*

Indeed, this was the only practical theory consistent with the constitution, a charter that failed even to mention parties. But equally important was the case made against party and faction by the late President, speaking to what he thought were the purposes of the constitution. From this perspective the only practical way in which one could eliminate their destructive spirit was to "reprobate" them. The new President John Adams agreed and his maiden speech to the Congress was in the language of the non-party state:

> It is impossible to conceal from ourselves, or the world, what has been before observed, that endeavours have been employed to foster and establish a division between the Government and people of the United States. To investigate the causes which have encouraged this attempt is not necessary: but to repel, by decided and united councils, insinuations so derogatory to the honour, and aggressions so dangerous to the constitution . . . is an indispensable duty.
>
> It must not be permitted to be doubted, whether the people of the United States will support the Government established by their free choice; or whether, by surrendering themselves to the direction of foreign and domestic factions, in opposition to their own Government, they will forfeit the honourable station they have hitherto maintained.[91]

Three months later the President continued his attack on the factions that threatened his administration:

> On August 7, 1797 Mr. Adams dined at Faneuil Hall, in Boston, with two hundred and fifty of his fellow citizens. An address was presented to him, which has this passage. "When domestic *factions* appear to have conspired with foreign intrigue, to destroy the peace of our country . . . at such a crisis we are excited, no less by our inclination than our duty, to reprobate and etc."
>
> To this yell of malice and stupidity, the President made a most

---

ner the late Election for a Chief Magistrate was Conducted throughout the States of the Union (Charleston, S.C., 1797), pp. 9, 11–16.

[91] *Messages and Papers of the Presidents*, op. cit., Vol. I, pp. 228–29. Special Session Message, 16 May 1797.

gracious reply. The address had *fourteen* lines upon faction. Mr. Adams rung the changes against faction through forty eight.[92]

Others were soon to take up the President's line, or had already done so. A speaker in Rhode Island told his audience that "two different parties have for a long time agitated and perplexed our national councils. Frivolous debates—tardy and timorous resolutions, have too much marked the character of our government . . ." As a result of these two factions, "this vast continent may be divided into petty republics, destitute of force and energy, dangerous only to themselves. . . . unite my children, and you may yet be an happy people. Divide, and your glory, honour, and national existence, are extinguished forever."[93] The speaker, concerned with union, believed that once party divisions began it would be impossible to constrict them. He saw the federal government splintering into any number of helpless entities.

Bache's *Aurora* and *Porcupine's Gazette* both indulged in reprobating the party spirit prevalent during the election, albeit from different perspectives. Bache pointed out a constitutional defect, one that—if it did not encourage the intrigue of faction—at least afforded it an opportunity:

> Notwithstanding all the *artifice* and *trick* of the cidevant Secretary of the Treasury, Mr. Adams obtained the major suffrages as President. It is a well known fact, that Pinckney was Hamilton's man; and so confident were the Hamiltonians of success, that the subject was mentioned at the present American Minister's table in London, as scarcely admitting of doubt. Things were so happily ordered in the estimation of these men, that the people of the United States were to be *tricked* into a President they did not want, and ousted of one they did want. The constitution favored such a design; and had the Hamiltonians succeeded in this state, their plan would have been successful. It was rumoured before the election, that the ci-devant Secretary wrote to a certain exciseman

[92] James Thomson Callender, *Sketches of the History of America*, op. cit., pp. 258–59.

[93] Paul Allen, *An Oration on the Necessity of Political Union at the Present Day* (Providence, 1797), pp. 6–7.

in this State, to use all his influence to carry the anti-Jefferson ticket, and it was said by those who appeared in the secret, that, if that ticket succeeded, another man besides Adams would be their choice. The unanimity of the votes in New-York and New-Jersey are strong proofs in favor of this plan; but as some eastern people are as cunning as a *Creole*, they were not to be duped by any insidious Cataline.

Then Porcupine went on to note that while "nothing was more infernally wicked than these insinuations. . . . Yet . . . Mr. Adams thinks the charge well founded."[94] As early as March of 1797, it had become apparent to most political observers that a deep split had occurred between the Hamiltonian faction and the Adams faction of the administration.

It had also become obvious to the Republicans that additional efforts would have to be made to reduce the strife of these factions. And as soon as the election results were known Jefferson initiated correspondence to that effect. Writing to Madison on 1 January 1797, he commented:

> I . . . have no feelings which would revolt at a secondary position to Mr. Adams. I am his junior in life, was his junior in Congress, his junior in the diplomatic line, his junior lately in the civil government. *Before* the receipt of your letter I had written the enclosed one to him. . . . If Mr. Adams can be induced to administer the government on its true principles, and to relinquish his bias to an English constitution, it is to be considered whether it would not be on the whole for the public good to come to a good understanding with him as to his future elections. He is perhaps the only sure barrier against Hamilton's getting in.[95]

Jefferson's primary concern here is with philosophical republican principles of government. In his modesty, there is no indication that he is going to set himself in opposition to the new President. If anything, he indicates the contrary, a willingness to submerge himself in the new administration.

[94] *Porcupine's Works*, op. cit., Vol. V, pp. 121–22.
[95] Jefferson to Madison, 1 Jan. 1797, *Writings*, Vol. IX, pp. 358–59.

This attempt to reconcile whatever factional differences may have existed between them had been a deep concern of Jefferson's for some time. As early as February 1796, Jefferson had written Adams a very soothing letter that ended on a decidedly nonpolitical note:

> I am glad to see that whatever grounds of apprehension may have appeared of a wish to govern us otherwise than on principles of reason and honesty, *we* are getting the better of them. I am sure, from the honesty of your heart, you join me in detestation of the corruption of the English government, and that no man on earth is more incapable than yourself of seeing that copied among us, willingly. I have been among those who feared the design to introduce it here, and it has been a strong reason with me for wishing there was an ocean of fire between that island and us. But away politics.[96]

Thus Jefferson, perhaps suspecting that Adams might become the next President, had written his old friend regarding his greatest fear. In December, Jefferson had written Madison that in the event of "an equal division" of electoral votes "it is both my duty and inclination, therefore, to relieve the embarrassment, should it happen: and in that case, I pray you and authorize you fully, to solicit on my behalf that Mr. Adams may be preferred. He has always been my senior from the commencement of our public life, and the expression of the public will being equal, this circumstance ought to give him the preference."[97] Not surprisingly, there was no mention of party here. On the contrary, Jefferson was doing his best to dampen down party spirit as much as possible. A few days later he penned a letter to Adams that disavowed his attachment to any party or faction, expressed confidence in Adams' election and even warned him about the factional intrigues within his own administration:

> The public and the papers have been much occupied lately in placing us in a point of opposition to each other. I trust with

[96] Jefferson to Adams, 28 Feb. 1796, *Letters*, Vol. I, p. 260.
[97] Jefferson to Madison, 17 Dec. 1796, *Writings*, Vol. IX, p. 351.

confidence that less of it has been felt by ourselves personally.
. . . your election to the first magistracy . . . with me . . . has
never been doubted. . . . Indeed it is possible that you may be
cheated of your succession by a trick worthy the subtlety of your
arch-friend of New York who has been able to make of your real
friends tools to defeat their and your just wishes.

Jefferson's closing remarks would indicate that if there were a
conclusion, it certainly did not include a concern with party
feeling:

No one then will congratulate you with purer disinterestedness
than myself. . . . that your administration may be filled with
glory, and happiness to yourself and advantage to us is the sincere
wish of one who though in the course of our own voyage through
life, various little incidents have happened or been contrived to
separate us, retains still for you the solid esteem of the moments
when we were working for our independence, and sentiments of
respect and affectionate attachment.[98]

In this same spirit Jefferson wrote Madison in late January,
recording his feelings concerning the new President. But what is
remarkable about this letter is the author's repudiation of the
factional strife of 1793 and his determination not to involve himself in anything resembling a party struggle again. He goes even
further, placing a limitation on his role as the Vice President, a
description that in large degree defined the office for his successors:

My letters inform me that Mr. Adams speaks of me with great
friendship, and with satisfaction in the prospect of administering
the government in concurrence with me. I am glad of that first
information, because though I saw that our ancient friendship was
affected by a little leaven, partly by his constitution, partly by the
contrivance of others, yet I never felt a diminution of confidence
in his integrity, and retained a solid affection for him. . . . As
to my participating in the administration, if by that he meant the
executive cabinet, both duty and inclination will shut that door to

[98] Jefferson to Adams, 28 Dec. 1796, ibid., pp. 355–57.

me. I cannot have a wish to see the scenes of 1793 revived as to myself, and to descend daily into the arena like a gladiator, to suffer martyrdom in every conflict. As to duty, the Constitution will know me as the member of a legislative body; and its principle is, that of a separation of legislative, executive and judiciary functions, except in cases specified. If this principle be not expressed in direct terms, yet it is clearly the spirit of the Constitution, and it ought to be so commented and acted on by every friend to free government.[99]

John Adams, in his turn, simply took it for granted that Jefferson would be above party strife: "I expect, from his ancient friendship, his good Sense and general good dispositions, a decorum of Conduct at least, if not as cordial and uniform a Support as I have given to my Predecessor . . ."[100] And there could be no doubt that Adams believed he had given full support to Washington, with no regard for party or factional considerations.

The attempt had thus been made to begin the new administration without the strife that had uncomfortably burdened the leaders of the first two administrations. Unfortunately, the attempt would prove to be a mere chance to stop, take an easy breath, and then become immersed in the politics of faction. Jefferson was by this time philosophical about the strife, the more so because, as he would say later, it did strange things to men's behavior. "The passions" were "too high," he wrote to Rutledge. "You and I have formerly seen warm debates and high political passions. But gentlemen of different politics would then speak to each other, and separate the business of the Senate from that of society. It is not so now. Men who have been intimate all their lives, cross the streets to avoid meeting, and turn their heads another way, lest they should be obliged to touch their hats."[101]

[99] Jefferson to Madison, 22 Jan. 1797, ibid., pp. 367–68; see also Jefferson to Elbridge Gerry, 13 May 1797, ibid., pp. 381–82.

[100] John Adams to Elbridge Gerry, 20 Feb. 1797, *Warren-Adams Letters, Being Chiefly a Correspondence among John Adams, Samuel Adams and James Warren*, Massachusetts Historical Society Collections, 73 (1925), p. 331.

[101] Jefferson to Edward Rutledge, 24 June 1797, *Writings*, Vol. IX, p. 411.

Indeed, the irrationality of this behavior troubled Jefferson and he looked for something better. In February, he had ruminated speculatively on the cause of this factional behavior and then made a prediction. With Washington's disappearance from the political scene, he believed the people would return to a spirit of harmony. But while it would prove to be a naïve prediction, it did define precisely the context in which the political struggles would take place for the next three years:

> Where a constitution, like ours, wears a mixed aspect of monarchy and republicanism, its citizens will naturally divide into two classes of sentiment, according as their tone of body or mind, their habits, connections and callings, induce them to wish to strengthen either the monarchical or the republican features of the constitution. Some will consider it as an elective monarchy, which had better be made hereditary, and therefore endeavor to lead towards that all the forms and principles of its administration. Others will view it as an energetic republic, turning in all its points on the pivot of free and frequent elections.
>
> I have no doubt we shall see a pretty rapid return of general harmony, and our citizens moving in phalanx in the paths of regular liberty, order, and a sacrosanct adherence to the Constitution.[102]

Jefferson obviously believed that John Adams intended to adhere to the prevailing administrative theory of the times—a unified government, a harmonious administration, and a tone in both that would quickly reduce the friction and discontent among the people. This was a step in the opposite direction from factional politics. Accordingly, he wrote Archibald Stuart that it was "most advisable to be silent till we see what turn the new administration will take."[103]

Meanwhile, Jefferson continued, philosophically and practically, to see the politics of his time in the context of republicanism versus monarchy. He was still obsessed with the fear of counter-

[102] Jefferson to James Sullivan, 9 Feb. 1797, ibid., pp. 377–78.

[103] Jefferson to Archibald Stuart, 4 Jan. 1797, *The Works of Thomas Jefferson* (Federal Edition), op. cit., Vol. VII, p. 99.

revolution in the young nation's institutions and a reversal of those principles established in the Revolution of 1776. His faith in the future of American independence oscillated wildly between extremes of optimism and pessimism. Thus he wrote to Aaron Burr in June, describing his lost hopes that the nation would have avoided the strife of faction. They had instead been "duped" into supporting the British faction in the executive. Indeed, Jefferson even wondered if the power of the revolutionary republican ideology was strong enough to overcome the spirit of faction and preserve the republic:

> I had always hoped, that the popularity of the late President being once withdrawn from active effect, the natural feelings of the people towards liberty would restore the equilibrium between the executive and legislative departments, which had been destroyed by the superior weight and effect of that popularity; and that their natural feelings of moral obligation would discountenance the ungrateful predilection of the executive in favor of Great Britain. . . .
> However, what with the English influence in the lower, and the Patroon influence in the upper part of your State, I presume little is to be hoped. If a prospect could be once opened upon us of the penetration of truth into the eastern States; if the people there, who are unquestionably republicans, could discover that they have been duped into the support of measures calculated to sap the very foundations of republicanism, we might still hope for salvation, and that it would come as of old, from the east. But will that region ever awake to the true state of things? Can the middle, southern and western States hold on till they awake? These are painful and doubtful questions. . . . [If] . . . you can give me a comfortable solution of them, it will relieve a mind devoted to the preservation of our republican government in the true form and spirit in which it was established, but almost oppressed with apprehensions that fraud will at length effect what force could not, and that what with currents and counter-currents, we shall, in the end, be driven back to the land from which we launched twenty years ago.[104]

[104] Jefferson to Aaron Burr, 17 June 1797, *Writings*, Vol. IX, pp. 402–4.

Burr knew exactly what the old patriot wanted to hear, because in his reply he suggested "the moment requires free communication among those who adhere to the principles of our revolution."[105] This exchange between the two set the stage, as it were, for the great debate that would take place in 1800. The principles of republicanism and their preservation became the principal theme. Jefferson would mention it time and time again, until, in the full splendor of his accession to power, he believed that that preservation had become a reality. However, when he had written his letter to Burr, his mind was filled with doubt. One of his last lines had been totally pessimistic: "Indeed, my dear Sir, we have been but a sturdy fish on the hook of a dexterous angler, who, letting us flounce till we have spent our force, brings us up at last."[106] The "angler" was Hamilton and his British faction; and Jefferson, his optimism failing, had expressed his apprehension that the angler's counterrevolution would culminate in the restoration of the British monarchy of 1775.

Despite good intentions, however, the spirit of party and faction continued to intrude upon the life of the Vice President. After the publication of the Mazzei letter, he warned one of his correspondents in a special postscript: "Take care that nothing from my letter gets into the newspapers."[107] To another he imparted: "the hostile use which is made of whatever can be laid hold of mine, obliges me to caution the friends to whom I write, never to let my letters get out of their own hands, lest they should get into the newspapers."[108] It is painfully obvious that Jefferson was doing everything in his power to dampen down the spirit of party, to add nothing to its fuel.

As Jefferson's letter to Mazzei surfaced, an opportunity presented itself for Jefferson and his colleagues to launch a counterattack against Hamilton and to rally republican supporters to his

---

[105] Burr to Jefferson, 21 June 1797, Jefferson Papers, CII, 17438 Lib. Cong.

[106] Jefferson to Burr, 3 Aug. 1797, *Writings*, Vol. IX, pp. 413–14.

[107] Jefferson to Colonel Bell, 18 May 1797, *Writings*, Vol. IX, p. 387.

[108] Jefferson to Peregrine Fitzhugh, 4 June 1797, Jefferson Papers, Duke University.

banner. After soliciting advice as to how to act, Jefferson chose to be silent on the basis that any public defense would "draw me at length into a publication of all (even the secret) transactions of the administration while I was in it; and embroil me personally with every member of the executive, with the judiciary, and with others still." This was the style of factional politics and Jefferson rejected it. His reaction to the Hamilton faction ran in a somewhat different pattern. Unwilling to make his objections public, he complained to a few trusted friends, placing his comments in the context of conspiracy: "they are endeavoring to submit us to the substance, as they already have to the *forms* of the British government; meaning by *forms*, the birthdays, levees, processions to parliament, inauguration pomposities, etc."[109] Indeed, these were the symbols of monarchy that had become accepted by the Adams administration. They contradicted that republican simplicity Jefferson wished to preserve in order to prevent the people from being overawed by their government. This reverence for plainness and simplicity was at the heart of Jefferson's understanding of the ethos of republicanism. And it was from this perspective that he was unable to hide his contempt for any executive who surrounded himself with the trappings of royalty and the equivalent of palace guards.

Moreover, that had been the advice of his chief collaborator. When asked how to handle the Mazzei letter, Madison had counseled his mentor according to the accepted theory of his time. He even cited Washington's attitude toward factional disputes as a precedent. It is "a ticklish experiment to say publicly yes or no to the interrogatories of party spirit. It may bring on dilemmas, not to be easily forseen, of disagreeable explanations or tacit confessions. Hitherto the Precedents have been the other way. . . . The late President was silent for many Years as to the letters imputed to him . . ."[110] Evidently, Madison believed the less said about matters relating to party issues, the better. Don't make the Mazzei

---

[109] Jefferson to Madison, 3 Aug. 1797, *Writings*, Vol. IX, p. 414.
[110] Madison to Jefferson, 5 Aug. 1797, Madison Papers, XX, 58 Lib. Cong.

letter an issue; don't even recognize faction and thereby elevate it to an undeserved status.

In terms of the natural divisions of Congress in 1797–98, it is clear that those which applied in 1787, during the debates over the constitution, were, for many, still in force. Jefferson's comments upon the origins of party and faction make perfectly clear his views on their significance and what they would do to the republic:

> It is true that a party has risen up among us, or rather has come among us, which is endeavoring to separate us from all friendly connection with France, to unite our destinies with those of Great Britain, and to assimilate our government to theirs. Our lenity in permitting the return of the old tories, gave the first body to this party; they have been increased by large importations of British merchants and factors, by American merchants dealing on British capital, and by stock dealers and banking companies, who, by the aid of a paper system, are enriching themselves to the ruin of our country, and swaying the government by their possession of the printing presses, which their wealth commands, and by other means, not always honorable to the character of our countrymen. Hitherto, their influence and their system have been irresistible, and they have raised up an executive power which is too strong for the Legislature. But I flatter myself they have passed their zenith.[111]

Federalist William Hindeman wrote "the Antis in our House count upon 51 on their side, We 55, so that if the Federal Members would all attend and be firm . . . the Power is with Us . . ."[112] Like Jay,[113] Hindeman had assessed the relationships of power using the terminology of the constitutional period. Theodore Sedgwick revealed his factional bias by dividing the House into "52 determined and rancorous Jacobins, and 54 who profess attachment to the government, or in other words, confidence in

[111] Jefferson to Col. Arthur Campbell, 1 Sept. 1797, *Writings*, Vol. IX, pp. 419–20.

[112] William Hindeman to Rufus King, 12 April 1798, *Life and Correspondence of Rufus King*, op. cit., Vol. II, p. 314.

[113] See Chapter II, p. 42.

the Executive . . ."[114] Sedgwick had made a succinct analysis:
there were those who professed allegiance to the government, and
there were those who, in his eyes, were undermining the government in true French revolutionary style. Whoever opposed Hamilton's factional policies was a "Jacobin," and the charge was made
with effect. Almost eleven months later Jefferson complained:

> Those who have no wish but for the peace of their country, and
> its independence of all foreign influence, have a hard struggle
> indeed, overwhelmed by a cry as loud and imposing as if it were
> true, of being under French influence, and this raised by a faction
> composed of English subjects residing among us, or such as are
> English in all their relations and sentiments.[115]

When Madison retired as the leader of the opposition, Albert
Gallatin took his place and the fortunes of republicanism began to
decline. Illness and a paucity of speakers for the opposition caused
Gallatin to say, "Our side of the House is so extremely weak in
speakers and in men of business that . . . Nicholas and myself
must stay, and at all events be ready to give our support to those
measures upon which the political salvation of the Union may
perhaps eventually depend."[116] Gallatin apparently believed that
the pressures against the opposition had reached such heights that
the future of the republic was at stake. This period of demoraliza-
tion was during the infamous XYZ affair, the time when Talleyrand had imposed a number of insults upon the American representatives. The reaction in America was to solidify favorable
opinion of the administration; and, equally, to change *en masse*
the population's ideas about the French Revolution. One Boston
divine stated in his sermon:

> The editors, patrons and abettors of those vehicles of slander upon
> our government—those wet nurses of a French faction in the

---

[114] Theodore Sedgwick to Rufus King, 9 April 1798, *Life and Correspondence of Rufus King*, op. cit., Vol. II, p. 310.

[115] Jefferson to General Gates, 30 May 1797, *Writings*, Vol. IX, p. 391.

[116] Albert Gallatin to his wife, 13 Feb. 1798, *The Writings of Albert
Gallatin*, op. cit., pp. 193–94.

bowels of our country, have no longer any cloak for their guilt. The late intelligence from our envoys has unmasked the traitorous views of the whole party, and has recovered all honest citizens from the delusion which had been imposed upon them.[117]

Events had changed dramatically in less than eight months. In June 1797, Jefferson had been guardedly optimistic regarding America's relations with the French republic. He had written Madison that "nothing less than the miraculous string of events which have taken place, to wit . . . bankruptcy of England, mutiny in her fleet and King's writing letters recommending peace, could have cooled the fury of the British faction. Even all that will not prevent considerable efforts still in both parties to show our teeth to France."[118] It was a prophetic letter, for with the coming of the XYZ affair, the "British faction" and the rise of party strife would reach unprecedented heights.

In this rise of the politics of faction, Madison, like Jefferson, saw the possibilities of counterrevolution. Within six months of Jefferson's prediction, Madison had written Monroe a warning, preparing him to expect the unthinkable: "You will be confronted with a progressive apostasy from the principles of our Revolution and Governments, which marked the period of your absence. If events should not be unpropitious to the monarchical party, you may prepare yourself for still more wonderful indications of its spirit and views. Those who tolerate at present the fashionable sentiments, will soon be ready to embrace and avow them."[119] Madison, Monroe, and Jefferson believed the British faction had gained such control that it might totally alter the principles of the government. In fact, Jefferson mentioned to Burr in June: "[our course] depends on events, and these are so incalculable, that I

---

[117] David Osgood, D.D., *Some Facts evincive of the atheistical, anarchical, and in other respects, immoral Principles of the French republicans stated in* A *Sermon* (Boston, 1798), p. 22.

[118] Jefferson to Madison, 15 June 1797, *Writings*, Vol. IX, p. 399.

[119] Madison to Monroe, 17 Dec. 1797, *The Letters and Other Writings of James Madison*, op. cit., Vol. II, p. 119.

consider the future character of our republic as in the air . . ."[120]

As the new year dawned, Jefferson sensed that the republic was in danger, its future more than just "in the air." On the second day of 1798 he wrote to a friend complaining about the factious tone of a publication directed at him: "I do not know whether you have seen the *furious abuse* of me in the Baltimore papers by a Mr. Luther Martin . . ."[121] This kind of abuse was something he attempted to avoid, but would nevertheless become increasingly involved in for the next two years. But abuse in the newspapers was one thing, congressional power was another. In the second session, the Congress passed a law for a provisional army, debated going to war with France[122] while suspending trade with that country, and made provisions for a Department and Secretary of the Navy.[123] The consequence of these bills—especially their tone—caused Jefferson to write Edmund Pendleton: "The present period . . . is the most eventful ever known since that of 1775, and will decide whether the principles established by that contest are to prevail, or give way to those they subverted."[124] Again it becomes obvious that Jefferson had in his mind the threat of counterrevolution in the principles of government. The weight of the recent legislation had given a military cast to the administration that threatened the meaning of the American Revolution.[125]

[120] Jefferson to Burr, 17 June 1797, *Writings*, Vol. IX, p. 403.

[121] Jefferson to Mann Page, Esq., 2 Jan. 1798, ibid., p. 428.

[122] Jefferson to Madison, 29 March 1798, *Writings*, Vol. X, p. 16.

[123] Jefferson to Madison, 26 April 1798, ibid., p. 31.

[124] Jefferson to E. Pendleton, 6 April 1798, ibid., p. 26.

[125] There were many, of course, who doubted Jefferson's sincerity and looked upon his concern for the principles of the American Revolution as a means to stir up propaganda for the opposition. One of these was Timothy Pickering, a Federalist, and as far as Jefferson was concerned a member of the British faction. "When the ashes of the controversies of the 1790's had cooled, a generation later, Timothy Pickering, . . . wrote that whatever popularity the Republicans had achieved was owing to their whipping up a love for the French and a hatred for the British, that in their tactics they had merely revived issues and passions which had been alive during the War for Inde-

These foreign measures, however, would be paled into insignificance by the domestic bills passed in that session. Jefferson knew that the prohibitions against preparations for "war measures *externally*" meant "consenting to every rational measure of *internal* defence and preparation." And in order to pay for the preparations, a land tax would be needed. This, of course, would provide "one party" the excuse "to make it a new source of patronage and expense."[126] To Jefferson, it all appeared to be in the tradition of the British system of corruption.

During the last week in April, Jefferson, as the presiding officer of the Senate, got wind of the "war party['s]" intentions, "in a fit of unguarded passion . . . to pass a citizen bill, an alien bill, and a sedition bill . . ." The alien bill would be proposed in hopes of reaching Albert Gallatin, the peerless leader in the House.[127] The sedition bill had as its object "the suppression of the Whig presses," and, Jefferson added, "Bache's has been particularly named." In addition to this new horror, Jefferson suspiciously described his version of the party machinations taking place in New York, indicating that there, Hamilton was as powerful as ever:

Hamilton is coming on as Senator from New York. There have been so much contrivance and combination in that, as to show there is some great object in hand. Troup, the district judge of New York, resigns towards the close of the session in their Assembly. The appointment of Mr. Hobart, then Senator, to succeed Troup, is not made by the President till after the Assembly had risen. Otherwise, they would have chosen the Senator in place of Hobart. Jay then names Hamilton Senator, but not till a day or two before his own election as Governor was to come on,

---

pendence." *A Re-Review of the Correspondence between the Honorable John Adams . . . and the late William Cunningham, Esq.* (Salem, 1824), p. 38. In Marshall Smelzer, "The Jacobin Frenzy: The Menace of Monarchy, Plutocracy and Anglophobia, 1789–1798," *Review of Politics*, Vol. 21 (1959).

126 Jefferson to Madison, 12 April 1798, *Writings*, Vol. X, pp. 27–28.
127 Jefferson to Madison, 26 April 1798, ibid., p. 31.

lest the unpopularity of the nomination should be in time to affect his own election.[128]

That Hamilton later refused the office[129] did not ease Jefferson's apprehension. He had been named the third leading military figure in America, behind Generals Knox and Pinckney. And though Washington was still nominally the commander-in-chief, it was acknowledged by everyone that he was too feeble to take the field. The responsibility would therefore fall upon Hamilton, and neither Jefferson nor Madison believed this line of succession had occurred accidentally. Adams evidently believed he had made the appointment only under pressure from Washington. In his official correspondence to the Secretary of War he wrote: ". . . there has been too much intrigue in this business with General Washington and me . . ."[130] The fear among the opposition was that Washington's commission was merely window dressing, and that in the event of an emergency, he would sound the alarm and then step aside for Hamilton.

For some, those who knew their English history, the fear was even greater. As George Nicholas put it:

[In England] Fairfax was the commander in chief of the army, he was a successful and a popular general, and a virtuous man. He was kept in office until the plans of those who meditated a change in government, were ripe for execution. They knew he would never consent to that change, and the command of the army was put into other hands. . . . What has happened, may happen again; and when we are calculating on its probability, we should recollect that the monarchy-loving Hamilton is now so fixed, as to be able, with *one-step*, to fill the place of our present commander in chief.[131]

128 Ibid., pp. 32–33.

129 Jefferson to Madison, 3 May 1798, *Writings*, Vol. X, p. 35.

130 Adams to J. McHenry, 29 Aug. 1798, *Works*, Vol. VIII, p. 588.

131 A *Letter from George Nicholas of Kentucky to His Friend in Virginia Justifying the Conduct of the Citizens of Kentucky as to some of the measures of the General Government* . . . (Lexington, Ky.: John Bradford, 1798), pp. 30–31. No date attached.

This fear was seen not only by George Nicholas, a friend of Jefferson's and Madison's and a fervent republican philosopher, it was corroborated years later by none other than John Adams himself:

> . . . the British faction was determined to have a war with France, and Alexander Hamilton at the head of the army and *then* Pres. of US. Peace with France was therefore *treason* against their fundamental maxims and reasons of State. . . . These were their motives, and they exhausted all their wit in studies and labors to defeat the whole design. A war with France, an alliance with England, and Alexander Hamilton, the father of their speculating systems, at the head of our army and the state, were their hobbyhorse, their vision of sovereign felicity.[132]

Opposition to the alien and sedition bills occurred almost immediately, and Adams, as the symbolic head of the country, was confronted with the younger generation—protesting and demonstrating against his repressive legislation. James Madison too, outraged at least as much as the young people, registered his anger against the President. By the time he ended his letter, he had brought into question Adams' republican principles, even linking him with the ever-present potential for counterrevolution:

> Every answer he gives to his addressers unmasks more and more his principles and views. His language to the young men at Pha. is the most abominable and degrading that could fall from the lips of the first magistrate of an independent people, and particularly from a Revolutionary patriot. It throws some light on his meaning when he remarked to me, "that there was not a single principle the same in the American and French Revolutions," and on my alluding to the contrary sentiment of his predecessor expressed to Adet on the presentment of the Colours, added, "that it was false let who would express it." The abolition of Royalty was it seems not one of his Revolutionary principles. Whether he always made

[132] John Adams to William Cunningham, Esq., 20 March 1809, *Suppressed History*, p. 364.

this profession is best known to those, who knew him in the year 1776.[133]

In addition to the Alien and Sedition Acts, the administration passed a land tax, proposed a snuff tax and a carriage tax, and seemed to be preparing the way for a salt tax. Madison, whose pristine republicanism as well as his notion of sound politics was opposed in principle to almost any kind of taxation, wondered how the administration—intent on disrupting French-American commerce—expected the average citizen to pay. His contempt for the administration and Adams took on a sinister tone. Clearly, Madison believed the train of legislation passed by the new administration was a blatant appeal to party violence. Adams, he believed, had gone berserk. Moreover, he was afraid that Monroe, one of his closest friends, was about to be victimized by the "spirit of party revenge":

How far the views of the Govt. will be answd by annihilating the ability to pay a land tax at the very moment of imposing it, will be best explained by the experimt. Looking beyond the present moment it may be questioned whether the interests of G.B. will be as much advanced by the sacrifice of our trade with her enemies as may be intended. . . . There is too much passion, it seems in our Councils to calculate consequences of any sort. The only hope is that its violence by defeating itself may save the Country. The answers of Mr. Adams to his addressers form the most grotesque scene in the tragicomedy acting by the Govermt. They present not only the grossest contradictions to the maxims measures and language of his predecessor and the real principles and interests of his Constituents, but to himself. He is verifying compleately the last feature in the character drawn of him by Dr. F., however his title may stand to the two first, "Always an honest man, often a wise one, but sometimes wholly out of his senses." . . . Monroe is much at a loss what course to take in consequence of the wicked assault on him by Mr. A. and I am as much so as to the advice that ought to be given him. It deserves consideration perhaps that

[133] Madison to Jefferson, 20 May 1798, *The Writings of James Madison,* op. cit., Vol. VI, pp. 320–21.

if the least occasion be furnished for reviving Governmental attention to him, the spirit of party revenge may be wreaked thro' the forms of the Constitution.[134]

What Madison had concluded, and rather vehemently, was that the politics of faction had, by mid-1798, blurred the separation of powers. Control of the legislature by a vengeful faction had taken place; and with a sympathetic executive, they were capable of any violation of the constitution. Not surprisingly, this was, at least in theory, the culmination of the politics of faction. The "profound scholar and politician" of the Constitutional Convention began to see events taking the worst possible turn. Within the next six months the rage of party and the spirit of faction would descend upon the republic. Jefferson and Madison would write the Kentucky and Virginia Resolutions, introducing a new dimension to the factional struggle, and the opposition would become noticeably widespread.

As the year 1798 drew to a close and 1799 appeared, the nation saw and heard its writers and orators proclaiming "disaster lay ahead" if the spirit of party continued unabated. Even the Almanac for 1799 predicted disaster: "On the 10th of October next, a portentous comet (which with fear of change perplexes) will approach our political hemisphere; and if it cross upon us at the same instant as the Bulam fever, the Lord have mercy on us!"[135] New Englanders as well as Southerners reviled against party and faction. The Reverend Azel Backus thundered his denunciation of the "wiles of faction, these depths of Satan" in the same spirit that he might have spoken of Calvin's theory of predestination: "The perfection of a government will not save it from the evils of faction and party spirit." He added, "The divine government itself has long had its opposers."[136] The implication was clear: when

---

[134] Madison to Jefferson, 10 June 1798, ibid., pp. 324–25.

[135] "Almanac Predictions," *The Philadelphia Magazine and Review*, No. I, Vol. I (Jan. 1799), p. 156.

[136] Azel Backus, *Absalom's Conspiracy: A Sermon Preached at the General Election at Hartford in the State of Connecticut, May 10th, 1798* (Hartford, 1798), pp. 5–8.

factions arose, the republic was inevitably doomed and those who promoted faction and party, being equivalent to the devil, should be banished to hell. Jedidiah Morse was more succinct regarding the political theory of his time: "A spirit of *insubordination to civil authority* is another vice which has endangered the existence of our government. Having a constitution and rulers of our own choice . . . there cannot be even a plausible reason alleged to justify disrespect and disobedience." He concluded, "FACTION has been bold and open-mouthed!"[137] Another New Englander said that "nothing tends more directly to the misery, and destruction of a community than want of confidence, between rulers, and ruled. It is wise and prudent, in a republic, to keep up a watchful eye over those who are intrusted with the affairs of government: But all combinations of lesser bodies, to counteract or embarrass public measures, or control lawful authority, are both dangerous and detestable, as they tend to tumult and faction, and so to anarchy and confusion."[138]

Antiparty sentiment in the Middle States was expressed in exactly the same terms as it was in New England. A writer in New York wrote:

> The two parties . . . would do well to desist from calling each other by the unjust and irritable appellations of French faction, English faction, or Federalists, and Anti-Federalists, etc. As *Patriots*, as *Men*, and as *Christians*, they should henceforth endeavor to forget all past dissentions and animosities, and *all unite*, in supporting and defending our *excellent Constitution* and Government against the attacks of every foreign and domestic foe.[139]

Not only did the New Yorker wish to abolish all factions and unite around the constitution, he indicated by his selection of the

[137] Morse, *A Sermon on the Anniversary of Thanksgiving in Massachusetts*, op. cit., p. 14.

[138] Joseph Sumner, *A Sermon preached at Shrewsbury, November 28, 1799, on the Anniversary Thanksgiving in Massachusetts* (Brookfield, Mass., 1800), pp. 20–21.

[139] Donald Fraser, *Party-Spirit Exposed, or Remarks on the Times, by a Gentleman of New York* (New York, 1799), pp. 15–16.

names of the factions, that their origins went back to the debates over the constitution. All of these sentiments were merely reflections of a generally accepted view of civil society. Many of the outspoken political commentators saw, amidst the danger, a necessity to make a plea for unity, while at the same time excoriating the factions and their behavior. One of these, Alexander Addison, was a Philadelphia writer who told his audience:

> To remove our danger we must remove divisions, jealousies, and suspicions, so to remove these, we must silence slanderers, and set our faces against them. We have seen the sad effects, and the gross misrepresentations of those lying newspapers, lying pamphlets, lying letters and lying conversations, with which this country has been filled. . . . Silence these slanderers, and we shall be as happy as we are free, as united as we are happy, and as formidable as we are united.
>
> Finally, in order to remove the danger thereby threatened, it is our duty to endeavor to remove that impression, which our divisions have made on the French government. As they rest their hopes of injuring us on the belief that there is a party among ourselves devoted to their will; let us show them that there is no such party. Let us unite in one band of unity among ourselves, and confidence in our administration; and to testify this union and confidence to the world, let us unanimously sign an instrument expressing to our government our confidence in the rectitude of its measures . . .[140]

Even though Addison called for an impossible "instrument" of unanimity, his message was clear: there must be no opposition party and those who were liars and slanderers, i.e., the promoters of party, must be silenced. This certainly was the rationale behind the Alien and Sedition Acts, which, in their turn, would produce another rationale and reaction. Moreover, the latter was not long in surfacing. As opposition to the administration became

[140] Alexander Addison, Esq., *Oration on the Rise and Progress of the United States* (Philadelphia, 1798), pp. 40–41.

widespread, as the possibility of war with France heightened, as the outline of a concerted movement of factions and parties became obvious, the rhetoric of those opposed to party shifted from an emphasis upon administration to an emphasis upon the constitution. Hezekiah Packard, speaking for a concerned clergy, pointed to the coming "catastrophe" and urged a thorough house-cleaning of the republican ideologues in the administration. He did this, however, from his perspective on the constitution:

> . . . when disorganizing principles attempt the overthrow of church and state, the christian patriot takes the alarm and uses the greatest efforts to prevent the threatened catastrophe. . . .
>
> Owing to foreign influence and to the disorganizing schemes of a few designing men, some in our State legislatures and even in our national government, have discovered prominent features of a party spirit. And those who have been most active in causing divisions in our national councils, have been among the first to lament and to complain, *that our state governments and congresses are divided*. . . . Let this consideration make us jealous of those who cause divisions and occasion unreasonable opposition to lawful authority.[141]

Another writer, calling himself "A Friend to The Constitution," echoed the same message:

> . . . that spirit of party which generally animates an opposition, is no longer allowable when ceasing to be a mere opposition, it has become the government of the country, and has acquired the power of dictating the measures of the nation. . . . there is much danger of being still actuated by the spirit of revenge; by the spirit of party rather than that of the nation. To guard against this danger, which in republics has often produced such calamities, *which has seldom been more imminent than in the present moment*, all those who love real liberty ought, unmindful of former distinctions or animosities, to rally together round the standard

[141] Hezekiah Packard, *Federal Republicanism, Displayed in Two Discourses* (Boston, April 1799), Introduction, p. 34.

of the constitution, and form one indissoluble band for its protection.[142]

Indeed, this shift in focus, from merely denouncing party to an
argument that linked party to the certain destruction of the constitution and the federal union, contained within it a new dimension. The analyses that developed from 1799 on began to speculate
on the potential for revolution in America. The argument that
revolution was the inevitable result of faction and party maturing
in the body politic became standard fare for almost everyone who
commented on the political scene. On one side were those who
supported the administration's every action, regardless of its theoretical departure from the constitution; on the other side were
those who saw republicanism endangered and the constitution
rendered void by the acts of the administration. This latter group
tended to see political developments in terms of a conspiracy, or a
"design" against liberty and an effort to restore monarchy. The
suspicions on the other side, i.e., of those who supported law and
order, were wont to view all opposition to the administration in
terms of potential revolutionary activity.

The suspicions and fears manufactured on both sides during the
years leading up to 1800 were summarized by one of the most
vitriolic editors of the time. Yet even he—ironically attempting to
capsulize the consequences of party—failed to extricate himself
from the strife of faction in which all were immersed:

> According to the laudable customs of these virtuous and decent
> republicans, every principle of honor and honesty has . . . been
> totally laid aside. Mutual hatred, mutual calumny and reproach,
> have distinguished the canvass. Private vices and foibles have been
> exposed and exaggerated; private conversations have been repeated
> and published; nor has this rancor spared even private letters,
> written in the hours of confidence and friendship! In short, the
> contending ambition of two insignificant individuals has convulsed
> the whole country; . . . In the words of our Prospectus, "a

[142] "A Friend to The Constitution." Author Unknown, pp. 3, 46. Huntington Library description estimates it was "issued" about 1799–1800.

country, *once* the seat of peace and good neighborhood, is torn to pieces by faction: plunged, by intriguing demagogues, into never-ceasing hatred and strife; expiating the crime of rebellion against monarchy by enduring the tormenting, the degrading curse of republicanism."[143]

Another writer, in one of the clearest analyses of faction and party in this period, linked the devotees of party to those who were in opposition to the constitution:

Where there is a division of federalists and democrats, as the parties are now called, and the president, or the governor will make an attachment to the one party or the other a qualification to office, and a condition for a place, we have a right to charge him with being of that party. Nay, further, we have a right to condemn the practice as being a species of corruption, destructive to the rights of private judgement on public concerns; and as a mode, which cannot fail to create factions, and to maintain dangerous and bitter parties, as long as the government shall exist.

Those who expect to live by the president's patronage, finding the offices all full, will begin to intrigue for a new president, whose political principles are in direct opposition to the one in office. The men who view themselves as candidates, will of course open a controversy with him, and either explicitly, or implicitly, form contracts to promote the leaders of their party. Thus the constitution will be forsaken, and the plans and machinations of parties form the plan of administration.

Mr. Adams in his book, intitled the Defence of the American Constitutions, observes very truly, that a *majority may be a faction*. Whatever number of men shall associate together, for any purpose than that of maintaining the government on the principles, and by the forms of the constitution, is a faction. What necessity can there be for associations, either by express compact, or by implicit intrigue? We are all united in a form of government, which interests all alike, and which must be supported by the will of the whole. Does any one say, that parties, intrigues, armies, and a separate order of men, are necessary, because the people have not virtue enough to govern themselves, in

143 *Porcupine's Works*, op. cit., Vol. XII, p. 134.

an elective republic? *He who says this, is an antifederalist, and commits treason against the constitution.*

Continuing with his explanation of the ultimate danger of party and faction, the author describes the current situation in language that suggests the government is faced with a revolutionary crisis:

> It is asserted with confidence, that there are men in the United States, who have no faith or confidence in the present federal constitution; and from a variety of publications in several parts of the union, there is some reason to believe the fact. There seems in some productions to be a design to disaffect the southern with the northern states. Others seem to be endeavoring to divide the New England states from the others. Whatever pretensions such men may make, they are by no means *federalists*. The general constitution is a league, or covenant, between all the states, and he, whoever he is, that shall attempt in any manner to dissolve it, is an *antifederalist*.

Finally, the author places his theory of party in a perspective that Jefferson, Madison, and Monroe shared:

> When this idea [i.e., of party] is properly examined, it will appear to be quite unnatural to our systems of civil government, and *derogatory to all the principles, which have been advanced, in order to maintain our late glorious revolution*. It will appear to be a legitimate offspring of that tyranny which has so often deluged the world in blood. It is introduced at no other door, than that, which opens to receive the dangerous charge against the people of America, that they are incapable of preserving and enjoying a free government.[144]

A relationship between the rise of faction and the potential for revolution in the state had become apparent even to the ministry. One New England divine made an explicit connection between 1776 and 1799, believing that the nation was in a similar position:

[144] Impartial Citizen, A *Dissertation upon the Constitutional Freedom of the Press* (Boston, 1801), pp. 42, 44, 47.

. . . were the ministers of the gospel to keep politics out of the pulpit, they would neglect a valuable part of the christian system, and an important branch of their duty. . . . For when the ark of liberty is in danger, the ark of God cannot be safe.

In the year 1775, the provincial congress of Massachusetts wrote a letter to all the ministers of the gospel throughout the province expressed in these words,

"Reverend Sir,

"We cannot but acknowledge . . . In a day like this,—when all the friends of civil and religious liberty are exerting themselves to deliver this country from its present calamities, we cannot but place great hopes in an order of men, who have ever distinguished themselves in their country's cause; and we do therefore *recommend* to the ministers of the gospel in the several towns . . . that they assist us in avoiding that dreadful slavery with which we are threatened."

Our liberties are as dear to us now as they were then, and the doctrines of the gospel and the duties of christian ministers remain the same. And whatever is said against their preaching political discourses,—when the state of public affairs is critical and hazardous, must be either owing to ignorance, delusion or perverseness.[145]

As the revolutionary crisis deepened, the ministry would take on a new and paradoxical function, aiding the cause of faction, while excoriating those who subscribed to it. One clear example was Zechariah Lewis, who very succinctly recorded the dilemma of the New England Federalist: how to indulge in partisan rhetoric while invoking the spirit of revolution:

However flattering . . . may be the *apparent* situation of our Country, its *real* situation is imminently critical and dangerous. . . .

It is the love of just and rational government—a government that consults the happiness of the people, and not the love of monarchy, which is increasing "in this part of the Union." Let the attempt be made to establish, in New-England, monarchy—or,

[145] Hezekiah Packard, *Federal Republicanism, Displayed in Two Discourses,* op. cit., pp. 32–33.

what is more to be dreaded, anarchy—and the SPIRIT of SEVENTY-
SIX will fire every breast, and nerve every arm.

True republicanism we still admire. We love that genuine
liberty, which is founded on the principles of just and equal rights.
But we detest injustice and oppression in every form. We especially detest them, when they assume the garb of Republicanism.[146]

The belief that revolution was in the air went beyond New
England and permeated the remaining states in the Union. Even
in far-off Europe, the rumors of revolution had circulated in the
newspapers and dinner conversations of diplomats. In mid-1798,
John Quincy Adams wrote his mother that "a paragraph in the
Moniteur . . . says that the *friends of liberty* in the United
States, supported by a great part of the House of Representatives,
will probably not wait for the next elections, but in the mean time
will destroy the fatal influence of the President and Senate *by a
Revolution.*"[147]

Fisher Ames, describing the influence of faction during and
after Washington's years in office, said, "As soon as party found
the virtue and glory of Washington were obstacles, the attempt
was made . . . to surmount them both. For this, the greatest of
all his trials, we know he was prepared. He knew, that the government must possess sufficient strength from within or without, *or
fall victim to faction.*" Then Fisher Ames concluded with the
classic definition of a historical revolutionary situation: "Thus
party forms a state within a state, and is animated by rivalship,
fear and hatred of its superior."[148] Fisher Ames's brother, Nathaniel, analyzing the politics of the day from an opposite point of
view, nevertheless came up with the same conclusion. In a diary
entry dated January 1799, he wrote: "House and land tax of
Congress goes on heavily, causing great uneasiness. Some refuse

[146] Zechariah Lewis, *An Oration on the Apparent, and the Real Political
Situation of the United States* (New Haven, 1799), pp. 13, 21.

[147] John Quincy Adams to Abigail Adams, 27 June 1798, *The Writings of
John Quincy Adams*, op. cit., Vol. II, p. 323.

[148] Ames, *Works of Fisher Ames*, op. cit., p. 124.

and then to avoid the penalty have to conform. . . . Silent indignation hath not yet exploded—tho' hard threatened. I fear civil war must be the result of Government measures."[149]

A Hartford wit, caught up in the spirit of the times, wrote a New Year's poem entitled "The Political Green-House"—an undisguised warning that, by 1799, the seeds of revolution and rebellion had been sown:

Oft has the New-Year's Muse essayed, . . .
While Frenchmen live and Faction reigns
Her voice arrayed in awful rhyme,
Shall thunder down the steep of Time. . . .

Long had the Jeffersonian band,
Determined here (1800) to take their stand,
To us, their vile intrigues apart,
and old Connecticut subvert.

. . . with deep laid plots and cunning schemes,
Don Quixote, knight of woeful face,
Led on the Revolution Race,
. . . and that their heads were bent on brewing
Subjection, infamy and ruin.

When from the burning lake in, ire,
They sat their feet in solid fire,
To find if war, or sly pollution,
Could raise in heaven a revolution.

. . . Beyond the Apalachian height,
Let poor Kentucky shew her spite
Pass many a factious resolution,
To guard the Federal Constitution. . . .

To recollect one proposition
A Governor can preach Sedition.
Some entertain the wise opinion
That Faction lurks in the Old Dominion.

And that the fistula of Giles,
is only one of many wiles

149 "Nathaniel Ames, Diary." In Warren, *Jacobin and Junto*, op. cit., p. 123.

Which modern politicians play,
To shield their projects from the day,
And that manicure will quickly discern,
The farmer, found from stem to stern
Among his kindred spirits stand,
Hurling Rebellion o'er the land.[150]

As we review these statements on the possibility of revolution, known by all to be the inevitable consequence of the violence of faction, it is natural to recall Jefferson's remark immediately before the outbreak of the French Revolution: "All the world is run politically mad. Men, women, children talk nothing else . . ."[151] A similar statement could have been made by Jefferson beginning in 1798–99. Indeed, it appeared to contemporaries that the same course of events was overtaking America. Porcupine spoke for many in the period of the quasi-war with France:

> . . . above all, the alliance with Great Britain would cut up the French faction here. It is my sincere opinion, that they have formed the diabolical plan of *revolutionizing* (to use one of their execrable terms) the whole continent of America. They have their agents and partisans without number, and very often where we do not imagine. Their immoral and blasphemous principles have made a most alarming progress. They have explored the country to its utmost boundaries and its inmost recesses, and have left a partisan on every spot, ready to preach up *the holy right of insurrection*.[152]

As we have seen, this was an almost universal sentiment. Poets, lawyers, doctors, diplomats, ministers, newspaper editors, farmers and politicians—men of every walk and run of life—saw the rise of faction and party strife surging toward one major catastrophic event. While some of their statements were definitely rhetorical, often reflecting rumor and the wildest speculation, the fact remains that an incredibly large number of responsible individuals of

[150] Richard Alsop, *The Political Green-House for the Year 1798*, 1 Jan. 1799 (Hartford, Conn., 1799), pp. 3–14.
[151] Jefferson to Anne W. Bingham, 11 May 1788, *Papers*, Vol. 13, p. 151.
[152] *Porcupine's Works*, op. cit., Vol. VIII, p. 65.

every political persuasion warned their contemporaries about faction and the violence of party. The sheer volume of such statements in the literature of the period, plus their intensity, indicates
that their fears and concerns were genuine.

The real terror of faction that these men experienced cannot be
dismissed with the trite label of "emotionalism," as has been done
so frequently in the past merely because their expressions did not
fit into the neat pattern of a modern party structure. The fact is,
their eighteenth-century historical perspective—the only one they
could have known at the time—told them that the politics of
faction was a prelude to revolution and, perhaps, anarchy. This
was the familiar pattern that the violence of faction had blocked
out through history. Using this frame of reference, John Adams, in
an argument with Jefferson, gives eloquent testimony to his genuine fears of terror and their relationship to party. In a letter to
Jefferson, he describes party's vitiating influence on the body
politic. He despairs of ever making himself "understood by Posterity." Yet, if the foregoing analysis has been at all successful, the
reader, by now, should have little trouble sharing Adams' anxiety
as he describes the nation tottering on the brink of disaster
throughout most of the turbulent years we have examined:

> . . . I proceed to the Order of the day, which is the terrorism of
> a former day. . . . "The Sensations excited, in free yet firm
> Minds by the Terrorism of the day." You say, "none can conceive
> them who did not witness them, and they were felt by one party
> only."
>
> Upon this subject I despair of making myself understood by
> Posterity, by the present Age, and even by you. To collect and
> arrange the documents illustrative of it, would require as many
> Lives as those of a Cat. You never felt the Terrorism of Chaises
> Rebellion in Massachusetts. I believe you never felt the Terrorism
> of Gallatin's Insurrection in Pensilvania. You certainly never
> realized the Terrorism of Fries, most outrageous Riot and Rescue,
> as I call it, Treason, Rebellion as the World and great Judges and
> two Juries pronounced it. You certainly never felt the Terrorism,
> excited by Genet, in 1793, when ten thousand people in the

Streets of Philadelphia, day after day, threatened to drag Washington out of his House, and effect a Revolution in the Government, or compell it to declare War in favour of the French Revolution, and against England. The coolest and the firmest minds, even among the Quakers . . . have given their opinions to me, that nothing but the Yellow Fever . . . saved the United States from a total Revolution of Government. I have no doubt you was fast asleep in philosophical Tranquility, when ten thousand people, and perhaps many more, were parading the Streets of Philadelphia, on the Evening of my Fast Day; When even Governor Mifflin himself, thought it his Duty to order a Patrol of Horse and Foot to preserve the peace; when Markett Street was as full as Men could stand by one another, and even before my Door; when some of my Domesticks in Phrenzy, determined to sacrifice their Lives in my defence; when all were ready to make a desperate Salley among the multitude, and others were with difficulty and danger dragged back by the others; when I myself judged it prudent and necessary to order Chests of Arms from the War Office to be brought through bye Lanes and back Doors: determined to defend my House at the Expence of my Life, and the Lives of the few, very few Domesticks and Friends within it. What think you of Terrorism, Mr. Jefferson? Shall I investigate the Causes, the Motives, the Incentives of these Terrorisms? . . . But above all; shall I request you, to collect the circular Letters from Members of Congress in the middle and southern States to their Constituents? I would give all I am worth for a compleat Collection of all those circular Letters.[153]

In John Adams' mind the recollection of the terror had been overwhelming. The desire for the "circular Letters" recalled to him the revolutionary impact he believed those documents had. Indeed, they were the evidence he longed for to prove his case that party was synonymous with terror. His assessment, moreover, leaves little doubt as to the historical perspective he places on the idea of party. In the end, speaking as an old patriot, the repository of American ideals, Adams had expressed his sovereign contempt for those who would corrupt the election process in the pursuit of

[153] John Adams to Jefferson, 30 June 1813, *Letters*, Vol. II, pp. 346–47.

power. There can be no doubt that Jefferson, Madison, Monroe, and every man of quality would have agreed.

John Adams' brief survey of the old-style politics and the terror of party places this chapter's analysis of the politics of faction in perspective. In conclusion, one cannot help seeing through these statements of the most prominent men of the age—America's age of democratic revolutions—that the politics of faction and party were the most hated, detested, and feared phenomena of their times. Yet, paradoxically, that particular style of politics has eluded everyone who has attempted to come to grips with the meaning of revolution in the early national period. This failure to see the period as producing the political conditions necessary for the culmination of the American Revolution has blinded us in our attempts to understand the politics of the years 1790–1800. For indeed, if we are to comprehend the meaning of Jefferson's Revolution of 1800 and its importance in the future struggles for power in America, we must view the politics of faction as the key to understanding the next stage of America's historical development —viz., the politics of revolution. Only then will we be able to say, in the broadest historical sense, that we truly understand America's revolutionary heritage and the spirit of '76.

VII

The Kentucky and Virginia Resolutions and the Threats to the First Amendment

"There is in these States a faction, a numerous and desperate faction, resolved on the overthrow of the Federal Government; and the man who will not allow that there is *danger* to be apprehended, is either too great a fool to perceive it, or too great a coward to encounter it."
Porcupine's Gazette, 1799

By middle 1798 the Federalists and John Adams' administration had reached the high-water mark of their popularity. Bathed in the glow of the XYZ affair and the enthusiastic support that incident created, the Hamiltonians and the supporters of John Adams combined to pursue a plan that, considered in its entirety, appeared threatening to anyone who opposed a consolidation of power in the national government.

A navy department had been established, the army had been expanded, a Direct Tax Law had been passed, Hamilton was appointed Inspector General, government loans to support the military were announced, and finally, the Naturalization Act of 1798 and the Alien Act were passed, so it was thought, to intimidate the most vocal opponents of the administration. This spate of legislation was climaxed by a Sedition Act, which, designed to curtail the opposition presses, raised the specter of an attack upon the constitution and the fundamental liberties of the country.

Indeed, the Alien and Sedition Acts were perhaps the most important bills of the Adams administration if for no other reason than that they set the tone of politics for the next two years. And because they constituted a threat to the First Amendment freedoms and constitutionalism *per se*, they set into motion a train of events that consolidated opposition to the administration. Therefore, the connection between these political events of 1798–99 and their relation to the idea of revolution will be the main focus of this chapter.

But, first, let us review a few connecting links. We began by discussing the role that faction played in revolutions throughout history and especially in the eighteenth century. We described the essential features of a revolutionary society with its consequent polarization and strife. We examined Adams' and Jefferson's views of revolt and revolution and outlined particularly the latter's ambition to construct a theory of permanent, peaceful, and constitutional revolution. We analyzed the notion of conspiracy and counterrevolution and saw the stage set for both. We also explored Jefferson's concern for principles in detail: personal, political, constitutional, and revolutionary.

The reader must keep the preceding chapters in mind in order to understand the analysis. The best single metaphor I might suggest is the "systems" approach to understanding: almost every important political act from July 1798 to February 1801 must be seen not only on a continuum but in relationship. The tracing of the action or influence of one of these events upon subsequent events is crucial to the understanding of the dynamics of revolution in this period. In addition, I am asking the reader to expand his horizon even farther, to look upon the period 1790 to 1801 as a whole. Finally, I urge the reader to consider, from the standpoint of principle, the events of this period in the context of the American Revolution of 1776.

As noted above, one of the most significant features of the events of July 1798 was the imposition of direct taxes by the federal government. Because the power of direct taxation was considered a primary source of revenue by the states, and because every state had a tradition of internal taxation that had begun in the colonial era, they were naturally unwilling to allow the national government to use that power. In their own experience they knew that the power to tax was the power to destroy. And in 1798 the power of the federal government to augment its revenues beyond import duties was not universally acknowledged. Indeed, Hamilton had scrupulously avoided mentioning any such intention at the Convention and attempted to allay all fears that the national government would impose any direct taxes on property and land.[1]

The Acts for the Assessment and Collection of a Direct Tax on Lands, Houses and Slaves passed by Congress on July 9 and 14, 1798, were thus viewed with considerable apprehension in the rural areas of the country. Alexander Graydon placed the tax issue in perspective by saying that the new taxes on houses and lands smacked of the Stamp Act: "It was a Stamp Act that first excited our displeasure with the mother country: the very name of an excise was hateful to freemen." In Pennsylvania, which was shortly to experience a tax rebellion, Graydon reported that "the federalists . . . were as tyrannical as she [Great Britain] had been, and that this tax upon farms, houses and *windows*, was but the beginning of a system, which would soon extend to everything; and that we should have at length a tax upon horses, wagons and ploughs . . ." Indeed, looking back from a thirty-year perspective, Graydon stated unequivocally that "the tax on real property was the fatal blow to federalism in Pennsylvania."[2]

Jefferson had anticipated Hamilton's intentions of imposing

---

[1] For an excellent review of taxation policies during the period, see Neil Charles Potash, "A Critique of Federalist Finances: The Direct Tax 1798–1800," unpublished thesis, Univ. of Maryland, 1964.

[2] Graydon was not entirely wrong. Alexander Hamilton, whose influence during this period was nearly absolute, wrote Theodore Sedgwick, Speaker of the House of Representatives: "I would add taxes on stamps, collateral successions, new modifications of some articles of imports, and, let me add, saddle-

such a tax the previous year. Considering the sentiments of the nation, he had predicted that the net effect of the tax would be to "awaken the constituents, and call for an inspection into past proceedings."[3] But the "inspection" failed to materialize. As a result, in November of the following year Jefferson wrote a "political letter" to John Taylor: ". . . there is a most respectable part of our State who have been enveloped in the XYZ delusion, and who destroy our unanimity for the present moment. This disease of the imagination will pass over because the patients are essentially republicans. Indeed, the Doctor is now on his way to cure it, in the guise of a tax gatherer. But give time for the medicine to work, and for the repetition of stronger doses, which must be administered."[4]

Jefferson knew his constituency in the southern states and especially their reluctance to pay taxes of any kind. He also suspected that the dissatisfaction would extend from Virginia to Pennsylvania and as far north as Massachusetts. Thus, he would not have been unduly surprised when a citizen of Massachusetts complained bitterly of the new tax laws. Nathaniel Ames, brother of arch Federalist Fisher Ames, nevertheless submitted his tax bill. At the same time, he could not resist making a few caustic remarks on what he saw as a drastically changed political situation. In his diary he wrote:

> *January 23, 1799.* Called on by Nehemiah Fales for dimensions of my house and windows, and list of land for direct tax of High Federalist tyrant Government. I introduce it thus:
> "Nat. Ames (regretting the short dawn of rational liberty under the Confederation—deploring the blindness and apathy of that People who once dared to defy and trample on the minions of foreign tyrants, only to be trampled on by domestic traitors, in impudent junto, breaking the limits of their Sovereign—greeted

---

horses." Hamilton to Sedgwick, no date other than 1798, *Works of Alexander Hamilton*, op. cit., Vol. VIII, pp. 515–16.

[3] Jefferson to St. George Tucker, 28 Aug. 1797, *Writings*, Vol. IX, p. 419.

[4] Jefferson to John Taylor, 26 Nov. 1798, *Writings*, Vol. X, pp. 63–64.

with the tyrant songs of 'Energy of the Government'—'Tighten the Reins of Government,' only to stifle the cheering sound of the great Sovereign's voice—forced to yield, instead of to Law, to the mighty powers that be), exhibits this list and description of his house and land on the first day of October, 1798.

"1 Dwelling House 40 feet long—two stories high—30 feet wide —glass, etc.—198 feet glass—453 squares.

"1 Barn, 24 x 35. 7¾ acres Lot and Bog Meadow. Woodland, 10 acres Rocks and Bushes. 1 corn house 10 feet square."

January 29. The great Sovereign grumbles at unconstitutional tax.[5]

Jefferson's and Ames's comments were not without foundation. In order to collect the taxes the federal government had to assemble in each state a vast bureaucracy of assessors plus their assistants, surveyors, commissioners, and collectors. This task force would be compounded by a national level of bureaucracy to supervise and enforce the collections. For example, in Pennsylvania alone there were nine commissioners, forty-one principal assessors, four hundred and twenty assistant assessors, four inspectors of the revenue, thirty-nine supervisors of the collection, fourteen surveyors of the revenue, and twenty-five collectors—all working to execute the new tax law.[6]

As Jefferson had intuited, resistance to these laws would be spontaneous and overwhelming. In Pennsylvania, Fries's Rebellion broke out in February 1799 against those who attempted to enforce the new tax law. Liberty poles sprang up over the countryside and farmers as well as townsmen attended meetings dressed in the uniform of the Continental army and bearing arms.[7] Nearly the same conditions applied in many other parts of the country. Little revenue was collected in the southern states of North and South Carolina, Kentucky, and Tennessee; and in western Pennsylvania the collectors never met their quotas. In the northern part of the country, Massachusetts Federalist Fisher Ames saw this resistance as potentially revolutionary: "All forces, all revenue is

---

[5] Warren, *Jacobin and Junto*, op. cit., p. 124.

[6] Potash, "A Critique of Federalist Finances," op. cit., pp. 50–51.

[7] Wharton, *State Trials of the United States*, op. cit., pp. 517–31.

viewed by the factious as the power of a foe, and therefore they will try to strip the government of both, but it must have both or be a victim to the faction; and if our people cannot be brought to bear necessary taxes, and to maintain so small a force as our army, they are (and I am afraid they are) unfit for an independent government . . ."8

Fisher Ames, examining the government's efforts to collect taxes from a perspective of nearly two years, may have been right but for the wrong reasons. The fact that the resistance, apart from Fries's Rebellion, was not overt meant that the change was taking place in people's minds. For the conduct of the army produced outrages that were reported throughout the country. The consequence was that more animus was directed against the federal government than against those who refused to pay their taxes. Two editors, Jacob Schneider and William Duane, the latter editor of the *Aurora*, were severely beaten by the soldiers. This caused the President to write later that "the army was as unpopular as if it had been a ferocious wild beast let loose upon the nation to devour it. In newspapers, in pamphlets and in common conversation they were called cannibals. A thousand anecdotes, true or false, of their licentiousness were propagated and believed."9

Passed nearly simultaneously with the tax law were the Alien and Sedition Laws. The timing of their passage more than added to the uncertainty and suspicion of many citizens toward the federal government. In the minds of many the two laws even raised the specter of a conspiracy against the constitution. But their immediate effect was to polarize the national legislature. This evoked a suspicion that the extremists in Congress were launching a vendetta against the republicans. At least Jefferson thought so, for when the Alien Act was first introduced, he had written Madison that its authors, frustrated by the genius of Albert Gallatin, hoped "to reach him by this bill."10

8 Fisher Ames to Oliver Wolcott, 12 Jan. 1800, Gibbs, *Memoirs of the Administrations of Washington and Adams*, op. cit., Vol. II, p. 320.

9 John Adams to James Lloyd, 11 Feb. 1815, *Works*, Vol. X, p. 118.

10 Jefferson to James Madison, 26 April 1798, *Writings*, Vol. X, p. 31.

In many states, arguments over the constitutionality of these bills became not only heated, but to many the only important topics of discussion. And judging from the reaction of many southern politicians, the two acts were responsible for producing the most dangerous constitutional crisis the young nation had yet encountered. Thus, when the Sedition Act was linked with the Alien Act, Jefferson became truly alarmed. "Both," he wrote Madison, "are so palpably in the teeth of the Constitution as to show they [the extremist faction] mean to pay no respect to it."[11]

The Alien Act conferred upon the President the power to remove aliens from the United States, to imprison or fine them, or both. Thus, an alien who was deported as a result of the President's personal decision would be deprived of a trial by jury and his fundamental rights under the constitution. While the Alien Act was directed against a limited number of persons, it nevertheless caused many to become suspicious about the administration's intentions.

The Sedition Act was considered more dangerous, and therefore more volatile, than the Alien Act. Under it the federal government intended to punish any combination or conspiracy against itself with a punishment of six months to five years imprisonment and a fine of $5,000. The law also gave authority to the government to punish anyone for "seditious writings." These included any writings that might, in the eyes of the administration, be "false, scandalous and malicious" against the President, Congress, or the government. This charge was punishable "by a fine of $2,000 and imprisonment not exceeding two years." Thus, while the Alien Act "was made contingent upon a declaration of war," the Sedition Act was designed "to deal with domestic political opposition in time of peace."[12] The Sedition Law, many felt, plainly violated the First Amendment to the constitution.

Albert Gallatin saw it as a vicious factional device directly attacking the tenets of a free society. In effect, Adams and his

[11] Jefferson to James Madison, 7 June 1798, *The Works of Thomas Jefferson* (Federal Edition), op. cit., Vol. VIII, p. 434.

[12] James Morton Smith, *Freedom's Fetters* (Ithaca, New York, 1956), p. 94.

administration were attempting to "chill" the presses. And Gallatin, sensing this, revealed the administration's blatant use of propaganda in a speech on the floor of the House. The purpose of the bill, he said, was

> to enable one part to oppress the other. . . . Is it not their object to frighten and suppress all presses which they consider as contrary to their views; to prevent a free circulation of opinion; to suffer the people at large to hear only partial accounts, and but one side of the question; to delude and deceive them by partial information and through these means to perpetuate themselves in power?[13]

The political consequences of the Sedition Act then were enormous: a polarization of factions would occur in the national and state legislatures and ultimately in the entire society. Gallatin had rightly perceived this potential danger and had spoken eloquently against it.

Gallatin's alarm was shared by more than a few of his fellow republicans. Jefferson saw the bill not only in terms of dividing the state legislatures, but as a conspiracy against the constitution:

> The XYZ fever has considerably abated through the country, as I am informed, and the alien and sedition laws are working hard. I fancy that some of the State legislatures will take strong ground on this occasion. For my own part, I consider those laws as merely an experiment on the American mind, to see how far it will bear an avowed violation of the Constitution.[14]

James Madison also saw the Sedition Act in constitutional terms. It was, he said, a "death wound on the sovereignty of the States." By that he meant that the national government was assuming the powers of the states by inferring "that Congress

[13] Speech of 10 July 1798, quoted in Levy's *Freedom of Speech and Press in Early American History*, op. cit., p. 259. In a speech on 5 July 1798, Gallatin had referred to the bill "as a weapon used by a party now in power in order to perpetuate their authority and preserve their present places."

[14] Jefferson to Stevens Thomson Mason, 11 Oct. 1798, *Writings*, Vol. X, pp. 61–62.

possess[ed] . . . similar power[s] of legislation."[15] This was a warning of things to come. The extremists within the federal government would expand this logic and assert the right to usurp the common law. And, as this strategy on the part of the extreme Federalists unfolded, it caused Jefferson, Madison, and Gallatin to redouble their opposition.

When the Adams administration passed the infamous Alien and Sedition Laws in 1798, there were few men who foresaw their catalytic nature for the political upheaval that was to follow. But those few were indeed important men, the leaders of the several factions then prominent. Alexander Hamilton, who would later attempt to use the bills for his own ends, saw the consequences immediately. To Oliver Wolcott he wrote referring to the Sedition Law:

> I have this moment seen a bill brought into the Senate, entitled, "A Bill to define more particularly the crime of Treason," etc. There are provisions in this bill, which, according to a cursory view, appear to me highly exceptionable and such as, more than anything else, may endanger civil war . . . I hope sincerely the thing may not be hurried through. Let us not establish a tyranny. Energy is a very different thing from violence. If we make no false step, we shall be essentially united, but if we push things to an extreme, we shall then give to faction *body* and solidity.[16]

Thus, upon seeing the first draft of what would become the rallying point for the faction allied with Jefferson and Madison, the chief theoretician of High Federalism intuited the consequences. He saw the possibilities of a civil war and of the potential interpretation or construction that would be placed upon such legislation, viz., the erection of a "tyranny." Indeed, Hamilton astutely predicted that the passage of such legislation would increase the strength of factions and their potential for revolutionary violence. Accepting the basic premise of the Sedition Law,

[15] Levy, *Freedom of Speech and Press in Early American History*, op. cit., p. 266.
[16] Hamilton to Oliver Wolcott, 29 June 1798, *Works of Alexander Hamilton*, op. cit., Vol. VIII, p. 491.

Hamilton had, in a flash of rare insight, seen the danger as well as the opportunity within it. For whether pretended, imagined, manufactured or real, the uproar surrounding the passage and enforcement of that bill sounded an alarm that reverberated throughout the nation.

Only a few weeks before Hamilton counseled caution to his own faction, Jefferson had recorded in a highly conjectural letter an observation by John Taylor that it would not be "unwise now to estimate the separate mass of Virginia and North Carolina, with a view to their separate existence."[17] This was strong language; moreover, its main point—a theoretical one—indicated a willingness on the part of Taylor to destroy the Union. It is also implied that John Taylor, one of Jefferson's closest friends and a brilliant constitutional theorist, had concluded that the extremists in power were willing to test the limits of the Union, to raise the violence of faction and even precipitate a constitutional crisis, thus compelling the opposition to resort to scission. For Taylor the theoretical consequences of an all-out struggle for power between factions were obvious: it would tear the constitution apart and, without a constitution that guaranteed the rights of the republicans, the Union must be destroyed. But Jefferson, still probing the opposition for its weaknesses, was not ready or willing to go that far, even in theory. Jefferson cautioned Taylor that he should not be beguiled by the Hamiltonian policy of "divide and rule"; he should recognize that it was "the old practice of despots to use a part of the people to keep the rest in order." Further, he held out, but without any evidence, the hope that "time alone would bring round an order of things" more favorable. Finally, he conceded that "the principles" he cherished had been "lost" and, abandoning his usual cool and reasoned position, he begged Taylor to "have patience 'til luck turns."

But "luck" was hardly the kind of assurance that a constitutional scholar could or would accept. Nor did Jefferson really believe that this new order of things would soon appear. The

---

[17] Jefferson to John Taylor, 1 June 1798, *Writings*, Vol. X, p. 44.

Sedition Act had heated up the factions beyond cooling and Jefferson was obviously trying to calm the troubled mind of his friend. This was indeed a difficult task, for John Taylor knew as much about factional violence as any man alive. And, as we have seen, he had written several essays on the subject that revealed he had history as well as "cool reason" on his side.

Despite this, Jefferson attempted to soothe him. Regarding party divisions as inevitable in any society, Jefferson *speculated* that "perhaps" they served a purpose: they kept the people aware of the acts of their rulers. "But," he added (agreeing with Taylor's basic premise), "if on a temporary superiority of the one party, the other is to resort to a scission of the Union, no federal government can exist." This was the real question: Could a federal government or a federal constitution exist in the midst of excessive factional strife? Taylor had made up his mind that it could not. Jefferson, in June of 1798, disagreed and, in doing so, attempted to maintain a clear distinction between theory and practice. Knowing full well his friend's views on party, he asked him to suspend his practical judgment on the future of the Union while granting him his theoretical point. Indeed, Jefferson had even carried Taylor's point to its logical conclusion: "If to rid ourselves of the present rule of Massachusetts and Connecticut, we break the Union, will the evil stop there? . . . Immediately, we shall see a Pennsylvania and a Virginia party arise in the residuary confederacy, and the public mind will be distracted with the same party spirit. . . . If we reduce our Union to Virginia and North Carolina, immediately the conflict will be established between the representatives of these two states, and they will end by breaking into their simple units."[18] The problem of factional strife was an eternal one; moreover, the evil would hardly be remedied by breaking up the Union.

In truth, the prospects for preserving the Union appeared dim. In the same letter, Jefferson had made a running summary of the constitutional crises then impinging upon the young nation: "The

[18] Ibid., p. 45.

crisis with England, the public and authentic avowal of sentiments hostile to the leading principles of our Constitution, the prospect of a war, in which we shall stand alone, land tax, stamp tax, increase of public debt, etc." Each of these, in addition to the Alien and Sedition Laws, could be used to manufacture a separate constitutional crisis. And considered collectively, it appeared to many, especially those like John Taylor, that the constitutional crisis was already at hand.

Both Jefferson and Taylor knew, as did Madison, that the extremists within the administration had few scruples and would stop at nothing. Madison even noted in another context, but still applicable, that "the spirit of party revenge may be wreaked thro' the forms of the Constitution."[19] Jefferson made the same observation several months later. Discussing the contrast between his own principles and those of the administration, he wrote Samuel Smith: "There is no event, therefore, however atrocious, which may not be expected." In addition, he left no doubt that the worst might be on the horizon. He linked the dominant faction's "warring against the people" to the idea of a French revolutionary conspiracy: "I have contemplated every event which the Marratists of the day can perpetrate, and am prepared to meet every one in such a way, as shall not be derogatory either to the public liberty or my own personal honor."[20] Like Marat during the French Revolution, the High Federalists were pretending to be the friend of the people while preparing them for a loss of their liberty.

Assessing this grim situation, Jefferson prepared to meet the crisis in a truly revolutionary way. Working in complete secrecy, and collaborating with his closest friend, he drafted the Kentucky Resolutions sometime between July 21 and October 26 of 1798.[21] His state of mind, responsible for the tone of the Kentucky Resolutions, can be seen in a letter written during those days when he

[19] Madison to Jefferson, 10 June 1798, *The Writings of James Madison,* op. cit., Vol. VI, p. 324.

[20] Jefferson to Samuel Smith, 22 Aug. 1798, *Writings,* Vol. X, p. 57.

[21] Koch, *Jefferson and Madison,* op. cit., p. 187.

was mulling over the substance and style of that document. Referring to the Alien and Sedition Laws, he wrote:

> If this goes down, we shall immediately see attempted another act of Congress, declaring that the President shall continue in office during life, reserving to another occasion the transfer of the succession to his heirs, and the establishment of the Senate for life. At least, this may be the aim of the Oliverians, while Monk and the Cavaliers (who are perhaps the strongest) may be playing their game for the restoration of his most gracious Majesty George the Third. That these things are in contemplation, I have no doubt; nor can I be confident of their failure, after the dupery of which our countrymen have shown themselves susceptible.[22]

"The Oliverians" were, in Jefferson's eyes, the supporters of John Adams. "Monk and the Cavaliers" represented Hamilton, the Inspector General, who was waiting in the wings with his followers. Thus, from a republican point of view, it appeared that of the two factions in power one was jockeying for the throne and the hereditary power that accompanied it; the other simply wanted power and would be satisfied to restore the fallen monarch. In either case, there can be little doubt that Jefferson viewed the factions within the administration as he might have the Cromwellians—a threat to the constitution.

Goaded by these fears of conspiracy, Jefferson wrote a series of resolutions that, if passed by a state legislature, would dramatize the crisis. His plan was to have an old friend, Wilson Cary Nicholas, act as a third party and present his resolutions to a member of the North Carolina legislature. Instead, Nicholas gave them to John Breckinridge of Kentucky, a member of that state's legislature, who promptly introduced them. There they became known as the Kentucky Resolutions. Jefferson's logic, contained within the draft, was a dialectical approach to the constitution. It gave rise to a novel theory that the states had "by *compact* under the style and title of a Constitution for the United States and of

[22] Jefferson to Stevens Thomson Mason, 11 Oct. 1798, *Writings*, Vol. X, p. 62.

amendments thereto . . . constituted a General Government for special purposes, delegated to that Government certain definite powers, reserving each State to itself, the residuary mass of right to their own self-government; and that whensoever the General Government assumes undelegated powers, its acts are unauthoritative, void and of no force . . ."[23]

Jefferson was attempting here to place the focus of debate upon the constitution itself and not upon the government's ability or right to construe, interpret, or assume powers from it. The same logic would follow in the Virginia Resolutions. Hence, Jefferson and Madison were both attempting to deny any construction or interpretation of the constitution by the general government. Indeed, if there was to be any interpretation it would be done by the states, for "each party [i.e. state] has an equal right to judge for itself, as well as infractions as of the mode and measure of redress." This approach, if successful, would have curtailed the power of the national government and prevented any future expansion of power—especially at the expense of the states. As far as the controversy over the Alien Law was concerned, Jefferson's approach provided an example. The fourth resolution claimed it would have made "an act concerning aliens . . . altogether void and of no force."

These arguments, we must note, were cast as "principles" in the resolutions. The reason for this was that no definite plan of *immediate* practical action was contemplated. Their main purpose contained within the third resolution was to stimulate *reflection* upon the basic freedoms guaranteed by the constitution—especially those contained within the First Amendment. Other resolutions called attention to the Alien and Sedition Acts, the act against bank frauds, and the combination of powers vested in the President by these bills. In this manner the Kentucky Resolutions

[23] Kentucky Resolutions, Broadside, Huntington Library. For those readers who have not seen the Resolutions in their original form, they were printed on a single sheet approximately the size of one page of *The New York Times.* The text exhibited a short preamble followed by nine stated resolutions consisting of one or two paragraphs.

called attention to the major philosophical and constitutional concerns of the republicans. The purpose of these resolutions, moreover, revealed a basic union between theory and practice in Jefferson's strategy: he was essentially beginning, for very practical reasons, a debate on the principles of constitutionalism.

Within the Kentucky Resolutions Jefferson took extreme care to delineate *principles* of fundamental revolutionary importance. One was the right not only of the states, but *of the people,* to make decisions regarding the national government and the use of its power. Throughout the resolutions the term "the States, or to the people" recurs again and again. Jefferson wished the people to realize that the ultimate power in a republic lay with them and not with the government. This was consistent with his republican ideology. For, according to that ideology, the people could not divest themselves of their authority. No governmental or legislative body could usurp it; it therefore remained a reservoir of strength, a final appeal against tyranny and the force of government. This point would be made explicit in a companion piece written by Madison—the Virginia Resolutions.

Another principle lay in Jefferson's urging the "co-states" to turn to "their natural right" in the event of disagreement with the general government on "cases not made federal." Jefferson's use of the natural rights argument against everything not delegated specifically to the federal government meant almost everything that the general government was doing. By invoking the "natural right" doctrine, he hoped the states would "concur in declaring these acts void and of no force." It was not difficult to imagine what would follow if and when such a collision took place. The fact that the resolutions ended on a proper constitutional note, i.e., each "state requesting appeal at the next session of Congress" of the oppressive legislation, did not disguise the dialectical nature of Jefferson's ideas. Once a citizen admitted the unconstitutionality of the Alien and Sedition Laws, and then accepted the original compact theory, there was no middle ground. A citizen was either in favor of preserving the constitution and the idea of limited government or he must accept the growth of government's power *ad infinitum.*

The ninth, or final, resolution added to the dialogue the proper Socratic note that Jefferson had in mind. He purposely stated "that this Commonwealth does therefore call on its co-States for an expression of their sentiments on the acts concerning Aliens, and for the punishment of certain crimes herein before specified, plainly declaring whether these acts are or are not authorized by the Federal Compact?"

The method was clear. Jefferson hoped to have a friend of republicanism introduce that question in the legislature of every state, distribute to the people printed copies of the debates in their legislatures and print copies of the original records in the newspapers and pamphlets of all the states. The method followed was identical to that of the colonists in the 1770s and echoed precisely John Adams' prescription for revolution in America. Jefferson, through his authorship of the Compact Theory, was attempting nothing less than a revival, *in principle*, of the Spirit of Seventy-six. In fact, the very day after their passage, November 16th, and before a messenger could have physically conveyed the news to Monticello, he wrote Madison the following:

> I enclose you a copy of the draught of the Kentucky resolutions. I think we should distinctly affirm all the important principles they contain, so as to hold to that ground in future, and leave the matter in such a train as that we may not be committed absolutely to push the matter to extremities, and yet may be free *to push as far as events will render prudent*.[24]

Not only was the method clear, the reasoning was also: Jefferson had, in the midst of crisis, unleashed a powerful force in the society. It was an *idea* of resistance, peaceful and constitutional in nature, but profoundly revolutionary in purpose. And it was an idea that could be developed practically and prudently to a full

[24] Jefferson to Madison, 17 Nov. 1798, *Writings*, Vol. X, pp. 62–63. While Jefferson did not wish to push matters to the extreme his resolutions would nevertheless be interpreted in that light by those who wished to see the Alien and Sedition Laws enforced to the letter. Hence Robert Goodloe Harper claimed that the resolutions would produce "an armed opposition to these laws and consequently to this Government." *Annals of Congress*, V, 2430.

revolutionary potential. In retrospect, during the waning days of autumn, Jefferson along with Madison had put together the first building blocks of a revolution.

But, as the November skies darkened, so too did Jefferson's mood. Brooding atop his little hill near the Virginia mountains, he attempted to assess the mind of the nation and discovered much to his sorrow that it was not yet aware of the crisis. The exact nature of the crisis was found in the High Federalists' attacks upon the constitution. The administration was plainly acting in a manner that violated the principles of freedom and republicanism, or so Jefferson and his colleagues believed. And by assaulting the constitution on such a broad front, the extremist faction made it nearly impossible to deal with the many issues that needed clarification. This was especially true where public opinion was concerned and the lethargy that characterized that public was unnerving.

Thus, immediately after Jefferson had conceived the Kentucky Resolutions a new strategy began to unfold. About this time the most able republicans began writing long tracts dealing with the nature of the constitution, expounding its principles and attempting, in short, to make people realize that for a constitution to be meaningful and preserve liberty, it must be maintained in its purity. This, the republican strategists concluded, was the only way they could arouse public opinion. Accordingly, a resident of Hanover County, Virginia, in speaking against the Sedition Act, framed his argument in the constitutional language that would dominate American politics for the next two years:

> The Constitution is the basis of the public tranquility; the firmest support of public authority; the pledge of the liberty of the citizens: But this Constitution is a vain phantom, if not religiously observed. The nation ought then to watch very attentively, in order to render it equally respected, by the governors and governed: To attack the Constitution of a state is a capital crime against society and if those guilty of it are invested with authority, they add to this crime, a perfidious abuse of the power with which they are entrusted; the nation ought constantly to suppress these

abuses with all the vigour and vigilance the occasion requires. It is very uncommon to see the Constitution attacked, openly violated; it is against silent and slow attacks, that a nation ought to be particularly on its guard. Sudden revolutions strike the imaginations of man—we write histories of them and unfold their causes; but we neglect the changes that insensibly happen, by a long train of steps that are but little observed. It would be doing an important service to nations to shew from history, how states have entirely changed their nature and lost their original constitutions. This would waken the attention of the people; and from thence forward filled with this excellent maxim, no less essential in politics than in morals, they would no longer shut their eyes against innovations, which though inconsiderable in themselves, may serve as steps to mount to higher and more pernicious enterprises.[25]

Another pamphlet that dealt with the constitutional problems facing the nation was more explicit. George Nicholas of Kentucky wrote a letter to his "friend in Virginia" that received wide circulation. In it he reflected his own, as well as Jefferson's, pessimism, while distilling the nature of the constitutional crisis as the republicans saw it. To his "friend," a Federalist, he wrote:

I beseech you to inform me on what it is that you found your opinion, that "our liberties are not in danger." So far from my being able to concur with you in this way of thinking, after the most serious reflections on the subject, I am clearly of the opinion, that if the real difference between our government as fixed by our constitution, and an absolute government could be ascertained; it would be found that those who have administered our government, have already by their different violations of the constitution, and *of the republican principles on which it is founded*, done away and destroyed, much the greater and most powerful part, of the guards to liberty, which are contained in that constitution; and which originally constituted the essential difference between our government and a despotic government. And that if they have, in so short a time, with the means which they then had in their

[25] Nathaniel Pope, Jr., *A Speech delivered . . . in support of The Resolutions which he prepared and presented to The People of Hanover*, October 17, 1798. (Richmond, Va.: Printer Meriwether Jones, 1800), pp. 21–22.

power, and when they were opposed by *all* the constitutional barriers, been able to effect so much, that it will not now require any great effort on their part, to remove the remaining difference between the two governments; when their means of attack are increased in a twenty fold degree, and when the principal constitutional barriers are already laid prostrate at their feet: unless the people of America will rally around their constitution, for its protection.[26]

The crisis over American liberty was deepening. By the second week in December the Kentucky Resolutions had taken effect and in Virginia the state legislature began debating their own version of the constitutionality of the Alien and Sedition Laws. As Jefferson's strategy trickled down to the county level, a fever of resolutions had begun to heat up the political tempo of the state. In Dinwiddie County, for example, a number of citizens had published in the Richmond *Examiner* of December 6, 1798, parallel arguments to the Kentucky resolves. The major points of their resolutions were:

1. Opposition to standing armies. "A militia composed of the body of the people, is the proper, natural, and safe defence of a free state . . . regular armies, except in case of invasion, or the certain prospect of an invasion, are not only highly detrimental to the public welfare, but dangerous to liberty. . . . Military establishments are in their nature progressive, the vast expense attending them, producing discontent and disturbances, and these furnishing a pretext for providing a force still more formidable; thus finally occasioning the oppression, the ruin, the SLAVERY of the people."

2. Opposition to great naval armament "because it enlarges still more the fund for increasing executive influence: because the expense is incalculable . . . because this country cannot hope to protect its commerce by a fleet . . . or to guard from in-

---

[26] *A Letter from George Nicholas of Kentucky to his Friend in Virginia, Justifying the Conduct of the Citizens of Kentucky as to some of the measures of the General Government* . . . , op. cit., p. 6.

vasion a coast of fifteen hundred miles in extent. . . . When therefore the navy of the United States is competent to the protection . . . of our sea ports and coasting trade, from privateering and piratical depredations, it has attained the point, beyond which it ought not to go."

3. Opposition to "an alliance with any nation on earth." Republicans "reprobate . . . the practice of maintaining ministers resident in foreign countries, in the extent to which it is carried by the executive of the United States: because it adds still more to the already enormous mass of presidential patronage . . ."

4. Opposition to increasing the national debt on the grounds that "the only proper way to raise money for national purposes, is by taxes, duties, excises and imposts, and that the power of borrowing money, ought not to be exercised except in cases of absolute necessity; that if the money really be wanted, the people ought to be taxed to pay it; if not wanted, it ought not to be raised."

5. Opposition to the Alien Act as "unnecessary, repugnant to humanity, and contrary to the constitution."

6. Opposition to the Sedition Act as a "daring and unconstitutional violation of a sacred and essential right, without which, liberty, political science and national prosperity are at an end." "Freedom of the press is the great bulwark of liberty and can never be restrained but by a despotic government."[27]

The implications of these resolutions seem clear: they were the constitutional issues that Jefferson and Madison had chosen to rally supporters around them. Opposition to standing armies, naval armaments, increasing the power of the executive through debt or embassies abroad, and the Alien and Sedition Acts served to raise the average citizen's ire and compel him to take a stand.

In other counties of Virginia, similar broadsides were being printed and meetings were being held. "In the large and respectable county of Goochland, the people met on the 20th of August,

[27] See Noble Cunningham, Jr., "The Election of 1800," in *History of American Presidential Elections, 1798–1968*, op. cit., Vol. I, pp. 119–20.

to consult on the present crisis of American affairs and adopted by an almost unanimous vote resolutions expressive of their strongest disapprobation of the late acts of Congress and the President. There was a very full meeting, consisting of about 400. They also voted instructions to their Delegates in the State legislature, requesting them to move in their next session of Assembly, a Remonstrance to Congress, against the late obnoxious acts of government."[28] "The citizens of Albemarle were to meet on the 1st ult. (of September) to take the late acts of government into consideration."[29] Similarly, in Prince Edward County a meeting was held on the 20th of August,[30] and in Caroline County, the committee heading the meeting there asked "whether such measures as are not maturing in America have not begotten and supported despotism in other countries; and let us enquire of prudence, whether a reasonable defense does not depend exclusively on foresight? If *Monarchy* may be defined '*a power supported by force, corruption, and patronage,*' it suggests an alarming idea."[31]

These resolutions quickly found their way to other parts of the country in leaflets and in newspapers. In Philadelphia, for example, Bache's *Aurora* printed a popularized version. James Lyon, the republican editor in Vermont, noted with satisfaction that "accounts from Virginia, and the adjacent states, give us a happy prospect of reformation; the business is taken up with so much earnestness, we have reason to believe that those states will never sit down quietly under the usurpation and tyranny of federalism; in all their resolutions and correspondences, they utter not a syllable against the Federal constitution, but wish to defend it against Congressional violation. In the southwesterly parts of the State of New York, in the counties of Orange and Ulster, the work

[28] James Lyon, A *Republican Magazine or Repository of Political Truth* (Fairhaven, Vt., 1798), p. 10.

[29] Ibid., p. 10.

[30] Ibid., p. 167.

[31] Ibid., p. 177.

of reformation is also began . . . the standing army, sedition and alien laws are the principal objects of complaint . . ."[32] In Kentucky the citizens of Scott County met on June 27th,[33] and those of Woodford County on August 8th.[34] In October, the citizens of Knoxville, Tennessee, met and proclaimed the Alien Law "unconstitutional, oppressive and derogatory to our general compact, by taking away our trial by jury."[35] On August 15th, the "citizens of Fayette and counties adjacent convened in this town [Lexington], agreeably to a notice published in this the newspapers; the number present 4 or 5,000."[36] Such was the response Jefferson had in mind and hoped would occur in every county in America.

But the dynamic effect of the opposition's pamphlets provoked a reaction. Those journalists sympathetic to the administration's policies reacted hysterically to the Kentucky statement then being printed all over the country. Peter Porcupine even made a prediction of revolution:

> Now is the crisis advancing. The abandoned faction, devoted to France, have long been conspiring, and their conspiracy is at last brought near to an explosion. I have not the least doubt but they have fifty thousand men, provided with arms, in Pennsylvania alone. If vigorous measures are not taken; if the provisional army is not raised without delay, A CIVIL WAR, OR A SURRENDER OF INDEPENDENCE IS NOT AT MORE THAN A TWELVEMONTH'S DISTANCE.[37]

The ministry also added to the belief that a moment of crisis had arrived. And, as the leading shapers of public opinion, especially in New England, they carried immense influence among the common voters. One New England minister, Jedidiah Morse, had exclaimed in April, "That our present situation is uncommonly critical and perilous, all persons of reflection agree . . ." Hinting

[32] Ibid., p. 45.
[33] Ibid., p. 11.
[34] Ibid., p. 132.
[35] Ibid., p. 174.
[36] Ibid., p. 102.
[37] *Porcupine's Works*, op. cit., Vol. X, p. 16.

at the possibility of full-scale rebellion, he left no doubt as to where the revolutionary conspiracy derived its strength—it was Virginia. Then, alluding to the notorious society of the Illuminati, he said, in phrases that would become familiar to Americans nearly a century and a half later:

> I have in my possession complete and indubitable proof that such societies do exist . . . in the United States. I have, my brethren, an official, authenticated list of names, ages, places of nativity, professions etc. of the officers and members of a Society of the Illuminati . . . consisting of *one hundred* members instituted in Virginia, by the Grand Orient of France. This society has a deputy, whose name is on the list, who resides at the Mother Society in France, to communicate from thence all needfull information and instruction.[38]

Another minister, writing from Philadelphia, disagreed and pointed out that the danger sprang from New England. Indeed, the "New England Clubs" had become so influential since the French Revolution that "the sons and favorites of the Illuminati now hold seats in the Senate and House of Representatives in Congress."[39]

Besides the threats of revolutionary conspiracy that dinned the ears of congregations throughout New England, there were the fire-and-brimstone sermons calculated to scare the wits out of any God-fearing population. The Reverend Lathrop thundered to a Springfield audience:

> "the time when Satan most vigorously employs his corrupting and seducing arts, is usually a time of great perplexity and distress.

[38] Jedidiah Morse, D.D., A *Sermon exhibiting the Present Dangers and Consequent Duties of the Citizens of the United States of America* (Charlestown, Mass., 1799), pp. 9, 15–16. This had been a long-standing theme for Morse. In the previous year he had charged that "FOREIGN INTRIGUE . . . has been operating in this country for more than twenty years past to diminish our national limits, importance and resources etc," in A *Sermon on the Anniversary of Thanksgiving in Massachusetts*, op. cit.

[39] John Ogden, A *View of the New England Illuminati: Who are indefatigably engaged in Destroying the Religion and Government of the United States* (Philadelphia, 1799), 2d ed., p. 16.

Woe to the inhabitants of the earth and of the sea; for the devil is come down having great wrath because he knoweth that he hath but a short time." The present time exhibits a scene so familiar to the description of the text, that I cannot forbear to improve this passage for the warning of my fellow citizens in this dangerous period.[40]

The ferment brought the Hamiltonians to attention. Hamilton himself had written Harrison Gray Otis that "with a view to the possibility of internal disorders alone" the army ought to be brought up to its "authorized force." He also suggested that "the act respecting the eighty thousand militia ought likewise to be revived." Thus, for Hamilton, the standing army was not enough. "In these precarious times," he asserted, the government should be "armed with the whole of the force which has been voted."[41] Hamilton was obviously worried about resistance. When a Virginia Federalist, William Heth, volunteered his military services, Hamilton delayed his answer but praised him for not remaining "idle in a crisis of national danger." Then in a postscript he got to the main point: "What do the factions in your State really aim at?"[42]

One answer to Hamilton's query was provided by the General Assembly of Virginia who passed their own set of resolves. The Virginia Resolutions were substantially the same as the Kentucky Resolutions. They recognized the "compact theory" of the constitution, attacked "forced constructions of the constitutional charter" and the Alien and Sedition Acts, and in conclusion, urged the chief executives of the other states to communicate with Virginia's legislature agreement or disagreement on their constitutionality.

When the Virginia Assembly began debating the resolutions

[40] Joseph Lathrop, D.D., *A Sermon on the Dangers of the Times From Infidelity and Immorality; and especially From the Lately Discovered Conspiracy Against Religion and Government* (Springfield, Mass., Sept. 1798), p. 11.

[41] *Works of Alexander Hamilton*, op. cit., Vol. VIII, p. 326.

[42] Hamilton to William Heth, 18 Dec. 1798, ibid., p. 513.

formally, those who spoke for adoption were the foremost republican philosophers in the state. John Taylor of Caroline, who introduced the resolutions, began his commentary against the Alien and Sedition Laws by asserting starkly: "Liberty was in danger . . . and every effort should be made to repel attempts to subvert it." He observed, "If once we were to permit executive power to overleap its limits, where was it to stop? And, if the executive branch exercised powers not bestowed, it overleaped the Constitution." Taylor then asked, are "we approaching the system of Divine Right?" "*The precedent established by*" the Alien Law "*was dangerous*, both as it affected individuals, and as it affected states." It was "a power inclined to usurpation, to the injury of aliens, would be inclined to usurp, in the construction of the Constitution, to the injury of states; and that the precedent in the one case, would soon ripen into a law for justifying the other."

Taylor estimated that together, the two laws were "destructive of the most essential human rights." As to the "probable effects of those laws," he believed "they would establish executive influence, *and executive influence would produce a* REVOLUTION." The great constitutional scholar then pointed to the immediate danger to liberty. The combined effect of these laws would beget "fear." And, "if public opinion were to be directed by government by means of fines, penalties and punishments, on the one hand, and patronage on the other, public opinion itself would be made the stepping stone for usurpation." "*The most dangerous effect of those laws would be the abolition of the right to examine public servants.*"[43] These issues—fear, executive usurpation, government manipulation of public opinion, and especially the claim of executive privilege which resulted in a destruction of the people's right to know—were the most vital issues in a free society. On the eve of the passage of Virginia's famous resolutions, the most influential republican constitutional theorist behind Jefferson and Madison had raised the alarm and pointed to the consequences.

[43] *The Virginia Report of 1799–1800 Touching the Alien and Sedition Laws; together with the Virginia Resolutions of Dec. 21, 1798* (Richmond, Va., 1850), pp. 24–27. Italics added.

Taylor was not alone. A number of his fellow delegates rose up to attack the new laws. William Ruffin, member from Brunswick, stated that it "was the exercise of this kind of right by the British Parliament which involved us in a war with that government."[44] His implication was clear: if the federal government continued its oppressive policy of asserting its sovereignty over that of the states, war was a necessity. General Henry Lee, on the antirepublican side, complained that the resolutions "struck him as recommending resistance. They [the resolutions] declared the laws null and void. Our citizens thus thinking, would disobey the laws. This disobedience would be patronised by the State, and could not be submitted to by the United States. Insurrection would be the consequence. We have had one insurrection lately, and that without the patronage of the legislature. How much more likely might an insurrection happen, which seemed to be advised by the Assembly?"[45] From the Federalist point of view, the Virginia Assembly was promoting actual revolution. This perspective was brought to light when the fifty-eight Federalist members of the Virginia legislature published their own reply to the Virginia Resolutions. They concluded, "Let us not endeavor to disseminate among our fellow-citizens the most deadly hate against the government, on the preservation of which we firmly believe the peace and liberty of America to depend . . . it cannot but inflict a deep wound in the American mind to find the commonwealth of Virginia, exhibiting through her legislature, irresistible testimony of the degrading charge. . . . Hatred to government is unapt to beget a disposition to unite in the defence and more probably project other schemes coupling defence from invasion, with change of POLITICAL SYSTEM."[46]

The fear of revolution extended beyond the resolutions to an

[44] Ibid., p. 39.

[45] Ibid., p. 108.

[46] *An Address of the Fifty-Eight Federal Members of the Virginia Legislature to their Fellow Citizens, in January, 1799* (Augusta, Me., 1799), p. 33.

indictment of one of their chief sponsors. John Taylor of Caroline was one of the chief architects of the Virginia Resolutions and, along with Madison, in charge of guiding them through the legislature. A Virginia Federalist noted: "Times are alarming; civil dissensions, if not actual civil war, may be expected. Nobody can mistake the meaning of Taylor, of Caroline. He is the prime mover and is surrounded by those who move pretty much as he directs. One week more and all their projects will be out. . . . Another project is before the house, for arming *en masse* all the militia of the commonwealth—this is also the scheme of Taylor and his party—and who can doubt the object? It is not to prepare to defend the nation against a foreign foe, for their party boldly asserts that there is no such danger to be apprehended. What then is the object?"[47]

James Barbour, Madison's cohort and a future senator, "believed he should not use language too strong, was he to assert, that in . . . [these debates on the Alien and Sedition Acts] might be read the destinies of America: for issue was joined between monarchical principles on the one hand, and republican on the other; and they were the grand inquest who were to determine the controversy. For should so important a state as Virginia sanction the measures complained of . . . it would become a step-stone to further usurpation, until those great rights, which are guaranteed by nature and the Constitution, will be destroyed one by one, and a monarchy erected on the ruins thereof."[48]

There were many who spoke for or against the provocative nature of the resolutions, but Barbour's remarks pointed to the fears that Jefferson and Madison had entertained for nearly a decade. For he had addressed himself to the basic differences in ideology and principle outlined in the fourth resolution—the most

[47] "Extract of a letter from a gentleman of respectability in Richmond to his friends in this town, dated January 20, 1799," *Philadelphia Magazine and Review* (Jan. 1799), Huntington Library, p. 117.
[48] Ibid., p. 54.

oft-quoted sentence of the Virginia Resolutions. That resolution accused the federal government of attempting to

> *consolidate* the States by degrees into one sovereignty, the obvious tendency and inevitable result of which would be to transform the present republican system of the United States into an *absolute, or at best, a mixed monarchy.*[49]

A counterrevolution leading to monarchy or its equivalent was, in December 1798, a genuine fear and a clear and present danger to a majority of the Virginia delegates. As the news of the first Virginia Resolutions became widespread, a sense of alarm swept over the country. Suddenly Peter Porcupine's dire prediction was not as hysterical as it had appeared only three months earlier. In the first months of the new year, 1799, almost every seasoned national leader expressed his dismay at the dangerous turn of events. Patrick Henry wrote Archibald Blair, clerk of the Executive Council of the Virginia State Legislature:

> It is possible that most of the individuals who compose the contending factions are sincere and act from honest motives. But it is more probable that certain leaders meditate a *change in government*. To effect this, I see no way so practicable as dissolving the confederacy. And I am free to own, that in my judgement most of the measures lately pursued by the opposition party, directly and certainly lead to that end.[50]

Henry had, as an old revolutionary, sensed the danger in the Virginia and Kentucky Resolutions. In fact, he had lost little of his oratorical fire. In his last public speech he displayed that in theory, at least, he still maintained his patriotic fervor. Before a group of students at Hampden-Sydney College he said: "If I am asked what is to be done when a people feel themselves intolerably oppressed, my answer is ready: OVERTURN THE GOVERNMENT . . ." But Henry,

---

[49] Ibid., pp. 22–23.

[50] Patrick Henry to Archibald Blair, 8 Jan. 1799, *Patrick Henry*, op. cit., Vol. II, p. 591. Italics added. Henry's alarm was echoed by Justice James Iredell, who wrote that Virginia was "pursuing steps which directly lead to civil war." Iredell to his wife, 24 Jan. 1799, quoted in Griffith J. McRee's *Life and Correspondence of James Iredell* (New York, 1851), Vol. II, p. 543.

who would die in less than six months, was a tired and sick man. He not only disapproved of the resolutions, he feared the factional violence that would be produced by any future revolutionary struggle. Ironically, his fears paralleled Jefferson's and Madison's; for he warned that "if ever you recur to another change, you may bid adieu forever to representative government. You can never exchange the present government but for a monarchy."[51]

In less than a week Henry would have his fears reinforced by the one man he revered. George Washington had also seen the implications in Jefferson's and Madison's revolutionary strategy: "At such a crisis as this . . ." he wrote, "a certain party among us . . . endeavors . . . to disquiet the public mind . . . with unfounded alarms; to arraign every act of the administration; to set the people at variance with their government; and to embarrass all its measures . . . useless would it be to predict what must be the inevitable consequences of such policy, if it cannot be arrested."

There can be little doubt that he believed the resolutions were polarizing the people against their government. And Washington must have known or at least suspected that the authors of the resolutions were Jefferson and Madison, for he added parenthetically: "Unfortunately, . . . the State of Virginia has taken the lead in this opposition. I have said the *State,* because the conduct of its legislature in the eyes of the world will authorize the expression; and because it is an incontrovertible fact, that the principal leaders of the opposition dwell in it . . ."[52] Washington's analysis was correct in several ways. Not only was the State of Virginia taking the lead by announcing its own resolutions, her most important men were creating a dialogue that would give impetus to the revolution they felt must occur.

Jefferson began the new year by announcing the *principles* of his "political faith" in order to combat the anticipated "calumnies" and "falsehoods" that would be directed against him. Placing

[51] Ibid., p. 609.
[52] Washington to Patrick Henry, 15 Jan. 1799, *The Writings of George Washington,* op. cit., Vol. 37, pp. 87–88.

them in the context of the current political dissension, he made an effort to counter what he believed were the inevitable consequences of the administration's policies. He began by praising the idea of the constitution at the time of its adoption and, by implication, opposing what he believed it had become. He next addressed himself to the monarchical tendencies he saw emerging. Indeed, the entire statement is one that places the virtues of republican simplicity in stark contrast to the heavy-handed policies and swelling posture of the administration.

The letter then, is a philosophic statement as well as a complete program for revolution. It is also the kind of statement that can be properly integrated with the debates over the Kentucky and Virginia Resolutions and Jefferson's struggles against the Hamiltonians for the previous eight years. As such, it deserves to be quoted at length:

> I do then, with sincere zeal, wish an inviolable preservation of our present federal Constitution, according to the true sense in which it was adopted by the States, that in which it was advocated by its friends, and not that which its enemies apprehended, who therefore became its enemies; and I am opposed to the monarchising its features by the forms of its administration, with a view to conciliate a first transition to a President and Senate for life, and from that to an hereditary tenure of these offices, and thus to worm out the elective principle. I am for preserving to the States the powers not yielded by them to the Union, and to the legislature of the Union its constitutional share in the division of powers; and I am not for transferring all the powers of the States to the General Government, and those of that government to the executive branch. I am for a government rigorously frugal and simple, applying all the possible savings of the public revenue to the discharge of the national debt; and not for multiplication of officers and salaries merely to make partisans, and for increasing, by every device, the public debt, on the principle of its being a public blessing. I am for relying, for internal defence, on our militia solely, till actual invasion, and for such a naval force only as may protect our coasts and harbors from such depredations as we have experienced; and not for a standing army in time of peace,

which may overawe the public sentiment; nor for a navy, which, by its own expenses and the eternal wars in which it will implicate us, will grind us with public burthens, and sink us under them. I am for free commerce with all nations; political connection with none; and little or no diplomatic establishment. And I am not for linking ourselves by new treaties with the quarrels of Europe; entering that field of slaughter to preserve their balance, or joining in the confederacy of kings to war against the principles of liberty. I am for freedom of religion, . . . for freedom of the press, and against all violations of the Constitution to silence by force and not by reason the complaints or criticisms, just or unjust, of our citizens against the conduct of their agents. . . . These, my friend, are my principles; they are unquestionably the principles of the great body of our fellow-citizens . . .[53]

This famous letter, placed in the context of the previous chapters, is a summary view of the rights of American citizens as Jefferson saw them. It is an attempt, not to lay out a "party platform" as many historians have asserted, but, rather, to assert the principles that are necessary to preserve free government. In addition, it is a distillation of the problems then confronting the young republic, a recognition of the crises impinging upon it, and a critique of the Adams administration and an interpretation of its policies in January 1799.

John Jay was another "elder statesman" who sensed the approaching crisis. While his prediction for the new year augured ill for the country, he at least held out a ray of hope: "The seeds of trouble are sowing and germinating in our country. . . . Why and by whom, were the Kentucky and Virginia resolutions contrived, and for what purposes? I often think of Pandora's box: although it contained every kind of evil, yet it's said that *hope* was placed at the bottom. This is a singular fable, and it admits of many, and some of them very extensive applications."[54]

Hamilton viewed events from such a dire perspective that he

[53] Jefferson to Elbridge Gerry, 26 Jan. 1799, *Writings*, Vol. X, pp. 76–79.
[54] John Jay to Rev. Dr. Morse, 30 Jan. 1799, *The Life and Writings of John Jay*, op. cit., Vol. II, pp. 287–88.

was incapable of holding out hope. He could only speak of the "signs of gangrene" that had "begun" and become more "progressive" with each passing day. Choosing his audience carefully, in this case the Speaker of the House of Representatives, he railed against the republican "faction" and accused them of preparing for revolution against the government:

> It is . . . apparent that opposition to the government has acquired more system than formerly, is bolder in the avowal of its designs, less solicitous than it was to discriminate between the Constitution and the administration, and more open and more enterprising in its projects. The late attempt of Virginia and Kentucky to unite the State Legislatures in a direct resistance to certain laws of the Union can be considered in *no other light than as an attempt to change the government.*
>
> It is stated in addition that the opposition party in Virginia, the head-quarters of the faction, have followed up the hostile declarations which are to be found in the resolutions of their General Assembly by an *actual preparation of the means of supporting them by force,* that they have taken measures to put their militia on a more efficient footing—are preparing considerable arsenals and magazines, and (which is an unequivocal proof how much they are in earnest) have gone so far as to lay new taxes on their citizens. Amidst such serious indications of hostility, the safety and the duty of the supporters of the government call upon them to adopt *vigorous measures of counteraction. It will be wise* in them to *act upon the hypothesis that the opposers of the government are resolved,* if it shall be practicable, *to make its existence a question of force.*[55]

Hamilton had appended a program of "consolidating the strength of the government" that covered expanding the judiciary, improving "communications," increasing the "popularity of the government," and instituting a "society with funds" that would make loans and grants availabe to "agriculture and the arts." Yet

[55] Hamilton to Jonathan Dayton, Jan. 1799, *Works of Alexander Hamilton,* op. cit., Vol. VIII, pp. 517–22. The editor, H. C. Lodge, placed the date in late January 1799. Italics added.

dovetailed with these benign considerations, really nothing more than a public relations program, was a plan almost insidious in its suggested implementation. The main point of Hamilton's plan for the nation lay in his advocacy of the use of force against the rebellious Virginians.

Within a week or two Hamilton wrote an even stronger letter which revealed his true intentions. If ever Hamilton gave expression to his counterrevolutionary mentality, it was here: he explicitly accused Virginia of engaging in a revolutionary "conspiracy to overturn the government." Indeed, had his advice to Theodore Sedgwick been taken and applied, there would have resulted immediate civil war. On February 2, 1799, Hamilton wrote:

> What, my dear sir, are you going to do in Virginia? This is a very serious business, which will call for all the wisdom and firmness of the government. The following are the ideas which occur to me on the occasion. The first thing in all great operations of such a government as ours is to secure the opinion of the people. To this end the proceedings of Virginia and Kentucky, with the two laws complained of, should be referred to a special committee. That committee should make a report, exhibiting with great luminousness and particularly the reasons which support the constitutionality and expediency of those laws, the tendency of the doctrines advanced by Virginia and Kentucky to destroy the Constitution of the United States, and with calm dignity united with pathos *the full evidence which they afford of a regular conspiracy to overturn the government.* And the report should likewise dwell upon the inevitable effect, and probably the intention, of the proceedings to encourage hostile foreign powers to decline accommodation and proceed in hostility.
>
> The government must not merely defend itself, it must attack and arraign its enemies. But in all this there should be great care to distinguish the people of Virginia from their Legislature, and even the greater part of those who may have concurred in the Legislature from their chiefs, manifesting, indeed, a strong confidence in the good sense and patriotism of the people that they will not be the dupes of an insidious plan to disunite the people of America, to break down their Constitution, and expose them to

the enterprise of a foreign power. This report should conclude with a declaration that there is no cause for a repeal of the laws. . . . No pains or expense should be spared to disseminate this report. A little pamphlet containing it should find its way into every house in Virginia. This should be left to work and nothing to court a shock should be adopted. In the meantime the measures for raising the military force should proceed with activity. . . . When a clever force has been collected, let them be drawn toward Virginia, for which there is an obvious pretext, then let measures be taken to act upon the laws and put Virginia to the test of resistance.[56]

These letters to Dayton and Sedgwick reveal, in addition to the near panic that had struck the High Federalists, the true revolutionary nature of the Kentucky and Virginia Resolutions of 1798. Their effect was to establish a dialectic in the society that polarized a significant number of citizens against the administration in power. Specifically, the resolutions revealed a number of contradictions in principle between the most important factions in the society. But more important, they did so in a way that made the ends of the factions and the principles they represented appear unresolvable. The resolutions had, in a period of crisis, laid bare the conflicting assumptions of the society.

Hamilton, the leader of the High Federalist faction, accused the Virginia faction, and by implication Jefferson, of conspiracy against the government. By his own testimony, Hamilton viewed Jefferson and Madison as the leaders of a faction that was potentially revolutionary. This was consistent with Hamilton's view that the administration of a one-party state should not brook interference by a minority faction or, for that matter, brook any opposition at all. Virginia and Kentucky republicans were a minority faction, or so Hamilton believed; and they should therefore be crushed. To do otherwise was to violate the principle of majority rule and run the risk of the government becoming a cypher. Hamilton, who believed that energy and power were the

---

[56] Hamilton to Theodore Sedgwick, 2 Feb. 1799, ibid., p. 525. The "two laws" referred to are the Alien and Sedition Laws. Italics added.

main engines by which a government accomplished its ends, knew that he could not compromise. He refused to recognize the validity of any opposition and opposed the logic of resistance manifested in the resolutions.

Ignoring Virginia's constitutional right to raise the militia's standards and levy taxes, Hamilton interpreted their actions as a willingness, even an intention, to use force. He thus dismissed the logic and expressed commitments to the constitution and Union contained within the resolutions. This pointed to an inability on Hamilton's part to distinguish between a constitutional right and Virginia's *potential* to make war against the Union. This is not to say that the author of *The Federalist* was constitutionally naïve. On the contrary, it is a recognition that in February 1799, Hamilton's constitutional principles, contained within his theory of government and administration, simply would not allow even the germ of a spirit of resistance. We need only recall his earlier statement in 1790, regarding Virginia's protest against the assumption bill to place this in perspective: "This is the first symptom of a spirit which must either be killed or will kill the Constitution of the United States."

Jefferson, on the other hand, may have believed that Hamilton was wrongheaded about his principles of administration and view of the constitution; but he would have agreed that in a one-party state the administration should not tolerate factional opposition. The difference was that Jefferson believed Hamilton represented a faction himself, one that had gained control of the government and was, in addition to misusing the constitution, failing to live up to or abide by its principles. He could not compromise either. Thus, while Hamilton was accusing the Virginia faction of using the resolutions to destroy the Union, Jefferson was accusing Hamilton of promoting faction to destroy the constitution *and* the Union. Both perceptions of the constitution and the Union could not be right; thus, a dialectic between the competing factions must ensue.

In addition to these there were differences between their ideas of union and liberty. Hamilton's notion of the constitution was that it must preserve union at all costs, even at the expense of individual liberty. Jefferson's idea was that liberty was a primary, even an absolute, value. One was a commitment to the postrevolutionary society emphasizing values of stability and order. The other was a commitment to the revolutionary society emphasizing the values of liberty and denying power to the central government. The primary concerns of the first were considerations that gave rise to empire, commerce, and security; the second were equated with the basic ideals of the American Revolution.

The role that ideology played in furthering these ever-widening divisions revealed, in an even broader sense, that the two factions were irreconcilable. Hamilton's belief in an elitist theory of government and his fear that the common people might participate in its administration were in direct opposition to Jefferson's faith in the people and what he believed was their sacred right to direct their own public affairs. Jefferson's assumptions lay behind the basic appeal of the Virginia and Kentucky Resolutions: the people, not elites, were the true sovereigns in a republic. They were asked, along with their elected representatives, to consider what sins had been committed against the constitution. And the manner in which the sins were spelled out made the potential conflict all the more obvious: the lines being drawn between the many and the chosen few indicated that the two cities of revolution had appeared.

As we have seen, this potential conflict regarding opposing factions and constitutional principles had been obvious to republicans for some time. And, as we ponder Hamilton's "plan," plus his advice to Sedgwick, we can see that on this occasion the revolutionary nature of Jefferson's and Madison's strategy was brought home to him. As he looked into the future he could not help but see that the ability of Jefferson to appeal to a growing constituency was in stark contrast to a dwindling Federalist elite who had contempt for the masses and the emerging forces of democracy. The future balance of power in the nation, then, was painfully obvious to those Federalists who had eyes to see. And Hamilton, whose vision was rarely clouded, perceived that the dialectical nature of the Virginia and Kentucky Resolutions was producing a revolution of opinion against the government. Unable, in his own words, to intimidate the opposition presses short of tyranny, he had begun to entertain the idea of using force to accomplish his ends.

We must remember that Hamilton was the foremost military figure in America. His advice, therefore, carried considerable weight. This was especially true because there were many in Adams' administration whose loyalties were to Hamilton rather than to the President. Keeping this in mind, we can appreciate the potential impact that such a plan might have had among Adams' chief advisors. As far as the plan was concerned, Hamilton's intuition was serving him well. His suggestion for concerted action gave truth to Madison's fears that the constitution could be used as a mask to wreak vengeance on the friends of republicanism. Hamilton obviously wished the committees of Congress to *prejudge* their deliberations and authorize the use of naked force against Virginia. Clothed with legislative respectability, Hamilton intended to turn Jefferson's strategy against him: accuse the Virginians of violating the constitution, malign their intentions, link them with a foreign power, produce a report, and then disseminate it widely. But there was one major difference: Hamilton had regard for only one principle, viz., power. He wished from the outset to go farther than Jefferson, and his blatant advocacy of the use of "clever force" indicated that he intended to plunge the Union into a bloodbath.

The fact that Hamilton could mask his plan with the legitimate organs of government came as no surprise to the republicans. They had suspected for some time that his intentions were to exacerbate the crisis; and, as far as they were concerned, it was merely a question of the particular methods he would use. Madison believed, as early as January 1797, that there might be an interregnum declared.[57] In the ensuing two years little had occurred

[57] Madison to Jefferson, 8 Jan. 1797, *Letters and Other Writings of James Madison*, op. cit., Vol. II, p. 110.

that would cause him to change his mind. Thus, by late 1798, republican confidence had reached its nadir and anything was possible. James Thomson Callender, the artful republican propagandist, raised the possibility of the administration's ending the republican experiment by simply declaring an interregnum:

> The present Congress will cease to exist, on the 3d of March, 1799. On the 4th Mr. Adams may get a certificate from some confidential judge, that Virginia or Tennessee is in a state of rebellion. Whether the story be true or false, rests entirely within his breast. He directly calls out the militia . . . till the first Monday of December thereafter, he and his militia are absolute masters of America. . . . Thus nine months of a royal *interregnum* might readily put an end to the government.[58]

The timing of Callender's remarks was not limited to republicans. By March, rumors of revolution had so filled the air that Americans in Europe even heard of them. John Quincy Adams wrote, "Expectations in the United States are that an armed opposition from the disaffected quarters will take place. Mr. K[ing] himself does not think Virginia will attempt it for the present, but appears persuaded that an appeal to arms will before long be made." Adams hastened to add, however, that while he was "not altogether of this opinion," this was the first sample of "defiance to civil war."[59] But three months later, having "seen" a publication by William Giles of Virginia advocating a separation of the Union, John Quincy Adams could not be certain. In July, writing with definite unease, he told his mother "a separation is the greatest calamity that can befall us, and is alike to be deprecated by us all."[60]

[58] James Thomson Callender, *Sketches of the History of America*, op. cit., p. 120.

[59] John Quincy Adams to William Vans Murray, 30 March 1799, *The Writings of John Quincy Adams*, op. cit., Vol. II, p. 398.

[60] John Quincy Adams to Abigail Adams, 3 July 1799, ibid., p. 427. The "unimpeachable source" was Timothy Pickering, a confidant of Hamilton's. Pickering wrote Rufus King referring to "the mad and rebellious resolves of

The first seven months of the new year were considered crucial in the opposition's circles, and Jefferson, in the closing days of January, placed his revolutionary "engine" into high gear. Three days after his famous letter to Gerry, he attempted to enlist Edmund Pendleton's pen in the cause. Resorting to unusual flattery, he wrote the aging statesman, "Nobody in America can do it so well as yourself, in the . . . character of the father of your country . . ." The "it" referred to a pamphlet that was to include "the whole story," a "recapitulation" of how the extremists within the administration had strayed from the principles of republicanism.[61] Unfortunately, Jefferson's plea failed to activate Pendleton's pen.

Jefferson tendered the same advice to Madison: "This summer is the season for systematic energies and sacrifices. The engine is the press. Every man must lay his purse and his pen under contribution." Indeed, he urged Madison "to set apart a certain portion of every post day to write what may be proper for the public."[62] This was Jefferson's method of beginning a revolution in people's minds. He had noted earlier, in a letter to Colonel Nicholas Lewis, that "reason, not rashness [was] the only means of bringing our fellow-citizens to their true minds."[63] Thus, he warned Madison that the public "wish[ed] to hear *reason* instead of *disgusting blackguardism.*"[64]

Fearing that Madison was lagging, Jefferson's philosopher friend, John Taylor of Caroline, took up the slack. Discovering that Patrick Henry was to stand for election to the Assembly and that Madison intended to withdraw, he wrote the latter:

. . . Virginia and Kentucky. . . . The real object of the leading Jacobins has been declared. Giles, at the house of Mr. Burwell at Richmond, said expressly that he desired that the Union of the States might be severed." Timothy Pickering to Rufus King, 4 May 1799, *Life and Correspondence of Rufus King,* op. cit., Vol. III, p. 13.

[61] Jefferson to Edmund Pendleton, 29 Jan. 1799, *Writings,* Vol. X, p. 86.

[62] Jefferson to Madison, 5 Feb. 1799, ibid., p. 96.

[63] Jefferson to Col. Nicholas Lewis, 30 Jan. 1799, ibid., p. 89.

[64] Jefferson to Madison, 5 Feb. 1799, ibid., p. 96.

consider that Virginia is the hope of republicans throughout the Union, and that if Mr. Henry prevails in removing her resistance to monarchical measures, the whole body will be dispirited and fall a sudden and easy prey to the enemies of liberty.

Then, appealing to Madison's conscience, he added, "If you will not save yourself or your friends—yet save our country." As a final note he sounded the tocsin: "The public sentiment of Virginia is at a crisis—at the next assembly it will take a permanent form which will fix the fate of America."[65]

Jefferson's, Madison's, and Taylor's belief in sweet reason and their faith that the people would respond to reasonable appeals was obviously a reflection of Jefferson's experience in France. As the leader in this new political movement, he was determined to keep the forces of violence under control, to deal with the constitutional issues at hand. He well knew that one false step toward violence and the extremists would be able to use an equal, if not greater, force against him. His reasoning, therefore, was exactly parallel to that he had given La Fayette in France. Renewing his appeal to Edmund Pendleton, Jefferson outlined his perceptions of what was becoming a nationwide movement:

This state [Pennsylvania] is coming forward with a boldness not yet seen. Even the German counties of York and Lancaster, hitherto the most devoted, have come about, and by petitions with four thousand signers remonstrate against the alien and sedition laws, standing armies, and discretionary powers in the President. New York and Jersey are also getting into great agitation. In this State, we fear that the ill-designing may produce insurrection. Nothing could be so fatal. Anything like force would check the progress of the public opinion and rally them round the government. This is not the kind of opposition the American people will permit. But keep away all show of force, and they will bear down the evil propensities of the government, by the constitutional means of election and petition. If we can keep quiet,

[65] John Taylor to James Madison, 4 March 1799. W. C. Rives Papers. Quoted in Koch, *Jefferson and Madison*, op. cit., p. 195.

therefore, the tide now turning will take a steady and proper direction. Even in New Hampshire there are strong symptoms of a rising inquietude.[66]

These were the first optimistic words that had flowed from Jefferson's pen in over a decade. Only the day before he had written Archibald Stuart "a wonderful and rapid change is taking place in Pennsylvania, Jersey and New York."[67] By that he meant that the resolutions were beginning to take hold. Indeed, the strategy was proving so potent that Jefferson's optimism was nearly euphoric. To his friend Thomas Lomax he placed the "movement" in perspective: "You ask for any communication I may be able to make, which may administer comfort to you. I can give that which is solid. The spirit of 1776 is not dead. It has only been slumbering. The body of the American people is substantially republican."[68]

The connection to the American Revolution had been made. Jefferson saw himself fighting essentially the same struggle he had twenty-five years earlier. Then, as now, he had acted in the same context. His days were filled with writing pamphlets, forming committees, petitioning Congress and state legislatures, writing declarations, resolves, letters to the newspapers, etc. Now, with a more sophisticated view of revolution, he had launched a movement that had the same capacity to change society, albeit peacefully "by the constitutional means of election and petition."[69] And however demanding the drain on his limited amounts of energy had become, the progress shown by his "engine" in the

[66] Jefferson to Edmund Pendleton, 14 Feb. 1799, *Writings*, Vol. X, p. 105.

[67] Jefferson to Archibald Stuart, 13 Feb. 1799, ibid., p. 103.

[68] Jefferson to Thomas Lomax, 12 March 1799, ibid., p. 123.

[69] An example of the kind of effect Jefferson wished to create in Congress can be seen in his description to Bishop James Madison in late February 1799: "The tables of Congress are loaded with petitions. . . . Thirteen of the twenty-two counties of this State (Penna.) have already petitioned against the proceedings of the late Congress." Thus, if every state legislature, in addition to the national legislature, were so "loaded with petitions," the nation's representatives would hardly have time to discuss anything *but* the crisis that Jefferson saw coming. 27 Feb. 1799, *Writings*, Vol. X, p. 122.

southern, western, and Middle States, and "even in New Hampshire," demonstrated that an appeal to revolutionary principles was yet possible. The "spirit of 1776" was still in the air.

But the success that Jefferson had in awakening the spirit of revolution was unnerving to his opponents. They were unwilling, even in the House of Representatives, to abide by the tenets of reason, "confidence and responsibility," the "new fangled names" to which they gave lip service.[70] This appalled Jefferson, who described to Madison the obvious corruption of reason. When Gallatin attempted to speak against the Alien Law, "a scandalous scene" broke out. Representatives "enter[ed] into loud conversations, laugh[ing], cough[ing] etc. . . . It was impossible to proceed."[71] Disruption of the legislative process, especially in a manner that contradicted sweet reason, revealed the low intentions of the extremists. And Jefferson, presiding over the orderly conduct of the Senate, must have viewed their actions with contempt.

The extremists were, however, equally contemptuous. The politics of faction had blinded all but the most discriminating critics of which few were to be found. One writer noted: "The season . . . for *open* opposition to the Federal government was, for a long time, inauspicious. [But] the summer of 1799 warmed the dormant faction into life."[72] Such was Peter Porcupine's assessment of politics during the ensuing three months and it was decidedly accurate. Both Hamilton and Jefferson had determined that stronger measures were called for. Hamilton wrote the attorney general of New York, complaining that he had

> long been the object of the most malignant calumnies of the faction opposed to our government through the medium of the papers devoted to their views. *Hitherto, I have forborne to resort to the laws* for the punishment of the authors or abettors, and were I to consult personal considerations alone, I should continue

[70] Jefferson to James Madison, 26 Feb. 1799, ibid., p. 121.

[71] Jefferson to Chancellor Robert R. Livingston, 28 Feb. 1799, ibid., pp. 118–19.

[72] *Porcupine's Works*, op. cit., Vol. XI, p. 402.

in this course, repaying hatred with contempt. *But public motives now compel me to a different conduct.*

When we recall Hamilton's advice to Oliver Wolcott in June of 1798, the "moment" he had seen the Sedition Act, it is hard to take him seriously as he complains of others maligning him. He had been for as much repression as possible, short of actual tyranny. Now that he had given "faction body and solidity," he was facing the consequences of his own repressive policies. And however he was attempting to disguise his motives by referring to another standard of conduct, Hamilton was implicitly stating that he was willing to go *beyond the law* to see his critics punished. Referring to the Virginians he continued:

> The designs of that faction to overturn our government, and with it the great pillars of social security and happiness in this country, become every day more manifest, and have of late acquired a degree of system which renders them formidable.
>
> One principal engine for effecting the scheme is by audacious falsehoods to destroy the confidence of the people in all those who are in any degree conspicuous among the supporters of the government—*an engine which has been employed in time past with too much success,* and which, unless counteracted in future, is likely to be attended with very fatal consequences.
>
> To counteract it is therefore a duty to the community. Among the specimens of this contrivance, that which is the subject of the present letter demands peculiar attention. A bolder calumny—one more absolutely destitute of foundation—was never propagated, and its dangerous tendency needs no comment; being calculated to inspire the belief that the independence and liberty of the press are endangered by the intrigues of ambitious citizens . . .[73]

[73] Hamilton to Josiah O. Hoffman, 1799. No date is given, but the editor, H. C. Lodge, has the letter listed in the period after July 10 to September or October of 1799. *Works of Alexander Hamilton,* op. cit., Vol. VIII, p. 354. Italics added. Peter Porcupine's remarks paralleled exactly those of Hamilton: "There is in these States a faction, a numerous and desperate faction, resolved on the over throw of the Federal Government; and the man who will not allow that there is *danger* to be apprehended, is either too great a fool to perceive it, or too great a coward to encounter it." *Porcupine's Works,* Vol. X, p. 174.

While Hamilton recognized the growing success of Jefferson's constitutional approach to revolution, his demand for counterrevolution implied that he and his cohort, in pressing the Sedition Act, had gone too far. Yet the failure to connect his own ambitions with the charge of the republicans also meant that he misunderstood the nature of Jefferson's opposition and the reasons for his success. The fact that journalists were clapped into jail and the free press was threatened eluded Hamilton and his advisors. It was as if Hamilton and those around him were so blinded by power, they were unable to see that constitutional principles were involved.

Hamilton's adversary, however, never lost sight of those principles. By mid-August Jefferson voiced even greater fears for the preservation of the constitution. The state legislatures seemed oblivious of the growing constitutional crisis. Responding to the Virginia and Kentucky Resolutions of 1798 and Jefferson's original query, they viewed with alarm the powerful ideas that Jefferson and Madison had unleashed. Of the nine states that expressed their opinions, all condemned the resolutions, indicating that Jefferson and his cohort faced an uphill battle. Delaware called them "a very injustifiable interference with the general government . . . and of dangerous tendency . . ." Rhode Island referred to the "many evil and fatal consequences which may flow from the very unwarrantable resolutions . . ." Connecticut "disavowe[d] the *principles* contained in the . . . resolutions . . ." New York described them as "inflammatory and pernicious sentiments and doctrines . . . destructive to the Federal Government." New Hampshire expressed its disagreement by saying that "for mere speculative purposes," the Alien and Sedition Acts "are constitutional and in the present critical situation of the country, highly expedient." Vermont not only "highly disapproved," but said the resolutions were "dangerous in their tendency."[74] Maryland, referring to "the crisis," resolved that it "highly disapproved of the sentiments and opinions contained in the resolutions . . ."

[74] *The Virginia Report of 1799–1800*, op. cit., pp. 169–77.

Pennsylvania's Senate voted fourteen to eight to "refuse" to consider the Kentucky Resolutions and then expressed "confidence" in the President's "administration." What was common to each of the state legislatures was a definite fear regarding the potentially revolutionary ideas expressed in the resolutions.[75] Massachusetts put that concern into perspective by saying:

> should the . . . state of Virginia persist in the assumption of the right to declare the acts of the national government unconstitutional, and should she oppose successfully her force and will to those of the nation, the Constitution would be reduced to a mere cypher, to the form and pageantry of authority, without the energy of power . . . the Federal Government . . . would be the object of opposition and of remonstrance; while the people, convulsed and confused by the conflict between two hostile jurisdictions, enjoying the protection of neither, would be wearied into a submission to some bold leader, who would establish himself on the ruins of both.[76]

All of this, of course, was beside the point. For Jefferson believed that if the opposite—i.e., resistance to the government by the states—did not occur, the constitution would be nothing more than a cipher anyway. But opposition to his attempts to promote a debate on the principles of the constitution was trivial compared to the next shock he endured. The federal government's attempting to usurp the common law of the United States was, for him, the final blow. Any reservations he might have had regarding the intentions of the administration and its willingness to abide by the constitution vanished. He wrote to Edmund Randolph:

> Of all the doctrines which have ever been broached by the federal government, the novel one, of the common law being in force and cognizable as an existing law in their courts, is to me the most formidable. All their other assumptions of ungiven powers have been in detail. The bank law, the treaty doctrine, the sedition act, alien act, the undertaking to change the State laws of evidence

[75] *The Philadelphia Magazine and Review,* Jan. 1799, pp. 54–55.
[76] *The Virginia Report of 1799–1800,* op. cit., pp. 170–71.

in the State courts by certain parts of the stamp act, etc., etc., have been solitary, unconsequential, timid things, in comparison with the audacious, barefaced and sweeping pretension to a system of law for the United States, without the adoption of their Legislature, and so infinitively beyond their power to adopt. If this assumption be yielded to, the State courts may be yielded to, the State courts may be shut up . . .

Jefferson saw this alteration of the constitution as a naked grab for power. At stake were the legal existence of the states and those systems of justice, the state courts, which they had evolved. Moreover, if the national government made good its "new doctrine that the common law is the law of the United States, and that their courts have, of course, jurisdiction co-extensive with that law, that is to say, general over all cases and persons,"[77] what role *would* the states have? Their ability to limit the power of government would be nonexistent. For those who believed in the sanctity of republican government, embodied in the state governments and their constitutions, tyranny had appeared knocking at the door. Finally, Jefferson and his colleagues realized that this attempt to destroy the independence of the states meant, for all practical purposes, the end of constitutional government. For if the extremists within the administration were successful, one of the fundamental principles of western constitutionalism, i.e., the idea of limiting the power of government, would be destroyed. The proposal to usurp the common law was nothing less than a systemic approach to counterrevolution, one that only incidentally set the stage for despotism. With the principle of federalism at an end, with the power of the states destroyed and in their place the erection of a Leviathan—arrogating all power to itself—the great experiment to preserve liberty would be shattered.

Frightened by this prospect, Jefferson committed to paper one of the most crucial decisions of his entire life. Everything that he had previously written regarding the administration's policies can be

[77] Jefferson to Edmund Randolph, 18 Aug. 1799, *Writings*, Vol. X, pp. 125–29.

considered educational and politically safe, always with an eye to preserving the Union of the states. Now, and for the first time, Jefferson stated explicitly that he would destroy the Union rather than see the states become the creatures of the federal government.

Within five days of his letter to Randolph, he had devised a potent and dangerous strategy of revolution. By using the legal techniques of resolutions and appeals to legislatures and then timing them to coincide with a general election, Jefferson proposed to confront the administration head on. Despite his claims that this was a "hastily" sketched strategy, an insightful and bold three-pronged attack emerged: 1. standing determinedly upon the principles of republicanism outlined in his letter to Gerry and the Kentucky Resolutions, while forcing the states and the national Congress to meet him upon his chosen ground; 2. making a comparison between his new compact theory of the constitution and the consequences of growing federal power; and 3. like Hamilton, presenting an overture to the idea of union in order to neutralize the most vociferous critics of his movement.

The dynamics of his program, as well as its timing, were of the utmost importance. The dynamics ensured that these three elements would combine to produce a movement that was based on principles, constitutional in nature, yet hopefully, peaceful in intent. The timing of the program was designed, once it was released to the public, to come to fruition within ten or eleven months. Finally, the tone of his program was deemed perfect. While his rhetoric was "patient," "indulgent," "affectionate," and "conciliatory," it nevertheless laid the foundations for the Revolution of 1800. With only two substantive changes in his language, and these would come within two weeks as a result of Madison's influence, the program for 1800 was essentially complete. Jefferson thus confided to his closest friend:

. . . the opportunity is certainly a valuable one of producing a concert of action. I will in the mean time give you my ideas to reflect on. That the principles already advanced by Virginia and Kentucky are not to be yielded in silence, I presume we all agree. I should propose a declaration of Resolution by their legislatures on this plan.

1. Answer the reasonings of such states as have ventured into the field of reason, and that of the Committee of Congress. Here they have given us all the advantage we could wish. Take some notice of those states who have either not answered at all, or answered without reasoning.

2. Make a firm protestation against the principle and the precedent; and a reservation of the rights resulting to us from these palpable violations of the constitutional compact by the Federal government, and the approbation or acquiescence of the several co-states; so that we may hereafter do, what we might now rightfully do, whenever repetitions of these and other violations shall make it evident that the Federal government, disregarding the limitations of the federal compact, mean to exercise powers over us to which we have never assented.

3. Express in affectionate and conciliatory language our warm attachment to union with our sister-states, and to the instrument and principles by which we are united; that we are willing to sacrifice to this every thing except those rights of self-government the securing of which was the object of that compact; that not at all disposed to make every measure of error or wrong a cause of scission, we are willing to view with indulgence to wait with patience till those passions and delusions shall have passed over which the federal government have artfully and successfully excited to cover its own abuses and to conceal its designs; fully confident that the good sense of the American people and their attachment to those very rights which we are now vindicating will, before it shall be too late, rally with us round the true principles of our federal compact. *But determined, were we to be disappointed in this, to sever ourselves from that union* we so much value, rather than give up the rights of self-government . . .[78]

[78] Jefferson to Madison, 23 Aug. 1799. Quoted in Koch, *Jefferson and Madison*, op. cit., pp. 196–98. Despite the strategy and tactics of "scission" and the reserved-rights clause, the author notes the following: "In the perspective of Jefferson's massive correspondence over the years, this is one of the most extreme statements that he ever made. The context of the fateful remark

What is remarkable about this letter, in addition to Jefferson's mood, is that it represents a departure as well as a refinement of his strategy. It is couched in terms of pure revolutionary theory and in that sense is a sign of his deepening commitment—in principle—to the idea of revolution in America. But it is also highly practical and represents a plan of action. Perhaps this is why Madison journeyed to Monticello so hurriedly in order to defuse Jefferson's anger. Madison's visit resulted in a second letter that, less than two weeks later, altered in a minor way his radical propositions.[79]

But while Madison was able to tone down Jefferson's plan by eliminating the extreme statement regarding secession, he nevertheless did not change his basic strategy. Jefferson's assertion about severing the Union would, if the federal government persisted in usurping the power of the states, naturally follow his "agreed" upon adherence to the principles of the Virginia and Kentucky Resolutions. And a strict adherence to those principles was made explicit. Moreover, in the *end*, they were agreed upon by all the republicans. This is a crucial point because it means that the concessions Jefferson made to Madison were political, not theoretical. They did not compromise the aims of his movement; they merely made his principles more palatable.

The second modification in Jefferson's letter to Wilson Cary

---

reveals how far he was willing to go in fighting 'arbitrary' government. He was prepared to answer the dilemma: preserve civil liberties or cleave to the Union that proscribes them, by choosing the former. Thus, Jefferson placed no absolute value upon 'Union.' Compared to the extreme evil of the ruthless suppression of liberty, it appeared to him that the destruction of the compact that bound the states together was the lesser evil. This line of thought is in accord with his earlier judgment that only an Adam and Eve left upon earth, but left free, would be better than a host of men enslaved." P. 199.

[79] Jefferson to Wilson Cary Nicholas, 5 Sept. 1799, *Writings*, Vol. X, p. 131. Jefferson wrote: "Mr. M[adison] who came, as had been proposed, does not concur in the *reservation* proposed above; and from this I recede readily, not only in deference to his judgment, but because, as we should never think of separation but for repeated and enormous violations, so these, when they occur, will be cause enough of themselves."

Nicholas, after his conversation with Madison, described the above reference to the rights of the states as a "reservation." That is, it would be tantamount to saying that if the national government succeeded in destroying the state governments, then the states would reserve the right, in effect, to nullify their acts and secede from the Union. While it was not stated precisely "what we (the States) might now rightfully do," the language carried with it a threat either to secede from the Union or to disregard the acts of the national government—or both. The implications behind this strategy were twofold: 1. to contain the power of the federal government within restricted constitutional boundaries, and 2. to enable the states to confront a constitutional issue in such a way that they would continually educate the people regarding their rights.

In truth, however, Jefferson's "reservation" statement carried to a logical conclusion was, from a strategic point of view, academic; and from a tactical point of view it was politically wise to eliminate it and thus avoid unnecessary criticism. The subtle issues of "reservation" and those words that implied a doctrine of nullification would come up again; but for the present Madison had convinced Jefferson that it was advantageous to delete them.[80] Indeed, while working toward revolution it was unnecessary to state the obvious conclusion if the administration did not change its policy. And, for reasons that we have already discussed, Jefferson, as well as Madison, did not wish to endanger the possibilities of a peaceful revolution. Jefferson's acquiescence indicated that he was biding his time, preparing, along with Madison and Nicholas, for the next level of the revolutionary dialectic.

Realizing the limited nature of the successful Kentucky and

[80] It is interesting to note Madison's objections in light of the fact that he had used the word "interpose" in the third Virginia Resolution of 1798. "Interpose" was not as blatant as "nullify" nor an expressed statement of the "reservation" of specific rights, but it did imply much the same meaning. The difference, however, was important: though vague, it made the point of determined resistance and also made it possible to be flexible on matters of principle.

Virginia Resolutions, Jefferson knew that something more must be accomplished in order to mobilize public opinion. Accordingly, he wrote Nicholas that the sole "object of the present communication is to procure a concert in the general plan of action, as it is extremely desirable that Virginia and Kentucky should pursue the same track on this occasion."[81] Indeed, a general plan of action was taking shape. And although it cannot be proven, because the author—or authors—are unknown, the "general plan" referred to by Jefferson may have included, because of the climate of opinion at the time, another set of Kentucky Resolutions.

Before the year was out the Kentucky legislature would pass a second set of resolutions consistent with Jefferson's revolutionary strategy. Taking his advice to "answer the reasonings of such states as have ventured into the field of reason," i.e., on the unconstitutionality of the Alien and Sedition Laws, Kentucky did just that. Castigating their "sister states" ("Virginia only excepted"), the General Assembly went on, still consistent with Jefferson's advice, to state their "attachment to the Union" and refusal to acquiesce "in the doctrines and principles advanced and attempted" by the other states. In addition, they made a distinction between those who administered the constitution and the constitution itself, stating explicitly that their co-states had accepted "in principle and in construction" an argument that would "stop nothing short of despotism."

Asserting this dire conclusion, the Kentucky legislature then went on to announce that "a nullification" doctrine was the "rightful remedy." Reaffirming their own "principles" of 1798, the new set of resolutions expressed Kentucky's right to resist "in a constitutional manner" all further violations of the constitution.[82] In this way the resolutions of November 14, 1799, went beyond Kentucky's principled and constitutional resistance of 1798. Not only had the Kentucky legislators criticized their sister states for a failure to oppose the administration, they took it upon themselves

[81] Jefferson to Wilson Cary Nicholas, 5 Sept. 1799, ibid., p. 132.
[82] Text of the Kentucky Resolutions of 14 Nov. 1799, in E. D. Warfield, *The Kentucky Resolutions of 1798* (New York, 1894), pp. 123–26.

to declare a nullification doctrine. This dovetailed precisely with Jefferson's plan: to consolidate opinion among the people on the idea of resistance. And, indeed, this had taken place. Three weeks after the Kentucky Resolutions had passed, John Breckinridge, now the Speaker of the Kentucky House of Representatives, wrote Jefferson regarding the nullification clause: "In the lower House . . . there was not a dissenting voice." And while a few state senators had voiced their "considerable division," the future would find "the great mass of people . . . uncontaminated and firm" in their support.[83]

The outlines of Jefferson's strategy were becoming clearer. Finding it necessary to deal with a rapidly deteriorating national situation, he was being prodded by Madison to become more practical and less theoretical. The next ten months would see him responding to that pressure and also paying more attention to his role as a political figure. Although still maintaining the reins of leadership, he was forced to elevate himself above the rough and tumble of politics. As a result, when Virginia's next response to the constitutional crisis was being formulated, Jefferson discovered that his closest advisors, Madison and James Monroe, were against his direct participation. Unwilling to risk even the hint of a scandal involving Jefferson in a protest against the administration, they convinced him that he had to remain silent. Yet, in the month that Madison was researching and writing his famous *Virginia Report of 1800*, Jefferson could not help presenting him with a set of guidelines.

These guidelines revealed that Jefferson realized the revolutionary movement he had launched was entering a critical stage. His concern for principle was consistent with all his previous statements. But the burden of his advice to Madison concerns the dual roles of "force" and the "army." His letter also deals with the potential political reaction of his opponents. He is intent on maintaining, if not reinforcing, the factional divisions within the administration, to do nothing that would lead to their uniting in a

---

[83] John Breckinridge to Thomas Jefferson, 9 Dec. 1799, ibid., p. 123.

strong coalition. Indeed, his thoughts are reminiscent of the advice he had given Moustier, La Fayette, Dumas, and Crevecoeur only ten years earlier: above all, do nothing that may "hoop" your opponents together or cause the army to "shew" its seducing hand. Finally, he urges his friend to place entire faith in the elective process of the constitution.

In retrospect, Jefferson was following the advice that he had given to the French revolutionaries. He always believed that had the French abided by these basic tenets they would have produced a successful revolution. Thus, at this critical juncture, he gave Madison the benefit of his eminent practical revolutionary experience:

> Our objects, according to my ideas, should be these: 1) peace even with Great Britain; 2) a sincere cultivation of the Union; 3) the disbanding of the army on principles of economy and safety; 4) protestations against violations of the true principles of our constitution, merely to save them, and prevent precedent and acquiescence from being pleaded against them; but nothing to be said or done which shall look or lead to force, and give any pretext for keeping up the army. If we find the monarchical party really split into pure Monocrats and Anglomonocrats, we should leave to them alone to manage all those points of difference which they may chuse to take between themselves, only arbitrating between them by our votes, but doing nothing which may hoop them together.[84]

Madison responded to Jefferson's guidelines by writing the *Virginia Report of 1800*, one of the most important papers written by an American statesman. Making a thorough analysis of the constitution and the threats against it, Madison revealed why he was later called "the Father of the Constitution." In the first of these new Virginia Resolutions, he declared attachment to the constitution and the Union and then proceeded to review and reaffirm the principles of the resolutions of 1798.

The third resolution elaborated on the doctrine of "interposi-

---

[84] Jefferson to Madison, 26 Nov. 1799. Rives Papers, Lib. Cong. Quoted in Koch, *Jefferson and Madison*, op. cit., p. 203.

tion," claiming that the states had a "duty" to "arrest the . . . dangerous exercise of powers not granted (to the federal government) . . ." Madison continued that "the object of the interposition" doctrine was "to arrest the progress of usurpation, and maintain the authorities, rights, and liberties appertaining to the states." Along with interposition, Madison validated his commitment to Jefferson's compact theory, asserting that the states "being the parties to the constitutional compact, and in their sovereign capacity . . . [will] decide in the last resort, whether the compact made by them be violated; and . . . [whether] such questions as may be of sufficient magnitude to require their interposition."[85]

In the fourth resolution Madison took up the question of construction or interpreting the constitution. He stated that "a spirit has been manifested to enlarge the powers of the federal government, by forced construction, especially of certain general phrases; of which the effect will be to consolidate the states into one sovereignty, and the result a monarchy . . ." This "tendency" would result because it would enlarge the executive power and thus enable "the chief magistrate to secure his own re-election" as well as "regulate his successors."[86] Finally, Madison drove home his conclusion: the presidency would become such an "object of ambition as to make elections so tumultuous and corrupt, that the people would themselves demand an hereditary succession." The prediction was clear: bring about a concentration of power in the executive branch, blatantly corrupt the election process, raise the violence of party and faction, and the people would demand a stable and authoritarian government. Indeed, this was one of Jefferson's basic beliefs and a fundamental reason for adhering to a peaceful idea of revolution.

The issue of separation of powers was taken up in the sixth

[85] *The Virginia Report of 1799–1800*, op. cit., pp. 189–92.

[86] *Communications of the Legislature of Virginia respecting the Alien and Sedition Laws and Instructions in reference to Resolutions of the General Assembly, 21st Day of December, 1798* (Richmond, Va., 1800), Huntington Library, p. 48.

resolution. Making a painstaking analysis of the Alien and Sedition Laws, Madison believed that the Executive's right to deport aliens "unite[d] legislative, executive, and judicial power in the hands of the President." The Executive would be in a position to "define" by his own "will" "every circumstance of *danger, suspicion, and secret machination*." He would thus "judge" and "execute his own decrees." "This union of powers," said Madison, "subverts the general principles of free government, which require the three great functions to be kept in distinct hands." The President's signing of the Alien Act thus "subvert[ed] the particular organization and positive provisions of the Federal Constitution . . ."[87]

Madison next attacked the Sedition Act by addressing himself to the major problem of the common law and the constitution. Claiming that it enabled the general government to usurp falsely the common law that had been in force before the American Revolution, Madison said, "If it be understood that the common law is established by the Constitution, it follows that no part of the law can be altered by the legislature . . ." Further, if such a law were passed by the federal government, ". . . the whole code, with all its incongruities, barbarisms, and bloody maxims, would be inviolably saddled on the good people of the United States." He then placed the Sedition Act in perspective by saying it violated the principles of the American Revolution: "The fundamental principle of the Revolution was that the colonies were . . . united by a common executive, but not united by any common legislative sovereign."[88] The consequence of this "construction," or interpretation, i.e., "admitting the common law as the law of the United States," was in Madison's eyes fatal to the states: "The Administration of it would overwhelm the residuary sovereignty of the states and by one constructive operation, new model the whole political fabric of the country."[89]

---

[87] *The Virginia Report of 1799–1800*, op. cit., p. 210.

[88] Ibid., pp. 216, 212.

[89] *Communications of the Legislature of Virginia* . . ., op. cit., p. 73; *The Virginia Report of 1799–1800*, op. cit., p. 217.

James Madison's remorseless logic continued. Not only had he exposed the dangers of the administration's policies in terms of separation of powers, corruption of elections, a tendency to monarchy, the usurpation of the common law, the destruction of state sovereignty, and the violation of the principles of the American Revolution, he addressed himself to the relation of the Sedition Act to the First Amendment. The act, especially where freedom of the press was concerned, "abridged" the First Amendment. By recognizing no "material difference between a previous restraint, and a subsequent punishment" of a writer for his article, Madison accused the administration of going beyond the English in attempting to crush freedom. "It would be a mockery to say that no law should be passed, preventing publications from being made, but that laws might be passed for punishing them in case they should be made." Nor, he continued, would the press be the only victim. "The freedom of conscience, and of religion, are found in the same instruments which assert the freedom of the press. It will never be admitted that the meaning of the former, in the common law of England, is to limit their meaning in the United States."

The great constitutional genius was saying that attacking one of these freedoms, for example, "chilling the press," was the same as attacking them all.[90] Without an uninterrupted flow of critical ideas in the only media that existed, the newspapers, the free society could not survive. The people, denied access to information, would not be able to make intelligent decisions. In a very subtle way, all of the First Amendment freedoms were related. Indeed, the administration's passage of the Sedition Law, which attempted to stifle criticism of government policy, was highly ironic. The determination to enjoy freedom of speech, press, assembly, conscience, and religion had been the main object of the American Revolution. And, upon the exercise of these freedoms, especially where they involved criticism of government, Madison was explicit: "As respects our Revolution, . . . [it] was promoted

[90] *The Virginia Report of 1799–1800,* op. cit., pp. 222–30.

by canvassing the measures of government."[91] Madison revealed the administration's greatest fears: they were afraid of those very principles of freedom which had given rise to revolution in the first place. But more to the point, they were determined that they would not be overthrown by a similar process.[92]

Placing his faith in the language of the First Amendment and in the text of the Virginia ratifying convention, Madison repeated the statement: "The liberty of conscience and freedom of the press cannot be cancelled, abridged, restrained, or modified, by any authority of the United States." Thus, by passing the Sedition Law, the administration's policies contradicted Madison's understanding of the theory of the constitution. Plainly, the executive and legislative branches were in direct violation of the constitution. For Madison and Jefferson this was a dangerous situation; and Madison, speaking for his committee, concluded his resolution by saying, "The unconstitutional power exercised over the press by the Sedition Act ought, more than any other, to produce universal alarm." Knowing the damage that would be done to a free society resulting from an attack on the First Amendment freedoms by government, Madison reaffirmed the tenets of a free society. There was, he stated, no way in which "the responsibility of officers of government . . . [could] be secured without a free investigation of their conduct and motives." It was, therefore, "the right and duty of every citizen to make such investigation, and promulgate the results."[93] Thus, any administration that would deny information to the people or their representatives, in order to shield its "machinations" from their eyes, was in violation of the constitu-

[91] *Analysis of the Report of the Committee of the Virginia Assembly on the proceedings of sundry of the other States in Answer to their Resolutions* (Philadelphia, 1800), Huntington Library, p. 187.

[92] We must keep in mind the fact that before 1800 there had never been a complete change of power in government without violence and bloodshed. A transfer of the reins of government from one faction to another, thus, meant a violent revolution would occur.

[93] *Analysis of Report*, op. cit., p. 187; *The Virginia Report of 1799–1800*, op. cit., p. 225.

tion. It constituted, in other words, a threat to the stability, harmony, and freedom of the society.

The consequences of this administrative mentality, basically repressive in nature, were so obvious that Madison, without mentioning any names, revealed the motives of the extremists within the administration: ". . . in the several elections, during the continuance of the Sedition Act, it would tend to screen the incumbents of office from inquiry." "The right of election (which depends on full information) is the essence of a free government . . . [and] is impaired by the Sedition Act." "Competitors against incumbents in office have not an equal chance, the latter being shielded by the act" and "the people [could] not fully discuss and ascertain the relative merits of such competitors and incumbents."[94] The truth about the faction in power had now been revealed by Madison. The extremists did not care about ethics, about principles of government, about honest elections, or about the constitution. They were concerned solely with power and the people be damned. Indeed, as Madison's description cut through the rhetoric of the High Federalists, it appeared that the politics of faction had come home to roost.

Thus did James Madison outline the administration's attempt to undermine the constitution through its attack upon the First Amendment. By choking off the free flow of ideas, many of them critical of Federalist policies, the administration was not merely laying the groundwork for victory in successive elections; it was destroying the foundations of a free society. Both Madison and Jefferson knew that integrity in government must be absolute in order to command the respect and trust of the citizenry. And the electoral process was where these values were put to the test. Clearly, then, the Virginia Resolutions of 1799–1800 were an attempt to expose the High Federalists and their efforts to corrupt both the elections and the values that underlay them. Madison hoped to prove that by imposing their own brand of repression the

[94] *Analysis of Report,* op. cit., pp. 187, 226–27.

administration extremists were contradicting the principles of the constitution, of republicanism and of the American Revolution.

This concerted attack against freedom could not continue. Therefore, arresting the extremist faction's "evil doctrine, its dialectic, and related procedures"[95] assumed an immediate and critical importance. The obvious method of retaliation was the same as it had been in November of the previous year. Unleashing the idea of resistance in the original Kentucky Resolutions, Jefferson had written Madison that while "we may not be committed absolutely to push the matter to extremities, . . . [we] yet may be free to push as far as events will render prudent."[96] And Madison, into whose hands the writing of the *Report* had fallen, decided to "push" events in his own prudent way.[97]

Realizing that the danger to the constitution had become greater since Jefferson had written his strategic letter, Madison renewed the dialectic that Jefferson had begun. There was, however, one major difference and that was a detailed analysis of the administration's attack against the First Amendment. By doing this, Madison indicated a slight change in strategy. No longer was it necessary to stress the right of the states to protest. After a fourteen-month debate on the compact and states' rights theories, the point had been made. He was now placing the burden of proof on a corrupt administration.

This was not to say that Madison had abandoned the doctrine

[95] Koch, *Jefferson and Madison*, op. cit., p. 210. It is interesting that Professor Koch recognized an "evil doctrine and its dialectic" on the part of the Federalists. However, she failed to note any corresponding dialectic, evil or no, on the part of the republicans.

[96] Jefferson to Madison, 17 Nov. 1798, *Writings*, Vol. X, pp. 62–63.

[97] Evidently one Federalist believed that Madison had pushed events too far. In an *Analysis of Report*, Alexander Addison stated: "The resolutions, embracing a variety of topics, if not intended, were well calculated, as a declaration of war by the State of Virginia against the government of the United States; and the transmission of them to the several states was well calculated to combine every State, under the plausible pretext of preserving the constitution, in a system of hostility against the Union," op. cit., p. 3.

of states' rights. Indeed, in the closing words of the *Report*, he said he viewed them as the "intermediate" between the people and the government. This meant that Madison was taking his bearings from the period of the formation of the government, about which no one knew more. It meant that, in the dispute over the role states would play in the future federal government, he placed his faith in the rights they established at the time of ratification. His entire essay, then, reinforced that final point: the states had the responsibility to "descry the first symptoms of usurpation . . . and sound the alarm to the public." And if "this argument . . . was a proper one then . . .," he concluded, "it must be a proper one now . . ."[98]

The *Virginia Report* followed the format of the Virginia and Kentucky Resolutions of 1798 in dealing with the principles of a free society. It was consistent as well with Jefferson's instructions to Madison and Wilson Cary Nicholas in August and September, plus the guidelines Jefferson had given the former in the closing days of November 1799. The *Report* was calculated, moreover, to have its effects upon the public mind within the following ten months. Thus, we see Jefferson registering his impatience to get a copy of the *Report* to the public before the Virginia legislature could authorize it. He even wrote James Monroe, then governor of Virginia, "If you will send me one, we can have it reprinted here and sent out. Pray do it by the first post."[99] Not until late March would Jefferson feel satisfied enough to write the governor, "a great impression made here of the Resolutions has been sold off and dispersed into the other States."[100] Madison had accomplished a Herculean task. His great essay was now in the hands of those who could educate the people. And no one realized more than Jefferson how crucial it was to go beyond this and actually place Madison's *Report* in the hands of the people. Nor was there a single person in America who better understood that the critical

[98] *The Virginia Report of 1799–1800*, op. cit., p. 232.

[99] Jefferson to James Monroe, 6 Feb. 1800, *Writings*, Vol. VII, p. 424.

[100] Jefferson to James Monroe, 26 March 1800. Jefferson Papers, Lib. Cong. Quoted in Koch, *Jefferson and Madison*, op. cit., p. 205.

problem of revolutionary education was time, in addition to timing. Indeed, in the battle between the factions, if any revolution were to enjoy even the limited possibilities of success, both of these imperatives must be closely adhered to. Thus by April of 1800, Jefferson, with Madison's help, had met his schedule and the revolution was proceeding apace.

Indeed, it was essential in Jefferson's drive for power that Madison's scholarly analysis have the ability to reveal the ambitions of the extremists within the administration. His *Report*, a forceful argument against the consolidation of power in the national government, would cause those who read it to turn against the administration if they wished to preserve free government. This was necessary, even essential, for the revolution to succeed. The citizenry must see refuted the charges directed against the republican faction and those who loved liberty. One of these citizens, Tunis Wortman, summed up the essence of Jefferson's and Madison's approach to revolution as set forth in the *Report* this way:

It is a prejudice not unfrequently entertained, that the advocates of Public Liberty are restless, turbulent, and seditious; perpetually addicted to the pursuit of novelty, and ever watchful for the opportunity of Revolution. To remove a prejudice, at once so fatal and delusive, is a duty equally owing to the safety of the Government, and the permanent welfare of the People. Such an opinion may excite the apprehensions of administration, and lead them to the adoption of measures creative of discontent, and liable to terminate in the very evils they are studious to avoid; it may influence the weak, the timid, and the affluent, and induce them to oppose the benevolent efforts of Melioration directed to the general benefit. Philosophical Reformation is not a crude and visionary projector: Rashness is not her attribute, nor physical Force her weapon. Her province is to enlighten Society by candid and argumentative addresses to the understanding. She is the benefactor of the human race, imbued with wisdom, moderation, and clemency; and not "the destroying Angel," who would sacrifice one generation from uncertain prospects of benefit to the next. Her genuine task is to preserve the lives of millions, to respect the private possessions of the people, and forbid the sanguinary streams to flow. Her constant solicitude is not to invite mankind to assemble amid the ferocious din of arms, but in the peaceful temple of Reason and Reflection.[101]

Such was the meaning of a revolution dealing with the principles of government. And in this reasonable, practicable, and prudent way, Madison had adhered to Jefferson's model of a permanent, peaceful, and constitutional revolution. For as Madison so ingeniously put it in the last pages of his *Report:* "These declarations . . . are expressions of opinion, unaccompanied with any other effect than what they may produce on opinion by *exciting reflection.*"[102]

---

[101] Tunis Wortman, A *Treatise Concerning Political Inquiry and the Liberty of the Press* (New York, Jan. 1800), pp. 190–91.

[102] *The Virginia Report of 1799–1800,* op. cit., p. 230.

The Politics of the Revolution
of 1800

PRELUDE

"No measures will be too intemperate that tend to make
the citizens revolutionary enough to make the man of 1775
the man of 1800."

FISHER AMES, 1800

As the year 1800 appeared on the horizon, Alexander Hamilton
sketched the political portrait of the republic in starkly prophetic
terms. Addressing himself to the problems of faction, he lamented
the loss of Washington, expressed his pique with the President,
assessed the condition of Federalist political disorganization, and
then, announcing that the administration would eventually prevail, proceeded to draw a specter of revolution:

At home every thing is in the main well; except as to the perverseness and capriciousness of one, and the spirit of faction of many.

Our measures from the first cause are too much the effect of
momentary impulse. Vanity and jealousy exclude all counsel.
Passion wrests the helm from reason.

The irreparable loss of an inestimable man removes a control
which was felt, and was very salutary. The leading friends of the
government are in a sad dilemma. Shall they risk a serious schism
by an attempt to change? Or shall they annihilate themselves and
hazard their cause by continuing to uphold those who suspect or

hate them, and who are likely to pursue a course for no better reason than because it is contrary to that which they approve?

The spirit of faction is abated nowhere. In Virginia it is more violent than ever. It seems demonstrated that the leaders there, who possess completely all the powers of the local government, are resolved to possess those of the national, by the most dangerous combinations; and, if they cannot effect this, to resort to the employment of physical force.[1]

This was the mood of High Federalism in the wake of Washington's death. Somber, slightly confident but wary were the prevailing attitudes. But this mood would change rapidly as the political realities of the coming months crashed down upon fond hopes. For the emergence of a full-scale theory of revolution based on the principles of the Declaration of Independence would confront almost everyone who had expressed confidence in the spring of 1800.

The Virginia and Kentucky Resolutions of 1798 and 1799 had drawn the battle lines, and those who were commentators on public affairs sensed the mood of the nation. Almost everyone believed that the political skirmishes that had dominated the country for the previous decade threatened to erupt into a full-scale war. At stake were not simply a few offices or senatorial seats but a collision between two conflicting ideologies: democracy and republicanism versus aristocracy and a consolidating power that bore a striking resemblance to monarchy. These themes would be referred to again and again by the adherents of both sides. To be decided in "this contest over principles," as Jefferson noted, was a choice between two systems of administration, two interpretations of the constitution and the power of government, and two views of society and the way in which it would develop.

The economic arrangement of society into two competing groups, one industrial with shipping and mercantile interests, the other reflecting a basic agricultural interest, could not help but

[1] Hamilton to Rufus King, 5 Jan. 1800, *Works of Alexander Hamilton*, op. cit., Vol. X, pp. 358–59.

translate itself into the politics of the young republic. Individual liberty was equated with one of those interests; power, influence, empire, and even a return to a form of mixed monarchy were associated with the other. One view represented the "principles" of Thomas Jefferson, the other view the "system" of Alexander Hamilton. For many, 1800 was the most crucial point in the history of the young republic. As one writer phrased it: "The present period of our national concerns is as important in its nature and as eventful in its consequences, as the memorable epoch when the American people revolted from the oppressions of the British monarch."[2] To the supporters of Jefferson, as well as many who opposed him, the contest was simply the American Revolution continued to its final resolution. And this theme, above all others, dominated the political literature of the day. Appeals were made to the "Whigs of '76"[3] and those who had fought in the Revolution, "who [had] distinguished themselves throughout life in advancing the rights of man and particularly the preservation of our Republican Government."[4] The contest was seen as a life or death struggle for the new republic; a continuation of Federalist rule was equated with a return to monarchy.

Another development of major importance, one that recommended the attention of everyone, was the renewal of the old-style politics of faction that had waxed vigorously since the formation of the new government. The revival of revolutionary committees of correspondence and caucuses, of personal factions, phalanxes, of cliques and personal connections, of newspapers and circulars and pamphlet writing for propaganda purposes, of concern for secrecy, of charges of conspiracy and attempts to corrupt

[2] "To the People of New Jersey" (Princeton, N.J.), 30 Sept. 1800, Broadside. Printed in *History of American Presidential Elections, 1798–1968,* op. cit., Vol. I, p. 135.

[3] Newark(N.J.) *Centinel of Freedom,* 1 April 1800.

[4] *Republican Meeting, at a meeting of Republican Citizens of the County of Burlington at the house of Joshua Rainear in Springfield, the 20th of September, 1800* (Mount Holly, N.J., 1800), p. 2. Quoted in Cunningham, *The Jeffersonian Republicans,* op. cit., p. 155.

elections—all were made and brought about with an eye toward influencing a greatly polarized society. Accompanying these developments was a degree of political organization that had been unknown since the earliest days of the Revolution. One Federalist wrote, referring to the Jeffersonians in standard revolutionary terms: "The Jacobins appear to be completely organized throughout the United States. The principals have their agents dispersed in every direction; and the whole body act with a union. . . . Their exertions are bent to introduce into every department of the State governments unprincipled tools of a daring faction . . ."[5] Another Federalist confessed that he was as occupied "writing letters" as any "member of a *revolutionary* committee."[6] Fisher Ames stated that "no measures will be too intemperate that tend to make the citizens revolutionary enough to make the man of 1775 the man of 1800."[7] And looking back on the political forces that were arrayed against the Federalists over the previous four years, Josiah Quincy remarked that "a degree of organization has been effected in the opposite party unexampled, I suspect, in this country, since the revolutionary committees of 1775."[8] These were testimonials that the political forces in the country had begun to organize in a way that many had seen before in a particular context; and that was a forerunner to revolution.

By April of 1800 the committees of correspondence, societies, and clubs, so feared by the British in the 1770s and by the Federalists in 1793 and 1794, began to make their appearance across

[5] Theophilus Parsons to John Jay, 5 May 1800, *The Correspondence and Public Papers of John Jay, 1794–1826,* 4 vols., ed. H. P. Johnston (New York, 1890–93), Vol. IV, p. 270.

[6] Peter Van Schaak, quoted in Fischer, *The Revolution of American Conservatism,* op. cit., p. 52.

[7] *History of American Presidential Elections 1798–1968,* op. cit., Vol. I, p. 115.

[8] Josiah Quincy to John Quincy Adams, 23 Nov. 1804, in Adams Family Papers, Vol. 403. Quoted in Fischer, *The Revolution of American Conservatism,* op. cit., p. 59.

the nation. The old-style politics was based on tried and true tactics: committees were appointed in counties; they were urged to make declarations, to distribute circulars, and to inform the citizens in their districts. Not only did their organizing activity appear similar to that of the Revolution, their objectives did also. The republican faction had taken the initiative for good reason. They were in opposition to the government and, as we have seen, any opposition was considered by the government to be seditious, even revolutionary. As early as February 1798, Federalist John Nicholas had written Washington a note on his birthday: "The opposition to the government . . . is here 'systematized'—regular plans are formed, and correspondences . . . commenced against the unsuspecting and unmarshalled friends of government . . ." The words carried a meaning fraught with danger. Jefferson, "the great man on the Hill," he said, was "the very 'centre' of opposition, the 'rallying point,' the headquarters, the everything, of the enemies of the government."[9] Indeed, this emerging opposition to the administration was looked upon as something more than subversive. And when the same organizational activity followed the Kentucky and Virginia Resolutions, they were considered, as we saw in the last chapter, revolutionary. This was plain evidence that the Virginia faction meant to overthrow the government.

Hamilton at least believed this and had good reason for doing so. The Federalists' memories were not short. They recalled the Democratic societies that had flourished in 1793 and 1794 and had been so roundly condemned by the President. A writer in the *Gazette of the United States* had noted that:

Nobody will deny the usefulness of popular Societies, in cases of revolutions. The reason is obvious. By forming the people together into clubs, and giving to all those clubs, a central point of union, a bad government may be shaken down: for it has to oppose not scattered and dispirited complainers, who may be kept under the

[9] Colonel John Nicholas to George Washington, 22 Feb. 1798, in Manning Dauer, "The Two John Nicholases," *American Historical Review*, 45 (1940), p. 352.

harrow of the law, and demolished as fast as they show themselves, but it has to oppose an organized body, acting in phalanx, thus tyranny is pulled down because it is overmatched, and perhaps there is no other way to pull it down.[10]

Now, six years later, the same phenomenon had appeared. The preparations that took place in Virginia were nearly exact duplications of the revolutionary committees of correspondence with but one difference—they were peaceful in nature. Their organization was identical as was their intended purpose: to provide information to as many citizens as possible.[11] These committees took their guidance from the major figures in Virginia politics, Madison, Monroe, and Jefferson, the leaders who defined the strategy of political opposition. In the tradition of the old-style factional politics of the preceding generations, these leaders were assured of election. For example, in Virginia's bid for electoral votes, while it was decided to change the mode of election, i.e., to vote by a "ticket" instead of by districts, the outcome was the same. With great names like George Wythe, Edmund Pendleton, James Madison, and William Giles, the republican faction could expect to win handily. When Wythe decided to stand for office, Philip Nicholas wrote Jefferson: "This I rejoice at as it will give it [the ticket] great weight and dignity. And I cannot but augur well of a cause which calls out from their retirement such venerable patriots as

[10] "Reply of the Citizens of Hanover County, Virginia to the Circular Letters of the Democratic Society of Philadelphia," in *Gazette of the United States*, 15 Jan. 1794. Quoted in Buel, *Securing the Revolution*, op. cit., p. 128.

[11] Cunningham, *The Jeffersonian Republicans*, op. cit., pp. 144–74. Noble Cunningham, Jr., has brilliantly described the structure of these committees and their organization state by state. A "General Standing Committee" of five members was established at Richmond, and Philip Norborne Nicholas was made its chairman. This committee, entrusted with the overall direction of the campaign, was to act as a central committee of correspondence; committees of correspondence, composed generally of five members, were appointed in eighty-nine counties and in Norfolk borough. In a few counties, where republican forces were weak, the committees did not have their full complement of members; and in three counties no committees were appointed, presumably because there were no trusted party members in those areas.

Wythe and Pendleton."[12] Besides adding two dimensions, the "ticket" and the theme of America's revolutionary "patriots," Nicholas could have been writing about any election that Virginia had held for the past twenty-five, even fifty, years. The concept of who would appeal to the voter was one of a natural aristocracy—men whose families and fortunes had connected them with government and place for as long as the common people could remember.

Similar efforts took place in New York, Pennsylvania, and New Jersey. The object of the committees in all the states was the same. In Virginia, Nicholas wrote Jefferson: "We have begun our correspondence with the subcommittees and mean to keep up a regular intercourse upon the subjects which may seem to require it."[13] In Newark, New Jersey, the objects were "to consult and correspond with similar committees . . ."[14] In Bucks County, Pennsylvania, it was announced that meetings would be held at various taverns. "The object of these meetings is to collect information . . . and generally, to condense the rays of political light and reflect them strongly on all around."[15] A Pennsylvanian, John Beckley (originally a Virginian and an associate of Jefferson and Madison but now one of the leading political organizers of the day), acted as chairman of the committee of correspondence for the city and county of Philadelphia. He wrote pamphlets and letters to newspapers, ensured that the necessary information was sent to the right people, and frequented the coffee shops of Philadelphia in order to educate his fellow citizens. He acted exactly as Samuel Adams had done in Boston twenty-five years earlier—the peripa-

[12] Philip Norborne Nicholas to Jefferson, 2 Feb. 1800, Jefferson Papers, CVI, 1817, Lib. Cong. Quoted in Cunningham, *The Jeffersonian Republicans*, op. cit., p. 152.

[13] Philip N. Nicholas to Jefferson, 2 Feb. 1800, op. cit. Quoted in Cunningham, *The Jeffersonian Republicans*, op. cit., p. 153.

[14] Newark (N.J.) *Centinel of Freedom*, 1 April 1800. Quoted in Cunningham, *The Jeffersonian Republicans*, op. cit., pp. 155–56.

[15] Philadelphia *Aurora*, 6 Aug. 1800. Quoted in Cunningham, *The Jeffersonian Republicans*, op. cit., p. 160.

tetic revolutionary organizer, traveling from city to city, staying long enough to get an organization functioning and then moving on. The fact that he had been performing these functions from roughly 1779, serving in different capacities as Clerk of the Virginia House of Delegates and Clerk of the House of Representatives, before moving to Pennsylvania, meant that he was familiar with the techniques of political organization most congenial to Madison and Jefferson, his main benefactors.[16]

The functions of these committees and subcommittees on the state, county, and local township levels were the same: to facilitate the exchange of information, to print newspapers, circulars, pamphlets, and handbills, and to hold meetings. In some states, whatever organization emerged did so only at a local level, and little statewide organization manifested itself. This was true in Maryland, for example, where only three counties were organized[17] and where one, Frederick County, followed the basic pattern of the original revolutionary committees: ". . . a general county committee of five members in Frederick-town and in each district of the county . . . a Republican committee."[18] As resolutions were passed, issues decided and candidates chosen by the various factions, committees, and cliques, the results were communicated

---

[16] Charles, *The Origins of the American Party System,* op. cit., pp. 80–82. Charles states, "A great deal of the work usually attributed to Jefferson in organizing opposition to Federalists' measures . . . among the general public should be credited instead to John Beckley . . ." p. 80.

[17] Baltimore (Md.) *American,* 11 June 1800. Quoted in Cunningham, *The Jeffersonian Republicans,* op. cit., p. 158.

[18] Ibid., pp. 157–61. Noble Cunningham, Jr., has traced the details of this organization with patience and skill and in the process revealed an infrastructure of communication—from the state or county committee to the districts, then townships, and finally to the local meetings held in taverns, churches, and in individuals' homes. The parallel descriptions of the committees of correspondence during the 1770s are strikingly similar. Charles Sydnor in *American Revolutionaries in the Making* (New York, 1962), pp. 96–99, relates that the Virginia committee of correspondence established on March 12, 1773, consisted of five members of a standing committee: Thomas Jefferson, Dudley Digges, Dabney Carr, Patrick Henry, and Peyton Randolph. Of these five, two were still active in politics in 1799–1800.

to the people in the most expeditious fashion. It was indeed the standard decision-making process of the old school of politics: control rested in the hands of a few and the voters were presented with their choice. Individuals nominated themselves through advertisements in the newspapers; but almost exclusively, and in the southern states especially, it was the old family patriarchs, like the Pinckneys, men of established wealth and position, who dominated political affairs and won elections. Revolutionary patriots, like Christopher Gadsden, may have called themselves Federalists, but their allegiance was to the nation. They resented "faction," "party," "cabal," and any interference with their right to vote for the individual of their choice. Gadsden expressed his opinions thus:

> Every state carefully attending to its own duty in . . . the election for a President, and to that only, leaving all the other states to do the same, without the least meddling, directly or indirectly any where, would soon restore peace, harmony, good humour, and good mutual confidence amongst us all, upon a firm and lasting footing, and prove the best and most effectual gag to stop the mouths of those turbulent and dangerous cabals that have never ceased to spread misunderstandings and jealousies at every Presidential election.
>
> That epidemical itch for meddling [was a] ruinous diabolical curse to the whole union . . .[19]

Little more than a month later Gadsden denounced party spirit in traditional terms: "No directions can be preferable to those in General Washington's farewell address, which cannot be too much attended to." Reiterating his desire for the states to maintain their own independence, he remained "convinced that [if] each state had an equal right to vote as it pleased, . . . the cant names of federalist, anti-federalist, aristocrat, democrat, jacobin, etc., etc. [would] be heard no more."[20] A Connecticut man wrote

[19] Richard Walsh, *The Writings of Christopher Gadsden, 1746–1805* (Columbia, S.C., 1966), p. 292.

[20] Ibid., pp. 297–98. Printed in the *South Carolina State Gazette* and *Timothy's Daily Advertiser*, 29 Aug. 1800.

in September 1800, "I wish we might reject the words, *federal, anti-federal, democrat, aristocrat,* etc., and go back to our old language Whig and Tory."[21]

Another writer from Connecticut noted, "The terms republican and democratic are used synonymously throughout because the men who maintain the principles of 1776 are characterized by one or the other of these names, in different parts of the country."[22] That most people throughout the country rejected the labels of party and faction and identified with the candidate cannot be doubted. To many it mattered not what your faction was, for faction could not solve the nation's problems. A writer from Rhode Island said:

> The present . . . crisis in the affairs of the United States demands the dispassionate consideration of every individual citizen. It is not by the prevalence of this or that faction or system that nations have been found to thrive; but they, as well as individuals, have generally prospered according as they have followed the dictates of sound reason.[23]

And Jefferson, we have observed, believed that supporting the violence of faction was unreasonable. Indeed, if the leader of the opposition refused to recognize the legitimacy of party cant, party names, even party *per se*, it is unreasonable to assume that he would consciously work to create one of his own.

[21] Hartford (Conn.) *American Mercury*, 4 Sept. 1800. Quoted in Cunningham, *The Jeffersonian Republicans*, op. cit., p. 219. In his book *The Jeffersonian Republicans in Power* (Chapel Hill, N.C., 1963), p. 303, Cunningham noted that Jefferson "never recognized the validity of the Federalist party either while Adams was in office or as an opposition party during his own administration."

[22] Abraham Bishop, *Connecticut Republicanism: An Oration on the Extent and Power of Political Delusion* (New Haven, Conn., Sept. 1800), p. 7.

[23] "A Candid Address to the Freemen of the State of Rhode Island on the Subject of the Approaching Elections, from a Number of their Fellow Citizens" (Special Collections, Brown University). Quoted in *History of American Presidential Elections, 1798–1968*, op. cit., Vol. I, p. 140.

Two other similarities to the revolutionary era that one might note in 1800 are the post office and the press. The Jeffersonian faction had systematically refused to use the mails for important personal messages since May and June of 1797.[24] By November of 1799 Jefferson had written one of his chief political advisors:

> I cease from this time during the ensuing twelvemonth to write political letters, knowing that a campaign of slander is now open upon me, and believing that the postmasters will lend their inquisitorial aid to fish out any new matter of slander they can gratify the powers that be. I hope my friends will understand and approve the motives of my silence.[25]

To Madison he would write: "I shall trust the post offices with nothing confidential, persuaded that during the ensuing twelve months they will lend their inquisitorial aid to furnish matter for newspapers, I shall send you as usual printed communications, without saying anything confidential on them. You will of course understand the cause."[26] And as late as August 1800, he was warning his correspondents to let no letter "go out of your own hands, lest it should get into the newspapers."[27] Jefferson indicated by his caution that he knew the Federalist faction was not above an invasion of his privacy. Yet this was to be expected in an era which looked upon opposition to government as a revolutionary phenomenon. We must keep in mind the fact that this was before the days of a recognized "loyal party opposition." But while this form of political espionage placed limitations upon his

[24] Jefferson to Colonel Bell, 18 May 1797, and Jefferson to Peregrine Fitzhugh, 4 June 1797, op. cit. See also Jefferson to Archibald Stuart, 13 Feb. 1799, *Writings*, Vol. X, p. 104. He says simply, "Do not let my name appear in the [printed] matter."

[25] Jefferson to John Taylor of Caroline, 26 Nov. 1799, Jefferson Papers, Collections of the Mass. Historical Society, Ser. 7, I, 64. Quoted in Cunningham, *The Jeffersonian Republicans*, op. cit., p. 139.

[26] Jefferson to James Madison, 22 Nov. 1799, *Writings*, Vol. X, p. 133.

[27] Jefferson to Uriah McGregory, 13 Aug. 1800, ibid., p. 172.

ability to communicate with his important advisors, he compensated by making greater use of the press.[28] He knew from his earlier revolutionary experience in both America and France that no true change in a people's sentiments or opinions could take place without its aid. Indeed, as Jefferson converted the weapons that he had in his arsenal of experience, he discovered that his main battery was the engine of the press. This was a perception also shared by his adversaries, albeit late. Fisher Ames wrote in 1801:

> The newspapers are an overmatch for any Government. They will first overawe and then usurp it. This has been done; and the Jacobins owe their triumph to the unceasing use of this engine; not so much to skill in the use of it as by repetition . . .[29]

But the fact that the Federalists had overplayed their hand, had failed to account for the powerful engine of the press, and had even gone beyond the rules of the system and intimidated editors was not lost on Jefferson and his followers. Their efforts to establish printing presses "in almost every town and county of the country" was reported by a Federalist at the height of the contest.[30] Indeed, this was what Jefferson had in mind when months before the campaign he had done everything in his power to enlist the aid of Edmund Pendleton, Madison, Monroe, and others to write letters, contribute funds to establishing newspapers, and in general begin a coordinated information system. The lessons that

[28] Jefferson's recognition of this as a crucial matter was a carry-over from his earliest days as a revolutionary. In the 1770s he had pointed out to John Adams the critical role that a reliable post office played: "I wish the regulation of the post office adopted by Congress last September could be put in practice. . . . The speedy and frequent communication of intelligence is really of great consequence. . . . Our people merely for want of intelligence which they may rely on are become lethargic and insensible of the state they are in." Jefferson to John Adams, 16 May 1777, *Letters*, Vol. I, pp. 4–5.

[29] Fisher Ames to Timothy Dwight, 19 March 1801. Quoted in Warren, *Jacobin and Junto*, op. cit., p. 160.

[30] Uriah Tracy to Oliver Wolcott, 7 Aug. 1800, Gibbs, *Memoirs of the Administrations of Washington and Adams*, op. cit., Vol. II, pp. 399–400.

he had learned in France and America during the 1770s were yet in his mind. Revolution took place, after all, "in the minds . . . of . . . people," and no one knew this more profoundly than Jefferson. Accordingly, he staked nearly everything on the "engine of the press."

Another revolutionary device that became part of the contest of 1800 was the caucus. The caucus was common at the state level among the various committees of correspondence, much as it had been during the days of the Revolution. It had been the usual method of producing a political strategy in the old-style politics. As we have already described in a previous chapter, the application of the caucus to the national level had occurred only twice by 1800. Yet, the fact that the two meetings held by the Jeffersonians were strung out over a period of six years indicates the ambivalence that national politicians held for them. Further, their results fail to tell us much more than the fact that national legislators viewed them with mixed emotions, due primarily to their secretive, almost conspiratorial-revolutionary nature. As a result, at the national level, at least, they lacked discipline.

As Gallatin so clearly described the events: "On both occasions we were divided; and on both the members of the minority of each meeting were left at full liberty to vote as they pleased . . ."[31] When the Federalists held "a meeting of the whole federal party, on the subject of the ensuing election," Theodore Sedgwick was not certain that it would mean anything either. He noted that "if this agreement be faithfully executed we shall succeed, but otherwise we cannot escape the fangs of Jefferson."[32] As it would turn out, the divisions within the administration were so great that the agreement would later be viewed with indifference.

But the notion of the caucus as a revolutionary device had its advantages. On the state and local levels it was used to prevent the fractionalizing of supporters and to produce consensus. Its other

[31] *The Writings of Albert Gallatin,* op. cit., Vol. III, p. 553.
[32] Theodore Sedgwick to Rufus King, 11 May 1800, *Life and Correspondence of Rufus King,* op. cit., Vol. III, pp. 237–39.

functions were to ensure continuity of leadership and enable a faction to concoct a political strategy. This seemed to work at the lower levels, but at the national level its results, at least for the Federalists, were inconclusive. One might argue that Jefferson, Madison, Monroe, Taylor, et al., had already caucused, planned their strategy, and were producing a consensus by early 1800. The decisions made upon the Kentucky and Virginia Resolutions had been in the hands of a few men who agreed on policy objectives and were united. By comparison, the members of the administration hardly spoke to one another.

The fact that the Federalists were in the midst of a "conservative crisis" had become apparent to a few of the far-seeing Federalists as early as 1797. Fisher Ames had summed up the sad state of affairs to Hamilton, "We are broken to pieces."[33] By January 1800, Hamilton admitted that "vanity and jealousy [have] exclude[d] all counsel. . . . The leading friends of the government are in a sad dilemma."[34] The previous three years had seen the Federalists warring among themselves, splitting off into personal cliques and factions, and creating a situation that one of their more astute members called a state of "anarchy." "But," said Gouverneur Morris, "the thing which in my Opinion has done most mischief to the Federal party is the Ground given by some of them to believe that they wish to establish a monarchy."[35] Morris had accurately described the malady as well as the cause: between the statements attributed to John Adams regarding his affinity to British institutions and the actual tendency of the policies of Hamilton and those who were loyal to him in the cabinet, the tone of the administration had become increasingly arrogant and authoritarian. As this impression was relayed successively by repub-

---

[33] Fisher Ames to Alexander Hamilton, 26 Jan. 1797, *Works of Alexander Hamilton.* Quoted in Fischer, *The Revolution of American Conservatism,* op. cit., p. 52.

[34] Hamilton to Rufus King, 5 Jan. 1800, *Works of Alexander Hamilton,* op. cit., Vol. X, p. 358.

[35] Gouverneur Morris to Rufus King, 4 June 1800, *Life and Correspondence of Rufus King,* op. cit., Vol. III, p. 252.

lican editors after the Whiskey Rebellion, the direct tax, and the Alien and Sedition Acts, as well as the Virginia and Kentucky Resolutions, citizens began to wonder if there might be some truth to their assertions. As these charges were repeated, the burden of proof weighed more heavily on the administration with each successive crisis.

The split between the Adams and Hamilton factions within the administration can be traced to the period immediately following the election of 1796. As we have seen, Hamilton's power was near absolute in the waning days of Washington's administration, and he naturally brought under his influence a majority of cabinet members that remained in the new administration. For almost three and a half years Hamilton was to exert an influence from outside the government that would ultimately destroy the President's confidence in his closest advisors. Oliver Wolcott was Secretary of the Treasury and, more than any other man, owed his position to Hamilton. James McHenry was Secretary of War and the least competent member of Adams' cabinet. Unfortunately, McHenry's lack of abilities caused him to defer to the Inspector General, thus giving Hamilton hegemony over military as well as civil affairs. Timothy Pickering was a Secretary of State who disagreed with the most crucial part of the President's foreign policy—the U.S. attitude toward France. From the outset he took advice from Hamilton, even assisting him in 1800 by providing evidence to attack the President on his conduct of public affairs. As a result, Adams ultimately fired Pickering and replaced him with John Marshall.[36] All three—Wolcott, Pickering, and McHenry—were inherited from the last Washington cabinet, and Adams assumed that he would also inherit their loyalty. But whether unfortunate, or even naïve, Adams had reckoned without the genius of Alexander Hamilton. From roughly 1790 to 1800 the

---

[36] Adams reserved a special hostility for Pickering in later years. He wrote Jefferson in 1817, "My loving and beloved friend Pickering, has been pleased to inform the world that I have 'few friends.' I wanted to whip the rogue, and I had it in my power, if it had been in my will to do it, till the blood came." Adams to Jefferson, 19 April 1817, *Letters*, Vol. II, p. 508.

former Secretary of the Treasury was the motivating force behind the High Federalist faction. Fisher Ames, Rufus King, Robert Troup, George Cabot, Theodore Sedgwick, Gouverneur Morris, and almost every influential conservative in politics looked to Hamilton rather than Adams for leadership. This naturally led Hamilton to believe that he could extend his influence over the entire administration. He thus continued to advise Adams' cabinet and members of Congress without consulting the President.[37]

This state of affairs piqued John Adams, and when he began to make decisions that he believed were in the national interest without consulting his High Federalist advisors, the Hamiltonians were outraged. By middle May 1799, Adams took several steps at once, all of which could not help but anger his antagonists. Within a period of a few weeks Nathaniel Ames reported that he "turn[ed] out Tim[othy] Pickering from the Secretary of State's office, disband[ed] in concurrence with Congress the standing army, and . . . retract[ed] from high-handed explosions against France and Democracy."[38]

This was one of the first signs that Adams was beginning to assert his independence even though he believed it might tear the administration apart. When he attempted to avoid war with France by sending three envoys on a peace mission, he was rebuked by nearly the entire Federalist faction. Robert Troup wrote: "I have not met with a single person, who approves this measure in the present posture of affairs. . . . The President, we understand, has embarked in it not only without advice, but against the opinion of all his friends." For all his efforts to improve relations with France, the President had widened the split and raised the ire of the extremists. Robert Troup reported a consensus feeling that would ultimately become a policy: "an attempt will

[37] Martin Van Buren wrote, "If there was a single instance in which Hamilton, in his numerous letters of advice to the secretaries, requested them to submit his views to the consideration of the President, it has escaped my observation." *Inquiry into the Origin and Course of Political Parties in the United States,* op. cit., p. 118.

[38] Warren, *Jacobin and Junto,* op. cit., p. 150.

certainly be made, by the best friends of the government, to get rid of Mr. Adams . . ."[39] Theodore Sedgwick echoed the same theme to King: "A total loss of confidence among the best friends of the government, in the wisdom and prudence, of the P——T, a belief that he is influenced by caprice above, or by the advice of men of intrigue, who have infused into his mind an incurable jealousy . . . [has taken place]. It is also expected that an irreconcilable division will in consequence of this state of things take place among the federalists, the effects of which will be incalculably mischievous . . . or what is still, if possible, worse an increase of strength to the opposing *faction*."[40]

That division by June of 1800 was irreconcilable and was known to a few leaders only. But as the summer wore on, the complex intrigues led by Hamilton et al., behind Adams' back, had made it obvious to everyone. The only difference now was that the President began to force the issue. More and more he aligned himself with the Jeffersonians and recalled his earlier days in the Revolution. Fisher Ames wrote sarcastically that "the President of the United States lately . . . gave as a volunteer toast 'the proscribed Patriots Hancock and Adams.' " Ames continued:

> The great man has been south as far as Alexandria making his addressers acquainted with his revolutionary merits. . . . Whether these answers and toasts are to be considered as the first steps towards reviving the revolutionary spirit you must judge for yourself; his language is bitter even to outrage and swearing and calling names against many who once were and I believe still are thought as good as any men in the Country, he inveighs against the British faction and the Essex Junto like one possessed.
> . . . In the mean time, every exertion is making to spread the passions that enrage and almost madden him, and it seems to be expected that the ferment of the people awe the Genl. Court in

[39] R. Troup to R. King, 6 Nov. 1799, *Life and Correspondence of Rufus King*, op. cit., Vol. III, pp. 141–42; see also R. Troup to R. King, 9 March 1800, ibid., pp. 208–9.

[40] Theodore Sedgwick to R. King, 15 Nov. 1799, ibid., p. 146. See also George Cabot to R. King, 20 Jan. 1800, ibid., p. 183.

Nov. next to choose Electors who will vote for Mr. A & throw
away the votes for the other Candidate. This game will be played
in Connecticut, N. Hampshire and R. Island. . . . Whether this
fervor will melt the tender hearts of the Jacobins is not clear. At
present it seems they are not disposed to give up their old favorite
and chief for a new one whose repentance and conversion are
rather late. But I think it probable that his sincerity will be made
more and more manifest till they perceive that he is no longer
the supporter of, or supported by, the federalists. Then perhaps
they will take him, if they find they cannot carry their own
candidate.[41]

To Timothy Pickering, Ames had previously written, "He
[Adams] is a revolutionist from temperament, habit, and, lately,
what he thinks policy. He is too much irritated against many, if
not most, of the principal sound men of the country even to
bestow on them his confidence or retrieve them. In particular, he
is implacable against a certain great little man whom we mutually
respect [i.e., Hamilton]."[42] George Cabot complained to King
that Adams' behavior had changed: ". . . he sometimes praises us
in strong terms; at others he denounces us in a manner that outrages all decency. . . . I am made one of the '*damned faction*' by
the opinions I am known to maintain."[43]

Thus, as Joseph Charles suggests, it would appear that the key
to understanding this period is the struggle that was "taking place
in Adams's mind as to how far he would go with the High Federalists." Adams' idea of an equilibrium, both in terms of a
constitution and the factions in society, seems to have asserted
itself here. As we have seen, Adams had contempt for party
intrigue, and it is logical that he would have been disgusted with
Hamilton. It is also logical that as Adams began to revive his

[41] F. Ames to R. King, 15 July 1800, ibid., pp. 275–76.

[42] F. Ames to Timothy Pickering, 19 Oct. 1799, quoted in Warren, *Jacobin
and Junto*, op. cit., p. 149.

[43] George Cabot to Rufus King, 9 Aug. 1800, *Life and Correspondence of
Rufus King*, op. cit., Vol. III, pp. 291–92.

revolutionary ideals, at least in terms of rhetoric, he would move closer to the Jeffersonians and bridge the gap between himself and the hated Jacobins.[44] Indeed, the possibility of such a coalition was not only real, it had been maintained at least in theory in Jefferson's mind. Before Adams had even taken office, Jefferson had informed him of the attempts that would be made to separate the two. He warned the incoming President that "the public and the papers have been much occupied lately in placing us in a point of opposition to each other." "I trust with confidence that less of it has been felt by ourselves personally." Yet more important were the warnings that Jefferson conveyed to Adams regarding the intrigues of the Hamilton faction—all of which would be borne out in the next four years. Implying that even after the election a danger still existed for Adams, Jefferson revealed the intentions of Hamilton:

> Indeed it is possible that you may be cheated of your succession by a trick worthy the subtlety of your arch-friend of New York who has been able to make of your real friends tools to defeat their and your just wishes. Most probably he will be disappointed as to you; and my inclinations place me out of his reach.

He closed with another reminder that "various little incidents have happened or been contrived to separate us . . ."[45]

Jefferson not only expressed his concern to Adams but indicated to Madison that he had written a special letter assuring the President of his support. Following the mention of their earlier revolutionary experience, which Jefferson alluded to, he found a political reason for making the overture: "He [Adams] is perhaps the only sure barrier against Hamilton's getting in." Madison failed to

----

[44] Charles, *The Origins of the American Party System*, op. cit., p. 73. Adams and Jefferson, Charles asserts, may have "joined forces against Hamilton at any time prior to the XYZ Affair." And the "support which both Adams and John Quincy Adams gave Jefferson after 1803–1804" indicates "the ever present possibility of a coalition between the two was the High Federalist nightmare from 1797 on."

[45] Jefferson to John Adams, 28 Dec. 1796, *Writings*, Vol. IX, pp. 356–57.

deliver the letter, claiming that "a probability" existed that Jefferson might oppose Adams and his administration, and "giving written possession to him of the degree of compliment and confidence which your personal delicacy and friendship have suggested" could prove embarrassing.[46] That Adams reciprocated with similar feelings can be seen in Jefferson's own words: "My letters inform me that Mr. Adams speaks of me with great friendship and with satisfaction in the prospect of administering the government in concurrence with me." In Jefferson's last comment in this exchange with Madison, he places his relationship with Adams in perspective; it is concerned with "harmony" and service to the nation. Thus, the working relationship Jefferson envisioned would hopefully serve those ends:

> Mr. Adams and myself were cordial friends from the beginning of the revolution. Since our return from Europe, some little incidents have happened, which were capable of affecting a jealous mind like his. His deviation from that line of politics on which we had been united, has not made me less sensible of the rectitude of his heart; and I wished him to know this, and also another truth, that I am sincerely pleased at having escaped the late draught for the helm, and have not a wish which he stands in the way of. That he should be convinced of these truths, is important to our mutual satisfaction, and perhaps to the harmony and good of the public service.[47]

Adams and Jefferson had every reason for believing that they could cooperate fully in the new administration. Together they shared the ideals of the Revolution, distrusted power, regarded the constitution and a republican form of government as essential for the liberty of the country, detested factions, wanted peace with France, and despised Hamilton while recognizing his growing

---

[46] Jefferson to Madison, 1 Jan. 1797, ibid., p. 359; see also J. Madison to Jefferson, 15 Jan. 1797, *The Letters and Other Writings of James Madison,* op. cit., Vol. II, p. 111.

[47] Jefferson to Madison, 22 Jan. 1797, *Writings*, Vol. IX, p. 367. Jefferson to Madison, 30 Jan. 1797, ibid., p. 375.

influence in the government. Thus, it is inconceivable that in their common quest for fame—which both identified with the success of the American Revolution—either would wish to see it and the republic it had produced fail. On the contrary, both would cooperate in order to ensure its success. Despite Adams' signing of the Alien and Sedition Acts, Jefferson wrote fifteen years later that:

> In truth, my dear Sir, we were far from considering you as the author of all the measures we blamed. They were placed under the protection of your name, but we were satisfied they wanted much of your approbation. We ascribed them to their real authors, the Pickerings, the Wolcotts, the Tracys, the Sedgwicks, et id genus omne ["and all of their kind"], with whom we supposed you in a state of Duresse. I well remember a conversation with you, in the morning of the day on which you nominated to the Senate a substitute for Pickering, in which you expressed a just impatience under "the legacy of Secretaries which Gen. Washington had left you" and whom you seemed therefore to consider as under public protection. Many other incidents shewed how differently you would have acted with less impassioned advisers; and subsequent events have proved that your minds were not together. You would do me great injustice therefore by taking to yourself what was intended for men who were then your secret, as they are now your open enemies. Should you write on the subject, as you propose, I am sure we shall see you place yourself farther from them than from us.[48]

With this perspective in mind it is possible to view the events leading up to the election of 1800 in a different manner than has formerly been related. The focus of the political struggle is not between two embryonic political parties, Federalist and Republican, which exist almost exclusively in the minds of twentieth-century historians. The focus, rather, is at two levels: 1. between the various factions that supported Jefferson, Adams, Hamilton, Charles C. Pinckney, and Aaron Burr—all reflecting an old-style

---

[48] Jefferson to Adams, 15 June 1813, *Letters*, Vol. II, p. 332.

traditional politics of faction; and 2. a contest between the ideas and principles of Jefferson and those ascribed to the Federalist administration, but not necessarily including John Adams. With the realization that Adams had been abandoned by many, if not most, of the prominent Federalists and that he was expected to repel the attacks of Jeffersonians and Hamiltonians alike while maintaining national unity in a period of crisis, we can better understand Adams' reversion to two themes that he knew would have broad popular support and undercut the strength of the extremists: viz., the republican ideology of the American Revolution and the danger of faction.

These were two well-chosen themes, especially the latter. The degree to which intrigue, manipulation, and outright attempts to deny the people's will dominated the elections of 1800 had become apparent at both the state and national level. To many observers it was a sign that the republic was breaking down. Perhaps more important, it gave credibility to the opposition's charges that the constitution was a dead parchment in the hands of the Federalists. This tended, more than anything else, to force both the Federalists and the Jeffersonians to consider extreme measures. The first of these attempts was by James Ross of Pennsylvania, a senator who introduced a bill designed to secure the electoral votes of Pennsylvania for the Federalists. Ostensibly entitled a "Bill Prescribing the mode of deciding disputed Elections, of President and Vice President of the United States," it was a blatant attempt to corrupt the electoral process. *The Kentucky Gazette* described it accurately:

A bill is now under consideration in the senate, and which I have no doubt will pass through that branch of the legislature, calculated to do much mischief, and finally to set aside the Constitution so far as relates to the election of the President. It proposes that each house of Congress shall by ballot elect six members who shall form a committee [6 from the Senate; 6 from the House] with the Chief Judge of the U.S. their chairman, for the purpose of examining and deciding on all contested elections, and with closed doors shall examine all the returns, and determine on the legality of any of the state proceedings as respects their mode of appointing electors. I think this the most alarming feature which has been exhibited from that quarter at any time heretofore.[49]

The arch-conservative William Cobbett had strong words for it: "This Bill was a sweeper. It would, had it passed into a law, have, in reality, placed the election of the President *in the hands of the Senate alone.* . . . To lead the sovereign people through the farce of an election, when the choice was finally to be made by thirteen men, *seven* of whom were to be nominated by the Senate, was a departure from the *frankness,* which has been said to be the characteristics of republicans."

When Senator Charles Pinckney released the text of the bill "to the Printer of the Aurora," the editor "published it with very severe . . . remarks. The Senate summoned the man before them. He attended, and after certain interrogatories, was ordered to attend on a subsequent day to receive his sentence. He asked for counsel, which was granted him, with the proviso, that the counsel should *not be permitted to question the jurisdiction of the Senate,* nor to urge any matter but *in mitigation.* The counsel, with the approbation of their client, refused to appear thus shackled, and their letters of refusal, being published in the newspapers, produced great effect."[50] The consequences were that the Senate had effectually deprived the editor of his civil liberties, combined the functions of a judge and a jury, and raised the specter of legislative tyranny.

Madison, always noting the subtleties of any legislative or constitutional maneuver, was outraged by the Senate's conduct. He saw the Ross bill "bid[ding] defiance to any possible parchment securities against usurpation." "Should the spirit of the Bill be followed up," he said, "it is impossible to say how far the

[49] *The Kentucky Gazette,* Thursday, 27 March 1800 (extract of a letter from Philadelphia dated 21 Feb. 1800), signed "K. Herald."

[50] *Porcupine's Works,* op. cit., Vol. XII, pp. 41–42. The editor, William Duane, left town until the legislative session ended and thus avoided punishment.

choice of the Executive may be drawn out of the constitutional hands and subjected to the management of the legislature. . . . If this licentiousness in constructive perversions of the Constitution continue to increase, we shall soon have to look . . . not [to] the charter of the people, for the form, as well as the powers of our Government."[51] In short, Madison saw the Federalists attempting to destroy the constitution. The effort by Ross and others was eventually defeated, but not until the Jeffersonians were sufficiently alarmed. Madison with his great knowledge and inside views of the intentions of the legislators passed the word to Jefferson: the Federalists would stop at nothing, and thus a legislative conspiracy to preserve their power was not out of the question. Madison, not given to wild statements, regarded the present climate in the government as an extremely dangerous one. The month before he expressed his sentiments on the Ross bill, he alluded to the potential for counterrevolution in America. Referring to France and the "melancholy evidence" that indicated "the destiny of the[ir] Revolution is transferred from the Civil to the military authority," he turned to his own country:

> Whether the lesson will have the proper effect here in turning the public attention to the danger of military usurpation, or of intrigues between political and military leaders, is more than I can say. A stronger one was, perhaps, never given, nor a Country more in a situation to profit by it.[52]

Jefferson's reaction to this crisis was similar to Madison's. Expressing a sense of relief over the relaxation of tensions in Europe, he then focused on the American situation: "We have great need for the ensuing twelve months to be left to ourselves. The enemies of our Constitution are preparing a fearful operation, and the dissensions in this State are too likely to bring things to the

---

[51] J. Madison to Jefferson, 15 March 1800, *The Letters and Other Writings of James Madison*, op. cit., Vol. II, p. 157.

[52] J. Madison to Jefferson, 14 Feb. 1800, ibid., p. 156. See Jefferson to Samuel Adams, 26 Feb. 1800, *Writings*, Vol. X, p. 154.

situation they wish, when our Bonaparte, surrounded by his comrades in arms, may step in to give us political salvation in his way. It behooves our citizens to be on their guard, to be firm in their principles. . . . We are able to preserve our self-government if we will but think so."[53]

But for every Jeffersonian who feared intrigue, there was a Federalist to match him. Hamilton, at the beginning of the new year, had spoken of the "crisis" and mutual jealousies that existed in the highest circles.[54] Oliver Wolcott had noted that the new Congress, sensing the national urgency, acted like a "conclave of cardinals, intriguing for the election of a Pope."[55] Within seven months the intrigue of faction would have so captured the imagination of Ames that even he expressed uncertainty: "Never was there a more singular and mysterious state of parties. The plot of an old Spanish play is not more complicated with underplot. I scarcely trust myself with the attempt to unfold it."[56]

Ames had good reason to allude to the themes of plot and underplot, for by July of 1800 the politics of the nation had been thrown into such consternation that anything was possible. The April elections in New York to determine that state's presidential electors had revealed to what lengths the Hamiltonians were prepared to go in disregarding the constitution and the sanctity of the election laws. Many people knew, or at least suspected, that the New York elections would decide the contest, and both sides spent all their energies in order to achieve victory. Jefferson knew in early January, from his communications with Burr, that the New York election would be crucial, and he felt compelled to disregard his "delicacy to be silent on this subject." Not only New

---

[53] Jefferson to T. M. Randolph, 2 Feb. 1800, ibid., p. 151.

[54] Alexander Hamilton to Rufus King, 5 Jan. 1800, *Works of Alexander Hamilton*, op. cit., Vol. VI, p. 416.

[55] Oliver Wolcott to Fisher Ames, 29 Dec. 1799, Gibbs, *Memoirs of the Administrations of Washington and Adams*, op. cit., Vol. II, p. 316.

[56] Fisher Ames to Rufus King, 15 July 1800, *Life and Correspondence of Rufus King*, op. cit., Vol. III, p. 275.

York but also New Jersey seemed to be in the republican camp.[57]
By March, Jefferson had detected dissensions among the opposition: "The federalists begin to be very seriously alarmed about
their election next fall. Their speeches in private, as well as their
public and private demeanor to me, indicate it strongly." Again,
after expressing confidence in New Jersey, he added: "In New
York all depends on the success of the city election . . ." By
placing "Governor Clinton, General Gates, and some other old
revolutionary characters . . . on the republican ticket," he hoped
to revive the theme and the principles he wished to preserve. It
was a gamble, and, though "Burr, [Brockholst] Livingston, etc.,
entertain[ed] no doubt on the event of that election," Jefferson
was still pessimistic.

In fact, Jefferson was so pessimistic that he was contemplating
throwing "prudence" to the winds.[58] Addressing himself to the
urgency of the national crisis that both he and Madison perceived,
he fell back upon an old revolutionary strategy: the announcing of
a Declaration that, in rhetorical form, would parallel the Declaration of Independence. He thus wrote to Philip Nicholas:

> It is too early to think of a declaratory act as yet, but the time is
> approaching and not distant. . . . As soon as it can be depended
> on, we must have "a Declaration of the principles of the Con-
> stitution" in nature of a Declaration of rights, in all points in
> which it has been violated.[59]

[57] Jefferson to James Monroe, 12 Jan. 1800, *Writings*, Vol. X, pp. 136–37.
See also Matthew L. Davis, *Memoirs of Aaron Burr* (New York, 1855), Vol.
II, p. 55. He quotes Jefferson to Madison, 4 March 1800: "In any event, we
must say, that if the city election of New York is in favor of the republican
ticket, the issue will be republican; if the federal ticket for the city of New
York prevails, the probabilities will be in favor of a federal issue . . ."

[58] Jefferson to Madison, 4 March 1800, *Writings*, Vol. X, pp. 157–59. On
the other hand, Madison wished to follow a "steady adherence to the principles
of prudence." "It would be doubly unwise to depart from this course at a
moment when the party which has done the mischief is so industriously cooperating in its own destruction." Madison to James Monroe, 23 May 1800,
The Letters and Other Writings of James Madison, op. cit., Vol. II, p. 160.

[59] Jefferson to Philip N. Nicholas, 7 April 1800, *Writings*, Vol. X, p. 163.

The conversion of this revolutionary device to an elective situation was interesting and from an ideological standpoint would have split the national Congress (where Jefferson wished it to take place) into two major factions: one for the principles of republicanism, the other against them. It was an inflammatory suggestion, one that would polarize the legislature, and if it trickled down to the state legislatures, the society as well. But this suggestion reveals Jefferson's revolutionary state of mind before he knew the outcome of the election in New York.

Preparations for the election in New York City had been from the start almost totally in the hands of Aaron Burr, "a man whose intrigue and management [was] most astonishing . . ."[60] In the typical old-style politics of faction, Burr had personally assembled the republican slate and called together a meeting to support it. Burr's one-man show was the essence of a personal faction. He directed the nominating process thus:

> As soon as the room begins to fill up, I will nominate Daniel Smith as chairman, and put the question quickly. Daniel being in the chair, you must nominate one member, I will nominate one . . . and other . . . and in this way, we will get them nominated. We must then have some inspiring speeches, close the meeting, and retire. We must then have a caucus and invite some of our most active and patriotic Democrats, both young and old, appoint meetings in the different wards, select speakers to address each, and keep up frequent meetings at Tammany Hall until the election.[61]

Indeed, as Jefferson had noted, the slate consisted of the most famous and distinguished revolutionary figures that could be found to lend their name to the republican cause. Thus the republican strategy in New York was to field a group of candidates

---

[60] Matthew L. Davis to Albert Gallatin, 29 March 1800, Gallatin Papers, box 5, N.Y. Hist. Soc. Quoted in Cunningham, *The Jeffersonian Republicans,* op. cit., p. 177.

[61] Mordecai Myers, *Reminiscences 1780–1814* (Washington, D.C., 1900), p. 11. Quoted in Herbert S. Parmet and Marie B. Hecht's *Aaron Burr: Portrait of an Ambitious Man* (New York, 1967), p. 149.

so illustrious that the average citizen would vote for long-familiar names. The strategy worked, and in addition to a surging of republican fortunes, Aaron Burr emerged as one of the foremost political figures in the nation.[62] But despite the fact that Burr had conducted himself in exemplary fashion as far as the Jeffersonians were concerned, the victory would prove in the long run to be a mixed blessing.

The impact of republican success was anathema to the Federalists. Repudiated at the polls and sensing the disaster that lay ahead if the verdict was not reversed, the Federalists immediately held a "select and confidential caucus . . ." Matthew Davis, one of the most active participants on the republican side, stated that the purpose of the caucus was:

> To solicit Governor [John] Jay to convene the existing legislative forthwith, for the purpose of changing the mode of choosing electors for president, and placing it in the hands of the people by districts. The effect of such a measure would have been to neutralize the State of New York, and . . . would have secured to the federal party their president and vice-president.

The news of the caucus was relayed to William Duane, editor of the *Aurora*, who promptly published an account of the meeting. The Federalists immediately denounced the author as a "jacobin calumniator, and the whole story was pronounced a vile fabrication. One of the New York City papers reprinted the letter . . . and close[d] its commentary on it: 'Where is the American who *will not detest the author of this infamous lie?* If there is a man to be found who will sanction this publication, he is worse than the worst of Jacobins.' "[63] The effort was worthy of a twentieth-century public relations expert crassly manipulating primary elections. The "infamous lie" turned out to be the truth. None other than the intellectual leader of the Federalists had stooped to such a low level that he was willing, through force and through fraud, to subvert the sanctity of the constitutional process.

[62] Davis, *Memoirs of Aaron Burr*, op. cit., Vol. II, pp. 55–64.
[63] Davis, *Memoirs of Aaron Burr*, op. cit., Vol. II, p. 61.

Alexander Hamilton began to set the wheels of faction into motion by writing a letter to John Jay, the Governor of New York:

> You have been informed of the loss of our election in this city. The moral certainty therefore is that there will be an antifederal majority in the ensuing Legislature; and the very high probability is that this will bring Jefferson into the chief magistracy, unless it be prevented by the measure which I shall now submit to your consideration, namely, the immediate calling together of the existing Legislature.
>
> I am aware that there are weighty objections to the measure, but the reasons for it appear to me to outweigh the objections; and in times like these in which we live, it will not do to be over-scrupulous. It is easy to sacrifice the substantial interests of society by a strict adherence to ordinary rules.

Then Hamilton, completely overlooking the fact that he had requested Jay to commit an immoral act against law and the constitution, i.e., those "ordinary rules," alluded to the integrity of the Governor and artfully suggested, "I shall not be supposed to mean that anything ought to be done which integrity will forbid . . ." The constitutional rules, he suggested, "ought to yield to the extraordinary nature of the crisis." "They ought not to hinder the taking of a *legal and constitutional* step," he said, which would not be in accordance with the constitution.[64]

Hamilton had concluded that the ends justify the means, and in the following sentence he told why: "[we must] prevent [Jefferson], an atheist in religion, and a fanatic in politics, from getting possession of the helm of state." Reasoning "from indubitable facts" he lectured Jay on his naïveté and led the Governor to

[64] This directly contradicted Hamilton's logic during the Whiskey Rebellion. Then he noted, referring to those who merely refused to pay what they considered an unconstitutional tax on home brew, "You will observe an avowed object is to '*obstruct* the *operation* of the law.' This is attempted to be qualified by a pretense of doing it by 'every legal measure.' But 'legal measures' 'to obstruct the operation of the law' is a contradiction in terms." Hamilton to John Jay, 3 Sept. 1792, *The Life and Writings of John Jay,* op. cit., Vol. II, p. 211.

believe that the consequences of not taking his advice would be revolution!

> You, sir, know in a great degree the anti-federal party; but I fear you do not know them as well as I do. It is a composition, indeed, of very incongruous materials; but all tending to mischief—some of them, to the OVERTHROW of the GOVERNMENT, by stripping it of its due energies; others of them, to a REVOLUTION, after the manner of BONAPARTE. I speak from indubitable facts, not from conjectures and inferences.

Following this attempt at intimidation, Hamilton softened his language and appealed to Jay's political constituency. Calling the legislature into session would "be approved by all the federal party" and be "justified by unequivocal reasons of *Public Safety*." Hamilton went on to rationalize his suggestion for all mankind: "The reasonable part of the world will, I believe, approve it. They will see it as a proceeding out of the common course, but warranted by the particular nature of the crisis and the great cause of social order." Blinded by his fury, his hatred of Jefferson and Burr, and the prospects of losing power, Hamilton had even gone so far as to accept a version of Jefferson's and Madison's "interposition theory" in the Virginia and Kentucky Resolutions. Then, being so bold as to instruct Jay in minute detail as to how to corrupt the electoral process, he wrote:

> In your communication to the Legislature they ought to be told that temporary circumstances had rendered it probable that, without their interposition, the executive authority of the general government would be transferred to hands hostile to the system heretofore pursued with so much success, and dangerous to the peace, happiness, and order of the country; that under this impression, from facts convincing to your own mind, you had thought it your duty to give the existing Legislature an opportunity for deliberating whether it would not be proper to interpose, and endeavor to prevent so great an evil by referring the choice of electors to the people distributed into districts.

Finally, Hamilton revealed his contempt for popular government by describing the violence of party, incidentally accepting

Jefferson's idea in nearly identical language of why party must be suppressed. He then noted with condescension the inevitable cycle of revolutions to which he believed republican, i.e., popular, governments were subject.

Indeed, at this point it is obvious that Hamilton perceived Jefferson's Revolution of 1800 had already begun.

> In weighing this suggestion you will doubtless bear in mind *that popular government must certainly be overturned*, and, while they endure, prove engines of mischief, if one party will call to its aid all the resources which vice can give, and if the other (however pressing the emergency) confines itself within all the ordinary forms of delicacy and decorum.
>
> The Legislature can be brought together in three weeks, so that there will be full time for the object; but none ought to be lost. Think well, my dear sir, of this proposition—appreciate the extreme danger of the crisis.[65]

The "crisis" was one of magnitude, and as rumors filled the air as well as the newspapers of the nation, many believed the republic was on the brink of civil war. William Cobbett was one of those who, ordinarily supporting the High Federalists in every undertaking, nevertheless drew the line. His confidence in John Jay proved worthy:

> It was said that Mr. Jay, the governor of New York, foreseeing that the legislature of that state would choose electors favorable to Mr. Jefferson, was resolved not to call a session, and thus deprive, the state of its voice in the election. But, so bold, and, indeed, so unlawful a measure, is not to be expected from Mr. Jay, who, though he might prevent the election of Jefferson, would

[65] Alexander Hamilton to John Jay, 7 May 1800, *Works of Alexander Hamilton*, op. cit., Vol. X, pp. 371–74. Italics mine. If Hamilton did not see it, his closest friend had predicted the disaster nearly a year earlier. "Burr has for two years past been a member of the Assembly, and by his arts and intrigues, he has done a great deal toward *revolutionizing* the state. It became an object of primary and essential importance to put him and his party to flight." Robert Troup to Rufus King, 6 May 1799, *Life and Correspondence of Rufus King*, op. cit., Vol. III, p. 14.

certainly stain his own character, and very probably plunge the country into an immediate civil war.[66]

In fact, John Jay, much to his credit, did not even send a reply. He scrawled across the top of Hamilton's "proposition" the most succinct condemnation of party and faction penned by an American statesman: "Proposing a measure for party purposes which it would not become me to adopt."[67]

The loss of the city elections in New York had stung the Hamiltonian faction into action. Besides the letter to Jay, Hamilton initiated a change in strategy which was disastrous in its implications. Because the Jeffersonians would control the New York elections, he wrote, "the policy which I was desirous of pursuing in the last election is now recommended by motives of additional cogency." By that he meant that the Federalists must now begin to support an alternative to the President, preferably a man who would do Hamilton's bidding. Knowing that he could not simply ignore Adams and jettison him without atomizing the Federalist organization, he suggested to Theodore Sedgwick: "To support *Adams* and [Gen. Charles Cotesworth] *Pinckney* equally is the only thing that can possibly save us from the fangs of *Jefferson*."[68]

Thus Hamilton began his attack upon the President. Claiming

[66] *Porcupine's Works,* op. cit., Vol. XII, p. 139.

[67] Editor's footnote, *Works of Alexander Hamilton,* op. cit., Vol. X, p. 374. The fact was that Hamilton was wrong in any event and was guilty of those very things he had accused the Jeffersonians of promoting. At the formation of the government in 1788, Hamilton had foreseen this possibility. Convinced of his own ability to stay in power, he never dreamed that he was describing his own actions a decade later. For in a prophetic statement, which, had he read it in May of 1800, might have turned the color of his cheeks, he wrote: "A spirit of faction, which is apt to mingle its poison in the deliberations of all bodies of men, will often hurry the persons of whom they are composed into improprieties and excesses for which they would blush in a private capacity." *Federalist,* #14.

[68] Hamilton to Theodore Sedgwick, 4 May 1800, *ibid.,* p. 371. See also Hamilton to Sedgwick, 8 May 1800, *ibid.,* p. 374. See also Timothy Pickering to William L. Smith, 7 May 1800, Pickering Papers, XIII, Mass. Hist. Soc.

that "most of the most influential men of that party [the Federalist] consider him as a very *unfit* and *incapable* character," Hamilton began sowing the seeds of doubt. He subtly initiated a linkage between Adams and Jefferson in the minds of the hard-core Federalists:

For my individual part my mind is made up. I will never more be responsible for him by my direct support, even though the consequence should be the election of Jefferson.

If we must have an *enemy* at the head of the government, let it be one whom we can oppose, and for whom we are not responsible, who will not involve our party in the disgrace of his foolish and bad measures. Under Adams, as under Jefferson, the government will sink. The party in the hands of whose chief it shall sink will sink with it, and the advantage will all be on the side of his adversaries.

'Tis a notable expedient for keeping the federal party together, to have at the head of it a man who hates and is despised by those men of it, who, in time past, have been its most efficient supporters. If the cause is to be sacrificed to a weak and perverse man, I withdraw from the party. . . . The only way to prevent a fatal schism in the federal party is to support General Pinckney in good earnest.[69]

After making up his mind to abandon Adams, Hamilton conceived a new treachery—political espionage! He would steal the President's papers in order to discover evidence to use against him. Informed in advance that Timothy Pickering and James McHenry were about to resign from the cabinet, Hamilton wrote a confidential message to the Secretary of State:

I perceive that you as well as McHenry are quitting the administration. I am not informed how all this has been, though I con-

[69] Hamilton to Sedgwick, 10 May 1800, *Works of Alexander Hamilton,* op. cit., Vol. X, p. 375. Secretary of War McHenry's actual resignation was 6 May 1800, but was made effective on 1 June 1800. James McHenry to John McHenry, 20 May 1800, Gibbs, *Memoirs of the Administrations of Washington and Adams,* op. cit., Vol. II, p. 346.

jecture. Allow me to suggest that you ought to take with you copies and extracts of all such documents as will enable you to explain both Jefferson and Adams. You are aware of a very curious journal of the latter when he was in Europe—a tissue of weakness and vanity.[70]

This amounted to a shocking arrogance on the part of Hamilton. Not only had Hamilton evidenced no respect for the law, he was now willing to invade the private papers of the President and use the contents of his personal journal to smear his name across the country. It is obvious that at this time Hamilton had decided to write an attack against Adams and only wanted information. In July he revealed his intentions to Wolcott. He would limit his readership to the "most discreet" members of the "second class" Federalists:

> It is essential to inform the most discreet of this description of the facts which denote unfitness in Mr. Adams. I have promised confidential friends a correct statement. To be able to give it, I must derive aid from you, and anything you may write shall, if you please, be returned to you. But you must be exact, and much in detail.[71]

This eighteenth-century equivalent of a modern-day "bugging operation" found Hamilton's clique inside the highest circles of government and in a position to convey any and all secrets to which they might have access. Hamilton's anger and frustration over the loss of the New York electoral votes had now spilled over to include Adams as well as Jefferson. The fact that Adams had refused to appoint him commander-in-chief and had actually "argued the propriety of changing the commander-in-chief every

---

[70] Hamilton to Timothy Pickering, 14 May 1800, *Works of Alexander Hamilton*, op. cit., Vol. X, p. 376. Pickering was forced to resign 12 May 1800. Gibbs, *Memoirs of the Administrations of Washington and Adams*, Vol. II, p. 348.

[71] Hamilton to Oliver Wolcott, 1 July 1800, *Works of Alexander Hamilton*, op. cit., Vol. X, p. 377.

year" had galled Hamilton.[72] Adams' pardon of John Fries had appeared to Hamilton a contemptible bid for popularity, as did the President's sending of William Vans Murray to reopen negotiations with France. All were against the advice of Hamilton and his supporters. Finally, when Adams dismissed the secretaries of State and War and supported the disbanding of the army in quick succession, he struck a blow so hard that Hamilton felt compelled to hit back.[73] Retaliation took the form of a direct letter to the President, a prelude to the pamphlet which Hamilton was preparing. Thus Hamilton, attempting to engage the President in a polemic, accused Adams of "asserting the existence of a British faction in this country, embracing a number of leading or influential characters of the federal party, as usually denominated; and that you have sometimes named me . . ."[74]

Adams, of course, was too shrewd a politician to rise to Hamilton's provocation. Hamilton had literally accused the President of having his friends attack him for "electioneering purposes." Indeed, Hamilton was afraid of the association that would be made between himself, Charles Cotesworth Pinckney, and anyone else that could be implicated with the charge of a "British faction." While the President and his followers denounced the movement to link him with General Pinckney, Hamilton contemplated extending his own audience from the "second class" of Federalists to the public at large. "I have serious thoughts of giving to the public

[72] James Cheetham, *An Answer to Alexander Hamilton's Letter Concerning the Public Conduct and Character of John Adams, Esq.* (New York, 1800). Cheetham noted that Adams' sentiments "demonstrate[d] a prudent jealousy so essentially necessary in revolutionary times. . . . A standing soldiery will become attached to their chief, and an ambitious chief, when a favourable opportunity occurs, will strike at the vitals of his country . . ." Pp. 5–6.

[73] Hamilton actually implied that Adams fired Pickering because he "had been for some time particularly odious to the opposition party [the republicans], [and] it was determined to proceed to extremeties." Gibbs, *Memoirs of the Administrations of Washington and Adams,* op. cit., Vol. II, p. 352.

[74] Hamilton to John Adams, 1 Aug. 1800, *Works of Alexander Hamilton,* op. cit., Vol. X, p. 382.

my opinion respecting Mr. Adams, with my reasons, in a letter to a friend, with my signature." He then asked Wolcott, "What say you to this measure? I could predicate it on the fact that I am abused by the friends of Mr. Adams, who ascribe my opposition to pique and disappointment; and could give it the shape of a defense of myself."[75] While this was not the character that Hamilton's pamphlet would ultimately take, he had dropped the seeds of the idea in the minds of those whom he must depend upon for support. By late August Hamilton realized that he must do something to offset Adams and to energize the campaign for Pinckney.

> We fight Adams on very unequal grounds, because we do not declare the motives of our dislike. The exposition of these is very important—but how? I would make it and put my name to it, but I cannot do it without being conclusively inferred that as to very material facts I must have derived my information from members of the administration. Yet, without this, we have the air of mere caballers, and shall be completely run down in the public opinon.[76]

And "run down" they were. The President's charges denouncing the Hamiltonians were beginning to take hold if for no other reason than that they substantiated what the Jeffersonians had been saying all along.

Others within the Federalist hierarchy had also witnessed the tendency of Adams' supporters to denigrate the Hamiltonians and steer a middle course closer to Jefferson. Fisher Ames wrote referring to Adams, "The friends of a certain great man are trying to

---

[75] Hamilton to Oliver Wolcott, 3 Aug. 1800, ibid., p. 383. Wolcott's reply merely served to inflame Hamilton against the man who would ultimately do him the most damage: "Nothing is more certain than that the Jacobins, seconded by Mr. Adams' personal friends, will fix the imputation of a British monarchical faction on a number of the most high-minded and independent gentlemen of the country." Wolcott to Hamilton, 10 Aug. 1800, Gibbs, *Memoirs of the Administrations of Washington and Adams*, op. cit., Vol. II, p. 400.

[76] Hamilton to James McHenry, 27 Aug. 1800, *Works of Alexander Hamilton*, op. cit., Vol. X, pp. 388–89.

rouse the revolutionary spirit, to awaken personal local party and national prejudices to secure for him the concentration of all the chances of the political game." Indeed, Ames feared actual revolution: "Everything smoaks with political fermentation in the U.S. You must watch and pray for the country, that we may not have a war with Great Britain, which would augment the danger of revolution exceedingly, both to Great Britain and the U.S." But Ames had noted something else that presented a more immediate problem to Hamilton: "Whether Mr. Adams is willing to be Vice under Jefferson is a problem and opinions in respect to its solutions are various. He acts as if he did not hate nor dread Jefferson, and *it is clear that his friends pursue a course in conversations and in the papers which can help nobody's cause but Jefferson's.* Indeed the Adams writers offer to fraternise with Jacobins whom they denominate old friends and openly rail against the 'exclusive Federalists,' 'Hamiltonians,' 'Essex Junto,' 'Royalists,' 'British Partizans,' as they affect to call the men who stick to the good . . . old cause."[77] Not only was Adams openly hostile to Hamilton, he was aiding the hated Jefferson, ensuring his chances to obtain the presidency, and hoping that he might come in second. If Ames was correct, it signaled a fundamental change in Adams' political strategy. While Ames fell short of proving that "a *coalition* had been made," he nevertheless implied that Adams, for what he considered the good of the country, or a spirit of "revenge," was willing to abandon the Federalist faction with whom he had been identified since the first Washington administration.[78]

But a month later Ames was not so sure. In a long letter to King outlining the domestic political situation, he described the mutual

[77] Fisher Ames to Rufus King, 19 April 1800, 26 Aug. 1800, *Life and Correspondence of Rufus King*, op. cit., Vol. III, pp. 295–97.

[78] General Henry Lee in 1807 related that in 1800 "in the Fall," he had noted Adams' friendliness toward Jefferson at a dinner in Virginia. He cautioned the President that Jefferson "was using all his influence and intrigue to supercede him [Adams] in the presidential chair." Adams reacted with "displeasure" and replied that "he believed Mr. Jefferson more friendly toward him, than many who professed to be his friends." Gibbs, *Memoirs of the Administrations of Washington and Adams*, op. cit., Vol. II, p. 366.

admiration that had sprung up between Jefferson and Adams and the latter's identification with the principles of the American Revolution:

> Whether there is any ground, (and if any whether there is much) for the coalition charged upon the two heads of parties I will not decide. I think there is rather too much complacency on the part of our man towards his antagonist, and too little towards the intended second of the former. This proceeds from several causes—but chiefly from the lofty idea he entertains of his own superior wisdom and greatness which disdains to have either for a second or a successor any less personage than the first of the other side. He has also a strong revolutionary taint in his mind, admires the characters, principles and means which that revolutionary system exacts and for a short period seems to legitimate, and as you know holds cheap any reputation that was not then founded and top'd off. Accordingly he respects his rival and the Gazette here, absolutely devoted to him and in the hands of his personal friends exclusively, is silent and has been for some months in respect to that rival. His irreligion, wild philosophy and gimcrackery in politics are never mentioned. On the contrary the great man has been known to speak of him with much regard, and an affected indignation at the charge of irreligion, asking what has that to do with the public and adding that he is a good patriot, citizen and father. The good Lady his wife has been often talkative in a similar strain, and she is as complete a politician as any Lady in the old French Court.[79]

It seemed inconceivable to Fisher Ames that the President would hold himself above the Hamiltonian faction and jeopardize Federalist unity. As early as July George Cabot had expressed the opinion that "I have no doubt that Mr. Adams will favor the election of Jefferson in preference to a federal rival, as far as he dares . . ."[80] The fact that Adams had gained control of the *Gazette of the United States,* which was silent as to Jefferson, was indicative that a change in policy and in attitude had been

[79] Fisher Ames to Rufus King, 24 Sept. 1800, *Life and Correspondence of Rufus King,* op. cit., Vol. III, p. 304.

[80] George Cabot to Rufus King, 19 July 1800, ibid., p. 278.

adopted. And knowing Abigail Adams' fondness for Jefferson throughout a lifetime's correspondence, Ames's assessment of her political acumen would increase rather than decrease that possibility. For indeed, Adams had personally destroyed whatever unity the Federalists might have enjoyed. Theodore Sedgwick, one of the most astute observers among the arch-Federalists, remarked to King:

> He [the President] every where denounces the men, and almost all the men in whom he confided, at the beginning of his administration, as an oligarchish faction, who are combined to drive him from office, because they cannot govern him, and to appoint Pinckney, by whose agency, under the controul of this faction and particularly of Hamilton its head; the country is to be driven into a war with France and a more intimate, if not an indissoluble, union with great Britain. In consequence of these representations by him, which are diffused thro' this state by his friends, and more by the indefatigable industry of his enemies the jacobins, the federal party here has been disorganized, and every where thro' the nation its energies are paralized. By the most painful industry, and the most perfect union the friends of the Government had attained a height on which they appeared to be impregnably intrenched; but by the conduct of an individual, the whole force is disheartened, on one hand, and on the other the adversary is inspired with fresh confidence.[81]

Adams' decision to destroy the power of the Hamilton faction within his administration had been devastating. He had engineered the total collapse of federalism. Robert Troup writing to Rufus King put it starkly: "I cannot describe to you how broken and scattered your federal friends are! At present we have no rallying point; and no mortal can divine where or when we shall again collect our strength! . . . Shadows, clouds, and darkness rest on our future prospects. . . . My spirits, in spite of all my philosophy, cannot maintain the accustomed level."[82]

[81] Theodore Sedgwick to Rufus King, 26 Sept. 1800, ibid., p. 308.
[82] Robert Troup to Rufus King, 1 Oct. 1800, ibid., p. 315.

IX

The Politics of the Revolution
of 1800

REVOLUTION

" 'The progress of the horseman can only be proportioned
to the speed of his horse.' Had Hamilton, the 'commander-
in-chief' of both houses of Congress, of all the five heads of
departments of General Washington, and consequently of
the President of the United States, been aware of your
principle, and acted upon it, *the revolution of 1801 would
not have happened.* There is no rodomontade, no exaggeration . . . in this language. In essence, it is strictly true."

JOHN ADAMS to JAMES LLOYD,
24 April 1815

The collapse of the Federalists' façade of unity improved the
republicans' situation immensely. Yet it would be months before
they realized their gain and in the interim their opponents would
be compelled to play out their intended roles. Generally recognizing their shared prospect for a dismal political future, the supporters of Alexander Hamilton appeared paralyzed. But the leader
of the arch faction was determined to do something—anything—
to revive his flagging base of power.

Accordingly, Hamilton refined his attack upon President John
Adams and released it to a number of the Federalist leaders. He
seemed to ignore and discount the clouded predictions of what

such an attack would mean. His correspondence indicates that nearly every advisor he had disapproved of his plan. They appeared, almost to a man, to reflect the opinion of Fisher Ames, who believed that Adams had decided to aid Jefferson and scuttle the Federalists' ambitions. Reinforcing Ames was George Cabot, who wrote early in August that "if Adams prevails," it will be by his "sacrificing the old federal cause and all its advocates . . ."[1]

Be that as it may, by September Hamilton had become desperate. To Oliver Wolcott he reiterated his concern:

> You may depend on it, a very serious impression has been made on the public mind, by the partisans of Mr. Adams, to our disadvantage; that the facts hitherto known have very partially impaired the confidence of the body of the Federalists in Mr. Adams, who, for want of information, are disposed to regard his opponents as factious men. If this cannot be counteracted, our characters are the sacrifice.

Descrying "anonymity," the leader of the High Federalist faction was anxious to get a rebuttal into print for the eyes, at least, of Adams' supporters. Not wishing to implicate the source of his information, Hamilton was willing to "stand upon the credit of [his] own veracity." Thus seeking Wolcott's approval, he sent him a draft of the pamphlet asking him to "say quickly what is to be done, for there is no time to spare."[2] Again he wrote John Adams, virtually demanding a confrontation.[3] When the President maintained his silence, Hamilton released his essay entitled "A Letter from Alexander Hamilton concerning the Public Conduct and Character of John Adams, Esq., President of the United States."[4] It was Hamilton's intention that the circulation be

[1] George Cabot to Rufus King, 9 Aug. 1800, ibid., p. 292.

[2] Hamilton to Wolcott, 26 Sept. 1800, *Works of Alexander Hamilton*, op. cit., Vol. X, p. 389.

[3] Hamilton to John Adams, 1 Oct. 1800, ibid., p. 390.

[4] The pamphlet was published on 22 October 1800. A copy is printed in Hamilton's *Works*, Vol. VI, pp. 391–444.

private, but Burr obtained a copy and proceeded to have extracts printed in the *Aurora* and the *New London* (Conn.) *Bee*.[5]

The publication of Hamilton's essay created an immediate sensation, and the result was the complete disintegration of the Federalists, destroying any possibility of solidarity in the coming election. Instead of "sound[ing] the tocsin about Jefferson," as Fisher Ames had advised Wolcott,[6] it appeared that the campaign, as far as the Federalists were concerned, centered around a controversy between the President and Hamilton. The pamphlet was in many ways a series of accusations and personal innuendos, all calculated to bring into disrepute the four years of Adams' presidency. Hamilton's personal attack not only succeeded in throwing the Federalists into consternation, it alienated many of his closest friends. Evidently Hamilton had been so disposed to vent his anger against Adams that he refused to listen to his counsel. Ames of Massachusetts had argued against it, albeit indirectly. Robert Troup, one of Hamilton's closest confidants, expressed his dismay less than two weeks after its publication:

> The general impression at Albany among our friends was that it would be injurious and they lamented the publication of it. Upon my return home I find a much stronger disapprobation of it expressed every where. In point of imprudence it is coupled with the pamphlet formerly published by the General respecting himself; and not a man in the whole circle of our friends but condemns it. The impression it has made among our friends in other states, I have not yet learned. Our enemies are universally in triumph. I have little or no doubt the latter will lay the foundation of a serious opposition to General Hamilton amongst the federalists, and that his usefulness hereafter will be greatly lessened. Noah

[5] Davis, *Memoirs of Aaron Burr*, op. cit., Vol. II, pp. 65–66. In what was already an American political tradition, J. C. Hamilton, the General's son, wrote "a *spy* had been placed in Hamilton's office . . ." Hence, the republicans were not above doing things for party purposes which were unbecoming.

[6] Fisher Ames to Oliver Wolcott, 12 June 1800, Gibbs, *Memoirs of the Administrations of Washington and Adams*, op. cit., Vol. II, p. 368.

Webster is open mouthed against him, and is supposed to be the author of Aristides.

In a postscript, Troup added: "General Hamilton's letter appears to have been written and put into print without advising with any of his friends here."[7] Hamilton, however, was glorying in the furore that the letter had created and was oblivious of the defections of his friends. To Pickering he wrote: "You no doubt have seen my pamphlet respecting the conduct and character of President Adams. The press teems with replies, and I may finally think it expedient to publish a second time."[8]

But try as he might, Hamilton would not be able to keep up with the rising sentiment his attack had provoked. Replies were made by the supporters of Adams and the republicans published excerpts in all the states who had not chosen their electors. One of these, "An Answer to Alexander Hamilton's Letter Concerning the Public Conduct and Character of John Adams, Esq.," was particularly devastating. James Cheetham turned Hamilton's logic against him and accused him of making "ambition the principle lever of all [his] actions . . ." In a series of questions which were directed at Hamilton himself, he asked: "Who controuled the New York elections, and represented himself the umpire and leader of the federal party, it was a gentleman by the name of EGO, so notorious in every page of your pamphlet."

Cheetham made a succinct review of Hamilton's role in the New York elections and then portrayed the Federalists as every republican saw them and, indeed, as many Federalists had now begun to view themselves:

---

[7] Robert Troup to Rufus King, 9 Nov. 1800, *Life and Correspondence of Rufus King*, op. cit., Vol. III, pp. 331–32. See also Troup to King, 4 Dec. 1800, "This letter [Hamilton's] continues to be disapproved of here. I have not yet met with a dissenting voice here. . . . The letter has added much to his unpopularity here . . . likewise the case to the Eastward . . ." ibid., p. 340.

[8] Hamilton to Timothy Pickering, 13 Nov. 1800, *Works of Alexander Hamilton*, op. cit., Vol. X, p. 391.

Amidst all these prospects of Federal republican villany, our elections were invaded by bribes and by intrigue; the honest patriot became an outcast, and the daring enemies of the country, monopolized the suffrages of a deluded people. Men who had shared the first and highest honours of their country (not forgetting yourself) were peddling at the polls, with the most rancorous principles, and the most degrading falsehoods; . . . British agents, contractors and factors united in your plans, and enjoyed the pleasing dreams of monarchy, . . . The points you had gained by such base and dishonorable means gave you a majority in congress, and saddled the country with alien and sedition laws, conceived in the spirit of a transatlantic pattern; laws for which public necessity never called, but which served to shade and protect the follies and vices of administration; laws that were intended to hold a certain description of foreigners in awe, and to refrain the liberty of the press, the only certain guarantee of public freedom and national happiness. Take away this grand republican essential, and the elements of society are rooted out forever; but all your projects have proved abortive, and those connected with you are sinking into irretrievable disgrace. Now is the time, agreeable to your favorite author (Machiaeval) to bring the government back to its original principles. Now is the time to wash away its impurities, and to render it worthy of the American people.

Little was it expected that your party would have made an explosion so soon. Your seeming unity of action, intimated firmness, duration and design, and perhaps you might have calculated on unchangable perpetuity, if envy ambition, and the loaves and fishes had been out of the question; but there is a truth with which every mind must be impressed, it is as palpable and glaring as an age of experience can render it, that vice cannot long be confident, and that sooner or later it betrays itself and exposes its hideous deformities.[9]

Saddled with the taint of corrupting elections, the Hamiltonian faction failed in its attempts to unite itself to the "second level" Federalists who supported Adams. Perhaps as important was the

---

[9] Cheetham, *An Answer to Alexander Hamilton* . . . , op. cit., pp. 14, 15, 11, 12.

failure of Hamilton to accomplish his second objective in writing the pamphlet: to consolidate support behind General Charles Cotesworth Pinckney in the hopes that he would defeat Adams for the presidency. It was as Richard Stockton had told Oliver Wolcott six months before but in another context, when the Hamiltonians, furious over the dismissal of Pickering, supported him in opposition to the President. What was the reason for the abandonment of Adams, asked Stockton. "These men [the leaders of the Hamiltonian faction] have for four years been holding up Mr. Adams as one of the wisest and firmest men in the United States. What reason could be given for so sudden a change of sentiment."[10] Stockton's query had never been answered and Adams' place in the hearts of his countrymen remained firmly fixed. He was, said George Cabot, somehow "interwoven with the web of national government."[11]

The policy of gaining support for Pinckney had been attacked on several grounds. Sedgwick placed his finger on the main problem when he stated that the President himself had implied the reason for Pinckney's advancement: "because he could be easily influenced."[12] Many simply resented the attempt by Hamilton to draw a parallel between Pinckney and Washington. Pinckney was, in fact, little known when compared with Adams and Jefferson. He had none of the glamour that surrounded Burr and his one claim to statesmanship had been during the XYZ affair.[13] Tunis Wortman, one of the ablest spokesmen for the Jeffersonians, put the candidacy in perspective:

[10] Richard Stockton to Oliver Wolcott, 27 June 1800, Gibbs, *Memoirs of the Administrations of Washington and Adams*, op. cit., Vol. II, p. 374.

[11] George Cabot to Oliver Wolcott, 14 June 1800, ibid., p. 370.

[12] Theodore Sedgwick to Rufus King, 26 Sept. 1800, *Life and Correspondence of Rufus King*, op. cit., Vol. III, p. 308.

[13] Cheetham, *An Answer to Alexander Hamilton . . .*, op. cit., pp. 19–20. Unfortunately for Pinckney, his physical character lent itself to ridicule. James Cheetham, a Jeffersonian supporter, accused Hamilton of insulting the nation by offering him for the presidency and told an anecdote to make the point: "If Heliogabulus could insult the Roman Senate by introducing a horse to its councils, may not designing politicians have their views in advancing and pro-

I know not Mr. Pinckney, politically speaking, he is a man whom nobody knows, but it is perfectly understood that he is contemplated as a second *Bibulus* who permitted Caesar to govern. We can judge of the individual from the character of the party by whom he is supported, and the views by which such party is uniformly actuated. It is well known, that at the last election Mr. T. Pinckney was supported by Mr. Hamilton in preference to Mr. Adams; and the C. C. Pinckney is now the candidate of the exiled members of the present administration. It is a matter of notoriety, that an explosion has taken place in the cabinet, and that a violent schism has ensued between the leaders of the Federal party. The dismission, or rather the expulsion, of Mr. Pickering, evinces that a convulsion had taken place in our councils, which may probably form a distinguished era in our history. The President has not thought proper officially to furnish us with his reasons for the dismissal of the Secretary, but it is perfectly understood, that his obstinate opposition to the negotiation with France, and his manifest partiality for Mr. Pinckney, were the principal occasions of the variance. Since that period at least, the Federalists have become divided into two parties, actuated by different views, and governed by different leaders. The party of Messrs. Pinckney, Hamilton, and Pickering, is the most desperate and violent; its principal characteristics have been a hatred to France; predilection for England; an inflexible determination for war, and an invincible enmity to freedom and the constitution.[14]

None of the republican critics, however, could deter Hamilton from his dream that supporting Pinckney would ultimately prove successful. Far from seeing the shortcomings of his position, Hamilton merely reiterated his opposition to the President, hoping thereby that Pinckney would reap the benefits:

It may become advisable, in order to oppose their fears to their prejudices, for the middle States to declare that Mr. Adams will

---

moting the election of an animal more particularly distinguished by the length of his ears, than the energy of his mind."

[14] Tunis Wortman, *A Solemn Address to the Citizens of New York* (New York, 1800), pp. 31–32.

not be supported at all, when, seeing his success desperate, they would be driven to adhere to Pinckney. In this plan New Jersey, and even Connecticut, may be brought to concur. For both these States have generally lost confidence in Mr. Adams.[15]

But within six short months, Hamilton switched strategies, indicating that he had given up his attempt to defeat Jefferson and was now favoring him.[16] His hopes for Pinckney had not only failed to materialize, they were under heavy assault. A series of letters between Adams and the two Pinckneys published by Tench Coxe and later William Duane had identified Hamilton's candidate with the pro-British faction. The letters actually dealt with Thomas Pinckney's appointment as minister to Great Britain and his brother's subsequent appointment to "two highly confidential offices" in 1792. The assertion was made that the two brothers and "the Federal Government *had acted under the influence of British gold.*" Adams' reply, after a "recantation" was demanded by Thomas Pinckney, wholly exonerated the brothers; but the furor, so close to the election, made the acceptance of the candidate doubly difficult.[17] Hamilton's earlier strategy of supporting Adams with Pinckney had now—with the changed circumstances—placed him in an illogical, even untenable, position. To the intelligent voter it must have appeared sheer hypocrisy to endorse one candidate, repudiate another, and then suggest voting for both.

Thus Hamilton, in attempting to manipulate the choice of a President, had, within six short months, tried to destroy the election laws of the State of New York, committed an act of political espionage, alienated a vast number of Federalist supporters by unnecessarily attacking the conduct of the President, and lost sight of his original goal—the defeat of Thomas Jefferson. By December

[15] Hamilton to Charles Carroll, 1 July 1800, *Works of Alexander Hamilton*, op. cit., Vol. X, p. 379.

[16] Robert Troup to Rufus King, 4 Dec. 1800, *Life and Correspondence of Rufus King*, op. cit., Vol. III, p. 340. Troup wrote: "General Hamilton makes no secret of his opinion that Jefferson should be preferred to Adams."

[17] *Porcupine's Works*, op. cit., Vol. XII, pp. 143–49.

1800, on the eve of the presidential election, he was truly a desperate man. His stranglehold on the Federalist faction had been broken, and he faced the inescapable probability that he had committed political suicide. What was even worse was the prospect that he had driven John Adams into the arms of the republican faction. As Hamilton's friends were now saying to one another, their leader's strategy had culminated in uniting the two men he hated most: for nearly a decade both Adams and Jefferson had been his bitterest enemies.

Since all his carefully laid plans had gone awry, it was now a question of what could be done to prevent total disaster. His friends, having lost their positions of power and their ability to influence policy, appeared bewildered. James McHenry dimly grasped the significance of what was happening and relayed his insight to Rufus King: "Public men, you will observe, are changed and changing. Whether there will be a *total revolution* in measures also, time must discover. . . . It is also highly probable, that the government must in a little time be exclusively in the hands of the opposition. Who is to blame for all of this? The men who sincerely supported Mr. Adams or Mr. Adams, who insincerely deserted his supporters?"[18] Thus James McHenry, the man Hamilton had considered an incompetent, had the wisdom to understand that a fundamental revolution was taking place around him.

[18] James McHenry to Rufus King, 18 Dec. 1800, *Life and Correspondence of Rufus King*, op. cit., Vol. III, p. 350. McHenry's remark might have been prompted by none other than Alexander Hamilton, who, the *Aurora* reported, "on his late visit to New England, after drinking his favorite toast, 'A strong government,' he positively declared, that 'if Mr. Pinckney is not elected president, a *revolution* will be the consequence, and that within the next four years he will lose his head or be the leader of a triumphant army.'" Tunis Wortman, *A Solemn Address to the Citizens of New York*, op. cit., p. 33. The toast was repeated in many pieces of pro-Jefferson literature, for example in *Serious Facts, Opposed to "Serious Considerations": or, The Voice of Warning to Religious Republicans* (New York, Oct. 1800), p. 6. No author other than the pseudonym Marcus Brutus is known. Whether apocryphal or not, the *Aurora* reported an anecdote that parallels Hamilton's description to John Jay of what would happen in America if Jefferson were elected.

A member of the inner circle of the High Federalists, McHenry would naturally turn his attention to the discordant elements within his own faction. He could wonder, and even imply, that the disaster lay at the feet of a President who manifested contempt for the idea of party. But the revolution McHenry alluded to was more extensive than even he and his colleagues had imagined. It encompassed a breadth and depth of popular sentiment, an understanding that even these archconservatives had recognized, but only in part, and belatedly. The evidence was there; they had seen it coming and had only to piece it together. Unfortunately, the nature of revolution in all ages disguises itself to those in power in such a way that, when one occurs, they are almost always the most surprised. Such was the case of the High Federalists in December 1800.

The massive increase in political organizational activity and the increase in rhetoric among newspapers that spoke out against the government excited a ferment throughout 1799–1800. It seemed that "republicans," "democrats," "Jacobins," "disorganizers," and whatever other label was given to that faction were everywhere attempting to revolutionize politics in their locality. Fisher Ames in Massachusetts saw the specter as early as April 1799. Then he described the essence of a grass-roots, old-fashioned, popular revolutionary organization:

> At last jacobins have taken their post, and .*. . have intrenched themselves to assail our sober and orderly liberty. Here we see of late, indeed within a single year, an almost total change in the tacticks, and management of parties. The jacobins have at last made their own discipline perfect: they are trained, officered, regimented and formed to subordination, in a manner that our militia have never yet equalled. Emissaries are sent to every class of men, and even to every individual man, that can be gained. Every threshing floor, every husting, every party at work on a house-frame or raising a building, the very funerals are infected with bawlers or *whisperers against government.*[19]

---

[19] Ames, "Laocoon, No. 1," *Works of Fisher Ames*, op. cit., p. 101. Fisher Ames's brother, Nathaniel, saw the same forces working but approved of them.

This fear that the republican faction had begun to organize itself for political action all over the country was expressed time and again. Fisher Ames's description of the opposition as "whisperers against government" indicated the character he felt the opposition took. A writer in the *Salem* (Massachusetts) *Gazette* commented on the same phenomenon: "There is now on foot a plan of the Jacobins, which they are pursuing everywhere with the most indefatigable industry, to have a majority in our next legislature, who will favour the views of France, and the Virginia and Kentucky Resolutions . . . and there is much fear they will in many instances accomplish their ends."[20] As we have seen, in May 1799 Robert Troup realized that Aaron Burr had "done a great deal towards *revolutionizing* the State." His subsequent urging that the Federalists destroy Burr's base of power is evidence that they were aware of the consequences of republican organizing. Another New Yorker, Congressman William Bingham, noted that "the Party which is attached to them [the Jacobins] have a better System and more Industry than their opponents and . . . make a *greater Impression on the lower Class of People.*" Bingham was describing a popularly based revolutionary movement, in complete contrast to the elitism of the Federalists.[21] In Massachusetts, George Cabot saw the consequences of activity by the opposition: "The Jacobins have lately become more systematical, I think, in their electioneering projects, and have, in this part of the country, availed themselves greatly of those momentary discontents which naturally follow the promulgations of a new tax." Adding another sentence, he gave evidence that the Federalists saw the danger and

---

At about the same time (April 7) that the politician perceived the organized efforts of the Jeffersonians, the doctor noted that "Civil war [was] threatening all over the U.S. drown[ing] foreign disputes." Quoted in Warren, *Jacobin and Junto*, op. cit., p. 119. In January of 1799 Nathaniel Ames had written, "I fear civil war must be the result of government measures." Ibid., p. 123.

[20] *Salem Gazette*, 29 March 1799. Quoted in Warren, *Jacobin and Junto*, op. cit., p. 110.

[21] W. Bingham to R. King, 6 Aug. 1800, *Life and Correspondence of Rufus King*, op. cit., Vol. III, p. 285.

were attempting to stem the tide: "We are taking some pains," he said, "to keep the people steady . . ."[22] Also in Massachusetts was the recognition by Harrison Gray Otis that a revolution was not only on its way, it was long overdue: "The wonder with me," he said, "is, and always has been that the sovereign people have not long since been excited to revolutionary movements."[23]

In New Hampshire the Federalists around Portsmouth called their opponents the "arch faction." William Plumer wrote in his letterbook that the republicans, known also as "the memorialists," had established a newspaper "the very soul of which is *opposition to administration.*" In March 1800, Plumer observed that "the democrats, in this State, are unwearied in their measures to effect a change in every elective office from that of municipal to the Chief Magistrate. . . . They have alarmed the fears of many."[24] By midsummer it had become obvious to Federalists and republicans alike that the latter had become dangerously organized. Hamilton wrote that Aaron Burr was "intriguing with all his might in New Jersey, Rhode Island, and Vermont, and there is a possibility of success in his intrigues."[25] And Oliver Wolcott noted to Hamilton two months later, "Our country is so divided and agitated, as to be in some danger of civil commotions . . ."[26]

In Connecticut a Federalist writer attempted to sound the tocsin. The republicans have "boasted that they would yet *revolu-*

[22] George Cabot to Oliver Wolcott, 2 May 1799, Gibbs, *Memoirs of the Administrations of Washington and Adams,* op. cit., Vol. II, p. 239.

[23] Harrison Gray Otis to John Rutledge, 25 Aug. 1800, Rutledge Papers, So. Hist. Coll., University of North Carolina. Quoted in Fischer, *The Revolution of American Conservatism,* op. cit., p. 39.

[24] William Plumer to Jeremiah Smith, 14 June 1800, Plumer Letterbook, I, pp. 425–26, Lib. Cong.; Plumer to James Sheafe, 19 March 1800, ibid, pp. 410–11. Quoted in Cunningham, *The Jeffersonian Republicans,* op. cit., p. 203.

[25] Wolcott to Hamilton, 2 Oct. 1800, Gibbs, *The Memoirs of the Administrations of Washington and Adams,* op. cit., Vol. II, p. 431.

[26] Hamilton to James A. Bayard, 6 Aug. 1800, *Works of Alexander Hamilton,* op. cit., Vol. VII, p. 562.

tionize Connecticut, and the malignant work is now begun. . . .
And for these purposes, they are scattering *The Aurora, The Bee,*
the *Virginia Papers* and *The American Mercury*—for these purposes they are alarming us . . ."[27]

The *Connecticut Courant* stated in late September, "There is
scarcely a possibility that we shall escape a civil war . . ."[28] But it
was already too late. Even by June of 1800, Gideon Granger had
written Jefferson that "as it respects New England, . . . a mighty
revolution in opinion has taken place within one year."[29]

That was the kind of news calculated to lighten Jefferson's
heart. The changing of men's minds was his principal aim, and the
fact that this could be accomplished through the engine of the
press while still keeping an eye on the elections was proof that a
revolution could remain peaceful. It also reflected the wisdom of

[27] *Connecticut Courant*, 1 Sept. 1800. Quoted in Cunningham, *The
Jeffersonian Republicans*, op. cit., p. 206. Noble Cunningham marks the
observation here that "the Republicans in Connecticut appear to have been
active and united, *though they had no definite organization*" (p. 207). The
fact was Connecticut Republicans had by early June developed their political
organization to such perfection that Gideon Granger could report to Jefferson:
"Every possible exertion is making (tho everything is perfectly still) to effect
a change in the Senate and House of Representatives of the United States—
and also in our own state legislature. . . . *The whole arrangement rests upon
three of us.* We all think the chances equal at least, and yet during all these
things I cannot learn that they apprehend any such plan—from the habits of
our people and their mode of Electioneering everything is lost, unless the most
perfect secrecy is observed." Gideon Granger to Jefferson, 4 June 1800, Jefferson Papers, CVII, pp. 182, 198–99, Lib. Cong. Granger was describing the
peaceful equivalent of a revolutionary organization: secret, controlled by only
a few people determined in the old-style factional politics to keep things that
way. The organization was there; only it was invisible to those with nonrevolutionary lenses.

[28] Quoted in Charles O. Lerche, "Thomas Jefferson and the Election of
1800: A Case Study of the Political Smear," *William and Mary Quarterly*, 3rd
Ser., Vol. 5 (1948), p. 480.

[29] Gideon Granger to Jefferson, 4 June 1800, Jefferson Papers, CVII, pp.
182, 198–99, Lib. Cong. Quoted in Cunningham, *The Jeffersonian Republicans*, op. cit., p. 204.

placing the locus of opposition in the state governments. The sixteen states were the units that could cut into the strength of the Federalists by degrees. One would not have to confront a national government on every issue, a national army or administration. It was possible to gain control of those states that were already republican in sentiment, neutralize others, and isolate the few that were intransigent. Fisher Ames saw this strategy at work and was frightened. For his knowledge of the past told him that a violent revolution was in the making:

> Our government is feeble in its structure, and therefore factions are bold and powerful. The rival state governments are organized factions, and I have long seen, are systematically levying the force to subvert their common enemy. New York will be Jacobinized; Massachusetts is threatened with Gerry, who, though a weak creature, would unite the confidence of the anarchists and would gain and abuse a portion of his adversaries. Within the United States, I see the great states leaguing together under democratic governors; Jefferson and Co., at the head of a stronger faction than any government can struggle with long, or prevail against at last, unless by military force; for it is obvious to me, that all other modes of decision will be spurned as soon as the anties think they have force on their side.[30]

John Ward Fenno noticed as much when he wrote a political tract against the Jeffersonians. Seeing the state governments falling increasingly into the hands of the opposition, he wrote: "Under the auspices of a prudent ruler, we might proceed to other reformations [i.e., constitutional]. . . . Those pestiferous incitements to demagogy, the State Governments, might be abolished and their offices rendered dependent as they ought to be on the Government of the United States, instead of having it in their power as at present, to *organize revolts against that government.*"[31]

[30] Fisher Ames to Oliver Wolcott, 12 Jan. 1800, Gibbs, *Memoirs of the Administrations of Washington and Adams,* op. cit., Vol. II, p. 320.

[31] John Ward Fenno, *Desultory Reflections on the New Political Aspects of Public Affairs in the United States of America Since the Commencement of the Year* 1799 (New York, 1800), p. 52.

Fenno, the editor of the *Gazette of the United States,* saw the implications of the opposition's political organization. That Jefferson had consciously utilized the state governments to bring about a change in power was dawning on the Federalist sympathizers. Fenno, within the Federalist inner circle, was privy to the reactions by the Hamiltonians to the growing strength of the opposition faction. His criticism of Adams' lack of "prudence" in the face of revolution was the difference between the two Federalist factions: one would in defiance of the constitution abolish the state governments; the other was determined to maintain a respect for federalism and the constitution. Indeed, when John Adams gave his fourth annual address in November 1800, he asserted that Americans should "fortify and cling to those institutions" and criticized those who would promote "dangerous innovations which may diminish their influence."[32] Peter Porcupine's reaction was shared by the Hamiltonian faction amidst what both considered the terror of revolution:

> When we hear the President talk about the institutions, which have been the source of such felicity to America, we cannot help thinking, that he deals in the equivoque: and, while he really means the institutions of his forefathers, he leaves the world (and the ignorant of this country in particular) to think that he alludes to be republican institutions of the revolutionists. For a man seriously to talk about the felicity that had been produced by institutions which keep the nation everlastingly in a flame, would be absurd to the last degree. At the very time when he was making this speech, not less than five thousand mobs of citizens (upon a moderate computation) were engaged in political fray. There was not a county, not a parish, not a hamlet, not a neighbourhood of five families, the peace and felicity of which was not disturbed by the effects of the new institutions . . .[33]

But a recognition that a revolution was occurring in their midst would simply not have taken place if the rhetoric of politics had

[32] John Adams, "4th Annual Address," 22 Nov. 1800, *Messages and Papers of the Presidents,* op. cit., Vol. I, pp. 297–98.

[33] *Porcupine's Works,* op. cit., Vol. XII, p. 247.

not reached to the fundamentals of society. The opposition that had merely "whisper[ed] against government" in 1799, had by 1800 increased its decibel level to a clamor that was a constant din in the ears of the Federalists. The Virginia and Kentucky Resolutions had spoken of the basic societal contract, a certain sign that government was breaking down. And the rhetoric of these resolutions had taken a form that set the stage as well as the tone for 1800: opposition to government was to be based on principle and not party. Indeed, the principles involved were those of the constitution and American Revolution. The theme of adhering to the principles of the American Revolution was adopted totally by Jefferson and the republicans from 1796 on. The consistency of Jefferson's position from early 1796, when he wrote the letter to Philip Mazzei, to 1800 indicates that his was no expedient or factional device. The theme was adopted formally by John Adams only after January 1800, when he went into open opposition to Hamilton. Adams may have been attempting to separate himself from the charges of favoring monarchy; yet, he could have and, in good faith, most likely did realize the danger stalking republican institutions. Certainly by November 1800, at the time of his annual message, he wished to warn the public that a crisis was at hand.

As the contest between Jefferson, Adams, Pinckney, and Burr developed, religious as well as political pamphlet writers allowed their pens to go berserk. One writer, calling himself "a Christian Federalist," vividly described the revolutionary situation that would follow a Jeffersonian victory:

> Can serious and reflecting men look about them and doubt, that if Jefferson is elected, and the Jacobins get into authority, that those morals which protect our lives from the knife of the assassin —which guard the chastity of our wives and daughters from seduction and violence—defend our property from plunder and devastation, and shield our religion from contempt and profanation, will not be trampled upon and exploded.

Then, after reviewing the horrors of the French Revolution and referring to Jefferson as in essence a French revolutionary, he wrote: "Trace the history of the furious and bloody demagogues of the revolution, and then remark the correspondence with the acts of demagogues at home."[34] The lesson was clear: ministers feared a complete revolution in the manners, habits, and customs of society if Jefferson was elected. "Consider the effects [of] the election of any man avowing the principles of Mr. Jefferson," said the Reverend Dr. Linn. "The effect would be to destroy religion, introduce immorality, and loosen all the bonds of society."[35] But despite the exertions of the ministers, at least one politician observed that it "is not probable, however, that all that has been, or will be, written on this subject will deprive Jefferson of a single vote . . ."[36]

The political writers, however, had a much greater influence upon the public mind, especially where they charged that the principles of monarchy endangered American institutions. John Beckley reminded Americans:

Seceding from the principles avowed to the world as the basis of your republican institutions, the pillars of aristocracy have arisen, and in the dereliction of American truths, the world has been astonished at your retrograde turn and rapid advance to monarchy.

A review of past events will but present the painful spectacle of political apostacy, amidst the wreck of principle: and the creation of systems equally subversive of liberty, peace and happiness—new and unheard of doctrines have been advanced, precedents established, and laws enacted, which go to sap the very foundations of public liberty.[37]

---

[34] "A Short Address to Voters of Delaware," 21 Sept. 1800. Quoted in *History of American Presidential Elections, 1798–1968,* op. cit., Vol. I, pp. 150–51.

[35] Rev. Dr. William Linn, *Serious Considerations on the Election of a President Addressed to the Citizens of the U.S.* (New York, 1800), p. 24.

[36] Robert Troup to Rufus King, 14 Sept. 1800, *Life and Correspondence of Rufus King,* op. cit., Vol. III, p. 300.

[37] John Beckley, *Address to the People of the United States* (Philadelphia, 1800), p. 4.

Indeed, there were dozens of writers who could supply that "review of past events" in addition to Beckley. One writer remarked succinctly, "We have seen old Tories, the enemies of our revolution, recommended as the guardians of our country."[38] Even Jefferson was writing on the theme as late as December 14, 1800: "The Constitution to which we are all attached was meant to be republican, . . . yet we have seen it so interpreted and administered, as to be truly what the French have called, A *Monarchic Masque.*" If we cannot restore true republican principles, he asserted, "we shall be unable to realize the prospects held out to the people, and we must fall back into monarchism . . ."[39] Another simply stated, "There is a monarchical party in the United States, and that Mr. Hamilton and Mr. Adams belong to that party."[40]

The charge of monarchy was even more effective when it was linked to the system of administration and finance that had characterized England for the past two centuries. One author noted that the national debt had accumulated to "eighty millions of dollars. . . . But why was this done?" he asked, and continued,

> The answer is obvious; Mr. Hamilton and his party, knew very well that the people would never consent to a monarchy, and that his only chance was to introduce it by degrees; it was therefore necessary to assimilate the measures of administration as nearly as possible to those of a monarchy, and the funding system was one of the first steps. The genealogy of the business will stand briefly thus: the funding system begets and perpetualizes debt; debt begets intrigue, offices and corruption; those beget taxation; taxation begets the treasury; the treasury begets a swarm of Pickerings and Daytons; Pickerings and Daytons beget a standing army, and

[38] "To the People of New Jersey" (Princeton, N.J., Sept. 1800). Printed in *History of American Presidential Elections 1798–1968*, op. cit., Vol. I, p. 136.

[39] Jefferson to Robert R. Livingston, 14 Dec. 1800, *Writings*, Vol. X, p. 177. Jefferson to Samuel Adams, 26 Feb. 1800, ibid., p. 153; Jefferson to Gideon Granger, 13 Aug. 1800, ibid., p. 167.

[40] Marcus Brutus (pseud.), *Serious Facts, Opposed to "Serious Considerations": or, The Voice of Warning to Religious Republicans,* op. cit., p. 2.

a standing army begets monarchy, and monarchy begets an enslaved and impoverished people.[41]

Thus in Marcus Brutus' mind, the economic system introduced by Alexander Hamilton led straight to a reimposition of monarchy. Citing his reverence for the "course dictated by the spirit of our revolution," another writer referred to the Federal convention and then warned those who failed to take the subject seriously:

Are such suggestions to be lightly regarded when it is now known that a number of men, who have been our political leaders, were holding their meetings in the year 1787 to contrive ways and means for the establishment of what they termed, A *Confederated Monarchy?* When we read the speech of General Hamilton in the Federal Convention, and now find him at the head of our army? When we hear our leading men avow that this country can never be governed without an *Hereditary Monarch?* When we see the appropriate plans of *Monarchy* adopted by administration? When we read the federal papers filled with reflections on liberty and republicanism, and with praises of *Monarchial* government? When Fenno, the mouth-piece of the federal party has just published a scheme of a *Federated, Presidential, Monarchial Aristocracy?*

The author closed with the admonition: "If one half of my positions and conclusions be just, A *Monarchy is decidedly before us!*"[42]

A third version of this attempt to portray the seriousness of a counterrevolution in America dealt directly with the Hamiltonian system of administration and was calculated to link the Federalist supporters of Pinckney to the threat of monarchy:

There is abundance of testimony to prove that this party is not contented with our present limited government, but that it is their steady and uniform object to introduce a system essentially and radically different. The constitution proposed by Mr. Hamilton in the late general convention, was everything but federal; it

[41] Ibid., p. 4.
[42] Abraham Bishop, *Connecticut Republicanism: An Oration on the Extent and Power of Political Delusion,* op. cit., p. i.

went to the establishment of a permanent executive, and to the total subversion of the states. The Governors were to have been appointed by that herculean executive, and united America, ruined by the perfidy of one man, was again to have been prostrated before the throne of a powerful and almost absolute monarch!

That project is far from being abandoned—it has been revived in another form—the pamphlet of young Fenno, contemptible as it is, in every respect, betrays the object and purpose of his party. This boy, nurtured in the air of a court, and conversant with the designs and opinions of his patrons, has presumed to offer a system of government to the United States. It is true that this system does not possess originality, but is the servile counterpart of the *project* of Mr. Hamilton; it exhibits the same features and betrays the same views. An alliance offensive and defensive with Great Britain—perpetual war with France and Spain—foreign conquests—permanent naval and military establishments—an eternal, unextinguishable debt—a perpetual system of funding and speculation—the compleat annihilation of states—a division of the country into districts or provinces, to destroy even the memory of their existence—a president with unlimited powers—governors, or prefects of his appointment—a house of lords composed of such prefects—a permanent aristocracy—an enslaved, impoverished and miserable people.[43]

The "system" that Wortman alluded to was the same system that Jefferson and his colleagues had been warning their fellow Americans about for almost a decade. The campaign literature bristled with discussions about the principles of republican government and the principles of the constitution versus the principles of aristocracy and monarchy. John Adams was cited as having a bias toward the latter. As proof, passages from Adams' writings, statements overheard by prominent men, and his association over a long period with the Hamiltonian faction were cited. But the charges against Adams were negligible compared with similar charges in 1796. Besides, Adams had for nearly a year broken with the Hamiltonians and reminded all who would listen of his ex-

[43] Tunis Wortman, *A Solemn Address to the Citizens of New York*, op. cit., p. 33.

ploits during the Revolution. Jefferson, on the other hand, was constantly identified with the principles of the American Revolution, and in most of the campaign literature on the Antifederalist side was given credit for being the very author of its principles. In a typical campaign circular the following exhortation was made:

> Let us therefore, taking the Declaration of Independence in our hands, and carrying its principles in our hearts, let us resolve to support Thomas Jefferson, whose whole life has been a comment on its precepts, and an uniform pursuit of the great blessings of his country which it was first intended to establish.[44]

The rhetoric implicit in these political writings led to a sense of crisis, an inescapable feeling that in the results of this election hung the fate of popular government. The alarmed mood of many was captured eloquently by one of the greatest patriots of the American Revolution, Christopher Gadsden. But even more important than the sense of crisis was the insight that Gadsden revealed for the nation over the next six months:

> . . . 'tis impossible the union can much longer exist. But our Government must prove *an abortion*, or smothered in its earliest infancy, will afford to anti-republicans and future historians the strongest example ever heard of, of the instability and very short duration of such kind of government. Never was or could be a fairer trial than ours, *every step* in its formation taken in the most deliberate manner by the people, if such a republic should be self-destroyed (the only way such governments ever have been destroyed) and the few trustless desperados, disgraced, joined to an ambitious, artful, indefatigable Cataline amongst us, should they succeed in their designs, which God forbid, then adieu (in all probability) to any attempt for such governments in future.[45]

This wise old man, a supporter of the Union and of John Adams and Thomas Jefferson, of federalism and the republican form of

44 "To the People of New Jersey," op. cit., in *History of American Presidential Elections 1798–1968*, op. cit., Vol. I, pp. 135–36.

45 Christopher Gadsden, Essay "For the State Gazette," 8 Oct. 1800. Published in the *South Carolina Gazette* and *Timothy's Daily Advertiser*. In *The Writings of Christopher Gadsden, 1746–1805*, op. cit., p. 304.

government, had intuited the possibility of a conspiracy against liberty.

By December 1800, the young nation was in the grip of its most severe crisis. Federalist and republican, democrat and Jacobin—all believed that upon the outcome of the election hinged the fate of the republic. Every politician of national standing had been attempting to assess the outcome of the election. Hamilton, by August, had begun to speculate on the possibility of Pinckney and Adams losing and Jefferson or Burr becoming President. If it were the latter, Hamilton suggested, he "will certainly attempt to reform the government *à la Bonaparte.* He is as unprincipled and dangerous a man as any country can boast—as true a Cataline as ever met in a midnight conclave."[46] Hamilton was describing nothing less than a conspiracy against the republic. In a calmer, but equally fearful, way Jonathan Roberts wrote to his father: "Never has any question occurred which has involved more serious consequences than the present."[47]

Both of their premonitions would prove accurate. It was still felt by many during the last days of November that the election of one of the Federalist candidates was a possibility. Despite their divisions, the Federalists had, with the exception of Rhode Island, all of New England's electoral votes. When Pennsylvania reached an impasse, the crucial state became South Carolina. There, due to the efforts of Charles Pinckney[48] and Hamilton's pamphlets,[49]

[46] Hamilton to James A. Bayard, 6 Aug. 1800, *Works of Alexander Hamilton,* op. cit., Vol. X, p. 387.

[47] Jonathan Roberts to his father, 3 Dec. 1800, Roberts MS., Historical Society of Pennsylvania. Quoted in Morton Borden, *The Federalism of James A. Bayard,* op. cit., p. 77.

[48] Charles Pinckney to Jefferson, Dec. 1800, *American Historical Review,* 4 (1898), p. 122. Pinckney, with all due modesty, wrote, "Most of our friends believe that my exertions and influence . . . has in a great measure contributed to the decision . . ."

[49] Robert Troup to Rufus King, 31 Dec. 1800, *Life and Correspondence of Rufus King,* op. cit., Vol. III, p. 359. Troup claimed that Hamilton's pamphlet had "accomplished the democratical majority in the South Carolina Legislature."

the contest became fierce, and even led the Federalists to contemplate abandoning their factional differences and offering an "accommodation" to the republicans.[50] But whether the possibility of an offer was real or not, Pinckney and his fellow republicans depended on the democratic majority in the legislature to secure victory. That dependence was rewarded. For when the presidential electors were known, Jefferson's supporters were ecstatic: "Our Electors are chosen . . .," wrote Peter Freneau, "rejoice and let the good news be known. Our country is yet safe. The vote tomorrow will be Jefferson 8; Burr 7; Clinton 1. This I am told—it is not the wish to risque any person being higher than Jefferson."[51] But the country was far from safe and the results of the election were to presage the results in the other states as well. For it was soon realized, even before the results from all the states were in, that the Jeffersonians had carried the election.[52] In the final tally the vote stood Jefferson eight and Burr eight. It was a tie that indi-

[50] Timothy Pickering to Rufus King, 27 Dec. 1800, ibid., pp. 352–53. Pickering believed that "General Pinckney might have been chosen—at least have stood on a par with Mr. Jefferson, if the federalists in the legislature of So. Carolina would have consented to have placed Mr. Jefferson on the ticket: but the latter considered themselves pledged to vote for Mr. *Adams* and General Pinckney." Thus Hamilton's political strategy had backfired once more. For a slightly different interpretation of this, one which has the Federalists offering an accommodation and the republicans refusing, see Cunningham, *The Jeffersonian Republicans*, op. cit., pp. 234–36.

[51] Peter Freneau to Seth Paine, 2 Dec. 1800. Quoted in Cunningham, *The Jeffersonian Republicans*, op. cit., p. 236.

[52] Within two weeks Jefferson would write Madison: "Though as yet we do not know the actual votes of Tennessee, Kentucky and Vermont, yet we believe the votes to be on the whole, Jefferson seventy-three, Burr seventy-three, Adams sixty-five, Pinckney sixty-four. Rhode Island withdrew one from Pinckney [given to John Jay]. There is a possibility that Tennessee may withdraw one from Burr, and Burr writes that there may be one vote in Vermont for Jefferson. But I hold the latter impossible, and the former not probable; and that there will be an absolute parity between the two republican candidates." Jefferson to James Madison, 19 Dec. 1800, *Writings*, Vol. X, p. 184. Jefferson's information was accurate and reflected the final arrangement of electoral votes.

cated a lack of foresight on the part of the republicans for which they might pay dearly.

Jefferson immediately sensed the danger. He wrote Aaron Burr, discreetly informing him of his plans for the new administration. Lamenting the fact that Burr would not be in his cabinet, Jefferson implied that Burr must now act out his role as the Vice President—a role Jefferson believed to be severely limited. By instructing Burr in this manner Jefferson also implied that he had expected to emerge as the clear presidential choice. The reason he had not was only thinly veiled. The contest, he said, "was badly managed," and it was unfortunate "not to have arranged with certainty what seems to have been left to hazard." Then, alluding to the problem that was uppermost in his, and by now everyone else's, mind, he wrote: "It was the more material, because I understand several of the high-flying federalists have expressed their hope that the two republican tickets may be equal, and their determination in that case to prevent a choice by the House of Representatives, (which they are strong enough to do) and let the government devolve on a President of the Senate."[53]

By the second week of December it was realized that a tie between the two republican candidates had occurred. Rumors and speculations had filled the air, of which Jefferson's was only one of the first. No one knew what was going to happen. Hardly anyone even knew how to proceed. The constitution, by failing to make a distinction between a President and Vice President in the electoral votes, had failed to "enounce precisely the true expression of the public will";[54] and while it gave limited guidelines as to how a successor would be chosen, it was nevertheless an unprecedented state of affairs in the political history of the western world. One thing had become obvious to Jefferson and Madison, though, as it had to the more perceptive Federalists: their strategy of revolution had been a resounding success. For more than any other measure

---

[53] Jefferson to Colonel Aaron Burr, 15 Dec. 1800, ibid., p. 181.
[54] Jefferson to Tench Coxe, Esq., 31 Dec. 1800, ibid., p. 188.

the elections in the states had validated Jefferson's idea of the possibility of a permanent, peaceful, constitutional revolution in a republic. His idea of progressively organizing the states to obtain majorities in their legislatures, until a majority of the Union had been accomplished, was now a fact. Suddenly, for the want of a single electoral vote, the entire political strategy of peaceful revolution was in jeopardy.

Jefferson's and Madison's faith in the constitutional process and the limits to which they were willing to go in order to preserve republican government would now be put to the test. Would the House of Representatives obey their constitutional obligation and elect a new President? Or would faction rear its head and plunge an orderly constitutional process into an abyss of violence and intrigue? Hamilton had predicted a "revolution" if Pinckney was not elected. He had also predicted a conspiracy "*à la Bonaparte*" if the Federalists adhered to Burr.

That event, fresh in the minds of everyone, had seen General Napoleon Bonaparte drive the legislature from its halls at the point of a bayonet, dismiss the Directory, and, after overturning the constitution of the republic, declare himself emperor. Hamilton had in the same connection alluded to the sinister conspiratorial mentality of the Roman "Cataline." There was no mistaking his meaning: Burr would become Cataline if he were ever elevated to the presidency. Was either of these scenes possible? Indeed, what if the people's will, meaning their choice of Jefferson, was ignored while a dubious adherence to the constitution produced Burr or no President at all?

With these thoughts in mind Jefferson wrote his most trusted political advisor that "the federalists, . . . openly declare they will prevent an election, and will name a President of the Senate, *pro tem.* by what they say would only be a *Stretch* of the Constitution." Without further comment, he then revealed his intentions to be "liberal and accommodating" to John Adams, a question that had arisen before in their correspondence and one that Madison had been formally against. Obviously Jefferson believed at this time that the election, if it were to be held then, would be in his favor.[55]

Meanwhile, Madison, struggling with a sick father at his home in Orange, had written Governor James Monroe of the "inquietude prevailing in this quarter as to the precise issue of the election."[56] Unaware of the final election returns or the uproar that was being fomented in the new capital city, Madison next wrote to Jefferson matter-of-factly: in case of a tie electoral vote the choice for a President would "devolve [up]on the House of Representatives. . . . There can be no danger, I presume . . ." Madison, whose blind instincts were also constitutional, naturally assumed that the next level of decision making would automatically take over. But others did not necessarily see the same sequence. Already Madison alluded to a development responsible for the nightmare that would follow for the next two months. Madison's advice—that it would be "desirable" to "preclude" a tie vote "by the foresight of some of the Electors"—came approximately one month too late. He then alluded to a Burr confidant, "[David] Gelston, of New York, [who] assures me that there are two, if not three States, in which something to this effect may be looked for, but he does not name the States."[57]

---

[55] Jefferson to James Madison, 19 Dec. 1800, *Writings*, Vol. X, pp. 184–85.

[56] James Madison to Governor James Monroe, Dec. 1800, *The Letters and Other Writings of James Madison*, op. cit., Vol. II, p. 165.

[57] James Madison to Jefferson, 20 Dec. 1800, ibid., p. 165. See also Madison to James Monroe, 10 Nov. 1800, Madison MS., Lib. Cong. Madison would make the claim of false assurances twice in later years: once in a letter to Jefferson, 14 Jan. 1824, and in his autobiography: "It was with much difficulty that a unanimous vote could be obtained in the Virginia College of Electors for both [Jefferson and Burr] lest an equality might throw the choice into the House of Reps, or otherwise endanger the known object of the people. J. Madison had received assurances from a confidential friend of Burr that in a certain quarter votes would be thrown from B. with a view to secure a majority for Jefferson." Douglass Adair, ed., "James Madison's Autobiography," *William and Mary Quarterly*, Ser. 3, 2 (1945), p. 206. Madison was referring to Gelston's letter to him, 2 Nov. 1800, Presidential Papers, Lib. Cong. In that letter Gelston had written: "We are well aware from good information that three

This was a crucial issue and would cast its pall over events for the next four years. Jefferson had, in his earlier letter to Burr, disclaimed any intention of reducing Burr's total number of votes. This avowal was designed to serve a dual purpose: to gain Burr's personal confidence and to indicate to him that a repetition of the events of 1796, when Burr had received merely one vote from Virginia, had not occurred. Burr, however, was suspicious of Virginia's intentions; he had expressed his suspicions to Maria Gallatin, wife of the Pennsylvania congressman.[58]

Despite this background of mutual assurance amidst mutual suspicion, it was apparent that something had gone wrong. Within a week the inner circle of the Virginia clique began to suspect that a new Federalist intrigue was commencing. Jefferson summed up the situation: "After the most energetic efforts, crowned with success, we remain in the hands of our enemies by the want of foresight in the original arrangements."[59] Within eleven days Jefferson would reveal to Madison and Tench Coxe the image of a daring conspiracy: "The Federalists appear determined to prevent an election, and to pass a bill giving the government to Mr. Jay, appointed Chief Justice, or to Marshall as Secretary of State."[60] To his friend, Coxe, he added another dimension:

> The federalists . . . propose to prevent an election in Congress, and to transfer the government by an act to the C.J. (Jay) or Secretary of State, or to let it devolve on the President *pro tem.* of the Senate, till next December, which gives them another year's predominance, and the chances of future events. The re-

---

states, two at least, will give Mr. J. three or more votes, more than Mr. B. will have."

[58] Henry Adams, *Life of Albert Gallatin* (New York, 1943), p. 241. Noting a conversation she had had with Burr, she wrote: "Burr says he has no confidence in the Virginians, they once deceived him, and they are not to be trusted."

[59] Jefferson to James Monroe, 20 Dec. 1800, Monroe Papers, VI, 1000, Lib. Cong.

[60] Jefferson to Madison, 26 Dec. 1800, *Writings*, Vol. X, pp. 186–87.

publicans propose to press forward to an election. If they fail in this, a concert between the two higher candidates may prevent the dissolution of the government and danger of anarchy, by an operation, bungling indeed and imperfect, but better than letting the legislature take the nomination of the Executive entirely from the people.[61]

If one could describe Jefferson's reaction to all of this, it might be one of calm anger. His correspondence indicates that he rather expected the extreme Federalists might make another attempt at corruption, as they had in the New York elections. Yet this was of a magnitude far greater than simply the corruption of a single state. Before he could plan his strategy, though, he had to have more evidence, and what was as important, the opinions of those he trusted most.

Thus, in the last two weeks of December Jefferson had communicated with his major advisors, James Madison and James Monroe, on the emergence of the crisis. His correspondence indicates that despite his disappointment over the failure to arrange the electoral votes and avoid a tie, he nevertheless did not suspect, or at least say he suspected, Aaron Burr of intriguing with the Federalist faction. His main preoccupation was with a Federalist faction turning the government over to the Chief Justice or the President of the Senate. At best, he hoped to proceed with the election in the belief that he and Burr would be able to make an amicable arrangement between themselves over a future republican administration. He was thus demonstrating his willingness to sacrifice his personal ambition and serve as the Vice President for another four years. At worst, he saw the emergence of a legislative tyranny and a usurpation of the constitution that would still have a constitutional solution after a year. The observation that one cannot help making then is that Jefferson, faced with the possible destruction of nearly five years of hard political labor, was still willing to seek a solution through the constitutional and legislative machinery. Perhaps his mind was reminiscing on the scenes he had witnessed in France when the factions abandoned the constitu-

---

[61] Jefferson to Tench Coxe, Esq., 31 Dec. 1800, ibid., p. 188.

tional process for a trust in force. Indeed, opposing the violence of faction and intrigue with the force he might have at his own disposal seemed, at the close of 1800, the farthest thing from his mind.

This was not so on the part of the Federalists. On the contrary, the extremists, with the exception of Hamilton, were more than willing to cabal in an attempt to resurrect their fleeing fortunes. George Cabot observed to his friend abroad in the closing days of December that despite "the remarkable calm here . . . some of the Jacobins . . . feared Burr will be their Chief." He then gave evidence that he recognized a revolution had taken place, though he was not quite sure how far it would go. Referring to the Secretary of the Treasury's resignation, he said, "Wolcott leaves his office in excellent order—the public creditors are safe against everything but *total revolution* . . ."[62] Thus, the "calm" he referred to in the opening part of his letter was at best uncertain and perhaps the proverbial calm before a storm. Joseph Hale, a Federalist, noted that it had become "fashionable with feds to declare in favor of Mr. Burr."[63] And Oliver Wolcott noted simply, referring to the Federalists' choosing between Jefferson and Burr: "There will be intriguing here through the winter on a high scale."[64] Uriah Tracy, an arch-Federalist, wrote to the former Secretary of War, indicating that perhaps all was not lost: "Burr is a cunning man. If he cannot outwit all the Jeffersonians, I do not know the man."[65] From republicans came similar observations. Two weeks later Stevens Mason wrote to a Jeffersonian leader that "the desperate Feds, are hope[ful] of throwing things into confusion by defeating an election altogether, and making a President for us by act of Congress. This project has been the subject of

[62] George Cabot to Rufus King, 28 Dec. 1800, *Life and Correspondence of Rufus King*, op. cit., Vol. III, p. 354.

[63] Joseph Hale to Rufus King, 29 Dec. 1800, ibid., p. 357.

[64] Oliver Wolcott to his wife, 31 Dec. 1800, Gibbs, *Memoirs of the Administrations of Washington and Adams*, op. cit., Vol. II, p. 462.

[65] Uriah Tracy to James McHenry, 30 Dec. 1800, McHenry MS., Lib. Cong. Quoted in Morton Borden, *The Federalism of James A. Bayard*, op. cit., p. 81.

much caballing and caucusing."[66] One writer in the New York
Gazette and General Advertiser said Burr would become President
by "forming a faction among the dregs—the refuse of both
parties."[67] The truth was, several factions had now developed and
were contending against one another: Jefferson, Hamilton, Burr,
and Adams supporters often found themselves in violent disagreement. It thus appeared to many that the politics of faction
threatened to plunge the country into yet another constitutional
crisis.

Hamilton, whether from a fear of the violence to the nation
that might result from a successful elevation of Burr, or from
pique over Burr's role in defeating his plans in New York and
revealing the pamphlet on John Adams, or simply from a wish to
see Burr kicked upstairs, away from New York politics, and de-
posited in the vice-presidential chair, had been urgently writing his
most influential friends that they must prevent the choice of Burr.
On the same day that Jefferson wrote Madison of the Federalist
plan to deny the election, Hamilton appealed to his faithful friend
Wolcott: "Jefferson is to be preferred . . . as to Burr, there is
nothing in his favor. His private character is not defended by his
most partial friends. He is bankrupt beyond redemption, except by
the plunder of his country. His public principles have no other
spring or aim than his own aggrandizement, *per fas et nefas*. If he
can, he will certainly disturb our institutions, to secure to himself
permanent power, and with it wealth. He is truly the Catiline of
America . . ." With deadly calculation Hamilton continued de-
noting his sense of urgency:

> But early measures must be taken to fix on this point the opinions
> of the Federalists . . . Burr will find partisans. If the thing be
> neglected, he may possibly go far. Yet it may be well enough to
> throw out a line for him, in order to tempt him to start for the

[66] Stevens T. Mason to John Breckinridge, 15 Jan. [1801], Papers of Breckinridge Family, XVIII, 3156, Lib. Cong. Quoted in Cunningham, *The Jeffersonian Republicans*, op. cit., p. 242.

[67] Quoted in Parmet and Hecht, *Aaron Burr: Portrait of an Ambitious Man*,
op. cit., p. 164.

plate, and then *lay the foundation of dissension between the two chiefs*.[68]

Thus, in the midst of an emerging constitutional crisis, Hamilton was not above attempting still another devious strategy: paralyzing the new administration and ultimately producing deep divisions within it.[69]

The following day Hamilton gave a justification for his opposition to Burr: it would injure the Federalists generally by acquiring the "animosity" of Jefferson if they failed; and if they succeeded, placing a man in power who could give "success to the Jacobin system." Hamilton believed the Federalists deluded themselves if they thought they could win Burr to accept "federal views." He then described Burr's character by charging that once Burr was in power, he would do anything, and use anyone, good or bad, to "accomplish his ends." "Every step in his career proves that he has formed himself upon the model of Cataline, and he is too cold-blooded and too determined a conspirator even to change his plan." He then alluded to the fact that Burr had publicly toasted "Bonaparte" within the "last three or four weeks." The Federal-

[68] Hamilton to Oliver Wolcott, 16 Dec. 1800, *Works of Alexander Hamilton*, op. cit., Vol. X, pp. 392–93. Italics mine.

[69] In the historical literature of the "Election of 1800" little has been made of Hamilton's role in the intrigue between the various factions that were to decide whether Jefferson or Burr would acquire the presidency. Matthew Davis, in his attempt to exonerate Burr totally from any complicity whatever in the election intrigue barely mentions Hamilton's name. Noble Cunningham, in *The Jeffersonian Republicans*, positively denies that Hamilton had much influence in the election (p. 245). In a more recent study by Parmet and Hecht, *Aaron Burr: Portrait of an Ambitious Man*, Hamilton is still considered not to have been "particularly influential," p. 167. Morton Borden's account in *The Federalism of James A. Bayard*, op. cit., by far the most scholarly and reasonable explanation of the intricate negotiations between the factions, makes note of Hamilton at several points and recognizes that he may have at least influenced Bayard (see Borden's footnote 92, p. 221). None of the secondary accounts I have seen, however, mention Hamilton's conscious willingness to follow a policy of dividing the "two Chiefs," thereby promoting unnecessary intrigue among already dangerously divided factions and running the risk of plunging the country into civil war.

ists, he concluded, might as well bid "adieu to the Federal Troy, if they once introduce this Grecian horse into their citadel." Following this warning, Hamilton announced the stipulations that the Federalists ought to extract from Jefferson. They were to be important, so much so, that in the end they would decide whether or not the nation would be plunged into civil war. Hamilton laid down these propositions:

> 1st –The preservation of the actual fiscal system.
> 2nd–Adherence to the neutral plan.
> 3d –The preservation and gradual increase of the navy.
> 4th–The continuance of our friends in the offices they fill, except in the great departments, in which he ought to be left free.[70]

Within one short week Hamilton had attempted to alert those few leaders among the Federalists he could yet trust. His credibility as a political leader had been undermined by the attack against Adams,[71] yet he was able to make his case to Oliver Wolcott, Gouverneur Morris, James A. Bayard, Robert Troup, Timothy Pickering, Theodore Sedgwick, and others of influence.[72] Urging Morris to use his "opinion . . . freely," Hamilton had begun a desperate campaign to gain control over what he saw was an inevitable but dangerous process.[73] To James A. Bayard of Delaware he sounded the depth of the constitutional crisis: "Several letters to myself and others from the city of Washington, excite in

[70] Hamilton to Wolcott, 17 Dec. 1800, *Works of Alexander Hamilton,* op. cit., Vol. X, pp. 393–96; see also Hamilton to Theodore Sedgwick, 22 Dec. 1800, ibid., p. 397.

[71] See Robert Troup to Rufus King, 31 Dec. 1800, on the declining status of Hamilton as the unqualified leader of the Federalists. *Life and Correspondence of Rufus King,* op. cit., Vol. III, p. 359.

[72] Wolcott for example responded to Hamilton's letters of 16 Dec. by saying "that of the 16th I communicated to Mr. Marshall and Mr. Sedgwick." Oliver Wolcott to Hamilton, 25 Dec. 1800, Gibbs, *Memoirs of the Administrations of Washington and Adams,* op. cit., Vol. II, p. 460.

[73] Hamilton to Gouverneur Morris, 26 Dec. 1800, *Works of Alexander Hamilton,* op. cit., Vol. X, p. 401.

my mind extreme alarm on the subject of the future President." Then waxing hotly about Burr's character and abilities, Hamilton hit upon the arguments he believed would cause most sensible Federalists to think twice before supporting Burr: 1. Burr wanted permanent power, and 2. he would destroy "the system."

> The maintenance of the existing institutions will not suit him; because under them his power will be too narrow and too precarious. Yet the innovations he may attempt will not offer the substitute of a system durable and safe, calculated to give lasting prosperity, and to unite liberty with strength. It will be the system of the day, sufficient to serve his own turn, and not looking beyond himself. To execute this plan, as the good men of the country cannot be relied upon, the worst will be used. Let it not be imagined that the difficulties of execution will deter, or a calculation of interest restrain. The truth is, that under forms of government like ours, too much is practicable to men who will, without scruple, avail themselves of the bad passions of human nature.[74]

As the old year ended with the election in doubt and the prospect of a violent factional dispute on the horizon, John Quincy Adams summed up for many the mood that must have dominated the traditional Christmas spirit. Willing to admit that he might be in error, he nevertheless stated to his younger brother Thomas Boylston Adams:

> . . . it is impossible for me to avoid the supposition that the ultimate necessary consequence, if not the *ultimate object of both the extreme parties which divide us, will be a dissolution of the Union and a civil war.* Your father's policy was certainly to steer between the shoals on one side, and the rocks on the other. But as both factions have turned their arms against him, and the people themselves have abandoned him, there is too much reason to expect that the purpose common to the two opposite factions will be effected.[75]

---

[74] Hamilton to James A. Bayard, 27 Dec. 1800, ibid., p. 403.

[75] John Quincy Adams to Thomas Boylston Adams, 30 Dec. 1800, *The Writings of John Quincy Adams*, op. cit., Vol. VI, p. 491. Italics mine.

The first days of January saw the speculation regarding Burr heightened and a new note added. A letter from Burr to General Samuel Smith, M.C., in mid-December had allowed Smith to act as "proxy" for Burr. Written at a time when Burr believed a tie vote improbable, the letter "utterly disclaim[ed] all competition" against Jefferson. Further, Burr wrote, "be assured *that the federal party can entertain no wish for such an exchange.*"[76] But as soon as the deadlock became apparent to the Federalists, they disregarded the letter. James McHenry, writing to King on the second day of January, quoted Burr's letter to Smith and then observed:

> Some of our Federalists . . . seemed determined to run Burr notwithstanding this letter. They do not consider that in it he has committed himself, not to accept of the office of President, if elected by the House of Representatives. They think they understand Burr and that he will not be angry at being aided by the Federalists, to outwit the Jeffersonians. The fact is, the opposition are in the most violent state of apprehension lest Mr. Jefferson be chosen.[77]

The Federalists were divided in their approach to Burr. Many believed Burr malleable or that they had nothing to lose. Others simply feared what Jefferson might do and wished to frighten the republicans into "imbecility." Still others were serious and looked upon whatever negotiations might take place as a device to prevent the Jeffersonians from taking power. What bothered many, however, was the uncertainty that surrounded Burr himself. Robert Goodloe Harper, a congressman from South Carolina and an extreme Federalist, took pains to advise Burr, and his letter might explain the reticence that would later be attributed to him: "The language of the Democrats is that you will yield your pretensions to their favorite, and it is whispered that overtures to this end are to be, or are made by you. I advise you to take no step whatever, by which the choice of the House of Representatives can be

---

[76] Aaron Burr to General Samuel Smith, 16 Dec. 1800, Davis, *Memoirs of Aaron Burr*, op. cit., Vol. II, p. 75.

[77] J. McHenry to R. King, 2 Jan. 1801, *Life and Correspondence of Rufus King*, op. cit., Vol. III, p. 363.

impeded or embarrassed. Keep the game perfectly in your own hands but do not answer this letter, or any other that may be written to you by a Federal man, nor write to any of that party."[78]

Thus a bitter congressman had added to the factional fires a mere hint upon which clever politicians could build a monumental doubt. The rumors surrounding Federalist support for Burr began to mount. Gouverneur Morris had estimated at one point:

> It seems to be the general opinion that Colonel Burr will be chosen President by the House of Representatives. Many of them [the Federalists] think it highly dangerous that Mr. Jefferson should, in the present crisis, be placed in that office. They consider him as a theoretic man, who would bring the National Government back to something like the old Confederation. Mr. Nicholas comes today, and to him I state it as the opinion, not of light and fanciful but of serious and considerate men, that Burr must be preferred to Jefferson.[79]

The republicans attempted to stem the rising tide of doubt by sending Samuel Smith to meet again with Burr and obtain a declaration that he had no ambitions for the presidency and "to say he would not serve if elected . . ."[80] Smith ended his interview with the opposite impression. Burr was not only willing to serve as President, but had intimated the next morning that his republican "friends must join the federal vote" and vote him into the presidency, and Jefferson would then become Vice President.[81] Not only was the republican leadership repudiated by Burr himself, overtures were made to loyal Jeffersonians to gain their support. Jefferson recorded one incident that may have been made to others as well. Matthew Lyon of Vermont was approached by

[78] Robert Goodloe Harper to Aaron Burr, 24 Dec. 1800. Quoted in J. F. McLaughlin, *Matthew Lyon, the Hampden of Congress* (New York, 1900), pp. 385–86.

[79] *The Diary and Letters of Gouverneur Morris*, op. cit., Vol. II, pp. 396–97.

[80] Gabriel Christie to Samuel Smith, 19 Dec. 1802, Samuel Smith MS., Lib. Cong. Quoted in Borden, *The Federalism of James A. Bayard*, op. cit., p. 82.

[81] *The Anas, Writings*, Vol. I, entry of 2 Jan. 1804, pp. 442–43.

John Brown of Rhode Island, who, "urging him to vote for Colonel Burr," used these words: "What is it you want, Colonel Lyon? Is it office, is it money? Only say what you want, and you shall have it."[82] And while there was no direct connection proven between Burr and the solicitation, many republicans might draw an inference.

By the second week in January even the normally calm and unruffled Madison had begun to contemplate the excesses of the politics of faction. Writing to Jefferson, he avowed that:

> Desperate as some of the adverse party there may be, I can scarcely allow myself to believe that enough will not be found to frustrate the attempt to strangle the election of the people, and smuggle into the Chief Magistracy the choice of a *faction*. It would seem that every individual member who has any standing or stake in society, or any portion of virtue or sober understanding, must revolt at the tendency of such a maneuvre.

But his next thoughts bore directly on the crisis, suggesting several constitutional ways that it might be headed off. His first was to remind Jefferson that the President had it in his power to "appoint . . . as early a day as possible . . . for the succeeding House to meet and supply the omission." Then he proceeded to the possibility that appeared to every one who was aware of the consequences of the scene being played before them: "On the supposition of either . . . *an interegnum* in the Executive, or of a surreptitious intrusion into it, it becomes a question of the first order, what is the course demanded by the crisis?" Madison's answer revealed his pessimism of what the future would hold. He began by raising two more questions. The first dealt with his fear of a usurpation of executive authority and the vacuum that would be created by that act. He had little doubt, as we have seen, what that might lead to. The second dealt with a more subtle problem and as far as he was able to envision it, might provide a way to

---

[82] Ibid. Entry of 31 Dec. 1803, p. 442. An incident surrounding one David A. Ogden, who solicited support for Burr, was another example. See Nathan Schachner, *Jefferson* (New York, 1951), p. 653.

legitimate the constitutional will of the majority. Thus, Madison believed that his second suggestion would enable the young nation at least to maintain an attachment to the principles of constitutionalism:

> Will it be best to acquiesce in a suspension or usurpation of the Executive authority till the meeting of Congress in December next, or for Congress to be summoned by a joint proclamation or recommendation of the two characters having a majority of votes for President? My present judgment favors the latter expedient. The prerogative of convening the Legislature must reside in one or other of them, and if both concur, must substantially include the requisite will. The intentions of the people would undoubtedly be pursued. And if, in reference to the Constitution, the proceeding be not strictly regular, the irregularity will be less in form than any other adequate to the emergency, and will lie in form only, rather than substance; whereas the other remedies proposed are substantial violations of the will of the people, of the scope of the Constitution, and of the public order and interest.[83]

Madison's suggestions were an indication that he had fully understood the dangerous game being played by the legislators in Washington. Indeed, in the days immediately preceding the election, the situation had become grave and finally desperate. Two days before the balloting, Gouverneur Morris captured the tension and the uncertainty that gripped the members of every faction: "It is impossible to determine, which of the two candidates will be chosen President. Rumors are various and intrigues great."[84] Evidence of increasing support for Burr made Federalists like Hamilton shrill in their fulminations against Burr.[85] The Philadelphia *Aurora* on February 6 printed a letter stating, "We are

[83] Madison to Jefferson, 10 Jan. 1801, *The Letters and Other Writings of James Madison*, op. cit., Vol. II, pp. 166–67.

[84] Gouverneur Morris to Nicholas Low, 8 Feb. 1801, Jared Sparks, *Life of Gouverneur Morris* (Boston, 1832), Vol. III, p. 152.

[85] See Hamilton to Gouverneur Morris, 9 Jan. 1801, and to James A. Bayard, 16 Jan. 1801, *Works of Alexander Hamilton*, op. cit., Vol. X, pp. 408, 412–17. The latter is a masterful example of Hamilton's rhetorical ability and is the most skillful analysis of Burr and his philosophy I have seen.

credibly informed [from] Mr. Bayard of Delaware . . . that it is the intention of the Federalists *at all hazards* to attempt the defeat of Mr. Jefferson's election. This information the Editor had direct two days ago."[86] Republicans were equally determined. Congressman Joseph H. Nicholson wrote to a constituent that in the event of a usurpation, "Virginia would instantly proclaim herself out of the Union."[87] George Erving wrote James Monroe that the Federalist extremists, men like "Harper, Otis, Rutledge, etc. . . . flatter themselves that they can bring their federal troops to act as heretofore in a united Phalanx."[88]

But the supporters of Jefferson were also forming their own phalanx. Albert Gallatin, the Jeffersonian floor leader, conceived of a "plan" and with the consent of his fellow republicans presented it to Jefferson. In it he stated the objectives of the extremists: "1. To elect Mr. B[urr]; 2. To defeat the present election and order a new one; 3. To assume *executive* power during *interregnum*." Noting that any effort on the extremists' part to assume power was "clearly unconstitutional," he asked, "If they shall *usurp,* for unconstitutional assumption is usurpation, are we to submit or not? . . . Any assumption on their part is usurpation. Usurpation must be resisted by freemen whenever they have the power of resisting. To admit to a contrary doctrine would justify submission in every case, and encourage usurpation for ever hereafter. The mode of resisting seems to be the only question."

Gallatin went on to note that in the states controlled by the republicans it would be possible to resist and not risk civil war "by refusing to obey only those acts which may flow from the usurper as President." The wily Gallatin, who had "clogged the wheels of government" before, now revealed why he was so feared by the Federalists. He outlined a plan whereby the republicans would

[86] Philadelphia *Aurora,* 6 Feb. 1801. Quoted in Borden, *The Federalism of James A. Bayard,* op. cit., p. 219.

[87] Joseph H. Nicholson to a Constituent, 15 Jan. 1801, MS., Penna. Hist. Soc. Quoted in Schachner, *Jefferson,* op. cit., p. 654.

[88] George Erving to James Monroe, 25 Jan. 1801, Monroe MS., Lib. Cong. Quoted in Borden, *The Federalism of James A. Bayard,* op. cit., p. 87.

themselves consider preventing "every partial insurrection, [and] even individual act[s] of resistance, . . . refuse to obey every order from the usurper, such as a call for militia; declaring our intention to have the usurper punished according to law as soon as regular government shall have been established." As an alternative to this plan Gallatin suggested simply that the republicans not risk civil war and the ruin of republican institutions and "assume the executive power by a joint act of the two candidates or the relinquishment of all claims by one of them."

Next Gallatin submitted an "outline of our republican conduct":

1. Persevere in voting for Mr. J[efferson].
2. Use every endeavor to defeat any law on the subject.
3. Try to prevail on Mr. A[dams] to refuse his assent to any such law, and not to call the Senate on any account if there shall be no choice by the House.
4. The Republican Senators to secede from any illegal meeting of the Senate . . . in case no choice being made by the House.
5. To have a meeting, either self-created or of delegates appointed by the Legislatures of the Republican States, or only by the House of Representatives of those States where we have but one branch (*viz.*, New York, Pennsylvania, Maryland and South Carolina), in order to form an uniform plan of acting both in relation to a new election and to the usurpation if attempted.

Gallatin had considered every constitutional subtlety available. If that new election occurred, as suggested by the extremists, the republicans could protest it, or let matters take their course and hope to duplicate their success; or, they could leave the entire situation up to the next Congress, which would be republican controlled. Another tack was to call a new national election. By another strategy the republicans agreed to refuse to obey all orders of the usurper and obey only those they believed "should continue in operation." Still other options were open: attempting to persuade John Adams to call on Congress "to put an end to the interregnum, or to propose passing a law for that purpose"; to hasten the elections of Tennessee and Kentucky; to ask the legislatures of New York and Pennsylvania to appoint special electors. In all of their strategies, Gallatin noted, "the meeting [which would choose one of them] to be constituted and to act so as not to be considered as the result of an unconstitutional compact between the States." The consequences of each of these strategies were then "hypothe[sized]" in detail. But the main consideration throughout the long list of options was the determination on the part of the republicans to do nothing that might endanger republican institutions. Specifically, Gallatin stated that the republicans should do anything to prevent "an assumption of power not strictly warranted by the forms and substance of our constitutions being adopted, and adopted by *us* in any one case." While recognizing that "the remedy [was] . . . dangerous," they were determined to adhere to their principles and maintain the inviolability of the constitution. Everything depended on whether a "usurpation" took place. If it did, the Jeffersonians were prepared to go to desperate lengths.[89]

Such was the air of expectation that hung over the capital city when the new Congress convened. Fisher Ames, addressing himself to the state of the nation during this period, summed up the mood. He wished, of course, to describe only the Jeffersonians; but he was, in truth, describing the partisans of Burr and Hamilton as well:

A faction, whose union is perfect, whose spirit is desperate, addressing something persuasive to every prejudice, putting something combustible to every passion, granting some indulgence to every vice, promising those who dread the law to set them above it, to the mean whispering suspicion, to the ambitious offering power, to the rapacious, plunder, to the violent, revenge, to the envious, the abasement of all that is venerable, to innovators, the transmutation of all that is established, grouping together all that is folly, vice, and passion in the state, and forming of these

[89] "Plan at time of Balloting for Jefferson and Burr. Communicated to Nicholson and Mr. Jefferson," *The Writings of Albert Gallatin*, op. cit., Vol. I, pp. 18–23.

vile materials another state, *an imperium in imperio*— Behold this is our condition, these our terrours. And what are the resources for our safety?[90]

No one, at this point, could, or would tell. As John Vaughan had written Jefferson, "Our political destiny is suspended by a slender thread . . ."[91]

The House of Representatives was in session on 9 February amidst confusion and alarm. It was rumored that Governor Mc-Kean of Pennsylvania had declared that he would issue an executive order for all state officials to refuse to obey federal laws if Jefferson were not elected. For "Pennsylvania will protest against the proceeding, and will refuse to obey any laws that may be sanctioned by a President in whose election she has had no share."[92] A Jeffersonian supporter had proclaimed to the "assembled Congress of America":

> Dare to designate any Officer whatever, even temporarily, to administer the Government, in the event of a non-agreement on the part of the House of Representatives, and we will march and dethrone him as an Usurper.[93]

This was a threat that, if it meant anything at all, raised the specter of civil war. A link between Pennsylvania and Virginia was feared even before the election began. Thus Gallatin's plan, it

---

[90] Ames, "Laocoon No. 2," *Works of Fisher Ames*, op. cit., p. 112.

[91] John Vaughan to Jefferson, 10 Jan. 1801, Jefferson MS., Lib. Cong. Quoted in Borden, *The Federalism of James A. Bayard*, op. cit., p. 88.

[92] *Porcupine's Works*, op. cit., Vol. XII, p. 175. The rumor was probably fact if Jefferson's response to Governor McKean, 2 Feb. 1801, can be taken as an answer. In the letter, Jefferson addressed himself to the electoral corruption that had occurred in Pennsylvania, New York, and elsewhere. He mentioned that "it was too soon" to make a decision in "atrocious cases . . . of federal officers obstructing the operation of State governments. One thing I will say, that as to the future, interference with elections, whether of the State or General Government, by officers of the latter, should be deemed cause of removal; because the constitutional remedy by the elective principle becomes nothing, if it may be smothered by the enormous patronage of the General Government." *Writings*, Vol. X, p. 195.

[93] *Porcupine's Works*, op. cit., Vol. XII, p. 178.

seemed, was already half formed and would present the Burrites with a *fait accompli*. Governor Monroe's personal courier, and a man Jefferson trusted, described a plot by the Federalists in the preelection skirmishing. A series of resolutions had been passed relating to the election. On the final resolution an amendment was passed stating that "all elections shall be considered as *incidental* to the main power of voting by states, that each State shall have a vote. This was opposed by Messrs. Gallatin, Randolph, Nicholas and Macon." This raised the question of a new strategy pursued by the Federalists on the eve of the election. Samuel Tyler spoke for nearly everyone when he said, "It gave rise to very uneasy sensations not only with myself but those with whom I associate. In a word, the opinion as far as it can be formed by the most intelligent is—that they will unquestionably pursue precisely the same system of policy that the Senate of Pennsylvania did [i.e., deadlock] and that, in a caucus, which they held last night, it was resolved to put everything to the hazard."[94] Thus the strategy of the Federalists had become one of obstructionism. If they could deadlock the elections until March 4, the possibility existed that the nation would be without its constitutional executive, and the legislature could then appoint a President from among its members. The Federalists, it appeared, also had their own *fait accompli* in mind.

But neither Gallatin, McKean, Tyler, nor anyone else knew what the outcome would be. Morris had been accurate in his assessment; no one had any idea who would win the election. The delegates knew the Jeffersonians controlled a majority of the states but that they would fail to attain the necessary number prescribed by the constitution. Thus the first order of business was to reveal what everyone already knew: Jefferson and Burr were tied with 73 electoral votes apiece. With this formality over, the delegates

[94] Samuel Tyler to Governor James Monroe, 9 Feb. 1801, *William and Mary Quarterly*, 1st Ser., Vols. 1–3 (1892–95), pp. 102–3. Tyler was a former member of the Virginia House of Delegates in 1798–99, who had been sent by Monroe to the New York elections as an observer. He was then a member of the Governor's Council.

began the serious balloting by states. On the first ballot Jefferson received 55 votes and Burr 49. An eyewitness recalled, less than a week after the election, that "it was necessary to recommence the balloting, which was repeated up to 28 times with the same result throughout the day and night of the 11th."[95] Jefferson received eight electoral votes, Burr six. By the evening of the first day's voting the tension reached a breaking point.

Governor Monroe's courier, dating his dispatches by the hour, waited until "5 p.m." before he sent a description of the first day's balloting. On the first round Jefferson had received sixteen electoral votes from Virginia. On the second he lost ground and dropped to fourteen. Tyler then reported that the Federalists had made an attempt to "set aside the vote of Georgia on the ground of some informality." It was "rejected," but Jefferson's loss of votes and an attempt by the Federalists to nullify a state whose vote was obviously for Jefferson was an ominous trend. Tyler then gave his opinion that "the Republicans will remain firm and never relinquish . . . and that they will put everything to the hazard; the fact is this opp[osition] cannot elect Mr. Burr." Tyler then went on to report the fulfillment of Gallatin's plan which had been carried many steps farther. "In the event of extremities," he reported, "Penn[sylvania] has her courier here and the report is that she has 22,000 prepared to take up arms . . ." Events looked so critical that Tyler recommended an emergency session of the legislature to Monroe. That "the Ass[embly] of Virginia should be convened if things remain in S[tatus] quo for this week I should decide as prudent . . ."[96] Finally, Tyler, whose judgment

[95] An anonymous observer wrote a description of the election proceedings which was discovered by Professor Peter P. Hill of George Washington University in the Paris Archives and translated from the French in October 1968. The long letter was forwarded by the French Consul Joseph Philippe Le Tombe. The letter was published in the Los Angeles *Times*, 27 Oct. 1968, Sec. G, p. 2 (hereafter referred to as Eyewitness). See Appendix B for complete text.

[96] Samuel Tyler to James Monroe, 11 Feb. 1801, *William and Mary Quarterly*, 1st Ser., Vols. 1–3 (1892–95), p. 104.

both Jefferson[97] and Monroe respected, submitted a plan that portended civil war:

> Pennsy[lvania] and Virg[inia] should clasp hands, N[ew] York would join, and that a Congress composed of these States and all South of the Poto[mac] ought to be recommended; yet I would be understood to mean that this should be adopted only in last extremities: for I am clear the Feds will yield.[98]

Not only did the republicans agree on what should be done if the Federalists should resort to usurpation, but they had the troops. Pennsylvania with her thousands of militiamen, and Virginia with her militia, supported by all the states "south of the Potomac," would be a force that would overawe the federal government. This was especially true as Adams had so fortuitously "disbanded" the army a few months earlier. But what was more important was the fact that the republicans had informed the Federalists of their intentions. This was no empty threat. And while it came close to violating Jefferson's concern not to allow the army to "shew its force" in the midst of a constitutional revolution, it did intimidate the opposition forces and make them respect the sanctity of the electoral process. In addition, the suggestion reflected Jefferson's thinking in that it combined the implicit threat of force with the revolutionary idea of calling a Congress, the process that would automatically give constitutional legitimacy to a burgeoning revolution. It was, in fact, how the American Revolution had begun in 1774.

The first day's balloting saw the members vote a recess without suspending session. "With night fall, members called for food and bedding, and each party resolved to die at its post." The 12th saw the same procedure repeated with the results unchanged: "8 votes in favor of Jefferson; 6 votes for Burr; and Maryland and Vermont divided."[99] When the second day's balloting broke up, it had become apparent that because of the "determination of both sides

---

[97] Jefferson to James Monroe, 15 Feb. 1801, *Writings*, Vol. X, p. 201.

[98] Samuel Tyler to James Monroe, 11 Feb. 1801, op. cit.

[99] *Porcupine's Works*, op. cit., Vol. XII, p. 182.

to adhere to their man, they [the Representatives] have *done away* the resolution which required them to remain together, and adjourned to meet to-morrow at 11 o'clock." The policy of stalemate had made its formal appearance. A Federalist member of the House of Representatives from Maryland wrote, "Both parties appear determined to hold out. I think we shall succeed."[100] Each side believed that it would persevere, despite the fact that the votes representing the states remained the same. But a subtle change had taken place. In the individual electoral votes Burr had forged ahead. He now had fifty-four votes to Jefferson's fifty-one. Thus, while Jefferson had control of the states, it was clear that a majority of those voting favored Burr. The psychological trend was toward Burr and the Jeffersonians, knowing the consequences of a slow loss of yet a few more votes, became desperate.

The deadlock by the third day had even raised the tension beyond the confines of the House of Representatives. "Persons whom curiosity had brought to Washington, *more than a hundred thousand of them*, began to get impatient and to mutter at the obstinacy of the Federalists, saying that the representatives of that party were voting for Burr only to throw the country into confusion and to see if they could retain, in their own hands, . . . *power* . . ."[101]

Among them were many Federalists from the neighboring counties who "presented addresses to their representatives [John C.] Thomas and [William] Craik, instructing them to vote for Jefferson; but as yet they are far from having complied with this request—nevertheless, such is the scandalous conduct of certain members that the federalists themselves disapprove of it." With an eye toward their future prosperity, these "Washington locals" put pressure on Congressman John Chew Thomas "not to oppose the election of Mr. Jefferson." They were "damnably afraid that there will be no President, and consequently a *dissolution of the government, and then to Hell goes the Federal City*."[102]

[100] Ibid., pp. 184–85.
[101] Eyewitness. Italics mine.
[102] *Porcupine's Works*, op. cit., Vol. XII, pp. 186–87.

While those may have been the sentiments and fears of a limited few, a greater number realized the consequences of further obstruction. The eyewitness noted that most of these hundred thousand or more people "feared, and rightly, that with the exercise of presidential and vice presidential functions expiring on March 3, the United States would find itself without a government on the 4th. . . . and therefore if the Federalists continued to ballot in the same manner until March 4, the federal government would see itself threatened by a dissolution that must inevitably produce a civil war."[103]

Despite the fears and remonstrances, however, the vote of Maryland remained split, and the tally continued to show Jefferson eight and Burr six. The Maryland voters were both frustrated and shaken. A writer in the *American* wrote, "Let the Republicans wait patiently, till the 3d of March—If the *spirit of faction* shall then, by its opposition to the voice of the majority of the people and the states, put the Constitution afloat, God send them safe out of the storm they may raise."[104] By Saturday, the Federalists were charged with "threatening war" and rumors were to the effect that "the people of Philadelphia had seized upon the public arms . . ."[105] The politics of faction threatened to escalate into a violent revolutionary situation.

Nothing offered greater proof of this than the ultimatum that the republicans had presented to the obstructionists. Jefferson wrote James Monroe on Sunday, describing the course of events thus far. He revealed the intentions of the faction that opposed his election: "If they could have been permitted to pass a law for putting the government into the hands of an officer, they would

103 Eyewitness.

104 Baltimore (Md.) *American and Daily Advertiser*, 14 Feb. 1801. John Adams in later years would express his feelings on the violent expectations of the time. Writing of the turbulent events leading up to Jefferson's election, he stated: "Let me repeat to you once more, sir, the faction was dizzy. Their brains turned round. They know not, they saw not the precipice upon which they stood. . . . To dispatch all in a few words, a *civil war* was expected." John Adams to James Lloyd, 6 Feb. 1815, *Works*, Vol. X, p. 115.

105 *Porcupine's Works*, op. cit., Vol. XII, p. 190.

certainly have prevented an election." Knowing this, the republicans had made the ultimate threat: dissolution of the Union, revolution, and civil war. Jefferson's own measured words corroborate Samuel Tyler's suggestion as well as Albert Gallatin's plan; and his use of the plural indicates that a consensus had been gained:

> We thought it best to declare openly and firmly, one and all, that the day such an act was passed, *the Middle States would arm,* and that no such usurpation, *even for a single day, should be submitted to.* This first shook them; and they were completely alarmed at the resource for which we declared, to wit, a *convention to reorganize the government, and to amend it.* The very word convention gives them the horrors, . . . in the present democratical spirit of America . . .[106]

Indeed, Jefferson and his colleagues had thrown the fear of revolution into the minds and hearts of the Federalists: "In the present democratical spirit of America" was nothing less than a recognition that the spirit of revolution, like that of 1776, had now come alive. The threat was as desperate a gamble as men might make with their security and the peace of the body politic. It was not a statement that could be made and then abandoned. Its very logic meant that once uttered, the republicans must be willing to see it through to the end. But it had become necessary, even more so because of John Adams' seeming indifference to the plight of the nation. Jefferson had found the situation so desperate the day before that he personally "called on Mr. Adams." He recorded in *The Anas* that:

> I observed to him, that a very dangerous experiment was then in contemplation, to defeat the Presidential election by an act of Congress declaring the right of the Senate to name a President of the Senate, to devolve on him the government during any interregnum; that such a measure would probably produce resistance by force, and incalculable consequences, which it would be in his

---

[106] Jefferson to James Monroe, 15 Feb. 1801, *Writings*, Vol. X, p. 201. Italics mine.

power to prevent by negativing such an act. He seemed to think such an act justifiable, and observed, it was in my power to fix the election by a word in an instant, by declaring I would not turn out the federal officers, nor put down the navy, nor spunge the national debt. Finding his mind made up as to the *usurpation* of the government by the President of the Senate, I urged it no further, observed the world must judge as to myself of the future by the past . . .[107]

Adams, like Hamilton, was intent on gaining assurances from Jefferson that he would protect "the system." Jefferson in his turn was determined not be bound by any agreement whatsoever. He had, about the same time, made similar declarations to Dwight Foster of Massachusetts and to Gouverneur Morris, both of whom had presented him with Hamilton's original conditions. Thus a consensus among the Federalists seemed to have been arrived at for the first time in more than a year: unless Jefferson agreed to their three basic conditions, they were willing to risk plunging the country into civil war.

In the maneuvering that had taken place since the beginning of the election, Jefferson and his colleagues had done everything in their power to convince the Federalists that their opposition to the government had been based on principles, and they were not about to change that ground. But as the balloting continued day after day and the tension grew, solicitations were made to Jefferson and his colleagues with increasing fervor.

With Jefferson spurning offers of compromise by the President, Foster of Massachusetts, and Gouverneur Morris, a solution had to be found that was independent of the solid phalanxes of both republican and Federalist factions. Hamilton had written James A. Bayard of Delaware a long and devastating letter regarding the character and diabolical intentions of Burr.[108] Thus Bayard, even

---

[107] *The Anas, Writings*, Vol. I, p. 452. At the same time Adams and Hamilton, Jefferson wrote, wished "the will of the people" respected. Jefferson to Thomas Mann Randolph, 23 Feb. 1801, *Writings*, Vol. XVIII, p. 233.

[108] Hamilton to James A. Bayard, 16 Jan. 1801, *Works of Alexander Hamilton*, op. cit., Vol. X, pp. 412–19. See Appendix A below.

though he may have been disposed toward his Federalist colleagues and their attempts to gain concessions from Jefferson,
probably did not wish to see Burr elevated to the presidency. A
mutual friend of Bayard and Jefferson's had written to the latter in
late December:

> I do not know what intrigues under various shapes may be going
> on at headquarters [Washington] or what influence . . . the
> Federal Partizans, may have on the mind of my friend Bayard
> (I call him my friend, widely as we differ in our political course,
> with great truth and justice for in private life I have never met
> with a better) when he arrives, but I have lately heard him say
> repeatedly and in company, that in case of an equality of votes
> between yourself and Col. Burr he should not hesitate to vote for
> you and he has spoken frequently of the dignified impartiality
> observed by you in your conduct as President of the Senate with
> much approbation.[109]

At the same time that the republicans were entertaining their
hopes for his eventual defection, Bayard was apparently making
overtures to Edward Livingston and General Samuel Smith to gain
the states of New York and Maryland. Despite this, James A.
Bayard had become the one person in whom the Jeffersonians
believed they might place some hope. But Bayard had voted with
the obstructionists for the first five days of balloting and there was
little sign that he would change. The republicans' hopes were revived on Saturday the fourteenth, when it was rumored that Bayard
had informed his colleagues he intended to break the tie and vote
for Jefferson. The intrigue had deepened. Sometime on Friday
Bayard "applied to" John Nicholas of Virginia to gain assurance
for "certain points of the future administration [that] could be
understood and arranged with Mr. Jefferson." Bayard "proposed"
that Nicholas "consult Mr. Jefferson. This he declined, and said he
could do no more than give the assurance of his own opinion as to
the sentiments and designs of Mr. Jefferson and his friends. I told

---

[109] Caesar Rodney to Jefferson, 28 Dec. 1800, Jefferson MS., Lib. Cong.
See Borden, *The Federalism of James A. Bayard*, op. cit., p. 87.

him that was not sufficient—that we should not surrender without better terms. Upon this we separated; and I shortly after met with General Smith."[110]

Despite Bayard's refusal to surrender, a door had been opened. It was obvious that Bayard had now placed himself in a position to bargain with the opposition. In addition to the conditions originally laid down by Hamilton, he had asked for the continuance of two men in federal offices.[111] These were points of negotiation which, it seemed, Jefferson would never accept. Realizing this, one of Jefferson's supporters took it upon himself to change the balance of power. That evening (Friday), General Samuel Smith of Maryland added to the confusion and, by a strategy that smacked of not a little deception, initiated a new round of negotiations with Bayard. Speaking, as he claimed, in Jefferson's name,[112] he led the Delawarean to believe that he would speak to the leader of the republicans and gain assurances on each of his points. "The next day (Saturday) [I] told him that Mr. Jefferson had said he did not think that such offices ought to be dismissed on political grounds only . . ." This seemed an adequate assurance to Bayard, who then replied, according to Smith, "We will give the vote on Monday . . ."[113] But the republicans were destined for disappointment, for on Monday the sixteenth, Bayard maintained the solid front of the Federalist faction.[114]

The situation over the weekend had thus become one of total constitutional crisis. With more than a hundred thousand people in the capital city and rumors flying to the effect that others from

[110] Davis, *Memoirs of Aaron Burr*, op. cit., Vol. II, pp. 130–31.

[111] Ibid., p. 133.

[112] Ibid., pp. 135–37. This led to a controversy in which Jefferson later categorically denied any conversation between himself and Smith on the subject. See *The Anas, Writings*, Vol. I, p. 450.

[113] Davis, *Memoirs of Aaron Burr*, op. cit., Vol. II, pp. 133–37. General Smith's testimony was given in a deposition to the Supreme Court of the State of New York, *James Gillespie v. Abraham Smith*, 15 April 1806.

[114] For an explanation of Bayard's maneuvering, I am indebted to Morton Borden and his account in *The Federalism of James A. Bayard*, op. cit., pp. 87–96.

major cities were preparing to march on Washington, it was expected that the government might fall at any hour.

> . . . as the news of what was happening in the capitol spread through the country, the discontent of the moderates of both parties increased with rumors spreading that the Federalists' tenacity was aimed at some act of violence or usurpation such as using their 22-to-12 majority in the Senate to name a Federalist member of that body President ad interim, which would have been a violation of the Constitution—began to arm and organize themselves into companies for the purpose of marching on Washington to seize it from those who proposed the usurpation of government, as well as from the usurpers.
>
> Within a few days, they formed a very numerous body at Baltimore. The same movement took place in Virginia and in the more distant cities, like Philadelphia and New York . . .[115]

A sense of deep crisis gripped the capital. On Monday the specter of violence appeared: "The lobby of the chamber of the House of Representatives was cleared in consequence of the threats of some violent persons who had been stationed there."[116] Yet even this failed to deter the Federalists who again voted for Burr. At the close of the balloting on Monday evening, the tally remained Jefferson eight, Burr six.

Bayard's failure to respond to Smith's solicitation had shaken the republicans and they became grim. Amidst the confusion it

[115] Eyewitness. The eyewitness's testimony was later corroborated by Alexander Hamilton. ". . . it is believed to be an alarming fact that, while the question of presidential election was pending in the House of Representatives, parties were organizing in several of the cities in the event of there being no election, to cut off the leading Federalists and seize the government." Hamilton to James A. Bayard, 6 April 1802, *Works of Alexander Hamilton*, op. cit., Vol. X, p. 436. Another writer, Ezra Witter, spoke of "the threatened invasion of New England from the middle States, particularly Pennsylvania, unless they [the Federalists] withdrew their support from Mr. Burr. . . . Much was said of the number, and valor, and determination of Governor McKean's militia . . ." Ezra Witter, *Two Sermons on the Party Spirit and Divided State of the Country, Civil and Religious* (Springfield, Mass., 9 April 1801), p. 11.

[116] *Porcupine's Works*, op. cit., Vol. XII, p. 190.

was learned that "two Federalist members of the House received notes threatening them with death if they did not vote according to the will of the people. During the night, stones were thrown against the houses where other representatives of the same party were living, and there is no doubt whatsoever that their lives [were] in danger . . ."[117]

The mad confusion that followed these events created panic among the Federalists. One element that added to their uncertainty was the location of Burr. No one had seen him, talked to him, or even knew if he was still in Baltimore where he had allegedly gone. Bayard had called a caucus earlier that weekend to inquire if anyone knew when Burr might arrive. When no one replied, Bayard made a statement that "the opposite party—would persevere to the 4th of March . . . undismayed by whatever disasters might result." Therefore, without the personal assurance or even the knowledge of the intentions of the man he was supporting, "he could not consent that the 4th of March should arrive without a chief magistrate."[118] The failure of Burr to appear on the scene the following day increased the apprehensions of the Federalists. It was not certain that he ever would appear. But what was becoming a virtual certainty was the dissolution of the government.

The republicans had successfully convinced the Federalist faction that they would not relent and would see a dissolution of the government before conceding to their demands. This, coupled with their own threats of organizing a revolutionary convention, made the more rational members among them realize that continued opposition meant the constitution would be destroyed.

---

[117] Eyewitness. Ezra Witter noted "the threats and menaces, lately addressed to several members of Congress, because they voted for Mr. Burr instead of Mr. Jefferson, as President of the United States." *Two Sermons on the Party Spirit* . . . , op. cit., p. 11.

[118] *The Correspondence and Miscellanies of the Hon. John Cotton Smith*, ed., William W. Andrews (New York, 1847), pp. 219–20. The description of the caucus was made by Smith.

The pressures that built up within the Federalist ranks were described by the one man who, having done everything in his power to maintain his loyalty to party, finally cracked under the strain. In what was a revelation of the lengths to which faction would go in destroying the republic, James Bayard of Delaware described the last-minute pandemonium that gripped the extremists when he finally decided to change his vote. His rationale was a devastating blow against the excesses of party and faction and a tribute to what Jefferson and his fellow republicans had been claiming all along: the constitution, the republic, and republicans were inseparable. Bayard thus writes:

> When it was perfectly ascertained that Burr could not be elected I avowed that the only remaining object was to exclude Jefferson at the expense of the Constitution. According to an arrangement I had made with Maryland I came forward and avowed my intentions of putting an end to the contest. The clamor was prodigious. The reproaches vehement. I procured a meeting—explained myself and declared an inflexible intention to run no risk of the constitution. I told them that if necessary I had determined to become the victim of the measure. They might attempt to direct the vengeance of the Party against me but the danger of being a sacrifice could not shake my resolution. Some were appeased: others furious, and we broke up in confusion. A second meeting was no happier in its effect.[119]

The end came amidst a tremendous amount of confusion. The Federalists, frenetic in their desire to achieve agreement, held several caucuses which saw their unity shattered. By two o'clock on the afternoon of the seventeenth, they could no longer sustain their support for Burr. Bayard, sensing that the danger of delaying even one more ballot might plunge the nation into violence, declared his intentions of changing Delaware's vote. "The manner of the last ballot was arranged but a few minutes before the ballot was

[119] James A. Bayard to Samuel Bayard, 22 Feb. 1801, "Papers of James A. Bayard, 1796–1815," ed. Elizabeth Donnan, *Annual Report of the American Historical Association for the Year 1913*, Vol. II, pp. 131–32.

given."[120] The final vote was Jefferson ten, Burr four, and two states, Delaware and South Carolina, abstaining. Thomas Jefferson had finally acquired the necessary number to become President *constitutionally.*

Thus ended the deadlock and the threat of civil war. And in the words of the eyewitness, "Such has been the last effort of a faction which has governed the United States since Gen. Washington retired from office . . ."[121] The Revolution of 1800 had been achieved without the violence and bloodshed that appeared to engulf it. Jefferson's and Madison's theory of revolution had been validated in the final outcome of the election. Through their own form of "electoral caesarism," i.e., the peaceful organizing of a constitutional majority of the people, they had achieved what no other group of revolutionaries had gained in the entire course of western political history: a change in the power of government, from one party to another, without a tremendous cost in violence and bloodshed. Indeed, they had set a precedent that could be followed by the world as well as their own nation for all generations to come: the possibility of a permanent, peaceful, constitutional revolution.

But what was just as important, at least to Jefferson and the members of his generation, was that the American Revolution of 1776 had finally been consolidated. Fifteen days after the nearly catastrophic election in the House, Jefferson gave his Inaugural Address. Referring to the principles of that American Revolution, he said:

> These principles form the bright constellation which has gone before us and guided our steps through an age of revolution and reformation. The wisdom of our sages and blood of our heroes have been devoted to their attainment. They should be the creed of our political faith, the text of civic instruction, the touchstone by which to try the services of those we trust; and should we wander from them in moments of error or of alarm, let us hasten

120 James A. Bayard to Hamilton, 8 March 1801, *Works of Alexander Hamilton,* ed. J. C. Hamilton, 7 vols. (New York, 1851), Vol. VI, p. 523.
121 Eyewitness.

to retrace our steps and to regain the road which alone leads to peace, liberty and safety.[122]

Certainly he had regained the road by retracing the steps of the American Revolution and resurrecting the Spirit of Seventy-six. By appealing to the people he had literally renewed its promise. Indeed, he would later claim, and justly so, that "the Revolution of 1800 was as real a revolution in the principles of our government as that of 1776 was in its form; not effected indeed by the sword, as that, but by the rational and peaceable instrument of reform, the suffrage of the people."[123]

[122] "Inaugural Address," 4 March 1801, *Messages and Papers of the Presidents*, op. cit., Vol. I, p. 312.

[123] Jefferson to Spencer Roane, 6 Sept. 1819, *Writings*, Vol. XV, p. 212.

Epilogue

Twenty days after Jefferson's Inaugural Address, John Adams penned a letter to his successor that captured the new mood and spirit of the nation: "This part of the Union is in a state of perfect Tranquility and I see nothing to obscure your prospect of a quiet and prosperous Administration, which I heartily wish you."[1] In this short compass, John Adams paid tribute both to the Revolution of 1800 and to Thomas Jefferson. It was a tribute to the revolution because it underlined the remarkable achievement of a constitutional change of power without violence and bloodshed, a triumph of reason over armed might. The fact that a revolution had occurred and that a nation remained calm, even devoted to its institutions, was unprecedented in western political history. It was also an affirmation of Jefferson's conciliatory address which did more to mollify the majority of Adams' supporters than anyone dared dream. Jefferson's speech had been, above all, a repudiation of representation that had not been seen since the days of the former President. It appeared to many then, in the calm that followed, that both Adams and Jefferson had symbolically extended the olive branch.

There were many others who agreed with Adams. George Cabot wrote a similar observation to Rufus King: "We are all tranquil, as

[1] John Adams to Jefferson, 24 March 1801, *Letters*, Vol. I, p. 264.

they say at Paris, after a Revolution."[2] Cabot, one of Hamilton's staunchest supporters, had recognized the fact that a revolution had taken place. Another Hamiltonian, Robert Troup, placed an ideological stamp on the achievement: "Democracy has obtained at our late election a complete triumph over us. The Revolution in the public mind has even astonished the leaders of that party."[3] His was a confession that the old aristocratic form, the elitism of the Federalists, had been replaced by a new democratic appeal to the people. Government was to have a new tone and a new kind of representation that had not been seen since the days of the Revolution. Matthew Davis, another of the active participants in New York, described the revolution thus: ". . . the Revolution of 1800 . . . resulted in the overthrow of the federal party . . . ," and in "the election of Mr. Jefferson to the presidency."[4] And John Quincy Adams, noting the political force of the revolutionary movement, stated that if the Jeffersonians had so wished, it could "have overthrown Washington's administration as it did that of his successor acting upon its principles."[5]

Thus the Jeffersonians referred to their achievement as "the Civil Revolution of Eighteen Hundred," or, as Martin Van Buren, a youthful republican at the time and a future President, put it: "A name given to it by the victors on the assumption that, although the weapons were different, the principles which were involved in it and the spirit which achieved the triumph were akin to those which distinguished the Revolution by the sword."[6]

James Madison saw the revolutionary achievement in the same light and even speculated why he believed it had been successful. Expressing his confidence in the elected representatives of the

[2] George Cabot to Rufus King, 20 March 1801, *Life and Correspondence of Rufus King,* op. cit., Vol. III, p. 408.

[3] Robert Troup to Rufus King, 22 May 1801, ibid., p. 454.

[4] Davis, *Memoirs of Aaron Burr,* op. cit., Vol. II, p. 66.

[5] Quoted in Van Buren, *Inquiry into the Origin and Course of Political Parties in the United States,* op. cit., p. 259.

[6] Ibid., p. 246.

nation, his words are nearly identical to those of Jefferson written in France at the time of the American Constitutional Convention:

> It was thought not probable that the phalanx would hold out against the general revolt of its partisans out of doors, and without any military force to abet usurpation. How fortunate that the latter has been withheld! And what a lesson to America and the world is given by the efficacy of the public will, when there is no army to be turned against it.[7]

Madison's conclusion was a repudiation of force in the politics of any nation and an affirmation of the electoral process as a means of securing future revolutions.

But the historical achievement of producing a revolution through the ballot box and then ensuring that it would become the dominant mode of political change for the future was not shared by everyone, especially Jefferson's most bitter critics. One of these, Fisher Ames, described the revolution thus: "Foreigners who examine events with an eye of scrutiny, will not hesitate to foretell, that the change is no little cabinet scene, where one minister comes into power and another goes out, but a great moral *revolution*, proceeding from the vices and the passions of men, shifting officers today, that measures, and principles, and systems, may be shifted tomorrow."[8] Indeed, Fisher Ames had caught the essence of Jefferson's scheme: power could now change hands along with men, principles, and systems.

Yet Ames, who had anticipated this revolutionary development two years before, did not believe the Jeffersonians would ultimately maintain the peaceful nature of their revolution. In a series of essays he addressed himself not to the "calm" that had made its appearance, but to what he believed was the inevitable course of revolutions in history: "The question, therefore, seems to be, how

[7] Madison to Jefferson, 28 Feb. 1801, *The Letters and Other Writings of James Madison*, op. cit., Vol. II, p. 171.

[8] Ames, "Falkland, No. 1," published in *The Palladium*, Feb. 1801, *Works of Fisher Ames*, op. cit., p. 137.

far we shall probably travel in the revolutionary road; and whether there is any stopping place, any hope of taking breath, as we run towards the bottomless pit, into which the revolutionary fury is prone to descend. . . . Events may happen to baffle the schemes of Jacobinism; and if New England should not be sleepy or infatuated, of which there is unhappily, great danger, our adversaries will never be able to push the works of mischief to its consummation."[9]

Fearing that the Jeffersonians might attempt to accomplish just that, i.e., their true revolutionary ends, Ames went on, in another essay, to point out why the revolution had taken place. In a few lines he captured the essence of the old elitist Federalist viewpoint and described the role that faction had played:

> The Washington and Adams administration proceeded on the basis, that the government was organized, and clothed with power to rule according to the constitution; the democratic theorists insist, that the people, meaning themselves, have a good right to rule the government.
>
> By exciting the people to govern or to oppose the government, these leaders well know, that those who are thus irregularly permitted to act in their behalf, will engross all their power. Against this natural propensity to faction, a regular and vigorous government is the proper and only adequate security. Of course for that very reason, such a government will be hateful to faction, and will be, if possible, usurped and destroyed by it. For such usurpation the nature of liberty excites the desire, and affords the pretext and the means.
>
> Accordingly, we have seen a faction, bitter against the constitution in its passage, against the government in its administering the laws, and the magistrates and officers intrusted with the execution of them. They have struggled for the mastery, and after a persevering effort for twelve years, they have succeeded in the late great election. Will this party acquiesce, if the mere change of *men* should be the only fruit of their victory? No, the nature of faction itself, our observation of jacobinism in France, our knowledge of jacobin characters at home, forbid the idea.[10]

[9] Ames, "No Revolutionist," *Works of Fisher Ames*, op. cit., pp. 228–29.
[10] Ames, "Falkland, No. 3," *Works of Fisher Ames*, pp. 148–49.

This was a pessimistic view and undoubtedly there were many who worried that the politics of faction would ultimately plunge the nation into violent revolution. Said one writer:

It is to be hoped that the late change in our Federal Administration, may serve to abate the violence of that party rage, which threatens our ruin. Should those in *opposition* to the Revolution, find, as is most devoutly to be wished, that the change does not prove injurious to the nation—and should those in *favor* of it, find, as we have every reason to believe, their extravagant expectations frustrated—that the millennium is not immediately ushered in, and much the same natural and moral evils continue to scourge our country and the world, which existed before—when these things are discovered, it is hoped, that the inveteracy of party will in some measure subside, and that less opposition will be made, in future, whether a Federal or Antifederal pilot guide the bark of state. If this should not be the case, if party spirit should continue and increase, the most calamitous consequences are to be apprehended. Probably a civil war and the effusion of much blood may follow.[11]

Ezra Witter spoke for many, especially in New England, yet he had also explained one reason why the Revolution of 1800 had been so revolutionary. Certainly it was no "millennium"; but it was an unprecedented event in the history of man. Further, it promised a kind of millennium if only men would learn its lesson in their future political affairs. It held out an example that man could neutralize the revolutionary violence of faction and party spirit. Jefferson fully realized this and took pains in his address to signal the new approach to politics he had inaugurated. The phrase "we are all republicans—we are all federalists" was his way of answering the fears of those like Witter and stating his intentions to suppress the spirit of faction and party completely.[12] Jefferson had actually written John Dickinson, an old revolutionary patriot, two days after taking office: "I hope to see shortly a perfect consolidation, to effect which, nothing shall be spared on

---

[11] Ezra Witter, *Two Sermons on the Party Spirit* . . . , op. cit., p. 14.
[12] Jefferson to James Monroe, 7 March 1801, *Writings*, Vol. X, pp. 218–19.

my part, short of the abandonment of the principles of our revolution."[13] Thus the ideal that Jefferson held of the return to the principles of the American Revolution also meant a return to the one or non-party state.

Benjamin Rush likewise recognized Jefferson's intentions and he wrote the new President a week after he had taken office:

> You have opened a new era by your speech on the 4th of March in the history of the United States. Never have I seen the public mind more generally or more agreeably affected by any publication. Old friends who had been separated by party names and a *supposed* difference of *principle* in politics for many years shook hands with each other immediately after reading it, and discovered, for the first time, that they had differed in *opinion* only, about the best means of promoting the interest of their common country. It would require a page to contain the names of all the citizens (formerly called Federalists) who have spoken in the highest terms of your speech.[14]

Jefferson had accomplished what no other American, even the great Washington, had been able to do: crush party spirit. Moreover, the "new era" Jefferson had begun brought citizens together who had been artificially separated for years. The old revolutionary's hunch that a majority of the people had been "republicans" "all the time" was correct. He had attempted an experiment out of which he hoped to establish republican principles on a new and permanent foundation. He thus wrote "a long disquisition on politics" shortly after taking office:

> We can no longer say there is nothing new under the sun. For this whole chapter in the history of man is new. The great extent of our republic is new. Its sparse habitation is new. The mighty wave of public opinion which has rolled over it is new. But the most pleasing novelty is, its so quietly subsiding over such an extent of surface to its true level again. The order and good sense displayed in this recovery from delusion, and in the momentous

[13] Jefferson to John Dickinson, 6 March 1801, ibid., p. 217.
[14] Benjamin Rush to Jefferson, 12 March 1801, *Letters of Benjamin Rush*, ed. Lyman H. Butterfield, 2 vols. (Princeton, N.J., 1951), Vol. II, p. 831.

crisis which lately arose, really bespeak a strength of character in our nation which augurs well for the duration of our republic; and I am much better satisfied now of its stability than I was before it was tried.[15]

The idea of a "new order" of things was shared by Federalists and republicans generally, an accurate measure of the fact that a true revolution in people's minds had taken place. Tunis Wortman, perhaps the most gifted writer among them, next to Jefferson, summed up the attitude of nearly everyone who expressed optimism regarding the character of the revolution:

> The struggle is over. Despotism has expired. A new order of things commences. A brighter aera dawns upon our hopes—Liberty is triumphant. Our independence is secured,—and our glorious Revolution established forever.[16]

"To establish a beginning and to retrieve the past," says Jacques Ellul, "is the hallmark of a successful revolution." Indeed, it is a statement not too different from Polybius' observation recorded in the first chapter: "The beginning is not merely half of the whole, but reaches out toward the end." Both, in fact, were true of the Revolution of 1800. A new order. A centuries-old struggle between liberty and despotism issuing in the securing of the American Revolution and independence. Finally, the establishment of a new tradition: a bloodless Glorious Revolution in America in which the constitution was renewed.[17] These were ancient themes that

---

[15] Jefferson to Dr. Joseph Priestley, 21 March 1801, *Writings*, Vol. X, p. 229.

[16] Tunis Wortman, *An Address to the Republican Citizens of New York on the Inauguration of Thomas Jefferson* (New York, 4 March 1801), p. 6.

[17] In a description of revolution in the Roman era, Caleb D'Anvers made a case for the type of revolution that Jefferson had accomplished in 1800. "The Romans had been so liberal in bestowing the Rights of Citizens on Strangers, that the Power of their Elections began to fall into such Hands as the Constitution had not intended to trust with them. Quintus Fabius saw the growing Evil, and, being Censor, he took the opportunity, confined all these new Electors into four Tribes; put it out of their power to turn the elections as they had done, whilst their Number were divided among all the Tribes, freed

reached far back into history and at the same time were capable of producing a new beginning.

This "new era" meant that the possibilities of a counterrevolution had disappeared in the face of what would be an uninterrupted series of republican administrations for the next twenty-four years. In that sense, Jefferson had simply noted that the original struggle he had engaged in was finally over—after twenty-five years. At the same time, identifying the Revolution of 1800 with the original principles of the American Revolution ensured a continuity of America's future with its past. In this unique way, Jefferson had preserved the principles of the American Revolution.

Jefferson, Rush, Madison, Davis, Troup, Cabot, Ames, McHenry, both Adamses, Witter, Wortman, and, as we shall see, even Hamilton, all recognized the Revolution of 1800 and its remarkable historical achievement. The list could go on, but this written testimony by the principal political actors of the period reveals the extent to which they realized they had participated in an unusual political phenomenon. For what the Revolution of 1800 signified was the herald of a new political development for man: the successful translation of Jefferson's lifelong study of revolutions into a theory and praxis of permanent peaceful constitutional revolution.

The reasons for its being a true revolution will, upon reflection, be evident. One of the first was Jefferson's belief that he was acting on the principles of freedom, seeking to liberate his fellow man by political means. He constructed a viable politics of revolution that would not endanger freedom, with the understanding that freedom would be better preserved in a country that avoided unnecessary bloodshed. This had certainly been the lesson of the

---

his Country from this Danger; restored the Constitution, according to the true Intent and Meaning of it; and obtained, by universal Suffrage, the title of Maximus. If a spirit like this had prevailed among us, at the time [1688] we speak of, something like it ought to have been done; for the *Revolution* was in many Instances, and it ought to have been so in all, one of those *Renewals of Our Constitution*, that we have often mentioned." Caleb D'Anvers of Gray's Inn, Esq., *The Craftsman* (London, 1737), Vol. XIII, p. 135.

French Revolution for him and his contemporaries. And inasmuch as the Revolution of 1800 was a liberating experience from the violence of old, Jefferson had made a novel contribution at the level of the nation-state to world revolutionary theory. Henceforth, it would be possible to change a government's character, principles, form, and system by peaceful means.

Tom Paine had written in 1795 that "the revolutions that are now spreading themselves in the world have their origin . . . [in] a conflict between the representative system founded on the rights of the people, and the hereditary system founded in usurpation. . . . No other distinction reaches the whole of the principle."[18] Indeed, given the rhetoric of the period 1790 to 1800, it is difficult to imagine a better description of what Jefferson and his colleagues believed they were struggling, in principle, to accomplish. Their frequent assertion that they were in fact opposing a set of republican principles to those of monarchy or quasi-monarchy was an integral part of their revolutionary theory. Operating on that assumption, they could not help but believe that when the Revolution of 1800 was accomplished, they had secured the blessings of the American Revolution.

But there was another order of accomplishment in terms of revolutionary theory for which Jefferson could be proud: the successful fragmenting of power as a revolutionary goal. Jefferson realized that the result of most revolutions (and this is uniformly true of the nineteenth and twentieth centuries) was a consolidation of the power of the state. The consequence was that, paradoxically, a nation became less able to maximize its individual freedom *after* a revolution than *before*, and, instead, increased those very forms of despotism that enabled the state ultimately to destroy freedom.

In Jefferson's eyes the most significant lesson of the French Revolution was that a despotic state might follow revolution itself. Revolution then would become responsible not for an expansion

18 "Dissertation on First Principles of Government," *Paine*, Vol. 9, pp. 244–45.

of liberty, but for despotism. He therefore realized that the revolution must be made on the level of principle and against administrations and individuals, while simultaneously preserving those institutions that were congenial to liberty. Evil ministers, even usurping tyrants, might be personally attacked, but the forms of government that corresponded to the principles of a constitutional republic must be maintained. As he looked around him he saw republican principles disregarded in favor of authority, power, and military force. He viewed the centralization of authority in the presidency, the monarchist tendencies of Hamilton, and the expressions of many for a more powerful and forceful government as the signs of a counterrevolution.

Jefferson's notion of history was too impregnated with the expansion of liberty in his lifetime for this to come true without a struggle. For this reason he was determined to mount a revolution against the faction in power. His struggle was truly one that *negated* the most powerful forces of his time and one that would continue unabated to the present day. Accordingly, he continued that struggle until he produced a revolution that decentralized the power of the state and made it more useful in the eyes of individuals. Every plan that Jefferson proposed, every policy that he adopted, every principle he said he stood for, was calculated to achieve a dual purpose: preserve liberty and reduce the power of the state.

Another integral feature adopted to Jefferson's theory was the method of organizing the nation's polity, viz., federalism. This offered an opportunity to Jefferson that no single method of state organization had previously recognized; to wit, that the states would reserve to themselves certain critical powers of government, limit the power of the central government, and thus deprive it of any function or source of power that might enable it to usurp and/or control the power of the states. Thus, when the states instituted a change in principles, men, administration, or form, and then comprised a majority, they would have effected a revolution in opinion as well as in the constitutional form of the state. This was the spirit of Jefferson's idea of "the best government governs least," and it ensured, at least for Jefferson's generation, that a counterrevolution led by a faction in control of the national government would not succeed.

This is not to imply that Jefferson entertained a vision of the "withering away of the State." Such a Marxian notion would never have been accepted by him, especially one connected with the "dictatorship of the proletariat." Jefferson would have seen that as an unresolvable paradox and a guarantee that the latter would prevail. If anything, Jefferson wished to make it possible for a state to be constantly vulnerable to revolution. For he believed that only through the fear of revolution could a powerful executive be held in check and the liberties of the people continually respected. Jefferson may have intuited Lord Acton's dictum that "power corrupts and absolute power corrupts absolutely." For every political form he cherished was one designed to prevent that axiom from becoming a truism. Through the representative system, checks and balances, separation of powers, rotation in office, and the principle of federalism, the system was designed to maintain power in the hands of the people and not the state. Jefferson's Revolution of 1800 was an acting out of those constitutional principles.

Another theoretical point that emerged in the conduct of the Revolution of 1800 was Jefferson's emphasis upon constitutional machinery. This was a tribute to his and Madison's belief that the only means by which liberty could be preserved was through a strict adherence to constitutional guarantees. The notion that "revolutionary necessity" allowed a faction to abandon its principles, i.e., as Paine noted, to permit itself *"discretionary exercise of power* . . . in the commencement of a revolution," was not accepted by Jefferson. By meeting the standard of constitutional principles at every level of strategy—whether it was the theoretical Virginia and Kentucky Resolutions or the Constitutional Convention recommended by the republicans in the face of a virtual dissolution of the state—Jefferson and his followers avoided the trap of setting a precedent that violated either the spirit or the letter of the fundamental law. This adherence to the law of the constitution had its effect in a most fundamental way: it caused men to change their minds regarding the new regime, to recognize that it would honor a standard imposed upon all citizens. Had the same strict adherence to the constitution been true of the French revolutionaries, Paine asserted, violence would have been prevented, "the nation would then have had a bond of union, and every individual would have known the line of conduct he was to follow."[19] Thus gaining support from a majority of all the factions in the state was a measure of the success of the Revolution of 1800.

The fact is, real revolutions do not occur through individuals solely, nor through single acts of prolonged conspiracy. They occur when the power of government is in the process of disintegration, when factionalism has so paralyzed and torn apart the ruling authorities and when colliding interests have produced such instability that the regime no longer has the power to govern. When this occurs, as it certainly did in the closing years of the Adams administration, men must be willing to organize and achieve power. Only then do we see those signs that mark the successful revolutionary from the rebel: the possession of organizational skills and the ability to concretize the expressed ideals and aims of a revolution.

Jefferson and Madison possessed these skills in abundance. Witness their ability to produce and sustain a political organization over time, a "second city" whose dynamism had been missing from American politics for more than a generation. Witness their ability to take advantage of the forms of the American Revolution of 1776, to continue that struggle until its ideas and principles were substantively realized. This can be seen in their struggle to change people's minds through the use of the press, newspapers, pamphlets, circulars, the committees of correspondence, the transformation of the Sons of Liberty into Democratic societies and Jacobin clubs, the various constitutional resolutions promulgated through county governments and committees, and the use of state

19 Ibid., pp. 276–77.

assemblies to communicate alarm through their legislatures. A similar turn was given to issues: the charges of monarchy, corruption of the constitution and the administration, the arguments against specific bills such as the Alien and Sedition Acts, taxes, the army, the common law, the charges against evil and corrupt ministers that amounted to a conspiracy against liberty—all had their precedents twenty-five years earlier.

The final tribute to Jefferson's revolutionary organizational skills, however, lies not in his ability merely to imitate what had occurred before. Rather it lies in his imaginative use of a device that only he had seen: viz., "Electoral Caesarism." This revolutionary concept transformed the nature of revolution from a military endeavor and one that ended historically with the rule of a clique by force, to that of an appeal to the people to organize around a set of principles and values in opposition to a present government.[20]

Jefferson, through a series of new devices that spread his ideas to an audience of unprecedented size, convinced the people to translate their opposition into votes and then into a new administration affirming new principles. In this sense Jefferson succeeded in accomplishing what every revolutionary must do in order to be effective: he must conceive a strategy that will enable *the people* to negate the present or existing system. By a conversion of military to peaceful means, Jefferson produced a strategy and an organization whose means could be identified in spirit and prin-

[20] In the end even Hamilton had been convinced by Jefferson's success that the future lay in a more democratic kind of organization. In a letter to James A. Bayard he emphasized that in the future the Federalists must rely on "publications. Wherever it can be done, and there is a press, clubs should be formed to meet once a week, read the newspapers and prepare essays, paragraphs, etc. 2d. The use of all lawful means in *concert* to promote the election of *fit* men; a lively correspondence must be kept up between different societies. 3d. The promoting of institutions of a . . . useful nature in the management of Federalists. The populous cities ought particularly to be attended to. . . . The foregoing to be the principal engine . . ." Hamilton to James A. Bayard, 6 April 1802, *Works of Alexander Hamilton*, ed. H. C. Lodge, op. cit., Vol. X, p. 436.

ciple with the purposes of the revolution. It enabled the people to identify with the emerging democratic sentiment that was a "second city" within the body politic. In this critical way the capacity of the Jeffersonians to combine a revolutionary ideology and a dynamic political organization culminated in the first modern theory of a politics of revolution.

The leaders of the Revolution of 1800 recognized that the rhetoric of the opposition must be, by nature, democratic; that what the Federalists had seen merely as cant was in reality those forces that would dominate the rising tide of man's political affairs. With its emphasis upon individual liberty, equality, and democracy, all arrayed against elitism and the increasing power of the state, Jefferson's rhetorical skill gave voice to the hopes of men everywhere, from 1800 to the present.

That hope was really an ancient one, as old as the time when men became philosophers: it was that man might continue his struggle to form a more perfect state. Jefferson wrote in 1802: "It is impossible not to be sensible that we are acting for all mankind; that circumstances denied to others, but indulged to us, have imposed on us the duty of proving what is the degree of freedom and self-government in which a society may venture to leave its individual members."[21]

It is impossible to see Jefferson in any other light. Here was a revolutionary philosopher, *par excellence*, giving voice to his utopian dream that America, realizing her own revolutionary potential in 1800, might now provide a model for all mankind. Indeed, the essence of Jefferson's spirit and character can be found in the example he wished to set for posterity: a legacy, not of suppression, but of liberation. It was a profound belief that men everywhere wished to escape the boots and spurs of their oppressors and throw them off their backs.

This utopian revolutionary vision, a dream for all time, was caught in a sentence by one of Jefferson's supporters in the mid-

---

[21] Jefferson to Dr. Joseph Priestley, 19 June 1802, *Writings*, Vol. X, pp. 324–25.

1790s. And for this writer, of all the commentary that has been written about the man and his times, it is the one statement that has stood alone, capturing the essence of Jefferson, Madison, and the American Revolution: "Nobody but a set of philosophical politicians ever imagined the plan of opening all the ports in the world to all the vessels in the world, of interweaving and confounding the interests of all nations, of forming the inhabitants of the earth into one vast republic, of rendering the whole family of mankind enlightened, free and happy."[22]

After the Revolution of 1800 this "plan" of a "set of philosophical politicians" could be taken seriously. For the first time in history Jefferson and his friends had proven that the reasoning faculty of man could triumph over violence and armed force. They had demonstrated, in principle, that there existed the possibility of a permanent, peaceful, constitutional revolution in the political affairs of man.

[22] Pseudonym "Franklin," *Porcupine's Works*, op. cit., Vol. II, p. 285. Identified as Alexander Dallas, founder of the Philadelphia Democratic Society.

Appendixes
and Index

Appendix A

LETTER FROM ALEXANDER HAMILTON
TO JAMES A. BAYARD

New York
Jan. 16, 1801.

I was glad to find, my dear sir, by your letter that you had not yet determined to go with the current of the federal party in the support of Mr. Burr, and that you were resolved to hold yourself disengaged till the moment of final decision. Your resolution to separate yourself in this instance from the federal party, if your conviction shall be strong of the unfitness of Mr. Burr, is certainly laudable. So much does it coincide with my ideas, that if the party shall, by supporting Mr. Burr as President, adopt him for their official chief, I shall be obliged to consider myself as an *isolated* man. It will be impossible for me to reconcile with my notions of *honor* or policy the continuing to be of a party which, according to my apprehension, will have degraded itself and the country.

I am sure, nevertheless, that the motives of many will be good, and I shall never cease to esteem the individuals, though I shall deplore a step which, I fear, experience will show to be a very fatal one. Among the letters which I receive assigning the reasons *pro* and *con* for preferring Burr to J., I observe no small exaggeration to the prejudice of the latter, and some things taken for granted as

Works of Alexander Hamilton, ed. H. C. Lodge, op. cit., Vol. X, pp. 412–19.

to the former, which are at least questionable. Perhaps myself the first, at some expense of popularity, to unfold the true character of Jefferson, it is too late for me to become his apologist; nor can I have any disposition to do it.

I admit that his politics are tinctured with fanaticism; that he is too much in earnest in his democracy; that he has been a mischievous enemy to the principal measures of our past administration; that he is crafty and persevering in his objects; that he is not scrupulous about the means of success, nor very mindful of truth, and that he is a contemptible hypocrite. But it is not true, as is alleged, that he is an enemy to the power of the Executive, or that he is for confounding all the powers in the House of Representatives. It is a fact which I have frequently mentioned, that, while we were in the administration together, he was generally for a large construction of the Executive authority and not backward to act upon it in cases which coincided with his views. Let it be added that in his theoretic ideas he has considered as improper the participations of the Senate in the Executive authority. I have more than once made the reflection that, viewing himself as the reversioner, he was solicitous to come into the possession of a good estate. Nor is it true that Jefferson is zealot enough to do any thing in pursuance of his principles which will contravene his popularity or his interest. He is as likely as any man I know to temporize—to calculate what will be likely to promote his own reputation and advantage; and the probable result of such a temper is the preservation of systems, though originally opposed, which, being once established, could not be overturned without danger to the person who did it. To my mind a true estimate of Mr. Jefferson's character warrants the expectation of a temporizing rather than a violent system. That Jefferson has manifested a culpable predilection for France is certainly true; but I think it a question whether it did not proceed quite as much from her *popularity* among us as from sentiment, and, in proportion as that popularity is diminished, his zeal will cool. Add to this that there is no fair reason to suppose him capable of being corrupted, which is a security that he will not go beyond certain limits. It is not at all improbable that under the change of circumstances Jefferson's Gallicism has considerably abated.

As to Burr these things are admitted, and indeed cannot be denied, that he is a man of *extreme* and *irregular* ambition; that he is *selfish* to a degree which excludes all social affections, and that he is decidedly *profligate*. But it is said (1) that he is *artful* and *dexterous* to accomplish his ends; (2) that he holds no pernicious theories, but is a mere *matter-of-fact* man; (3) that his very selfishness[1] is a guard against mischievous foreign predilections; (4) that his *local situation* has enabled him to appreciate the utility of our commercial and fiscal systems, and the same quality of selfishness will lead him to support and invigorate them; (5) that he is now disliked by the Jacobins; that his elevation will be a mortal stab to them, breed an invincible hatred to him, and compel him to lead on the Federalists; (6) that Burr's ambition will be checked by his good sense, by the manifest impossibility of succeeding in any scheme of usurpation, and that, if attempted, there is nothing to fear from the attempt. These topics are, in my judgment, more plausible than solid. As to the first point, the fact must be admitted, but those qualities are objections rather than recommendations, when they are under the direction of bad principles. As to the second point, too much is taken for granted. If Burr's conversation is to be credited, he is not very far from being a visionary. He has quoted to me *Connecticut* as an example of the success of the democratic theory, and as authority, I have serious doubts whether it was not a good one. It is ascertained in some instances that he has talked perfect *Godwinism*. I have myself heard him speak with applause of the French system, as unshackling the mind and leaving it to its natural energies, and I have been present when he has contended against banking systems[2] with earnestness and with the same arguments that Jefferson would use.

The truth is, that Burr is a man of a very subtle imagination,

[1] It is always very dangerous to look at the *vices* of men for good.

[2] Yet he has lately, by a trick, established a *bank*—a perfect monster in its principles, but a very convenient instrument of *profit* and *influence*.

and a mind of this make is rarely free from ingenious whimsies. Yet I admit that he has no fixed theory, and that his peculiar notions will easily give way to his interest. But is it a recommendation to have *no theory?* Can that man be a systematic or able statesman who has none? I believe not. *No general principles* will hardly work much better than erroneous ones.

As to the third point, it is certain that Burr, generally speaking, has been as warm a partisan of France as Jefferson; that he has, in some instances, shown himself to be so with passion. But if it was from calculation, who will say that his calculations will not continue him so? His selfishness,[3] so far from being an obstacle, may be a prompter. If corrupt as well as selfish, he may be a partisan for gain. If ambitious as well as selfish, he may be a partisan for the sake of aid to his views. No man has trafficked more than he in the floating passions of the multitude. Hatred to Great Britain and attachment to France, in the public mind, will naturally lead a man of his selfishness, attached to place and power, to favor France and oppose Great Britain. The Gallicism of many of our patriots is to be thus resolved, and, in my opinion, it is morally certain that Burr will continue to be influenced by this calculation.

As to the fourth point, the instance I have cited with respect to banks, proves that the argument is not to be relied on. If there was much in it, why does Chancellor Livingston maintain that we ought not to cultivate navigation, but ought to let foreigners be our carriers? France is of the opinion too, and Burr, for some reason or other, will be very apt to be of the opinion of France.

As to the fifth point, nothing can be more fallacious. It is demonstrated by recent facts[4] that Burr is *solicitous* to *keep* upon *anti-federal* ground, to avoid compromitting himself by any engagements,[5] with the Federalists. With or without such engagements, he will easily persuade his former friends that he does stand

[3] Unprincipled selfishness is more apt to seek rapid gain in disorderly practices than slow advantages from orderly systems.

[4] My letter to Mr. Morris states some of them.

[5] He trusts to their *prejudices* and *hopes* for support.

on that ground, and after their first resentment they will be glad to rally under him. In the meantime he will take care not to disoblige them, and he will always court those among them who are best fitted for tools. He will never choose to lean on good men, because he knows that they will never support his bad projects; but instead of this he will endeavor to disorganize both parties, and to form out of them a third, composed of men fitted by their characters to be conspirators and instruments of such projects.

That this will be his future conduct may be inferred from his past plan, and from the admitted quality of irregular ambition. Let it be remembered that Mr. Burr has never appeared solicitous for fame, and that great ambition, unchecked by principle or the love of glory, is an unruly tyrant, which never can keep long in a course which good men will approve. As to the last point, the proposition is against the experience of all times. Ambition without principle never was long under the guidance of good sense. Besides that, really, the force of Mr. Burr's understanding is much overrated. He is far more *cunning* than *wise*, far more *dextrous* than *able*.

(*Very, very confidential.*—In my opinion he is inferior in real ability to Jefferson. There are also facts against the supposition. It is past all doubt that he has blamed me for not having improved the situation I once was in to change the government. That when answered that this could not have been done without guilt, he replied, "Les grandes âmes se soucient peu des petits moraux"; that when told the thing was never practicable from the genius and situation of the country, he answered, "That depends on the estimate we form of the human passions, and of the means of influencing them." Does this prove that Mr. Burr would consider a scheme of usurpation as visionary?)

The truth is, with great apparent coldness he is the most sanguine man in the world. He thinks every thing possible to adventure and perseverance, and, though I believe he will fail, I think it almost certain he will attempt usurpation, and the attempt will involve great mischief. But there is one point of view which seems to me decisive. If the Anti-federalists who prevailed in the election are left to take their own man, they remain responsible, and the Federalists remain *free, united,* and without *stain,* in a situation to resist, with effect, pernicious measures. If the Federalists substitute Burr, they adopt him and become answerable for him. Whatever may be the theory of the case abroad and at *home* (for so from the beginning will be taught), Mr. Burr will become *in fact* the man of our party; and if he acts ill, we must share in the blame and disgrace. By adopting him we do all we can to reconcile the minds of the Federalists to him, and we prepare them for the effectual operation of his arts. He will doubtless gain many of them, and the Federalists will become a disorganized and contemptible party. Can there be any serious question between the policy of leaving the Anti-federalists to be answerable for the elevation of an exceptionable man, and that of adopting ourselves and becoming answerable for a man who, on all hands, is acknowledged to be a complete Catiline? 'T is enough to state the question to indicate the answer, if reason, not passion, presides in the decision.

You may communicate this, and my former letter, to discreet and confidential friends.

Appendix B

❧

LETTER FOUND
IN FRENCH ARCHIVES

The possibility that Governor George C. Wallace could have won enough electoral votes to throw the 1968 presidential election into the House of Representatives evoked understandable interest in earlier House decisions, the first of which occurred in the Jefferson-Burr contest of 1801.

Although historians have long since satisfied their curiosity as to what went on in the House that February, they seem to have overlooked an interesting eyewitness account of the event tucked away in the archives of the French Foreign Ministry. In the *"correspondance politique"* is a copy of a letter written by an anonymous informant in Washington to the French consul general (a man named Le Tombe) in New York City. Le Tombe is forwarding the letter to the minister of foreign affairs. Although the writer is not identified, he is undoubtedly French. Moreover, there is no mistaking his fervor for Thomas Jefferson.

Letombe— Philadelphia,
No. 62 17 Ventose,
year 9 of the French Republic, one and indivisible.

Citizen Minister:
I have the honor to send you promptly a copy of a letter which has just been brought to me, dated

Peter P. Hill, "Story of Jefferson: Letter Found in French Archives," Los Angeles *Times*, 27 Oct. 1968. Copyright © 1967 by *The Washington Post*.

"Washington, 24 February 1801

". . . The opening of the various state ballot boxes having taken place on the 11th in the Senate chamber, where were gathered members of the House of Representatives, the votes as counted by one member of the first chamber and by two from the second were found to be, according to the Vice President's declaration,

For:

Thomas Jefferson	73
Aaron Burr	73
John Adams	65
C. C. Pinckney	64
John Jay	1

"Upon which the Vice President declared that Thomas Jefferson and Aaron Burr being equal in number of votes, it was for the House of Representatives to determine the choice.

"One should know that the Constitution holds that, in the election of a President, each elector names two candidates, one of whom may be from the state which he represents, but not both, and without designating which one of the two he wishes to be President, this question to be decided only by the resultant plurality of votes. One should know, too, that the Constitution also rules that when two candidates shall have an equal number of votes, with a plurality over the others at the same time, the House of Representatives shall elect one of the two, voting by state, but requiring that one of the candidates must have at least nine states in order to be elected President . . .

"It was morally certain, however, prior to the 11th of the month, that the two Republican candidates were equal in votes and, consequently, the two parties have been exerting all their efforts; the Republicans to assure the election of Jefferson, and the Federalists to prevent the election by giving their votes to Col. Burr, so that neither one of the two candidates would have the required majority, and thus to destroy the effect of this election in which the Federalist Party was beaten.

"The representatives were thus reassembled in their chamber

with their purposes in view and began at noon to vote by state. The result of the first ballot was 8 in favor of Jefferson, 6 for Burr and 2 states evenly divided between Jefferson and Burr. Since the Constitution requires a candidate to have 9 votes, and since neither one had obtained that number, it was necessary to recommence the balloting, which was repeated up to 28 times with the same result throughout the day and night of the 11th. The states voting for Jefferson were New York, New Jersey, Pennsylvania, Virginia, North Carolina, Georgia, Kentucky and Tennessee; for Burr, New Hampshire, Massachusetts, Connecticut, Rhode Island, Delaware and South Carolina; the divided states, Vermont and Maryland.

"With night fall, members called for food and bedding, and each party resolved to die at its post. (Joseph) Nicholson, a Republican member from Maryland, finding himself dangerously ill and knowing that the loss of his vote would give his state to the Federalists, had himself carried that morning . . . into the Capitol (the building where Congress assembles), where a room was prepared for him and where he had the perseverance to vote, from his bed, during all the balloting. The two parties, seeing that after 28 rounds of voting the result was always 8-6-2, decided at 7 o'clock on Tuesday morning to suspend the election for a few hours so that they could rest. They reassembled at 3 o'clock in the afternoon and voted 7 more times, always with the same result.

"Persons whom curiosity had brought to Washington, more than a hundred thousand of them, began to get impatient and to mutter at the obstinacy of the Federalists, saying that the representatives of that party were voting for Burr only to throw the country into confusion and to see if they could retain, in their own hands, the power which they had so long enjoyed, so much abused during four years and which the people had now obviously given to Jefferson. It was well known, and indeed reflected in the utterances of the Federalist press, that the Federalists detest Burr as much as they do Jefferson, and it was clear that their only object was to divide the votes so that Jefferson would not have the 9 states majority which the Constitution requires.

"The equality of votes between the two candidates (in the Vermont and Maryland delegations) stemmed from a criminal desire on the part of the Federalists to exclude Jefferson and Burr from the Presidency and Vice Presidency by elevating the second to the height of the first and thereby annulling the election of both.

"Now as soon as the news began to spread that the Federalists were persisting in their original stubbornness, the people saw the danger which this audacious conduct posed to the United States. They feared, and rightly, that with the exercise of presidential and vice presidential functions expiring on March 3, the United States would find itself without a government on the 4th. Even more to be feared was that the Constitution had not foreseen this eventuality and that consequently, it had prescribed no remedy for this evil, and therefore if the Federalists continued to ballot in the same manner until March 4, the federal government would see itself threatened by a dissolution that must inevitably produce a civil war.

"The moderates of each party and all those who had something to lose, viewing this prospect with alarm, gathered together from the counties surrounding Washington those men most noted for their patriotism and presented them with remonstrances addressed to their Federalist Party representatives, urging the latter not to jeopardize the safety and tranquility of the United States by adhering to views of personal and party interest, and in order to avert the fatal consequences that would result from their obstinacy, they should immediately give their votes to Jefferson. Although these remonstrances were signed even by the Federalist political enemies of Jefferson, the two Maryland representatives, [William] Craik and [John C.] Thomas, hearing the voice of their party rather than that of their constituents . . . voted on Friday and on Saturday in the same way, so that after a consistory of 4 days in which there had been more than 50 ballotings, the result was still the same: that is to say, 8 for Jefferson, 6 for Burr and 2 divided.

"But as the news of what was happening in the capitol spread through the country, the discontent of the moderates of both parties increased with rumors spreading that the Federalists' tenacity was aimed at some act of violence or usurpation such as using their 22-to-12 majority in the Senate to name a Federalist member of that body President ad interim, which would have been a violation of the Constitution—began to arm and organize themselves into companies for the purpose of marching on Washington to seize it from those who proposed the usurpation of government, as well as from the usurpers. Within a few days, they formed a very numerous body at Baltimore. The same movement took place in Virginia and in the more distant cities, like Philadelphia and New York . . .

"But the Federalists, realizing finally that public opinion had declared against them, saw that they would have to yield to the imperious cries of the people and vote for Jefferson, to whom, before yielding, they proposed a sort of capitulation, offering to give him their votes provided that he would guarantee to the principal Federalists a continuation in the public offices which they enjoyed. To this, Jefferson replied that he would think himself unworthy of the eminent post which the people had entrusted to him, if, to obtain it, he were to humiliate himself by agreeing to such a shameful set of terms. Consequently, the conference ceased and the Federalists continued the balloting on Monday and part of Tuesday, with the same result—8, 6 and 2. On Monday, two Federalist members of the House received anonymous notes threatening them with death if they did not vote according to the will of the people. During the night, stones were thrown against the houses where other representatives of the same party were living, and there is no doubt whatsoever that their lives would have been in danger if on Tuesday the 17th, after a conclave of 8 days, two of the states had not abandoned their support of Burr: that is to say, half the representatives of Maryland and Vermont.

"What followed during the balloting which took place on Tuesday at 2 o'clock was that Jefferson had 10 states and Burr 4, Delaware and South Carolina having cast blank ballots in order to void their votes. Consequently, Jefferson was immediately declared President, Burr Vice President, and special couriers were dispatched to all the states of the union in order to calm the disorders . . .

"Such has been the last effort of a faction which has governed the United States since Gen. Washington retired from office . . ."

Index

⌒⌒⌒

i

Index

A Note About the Author

Daniel Sisson, born in Washington, D.C., in 1937, received his B.A. in History from California State University at Long Beach, and his M.A. and Ph.D. in History from the Claremont Graduate School and University Center. Formerly a member of the staff of The Center for the Study of Democratic Institutions, he served there as Junior Fellow and Senior Research Assistant. He is also a faculty member of the Adult Education division of Santa Barbara City College, and a tutor in the International Community College. Mr. Sisson lives in Santa Barbara, and this book, his first, was his dissertation.

A Note on the Type

The Text of this book was set in Electra, a Linotype face designed by W. A. Dwiggins (1880–1956), who was responsible for so much that is good in contemporary book design. Although much of his early work was in advertising and he was the author of the standard volume *Layout in Advertising*, Mr. Dwiggins later devoted his prolific talents to book typography and type design and worked with great distinction in both fields. In addition to his designs for Electra, he created the Metro, Caledonia, and Eldorado series of type faces, as well as a number of experimental cuttings that have never been issued commercially.

Electra cannot be classified as either modern or old-style. It is not based on any historical model, nor does it echo a particular period or style. It avoids the extreme contrast between thick and thin elements that marks most modern faces and attempts to give a feeling of fluidity, power, and speed.

The book was composed, printed, and bound by American Book–Stratford Press, Inc., Saddlebrook, New Jersey.